The Genesis Exhibition

DO HO SUH

WALK THE HOUSE

Edited by Nabila Abdel Nabi and Dina Akhmadeeva
with Amie Corry

With contributions by Nabila Abdel Nabi,
Dina Akhmadeeva, Sean Anderson, Sarah Fine,
Monica Juneja, Janice Kerbel, Do Ho Suh,
Rirkrit Tiravanija, Dylan Trigg, Kira Wainstein

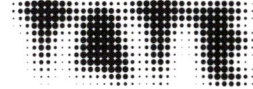

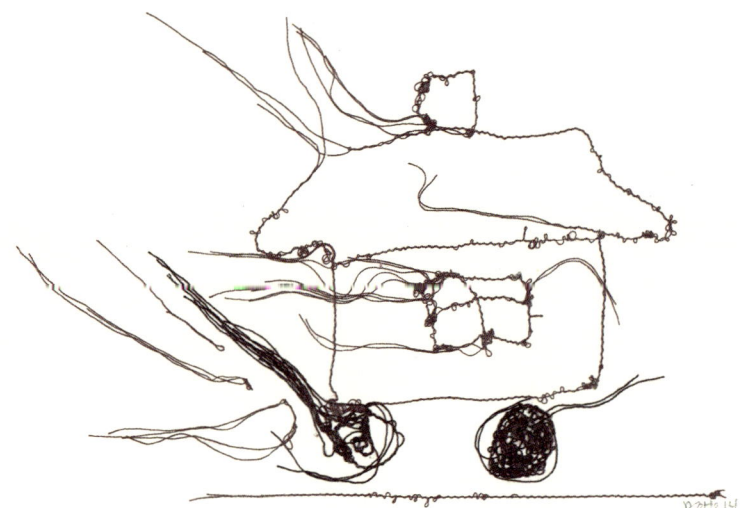

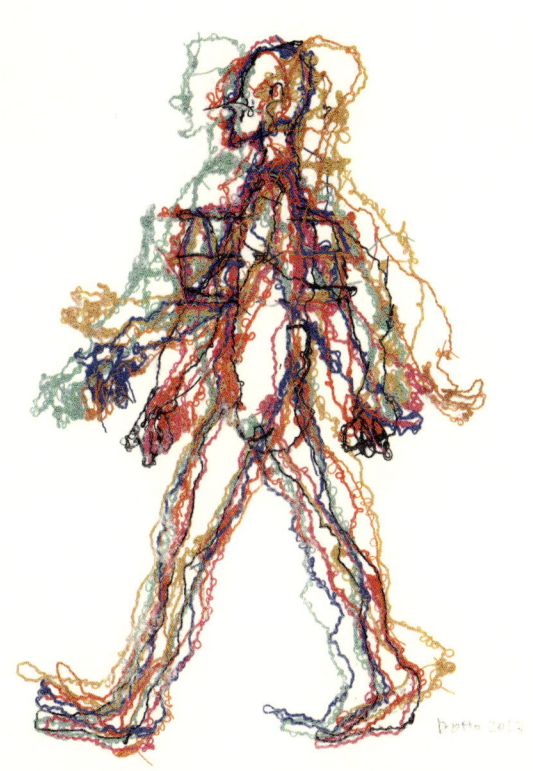

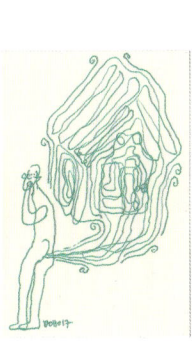

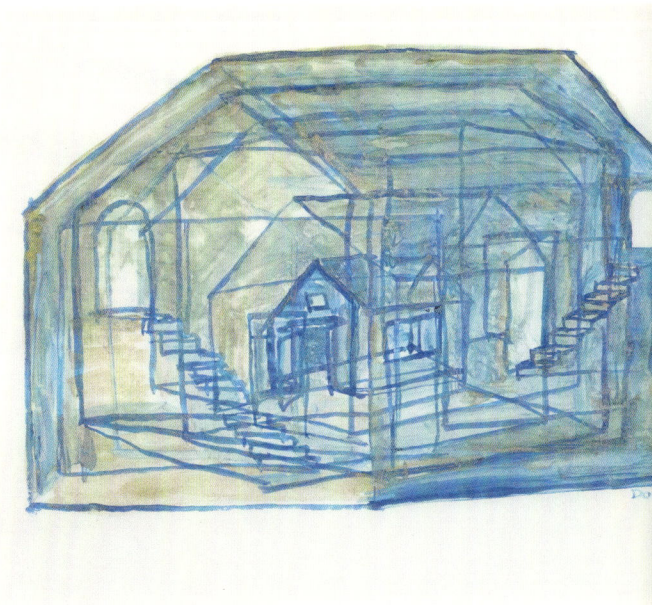

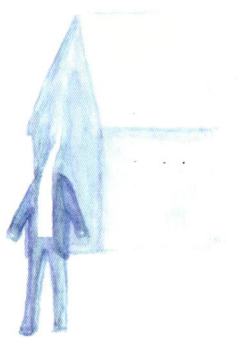

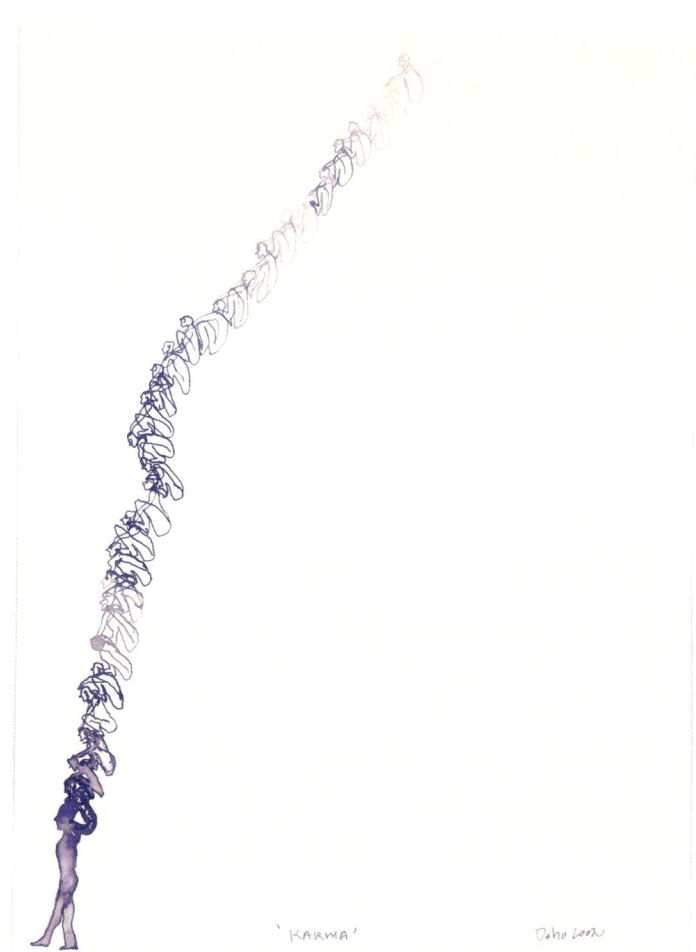

'KARMA'   Doho 2002

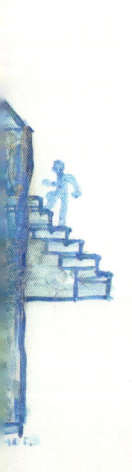

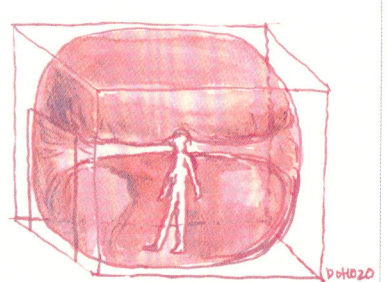

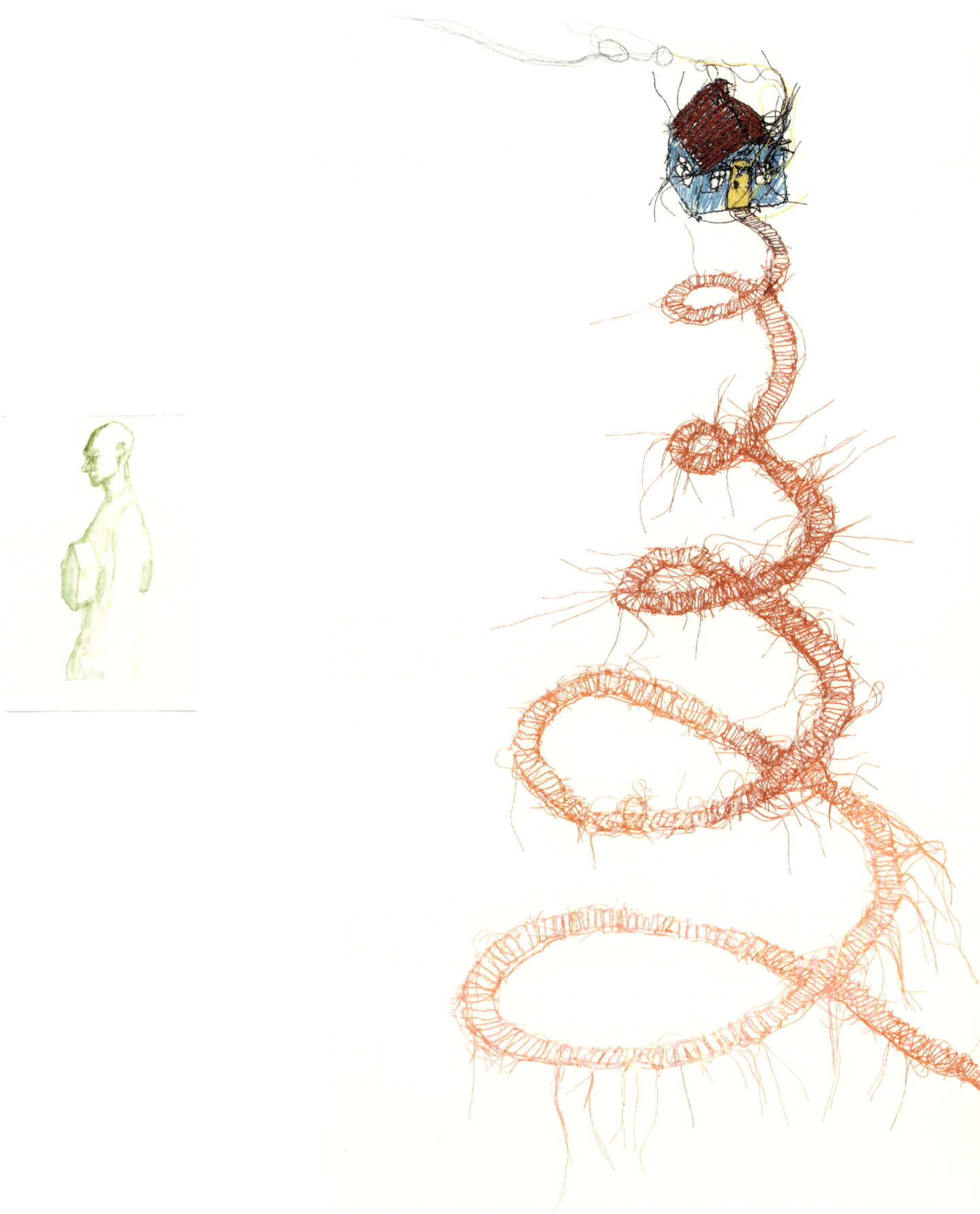

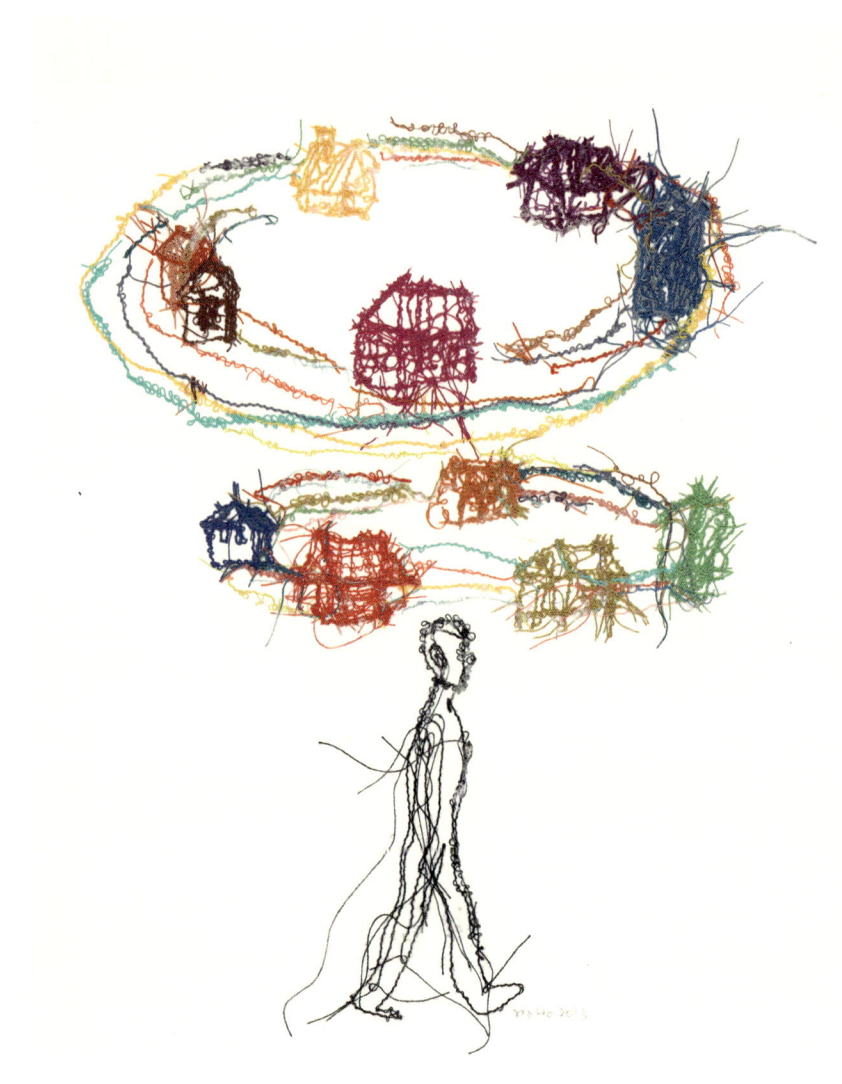

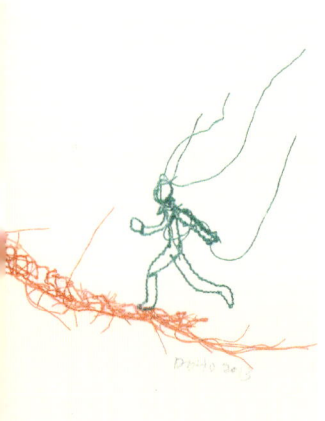

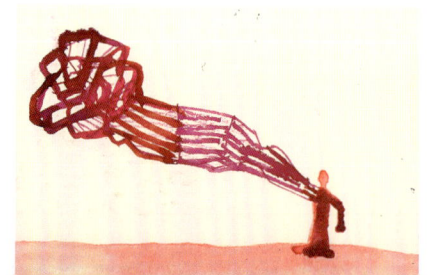

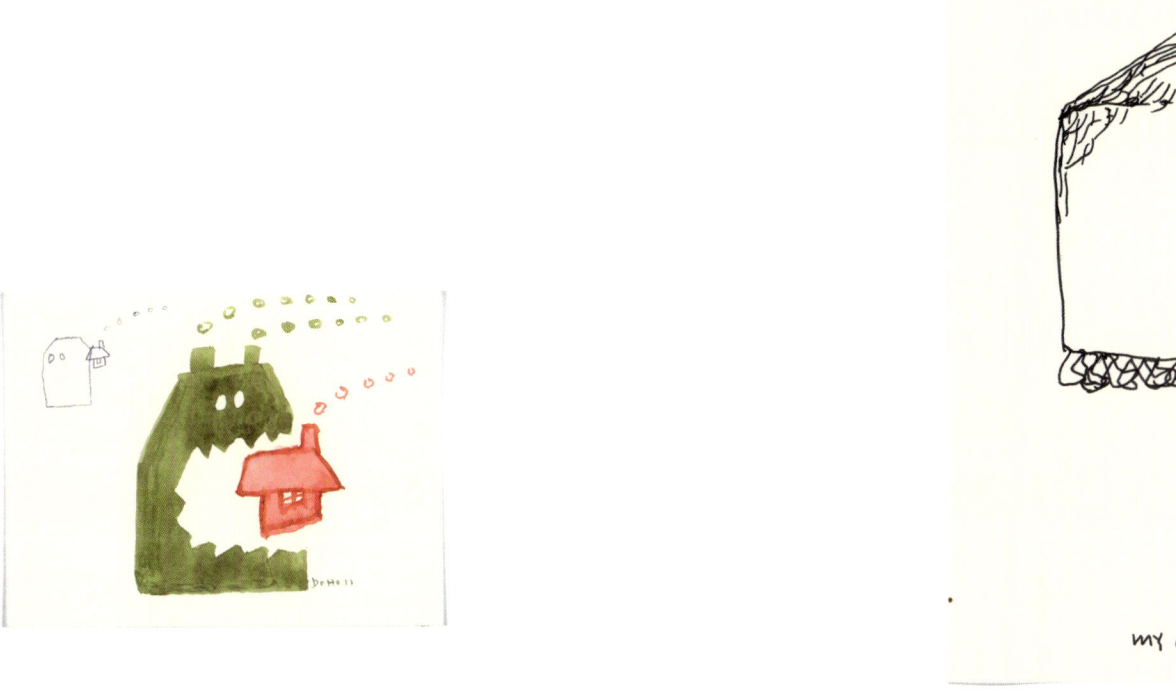

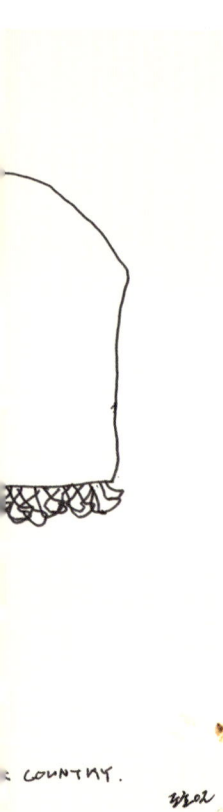

COUNTRY.

3/2/02

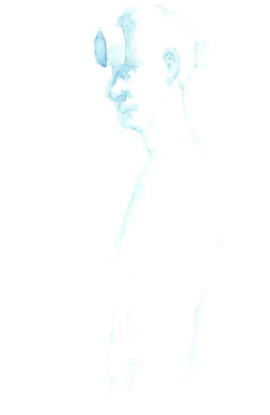

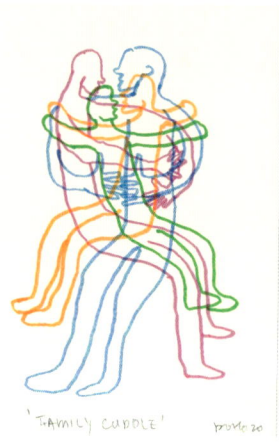

'FAMILY CUDDLE'

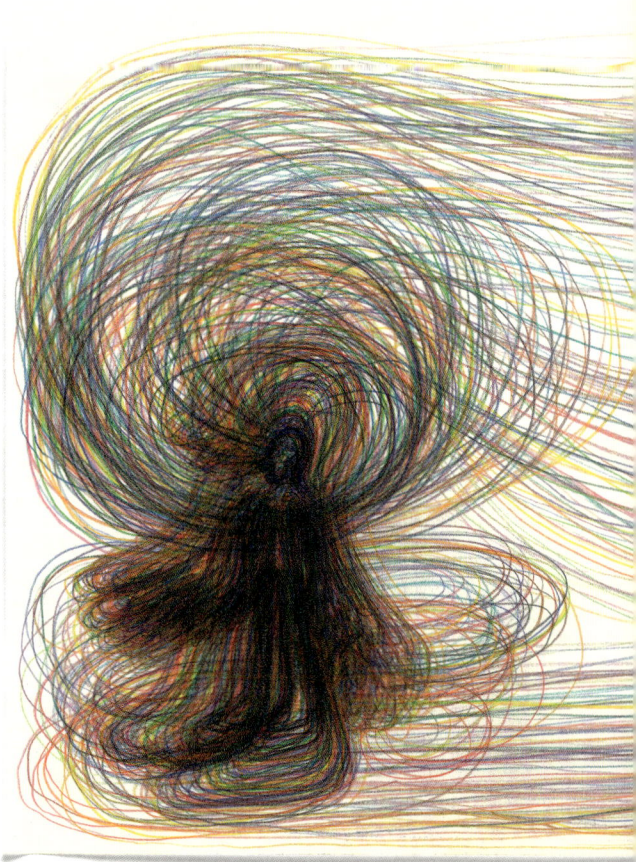

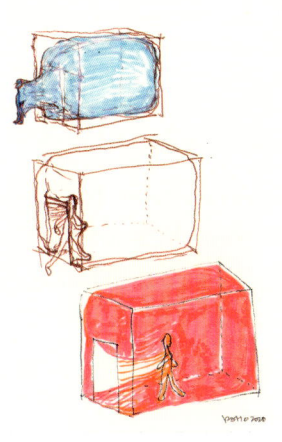

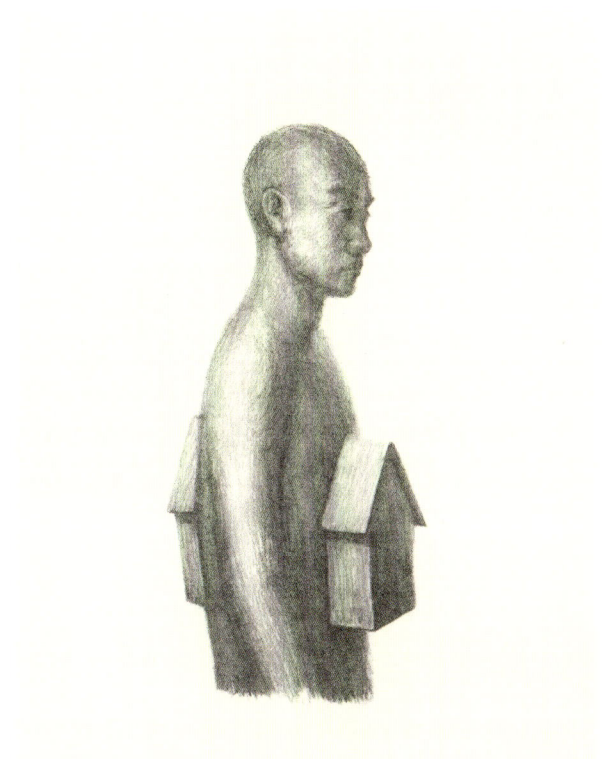

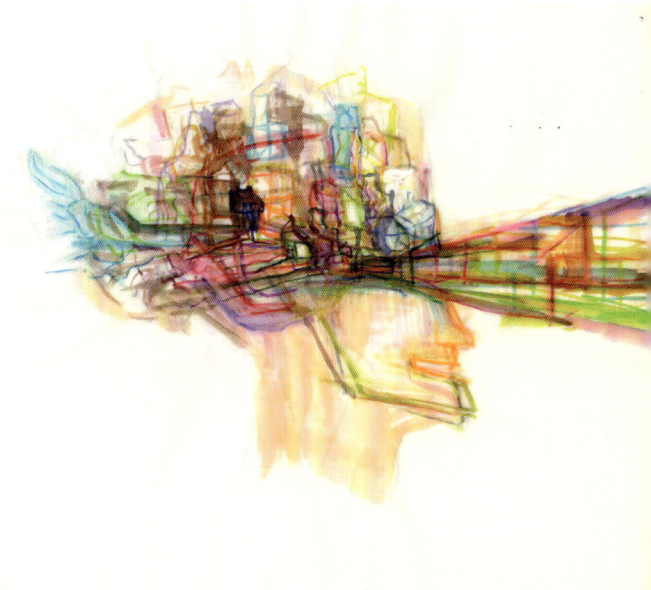

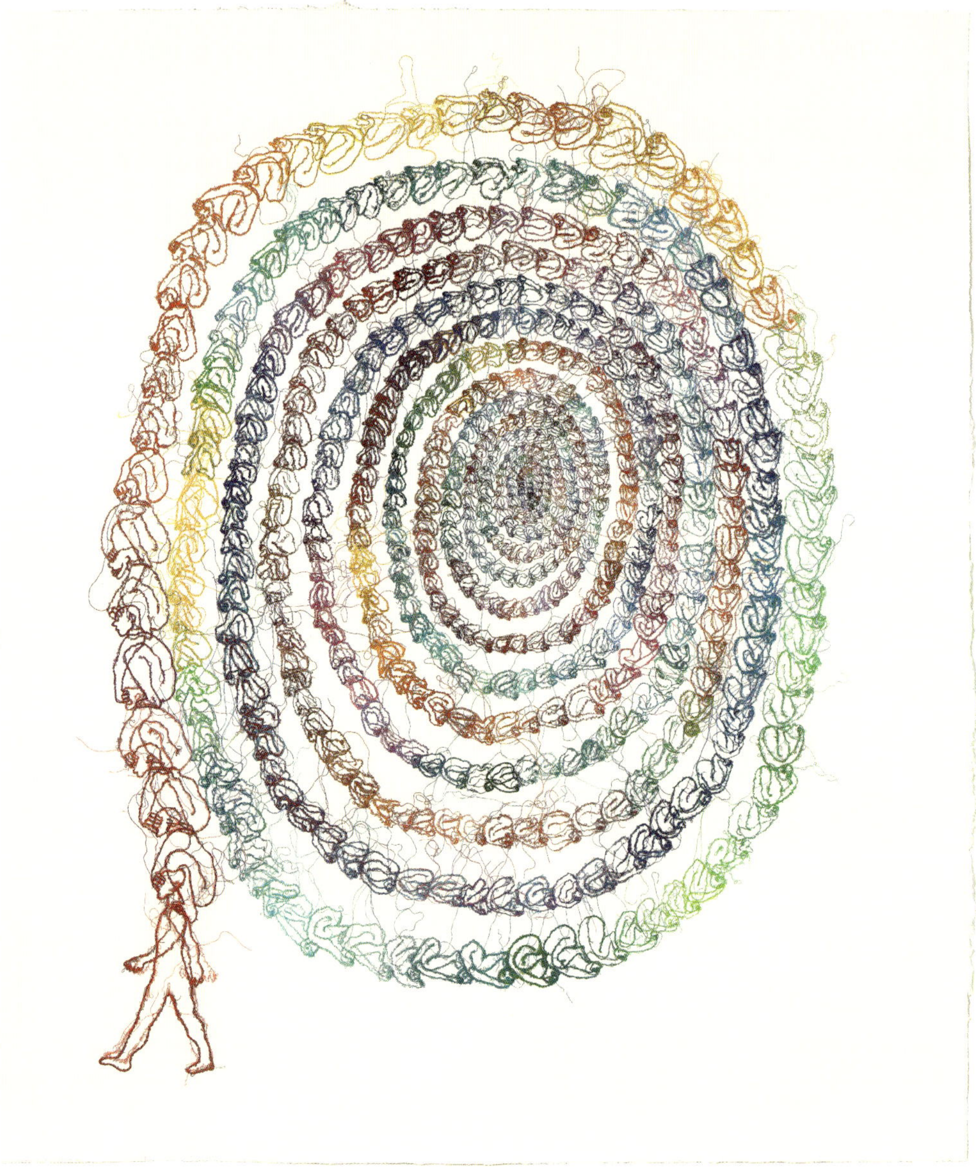

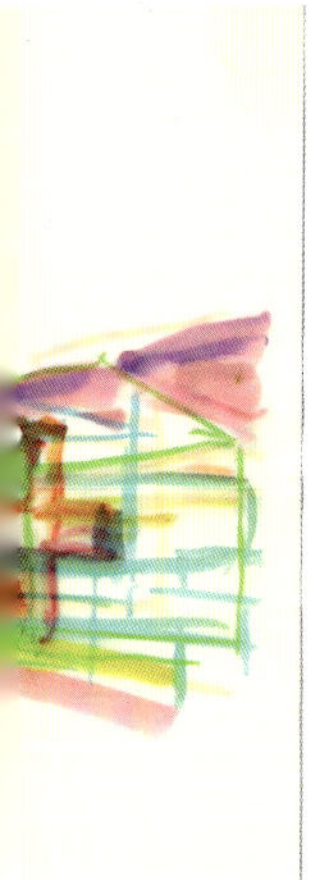

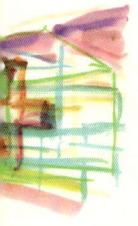

Over the course of history, advancements in technology, particularly the ability to move around and be present everywhere, have altered perceptions of space and time. While our need for mobility and hybridity creates augmented identities and ever-changing lives, we are also searching for a space where our memories can belong.

The Genesis Exhibition: Do Ho Suh: Walk the House is a comprehensive survey of Do Ho Suh's three-decade-long practice of travelling through cities such as Seoul, New York and London, all of which he has called 'home' at one stage of his life. Suh takes us on the artistic journey through his past and present homes to invite reflection on our own personal memories and the various spaces we have inhabited throughout our lives. Suh's continued act of tracing these memories explores the relationship between architecture, space, the body and the memories that shape who we are.

As one of the endeavours of Genesis Art Initiatives, *The Genesis Exhibition: Do Ho Suh: Walk the House* reaffirms our commitment to illuminating timeless issues that transcend spatial and temporal boundaries, as well as prompting audiences to discover the profound in the everyday by amplifying the voices of renowned visionaries.

We are honoured to expand Genesis Art Initiatives in Europe through our long-standing partnership with Tate by supporting the highly anticipated exhibition by Do Ho Suh at Tate Modern. We hope to spark valuable dialogues by supporting artistic experimentation that explores the complexities of our time.

We would like to express our heartfelt gratitude to Do Ho Suh for his inspiring practice and willingness to constantly break down boundaries to share timely yet timeless insights for our society. We would also like to thank Maria Balshaw and everyone at Tate for their invaluable contributions to this meaningful partnership.

Euisun Chung
Executive Chair, Hyundai Motor Group

Supporter's Foreword

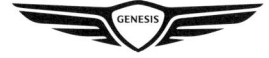

The title of Do Ho Suh's exhibition, *Walk the House*, is drawn from a Korean expression referring to the *hanok* – a house that could theoretically be disassembled, transported and reassembled at a new site. Reflecting this idea of a transportable home, Suh's immersive works examine the relationship between our memories and the spaces and places we inhabit. The artist has stated that, 'The space I'm interested in is not only a physical one, but an intangible, metaphorical, and psychological one. For me, "space" is that which encompasses everything.' While Suh's practice is highly personal, it also allows viewers to fill the works physically with their presence and psychologically with their experiences, inviting our own reflections on the enigma of home, identity and how we move through and inhabit the world around us.

The artist is perhaps best known for his fabric architectures – translucent 1:1 scale replicas of spaces in which he has lived and worked, which visitors are encouraged to wander through. His practice thus lays bare transcultural processes at every level, from the aesthetic collapsing of different time-spaces in his foldable architectures, to the very fabric from which the structures are made. The exhibition includes two ambitious new installations, configured for the Tate galleries. *Nest/s* 2024 colourfully weaves together domestic spaces from locations around the world, highlighting the porous nature of boundaries we traditionally think of as fixed. *Perfect Home: London, Horsham, New York, Berlin, Providence, Seoul* 2024, an outline of the artist's current home in London, is filled with brightly coloured architectural features, including doorknobs, light switches and electrical sockets, that playfully trace the spaces the artist and his family have previously lived in. Like many of Suh's works they also highlight the ways in which, regardless of where we are physically located, we are usually 'in' and 'of' a multiplicity of places.

The exhibition opens with Tate's collection work *Who Am We? (Multicoloured)* 2000 which has been installed as a wallpaper that envelops Tate Modern's concourse space. A mosaic of tens of thousands of tiny portrait photographs that Suh gathered over many years from sources including school yearbooks, it exemplifies the artist's reflections on the relation between individual and collective identity as a never-ending process of becoming.

Suh also extends his inquiries of space and movement to the ways in which public and private life are continually entangled and, contrary to the notion of home as a hermetic space, the 'out there' is also always 'in here.' His video works – *Robin Hood Gardens, Woolmore Street, London E14 0HG* 2018 and *Dong In Apartments* 2022 both evidence Do Ho's incredible attentiveness to process. Through photogrammetry, which stitches together images to produce a digital model of the physical world, Do Ho strives to explore the built environment as a living organism, an active witness to the traces left behind by past inhabitants.

The exhibition culminates in a space dedicated to Do Ho Suh's *Bridge Project* – an interrogation of the 'perfect home' hypothetically situated between New York, Seoul and London and how this intersects with real-world social, political and ecological issues. The exhibition thus ends on a question – the artist prompting us to ponder collectively *how do we build a world we call home?*

This exhibition has been developed in close collaboration with Do Ho Suh and his studio, through conversations beginning with former Director of Programme, the late Achim Borchardt-Hume, that have since been carried on by Nabila Abdel Nabi, Senior Curator, International Art (Hyundai Tate Research Centre: Transnational), Dina Akhmadeeva, Assistant Curator, International Art, Tate Modern, and Jarelle Francis, Exhibitions Assistant, Tate Modern. Special thanks also go to Catherine Wood, Director of Programme, Tate Modern, as well as Frances Morris, former Director, Tate Modern, Sook Kyung Lee, former Senior Curator, International Art, Tate Modern, and Kira Wainstein, former Research Assistant, Tate Modern. The exhibition would not have been possible without the incredible support and knowledge of Amie Corry, Kyle Bloxham Mundy, Nicola Chan, Elisa Lapenna, Louise Price and everyone in the artist's studio team. We are grateful to all the contributors: Sean Anderson, Sarah Fine, Monica Juneja, Janice Kerbel, Rirkrit Tiravanija, Dylan Trigg and Kira Wainstein. Our thanks also go to Marwan Kaabour for the beautiful design of this book, which so perfectly captures the dynamism of Do Ho Suh's practice.

I join the curators in thanking our many Tate colleagues who have contributed to the making of this exhibition, from art handling, registration, conservation, to learning, communications, digital, development and visitor services.

On behalf of Tate we would like to extend our deepest gratitude to Genesis for their generous support of this exhibition and towards the creation and repurposing of the works in the exhibition. Hyundai Motor has long supported Tate, and we're honoured to be growing this relationship through this new partnership with Genesis – coming together with our shared values of celebrating art as an authentic experience to discover the truly meaningful and valuable aspects of life. We are also grateful to The Genesis Exhibition: Do Ho Suh Supporters Circle: Lehmann Maupin, New York, Seoul and London; STPI – Creative Workshop & Gallery, Singapore; and Victoria Miro, for their committed support.

The exhibition has also been made possible by the provision of insurance through the Government Indemnity Scheme, and we thank HM Government for providing this, and the Department of Culture, Media and Sport and Arts Council England for arranging the indemnity.

Karin Hindsbo, Director, Tate Modern

On behalf of Do Ho Suh, we wish to acknowledge the numerous colleagues with whom we have had the honour to work during development and staging of this ambitious exhibition over the course of the past six years.

We are indebted to Do Ho Suh's studio team, with whom we have had the privilege to work closely: Amie Corry, Elisa Lapenna, Kyle Bloxham Mundy, Nicola Chan, Amandine Couot-Garibal and others. We extend our thanks to the teams at Daein, Image Bakery, MDM Props and all others involved in the technical production of Suh's installations. Our gratitude also goes to the artist's galleries: Lehmann Maupin and Victoria Miro.

At Tate Modern, we are grateful to Catherine Wood, Director of Programme, Amy Dillmann, Head of Programme Management, and Neil Casey, Head of Business and Operations for their insightful help and advice throughout the duration of the project. We express great thanks to Rita Machado, Exhibitions Registrar, for skillfully overseeing the loan and transportation of the works, and to Travis Miles, Senior Exhibitions Registrar, for his ongoing guidance. We are enormously grateful to Adam Wozniak, Senior Art Installation Manager, for deftly and imaginatively finding ways towards realising Do Ho Suh's visions within the spaces of Tate Modern, and to the skillful Art Handling team, overseen by Yaakov Gueta, Senior Art Handling Technician, for bringing the exhibition to life. We thank Phil Monk, Senior Design & Production Manager, for his overseeing of the design of the exhibition. Sincere thanks to Time-Based Media Conservator Alexandra Nichols; to Sculpture Conservator Elizabeth McDonald; to Paper Conservator Charity Fox, and to their respective teams, overseen by Cheryl Lynn, Deborah Cane and Jacqueline Moon, for working to bring this show to fruition with care. We express our thanks to Manuela Buttiglione, Programme Manager: Exhibitions, for carefully steering the organisational process of the exhibition, and to Jarelle Francis, Exhibitions Assistant and Kira Wainstein, former Research Assistant, for their invaluable support. We would like to acknowledge the thoughtful contributions from the following colleagues in Press and Marketing working on the project: Duncan Holden, Lucy McNabb, Megan Pottle, Hele Rhys, Hannah Rose, Joanna Sandler, Rachael Young. In the Corporate Partnerships team, we are thankful to Charlotte Reeves, Sophie Busby, Danielle Dikoko and Amy Goodman, as well as to Claire Gylphé, Ellie Rushforth, Sarah Monteath and the wider Development team. In the Learning team, we are grateful to Mark Miller, Rachel Noel and Sandra Sykorova for their work towards bringing Do Ho Suh's thinking beyond the walls of the exhibition. We extend our thanks to David Dibosa, Director of Research and Interpretation, for his ongoing reflections throughout the process of ideating and realising the exhibition, and to Gillian Wilson, Curator, Interpretation for her attentive collaboration in developing the show's interpretation narrative. Sincere thanks to Alessia Arcuri, Designer, for the exhibition's graphic design. Many thanks to Sandra McLean and to colleagues in the Visitor Experience team for bringing their insight from the early stages of developing the exhibition; to Alessandra Serri in the Legal team; to Enrico Tassi and Figgy Guyver at Tate Etc., to Irena Cater, Tylar Napolitano and Roma Clemie in the Engagement & Events team; to all in Tate Estates.

We reiterate our thanks to Nicola Bion, Senior Editor, for deftly and expertly steering the process of realising this publication, and to Roz Hill, Picture Researcher, and Juliette Dupire, Production Controller, for their work in bringing it to fruition. Sincere additional thanks to Amie Corry, Director of Publications, in Do Ho Suh's studio, for her editorial collaboration. We are grateful to Marwan Kaabour for imagining the book's design with immense sensitivity to Do Ho Suh's practice.

Nabila Abdel Nabi and Dina Akhmadeeva

Acknowledgements

Nabila Abdel Nabi and
Dina Akhmadeeva

Walk the House

'Site-specificity [that] becomes highly translatable and transportable'
Do Ho Suh[1]

To walk the house, or to make a house walk, is a now infrequently used Korean expression that the young Do Ho Suh heard from the master carpenter of his childhood home in Seoul. Aged nine at the time, Suh observed as his parents oversaw the building of a *hanok*, a 'traditional' Korean house, in an intentional effort to preserve this architectural form amid the waves of rapidly modernising architectural projects that were producing ever-growing high-rises in 1970s South Korea. Built with wooden joinery for structural support and rice paper for windows and doors, the *hanok* was a house that could be – and historically on occasion would be – 'walked': disassembled, transported and reassembled at a new site. Unravelling the fixity and rootedness of place, its modular form held the seeming contradiction around which Suh's decades-long practice has developed: tending to place site-sensitively, site-responsively and site-specifically, while offering the notional possibility of dislocating and transplanting it elsewhere. Suh's practice thus collapses the boundaries between the local and the global, the rooted and the mobile, the solid and the impermanent.

Suh moved to the US in 1991 following his BFA and MFA studies in Korean ink painting at Seoul National University. He studied first for a BFA in painting at the Rhode Island School of Design, then for an MFA in sculpture at Yale University. It was during this time that he developed the beginnings of an enquiry that would combine material and memory, space and body. Measurement became a method for Suh to give heightened attention to space as a substance in itself, which he brought together with the relative lightness of textile. In this combination of site-specificity of space and transportability of textile, Suh experimented with both intervention in space and its relocation. Some of these early experiments include *Room 516/516-I/516-II* 1994–5, a project of 'clothing' his studio in muslin, complete with ribs and zippers, allowing it to be erected elsewhere as a tent-like structure, and *Red Conjunction* 1995, in which a translucent red scrim-like fabric structure cut a corridor in half, calling attention to an otherwise overlooked space of transition.

It was during this time, too, that spaces through which Suh himself transited and that he carried with him became more visibly present in his artistic imagination. 'The experience of leaving home is what made me think and become aware of the notion of home for the first time', Suh has stated. 'It could therefore be said that home started to exist for me once I no longer had it. But if that is the case, where and when does home exist?'[2] Suh's use of readymade textiles intended for making Korean clothing – and their implied proximity to the human body – to produce his soft architectures serves as an apt material vehicle for

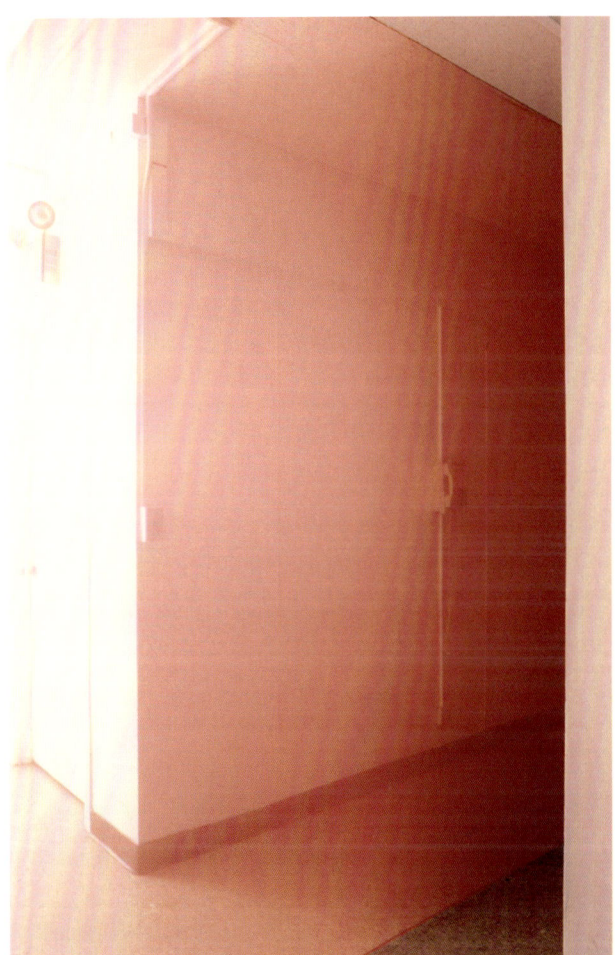

Red Conjunction 1995

shaping architectural spaces that exist as inseparable from how they were experienced, metabolised and remembered through the body.

Three cities Suh has called home over the course of his life – Seoul, New York and London – recur and accumulate throughout his oeuvre, materialising as expansive fabric architectures, as attentive and time-consuming rubbings of fixtures, room interiors and exteriors of buildings, as videos and installations that utilise experimental new technologies such as photogrammetry, 3D printing and robotics, and as both intimate and large-scale works on paper. These are spaces that have appeared, separately and together, in numerous exhibitions across the world, recognising Suh's responsiveness to increasingly interconnected, transnational, hybrid, migratory structures of contemporary existence. Whether locating himself in the Korean Pavilion of the 2001 Venice Biennale or the Los Angeles County Museum of Art in 2009 and 2019, the Leeum Museum of Art in Seoul in 2012 or the 21st Century Museum of Contemporary Art, Kanazawa, Japan the

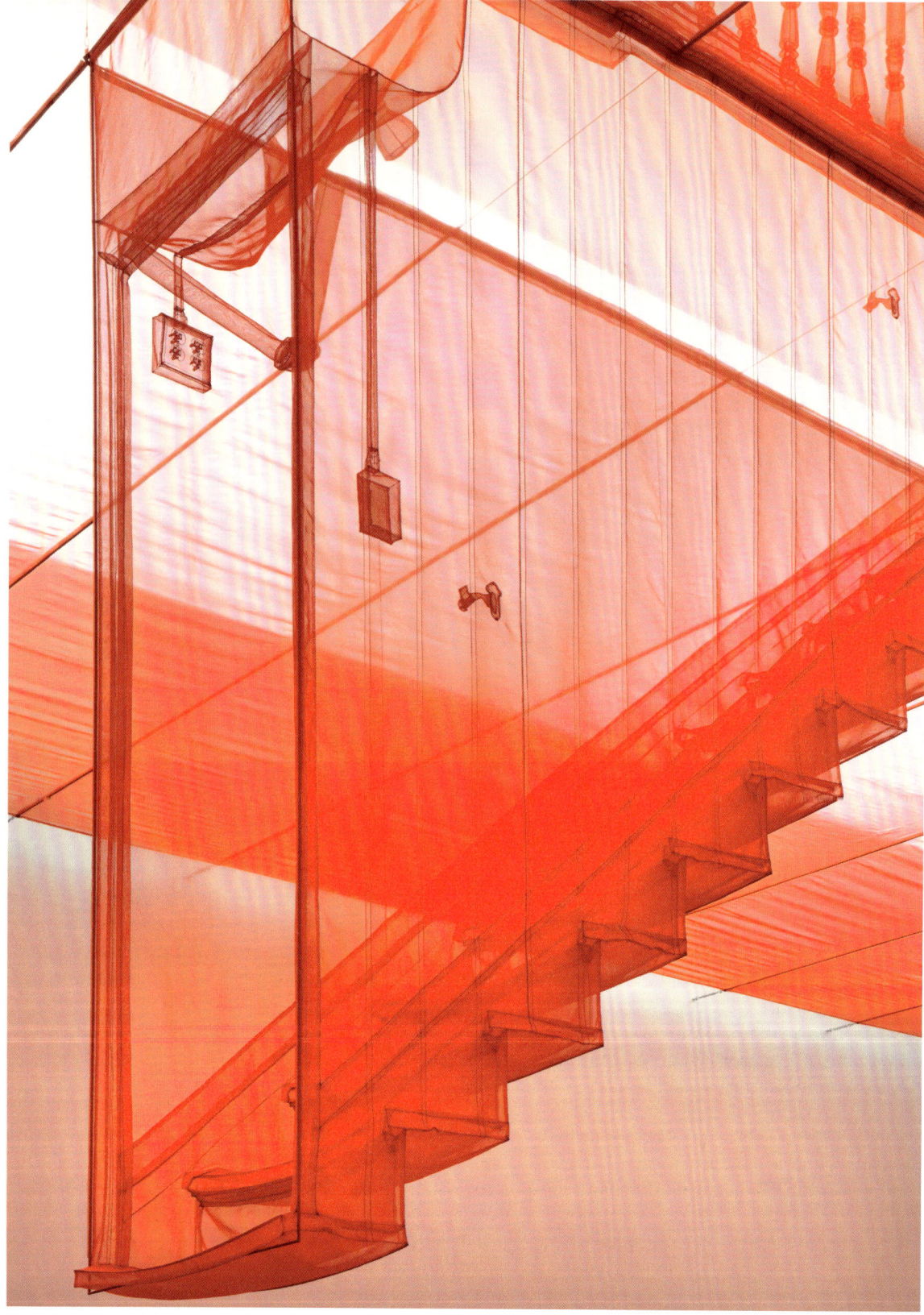

Staircase-III 2010

same year, the Museum of Contemporary Art Australia in Sydney in 2022 or the sites of his other acclaimed projects, Suh has unfolded, unravelled, unpacked and installed between their walls geographically impossible acts of spatial transposition and super-imposition, inviting visitors to perform similar feats of their own through the act of recollection. Suh's 'stand-ins' for those spaces – which the artist repeats and to which he returns across his work – simultaneously point to the very impossibility of relocating a space. The invitation to look inside ourselves for the spaces we carry within us is also an invitation to tend to the complexity and contradiction of emotions that might arise from this process, whether loss, longing, fond recollection, indifference or anger.

Staircase-III 2010 is based on the narrow stairs that once connected Suh's apartment to his landlord's in New York. A diaphanous staircase cascades down from a horizontal ceiling that bathes the entire gallery space in a warm red glow. The fabric panels that line the gallery's ceiling were measured to fit the space, and can be reconfigured each time the work is shown. In this work Suh was already challenging the very idea of a transportable artwork by grounding it within the specificity of the gallery, as well as challenging what he refers to as the 'permanence' of the institutional space. Through its potential for evolution, the work remains *alive* – able to shapeshift and adapt to the exhibiting gallery each time it is shown. Suh's interest in reproducing interstitial spaces, compelling for their contradictory ability to both connect and separate, is echoed in his attention to smaller domestic features, including doorknobs and light switches (items the artist terms 'specimens'), each of which becomes a portal to the past while holding physical space in the present.

Spatial acts are inherently temporal acts. By recreating these spaces in a spectral register, Do Ho Suh repeatedly folds in multiple temporalities. The large-scale work *Nest/s* 2024, a series of 'passages' traversed by the artist throughout his life, is also a material interrogation: *What are we moving towards?* In their translucency, the fabric architectures entwine space-making and place-making; bodies that move through them become part of the work as well as part of a wider constellation of bodies sharing the space and being momentarily in common. To move through these architectures is to psychically pass through structures of belonging that shift in scale, connecting our sense of place in the world through our own body to the planetary body, and all the national and transnational forms of belonging mapped across it.

Tate acquired Suh's *Staircase-III* in 2011, at a time when curators were interrogating the institution's reliance on the national frame and working to reconceive the museum as a polyphonous, transculturally constituted entity. A little

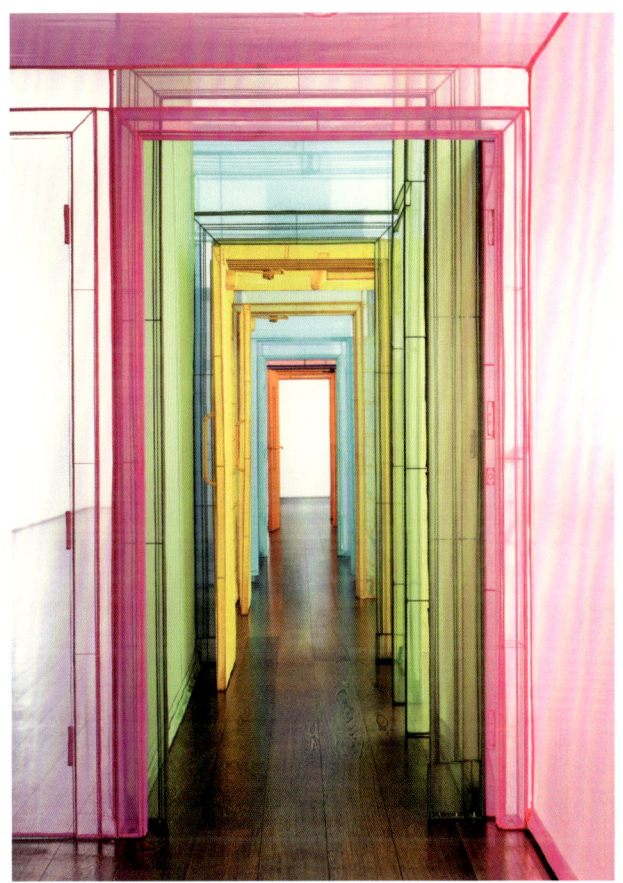

Hub series, installation view, Victoria Miro, London, 2017

over a decade later, Tate is renowned for its methodology, highlighting art's interconnectedness and the ways in which the movement of artists, artworks and ideas has increasingly defined artistic practice across the twentieth and twenty-first centuries. It is against this backdrop that *Staircase-III* was brought into the collection: materially and conceptually, this work orients our attention to the manifold ways we inhabit space at any one time, and the ways in which artists always bridge the distinct time-spaces they speak from with all the spaces they move through.

While seemingly crystallising the museum's transcultural ethos, *Staircase-III* – as with so many of Suh's works – also disrupts its entrenched structures. Suh has often worked in ways that tease museums' conventions, in this instance challenging the 'permanence' associated with bringing a work into the collection through the work's potential for continuous change each time it is displayed. Similarly, a mosaic of thousands of tiny portrait photographs collected from sources including school yearbooks, *Who am we? (Multicoloured)* 2000 becomes a series of enveloping wallpapers – second skins on the museum's interior walls, inextricable from the body of the museum and therefore the bodies that temporarily inhabit it.

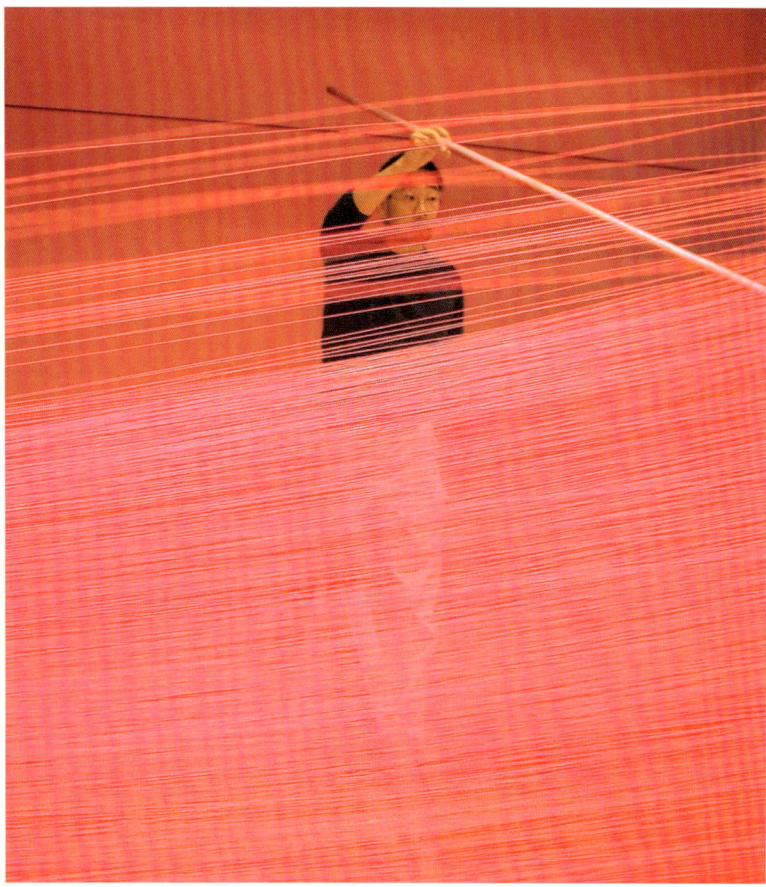

Do Ho Suh at work on *Paratrooper-I*, 2003

Suh has thought for decades about the role of art to reflect as well as create publics. Since 2016, he has resided predominantly in London and, as the city's built environment entered his practice, the artist found himself increasingly grappling with the 'fixity' of different forms across the urban landscape. Ever sensitive to the space surrounding him and to the effects of the built environment on one's psyche, Suh has explored the place-making conventions of public monuments – whose syntax, in the UK, remains largely singular, white, male and vertically oriented.

In 1998 Suh created *Public Figures*, which he describes as an anti-monumental form. As he notes:

> One of the exemplary structures of encounter between the individual and the public is the erection of statues of illustrious figures in public squares. I reexamine this conventional structure of a single larger-than-life size figure standing on an immobile pedestal and to which the passing public looks up. My rethinking displaces the site of the (heroic) individual by taking the figure from above to below the pedestal, reducing its size, making it anonymous, and multiplying it.[3]

Suh based his reconstituted monument on Korea's own history of oppression. In Korean, the term '*mincho*', which refers to the general public or oppressed people, is translated literally as 'public grass' – because, as Suh explains, 'it never dies, it continually renews'.[4] This notion of collective resilience encapsulates Suh's thinking about the role of the built environment in shaping a sense of collective memory, as well as its capacity to disrupt exclusionary social constructs by making space for the unacknowledged lives of people in defining those public spaces.

This book brings together a collective set of scholarly and artistic perspectives to locate Suh's practice within wider art historical, social, political and philosophical concerns, opening up new trajectories and illuminating lesser-known aspects of his wide-ranging body of work. Dylan Trigg situates Suh's structures in the space between materiality and

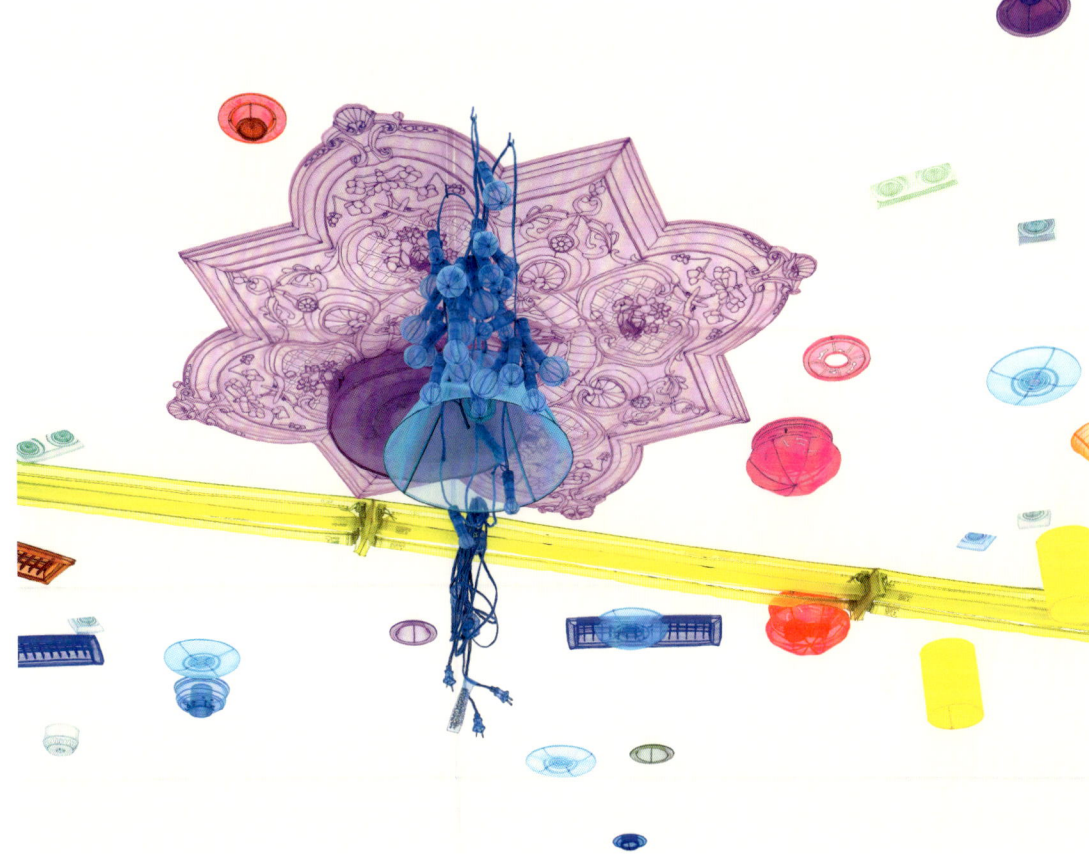

Perfect Home: London, Horsham, New York, Berlin, Providence, Seoul 2024 (detail)

the body, where home becomes the site through which memory and experience infiltrate and undo the abstract geometry of the built environment. Monica Juneja's thinking through the lens of the transcultural locates Suh's 'exilic sensibility' within wider currents of movement: of people, materials, labour and ideas. Sean Anderson's meditations on haunting and the ghostly confront the potent capacity for Suh's work to draw the viewer into multiple spaces and temporalities all at once. Locating Suh's work at the nexus of imagination and real-world politics of movement and inhabitation – territorial claims, jurisdiction, borders – Sarah Fine explores fictional spaces as ways to envisage other possible ways to be. Rirkrit Tiravanija's text playfully emphasises the semi-translucent, semi-opaque function of memory as he takes us to the US in the 1990s, narrating his first encounters with Do Ho Suh and his practice. Janice Kerbel and Do Ho Suh, whose friendship began in 1993 as residents at the Skowhegan School of Painting in Maine, discuss process, the persistent connection between time and space, and the development of Suh's practice across the last thirty years.

In a world defined by increased movement – voluntary and involuntary – Do Ho Suh's work outlines the cultural collisions that so many of us negotiate daily, as we leave our homes behind and seek new ones, continuously calibrating the boundaries between the worlds we make and remake and those made by others.

Notes

1   Do Ho Suh, lecture given at University College London as part of *Edge: Situated Practice in Art, Architecture and Urbanism*, 7 October 2017 (unpublished).

2   Ibid.

3   Do Ho Suh, quoted in Kelyn Soong, 'Take a Closer Look at a Surprising New Sculpture That Rethinks Who We Put on a Pedestal', *Smithsonian*, 30 April 2024, https://www.smithsonianmag.com/smithsonian-institution/take-a-closer-look-at-a-surprising-new-sculpture-that-rethinks-who-we-put-on-a-pedestal-180984243, accessed 31 Oct. 2024.

4   Ibid.

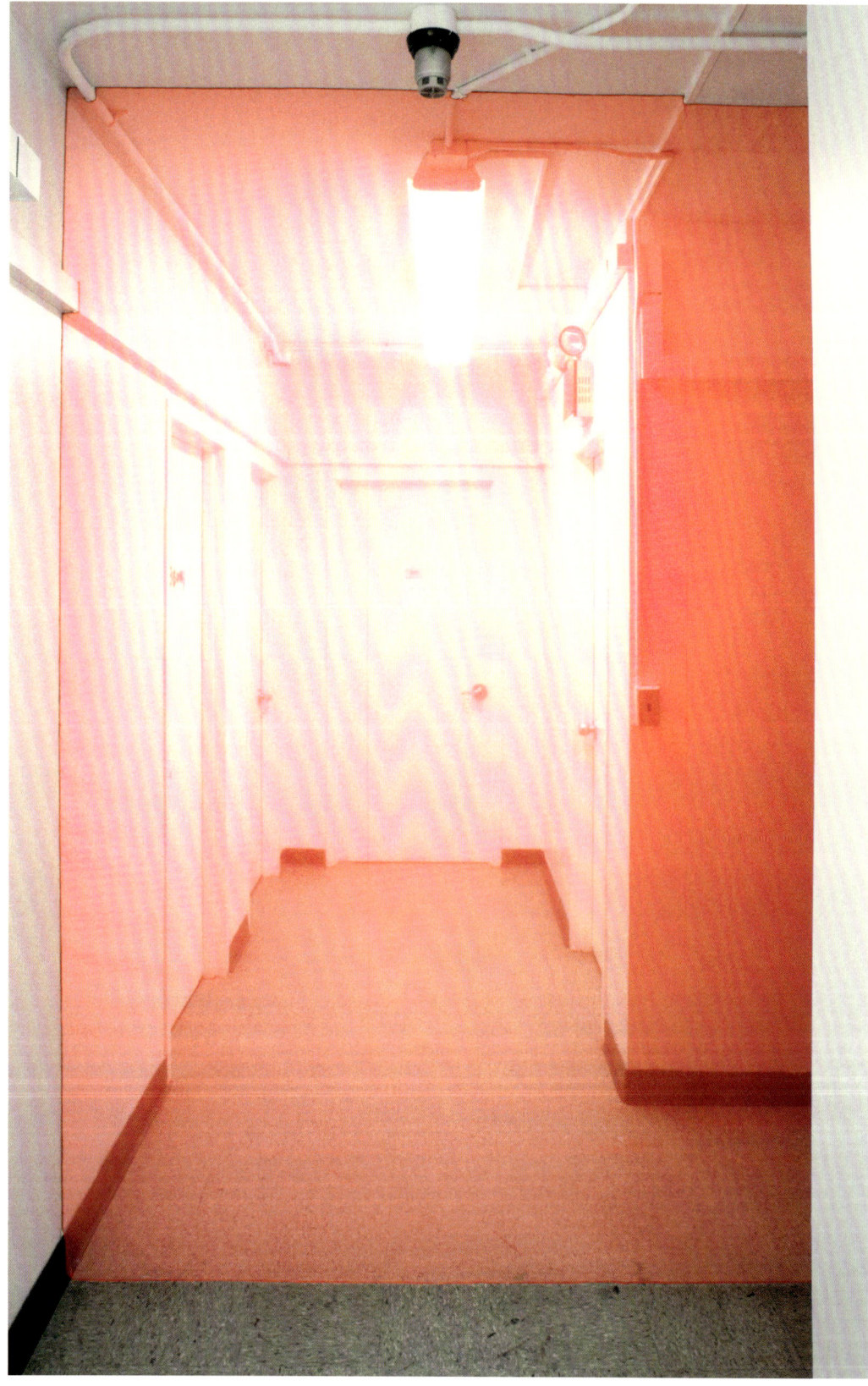

Red Conjunction 1995

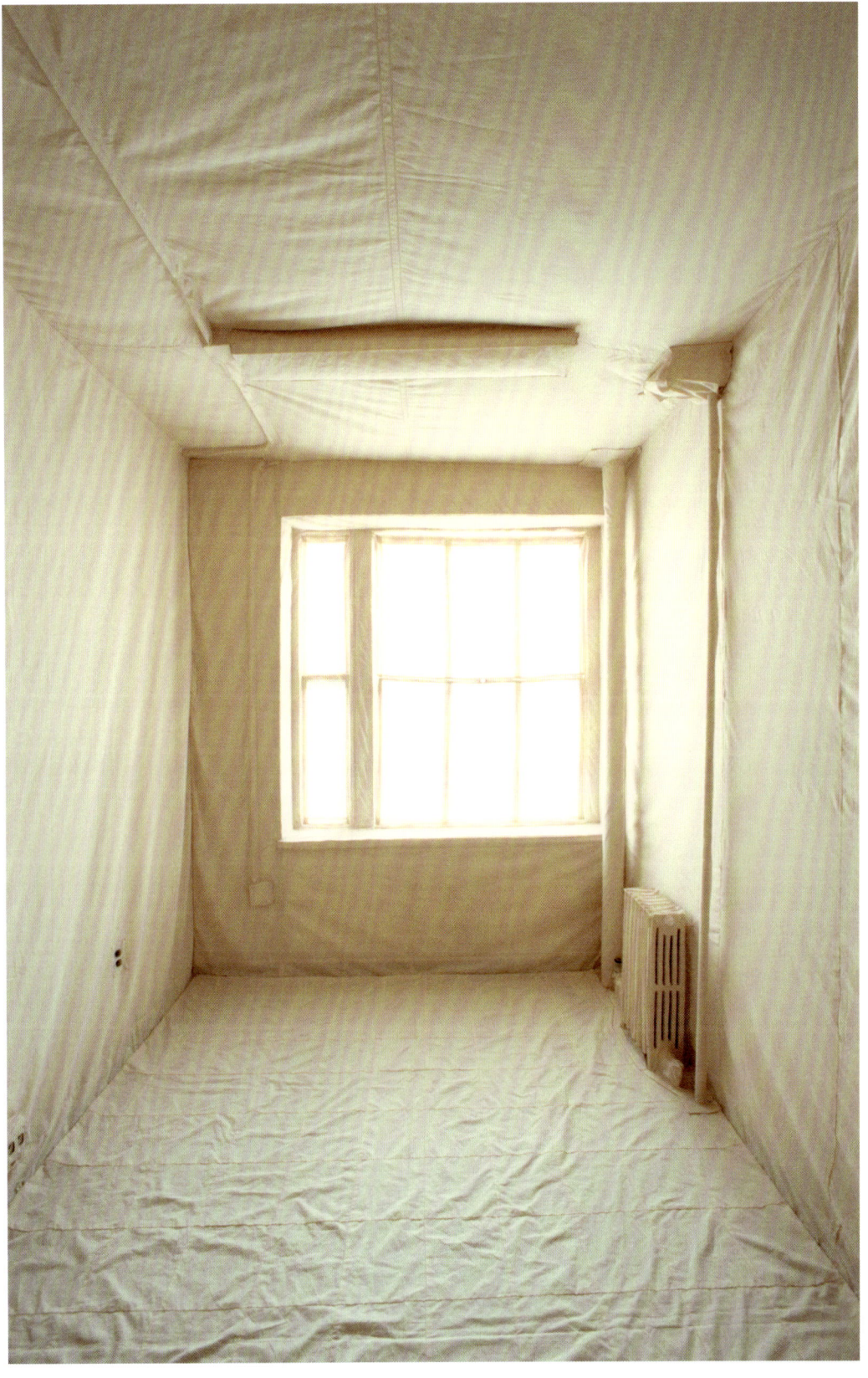

Room 516/516-I/516-II 1994–5

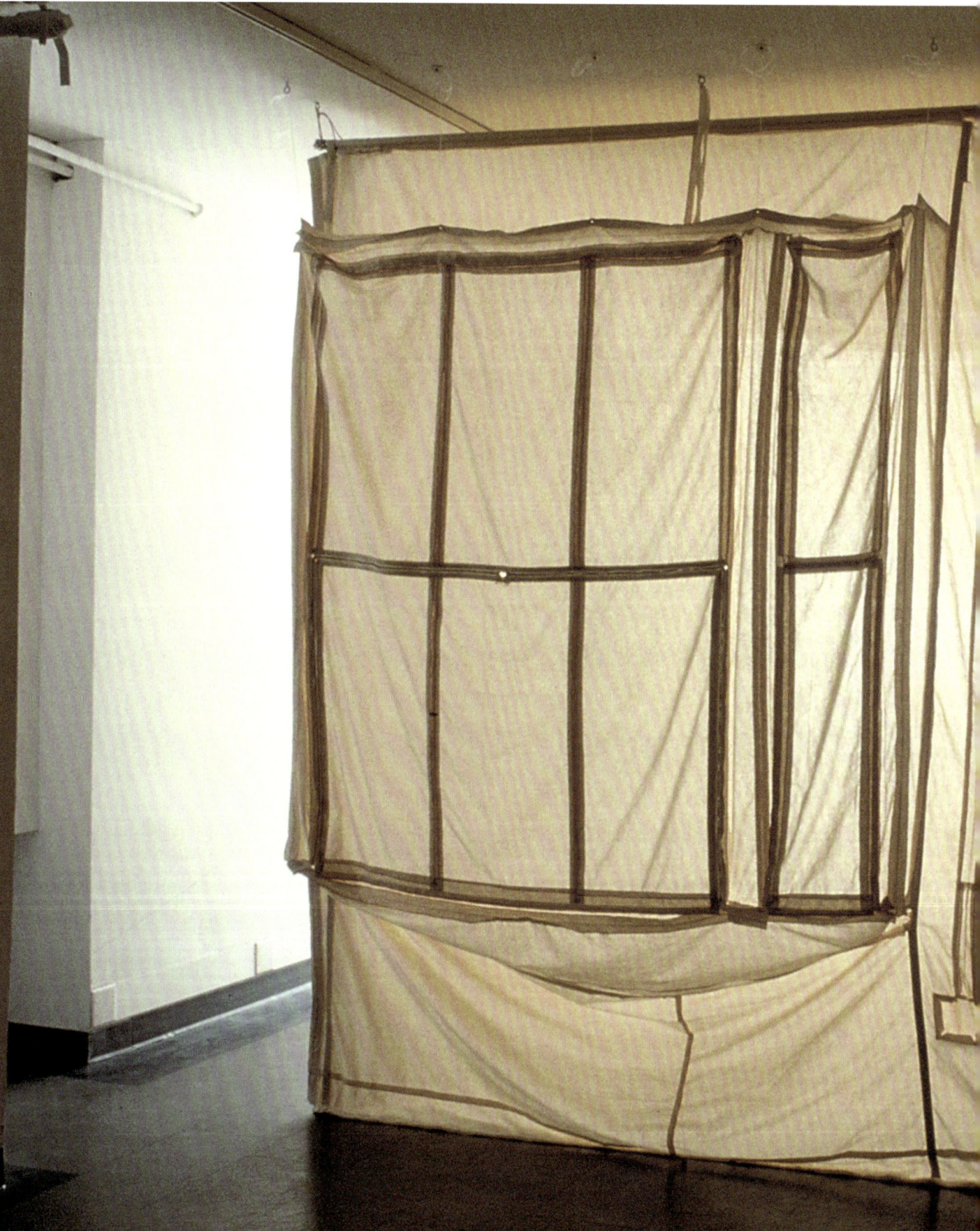

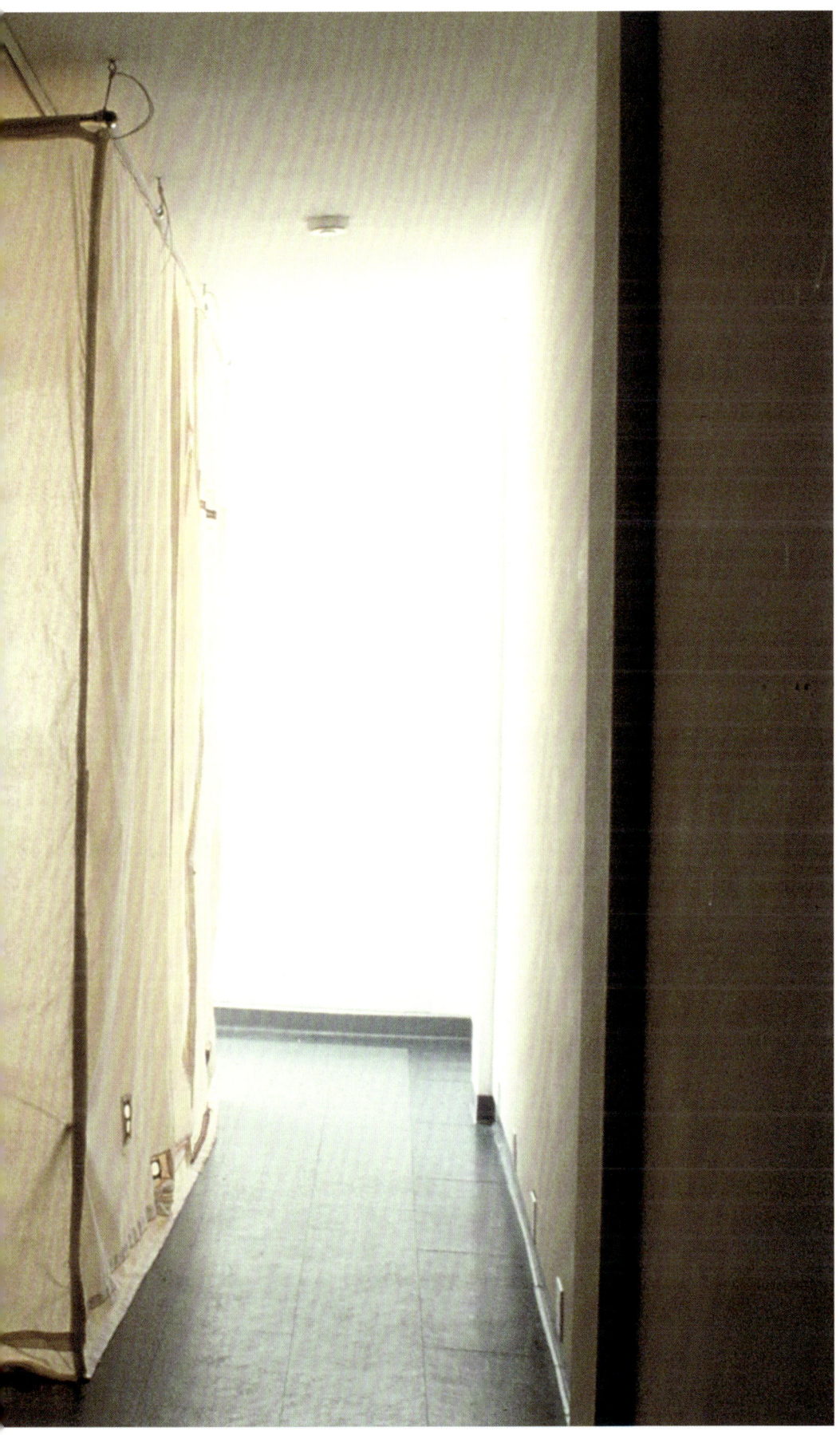

Room 516/516-I/516-II 1994–5

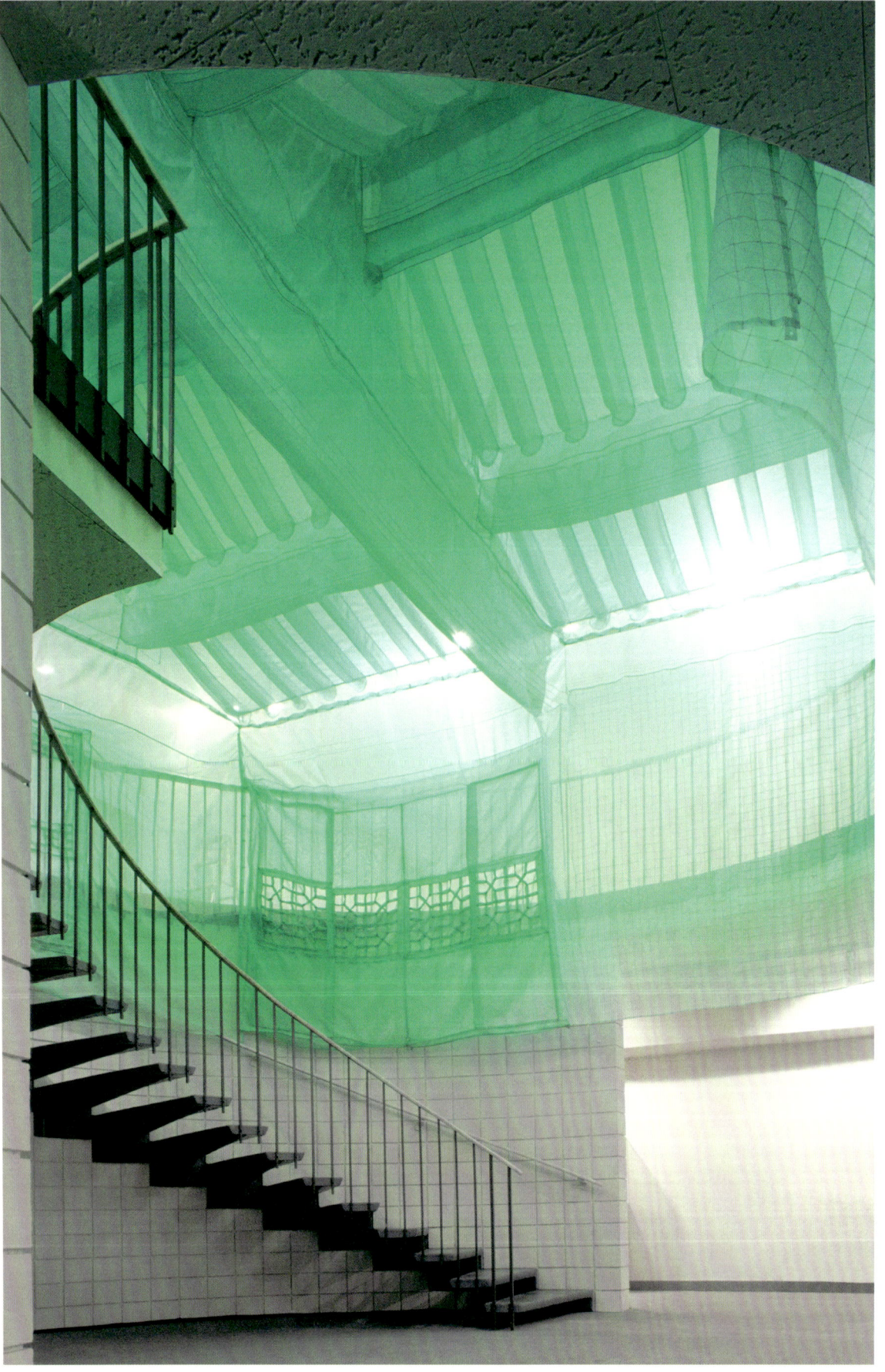

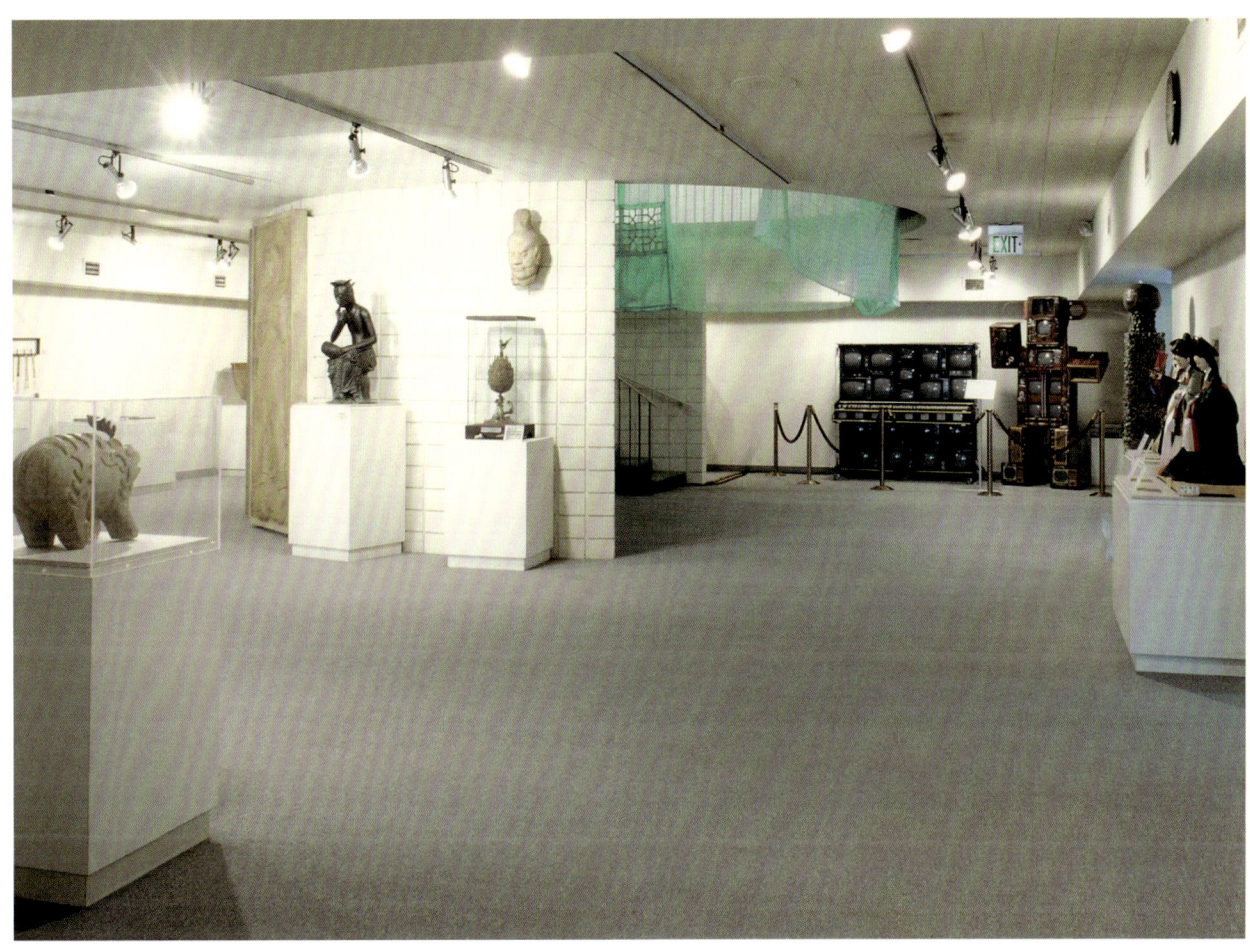

Opposite, above and overleaf: *Seoul Home/L.A. Home/New York Home/Baltimore Home/London Home/Seattle Home/L.A. Home* 1999, installation views, Korean Cultural Center, Los Angeles, 1999

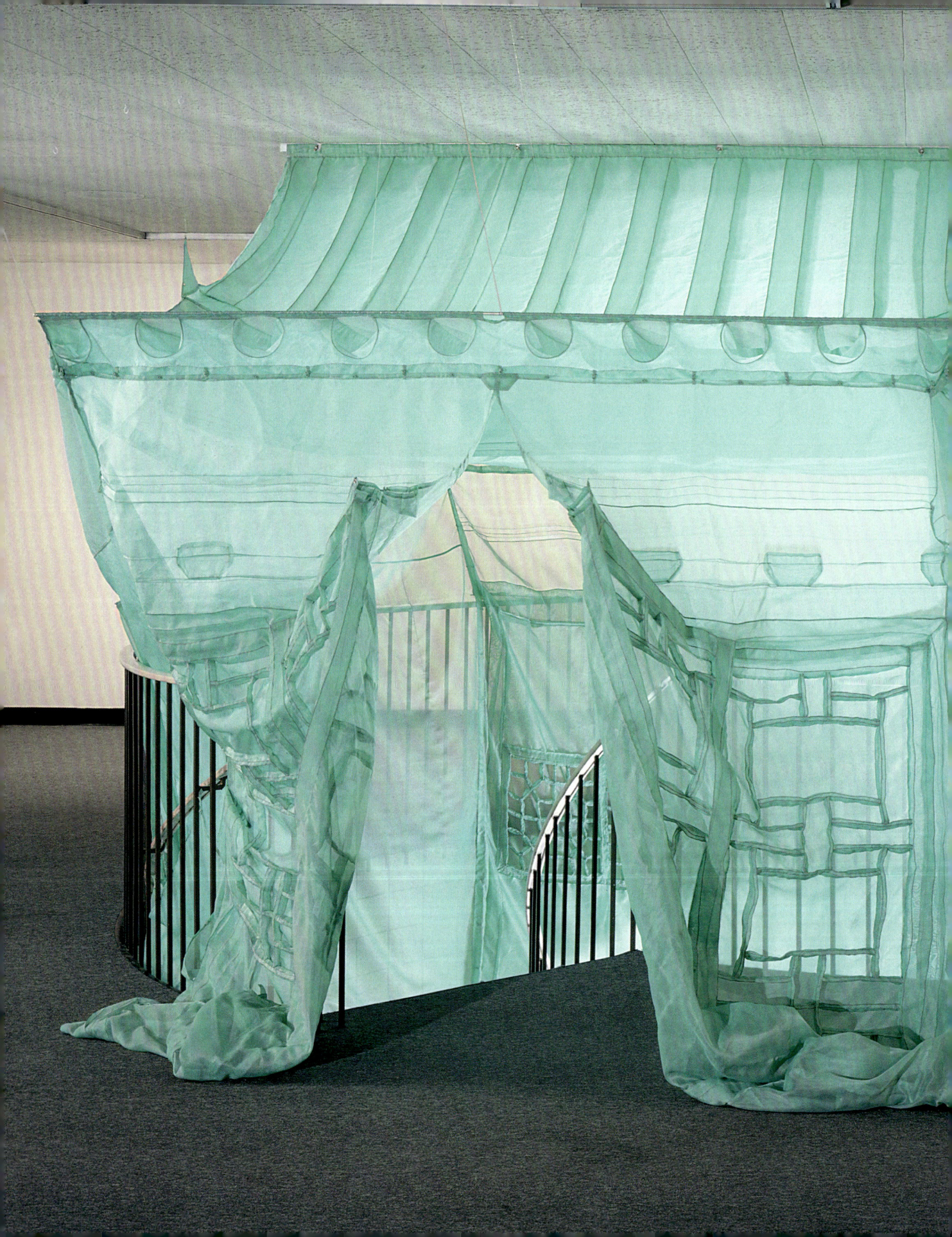

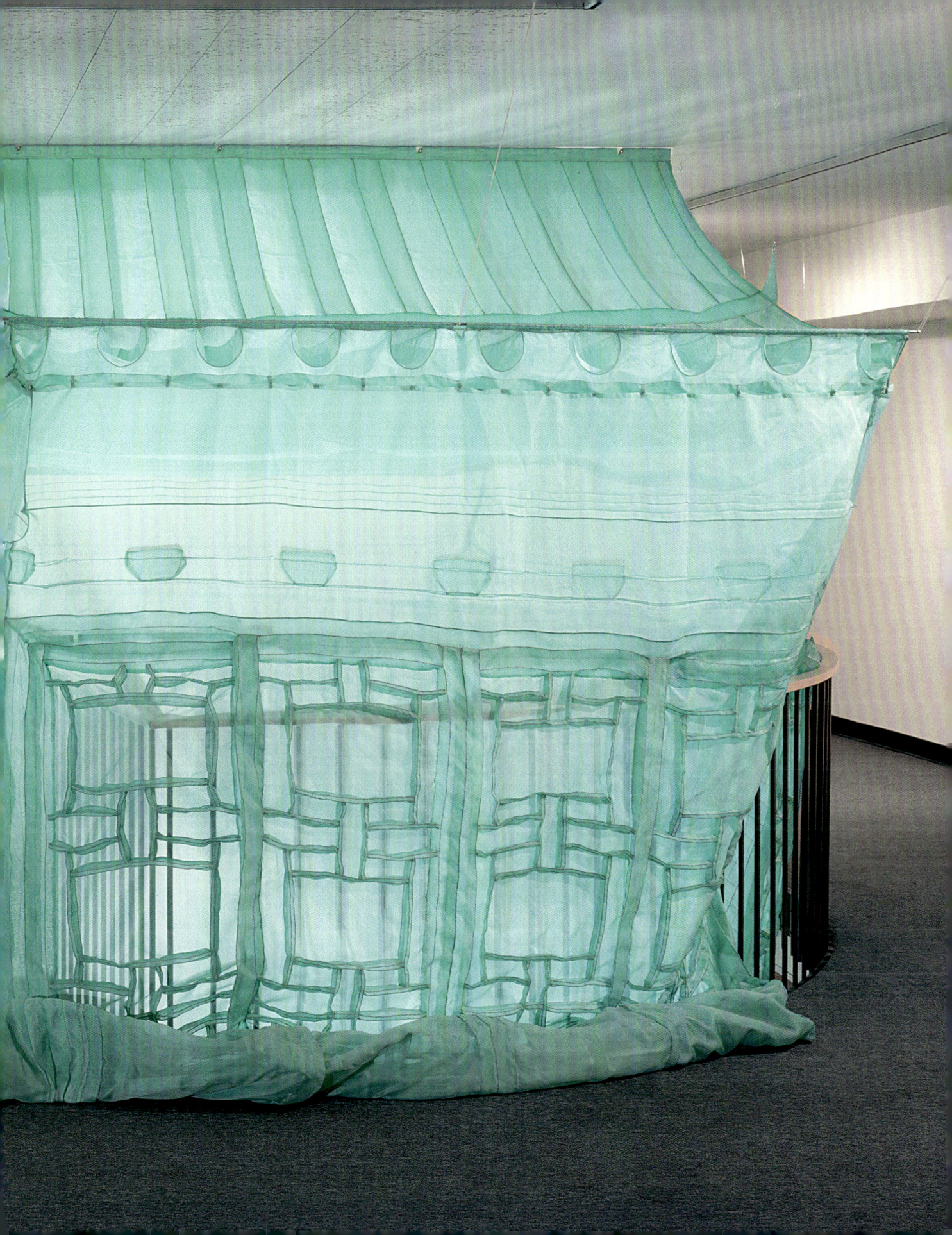

This wallpaper work is made up of tens of thousands of tiny portrait photographs that Suh collected over many years in Seoul from sources including school yearbooks. The images were scanned and then reduced to the smallest possible size at which their distinguishing features remained visible. From afar the wallpaper appears simply as a pattern of homogenised dots, but on closer inspection distinct faces appear as their details are revealed. This work is part of Suh's exploration of the relationship and tension between the individual and the collective, and his interest in what he describes as 'the minimum differential space that lets me be what/who I am and not you, or anyone else'. Exploring the construction of collective identity, the work makes visual the subsuming of the individual and their unique identity within a larger collective group. It also probes habits of looking and perception. The use of wallpaper as the medium plays with the notion of blending in; pasted as a backdrop or a second skin, the work is seamlessly incorporated into the museum's architecture, acting as a support for signage and wayfinding. (KW: Kira Wainstein)

Who Am We? (Multicoloured)

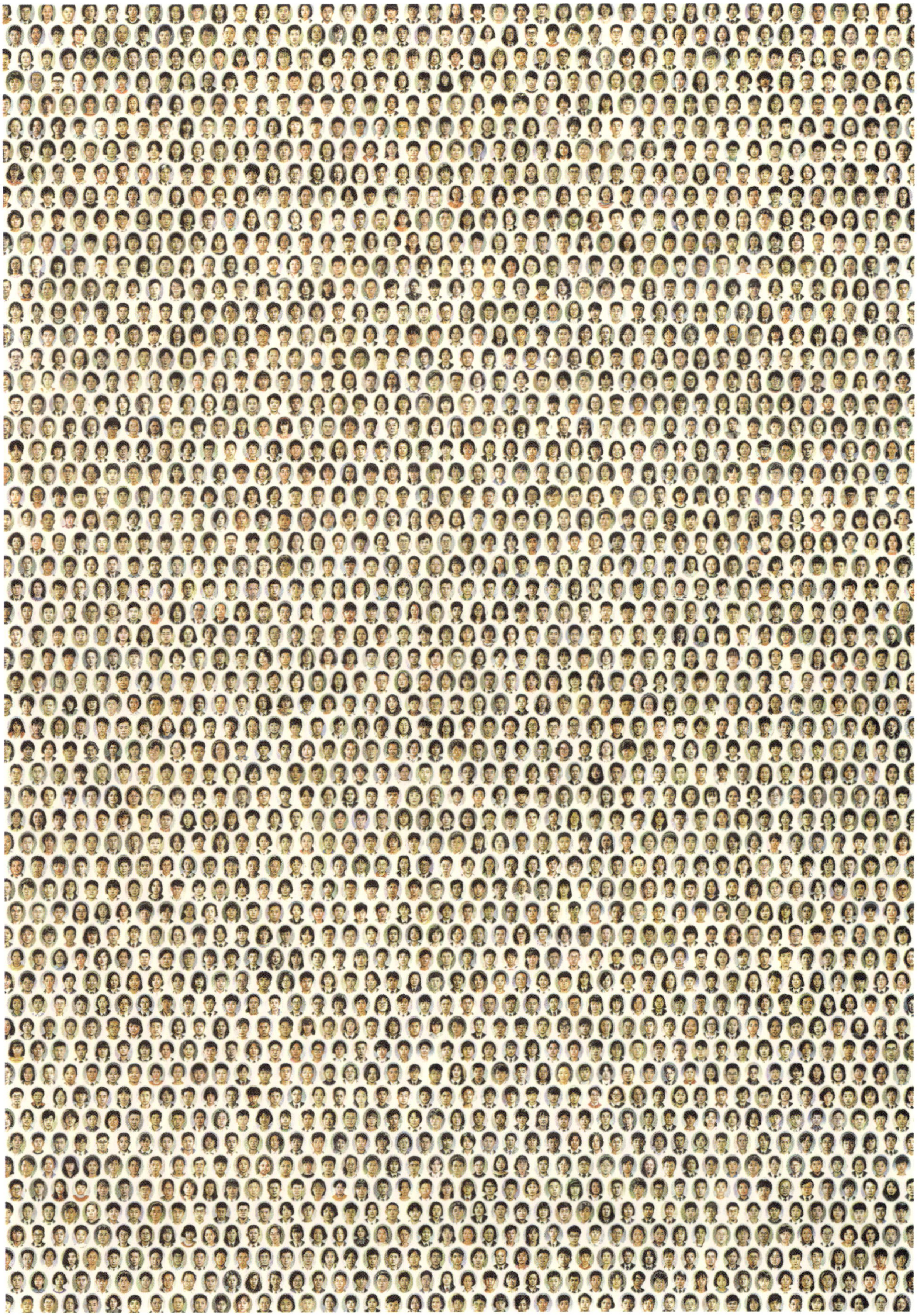

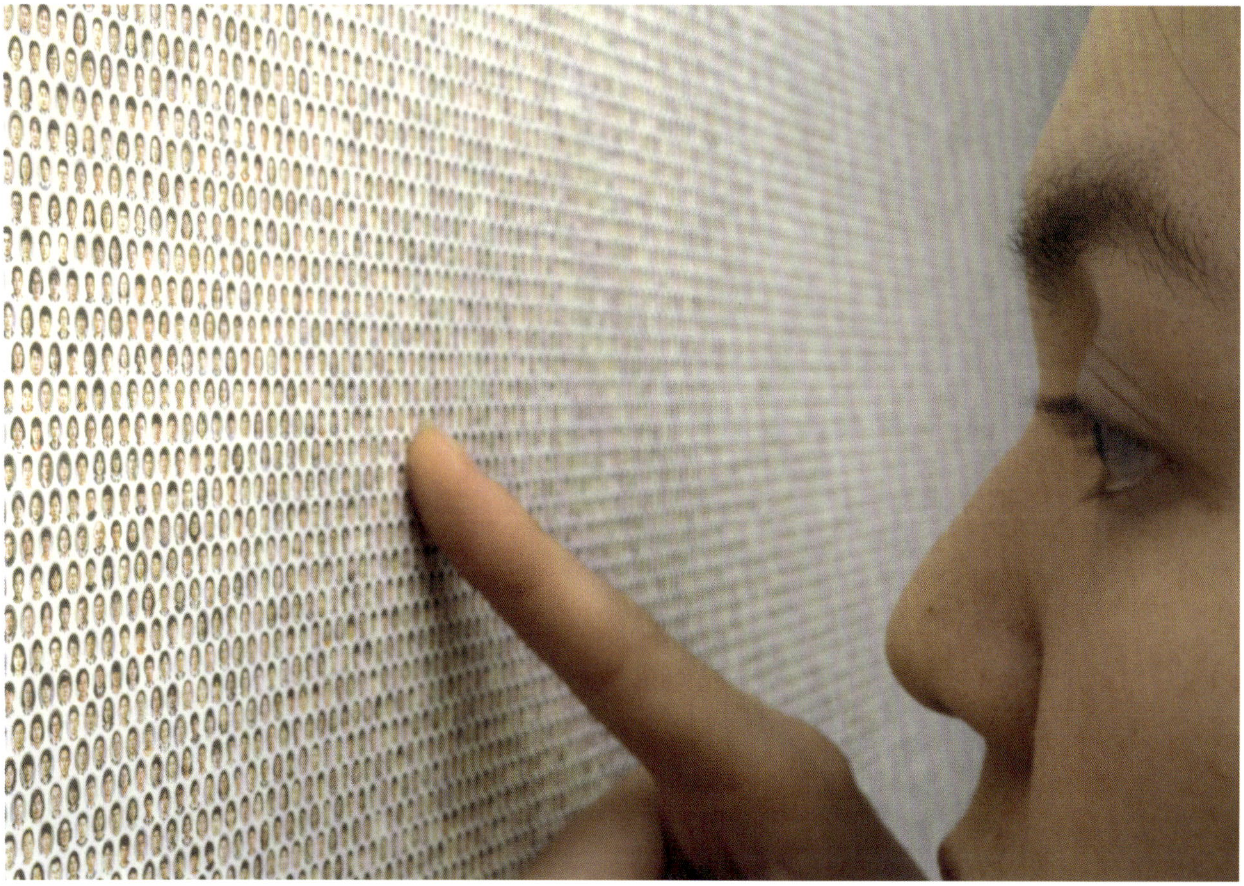

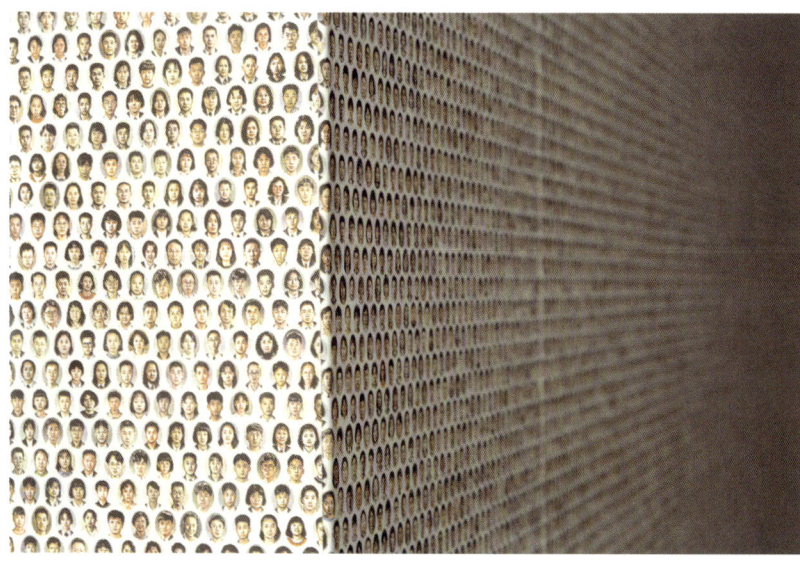

Above: *Who Am We? (Multicoloured)* 2000, installation view, Art Sonje Center, Seoul, 2003
Opposite: *Who Am We? (Multicoloured)* 2000, installation view, Museum of Contemporary Art, Chicago, 2024

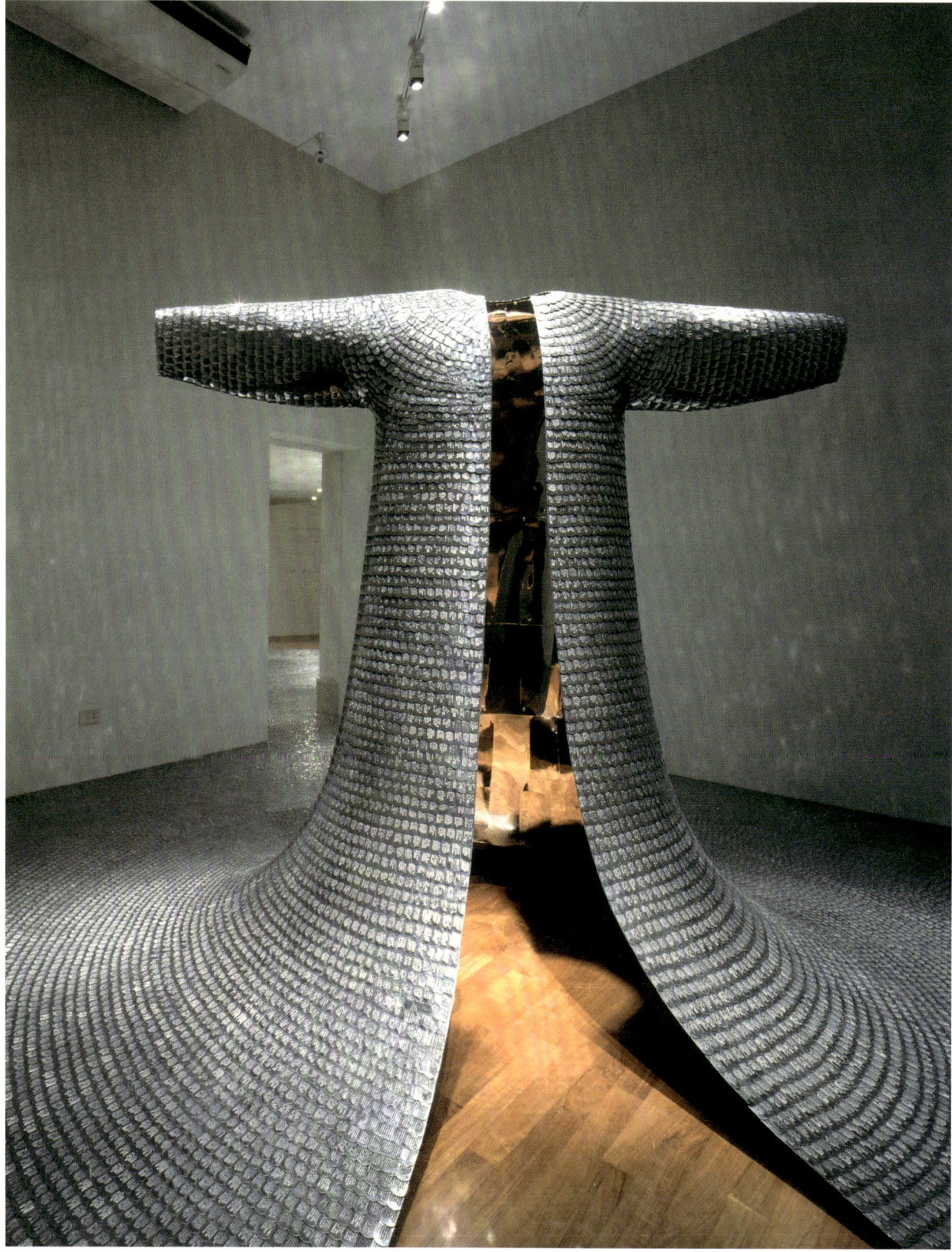

Some/One 2001, installation view, the 49th Venice Biennale, Korean Pavilion, 2001

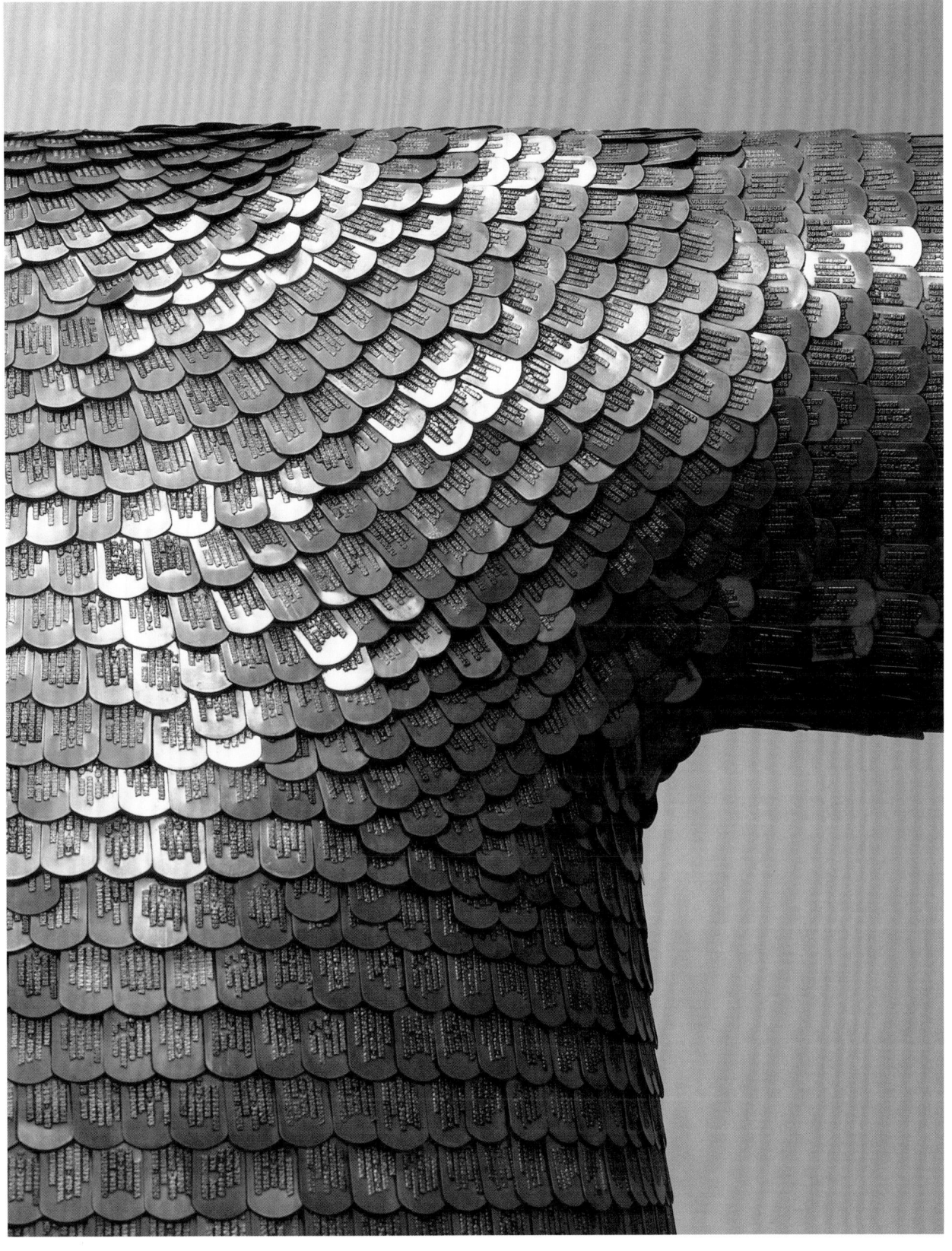

Rubbing/Loving: Company Housing of Gwangju Theater

This site-responsive work was created for the 2012 Gwangju Biennale. It is one of a series of rubbings Suh has made of domestic spaces in the city that lay empty following the Gwangju Uprising, a mass protest against the South Korean military government which took place in May 1980. Following a brutal suppression of the protest by the military, causing widespread casualties, the government covered up what had taken place, censoring news coverage, the publication of books, and even South Koreans' freedom to speak of it. Despite increasing awareness of the event in the last few decades, estimates for the number of civilians killed still vary. For this work, a rubbing of the interior of a residence belonging to cinema employees, Suh and a team of five assistants covered the space with paper, then rubbed the entire surface of the room with graphite. They wore blindfolds as they worked. Peculiarly, one corner of the space was missed by every member of the team. Of the collective experience of creating this work, Suh says: 'It was not a performance piece, but there was a deeply moving sense of ritual, or commemoration, that came from doing things together.' Tracing the shape of absence in the collective memory of South Korea, the work also speaks more specifically to the community of Gwangju who lived through the uprising, the lives lost, and the many stories which remain unknown. In an ongoing renegotiation of the space between two and three dimensions, Suh adapted the work in 2025, unfolding the room structure into a floorplan-like form (pictured overleaf). (KW)

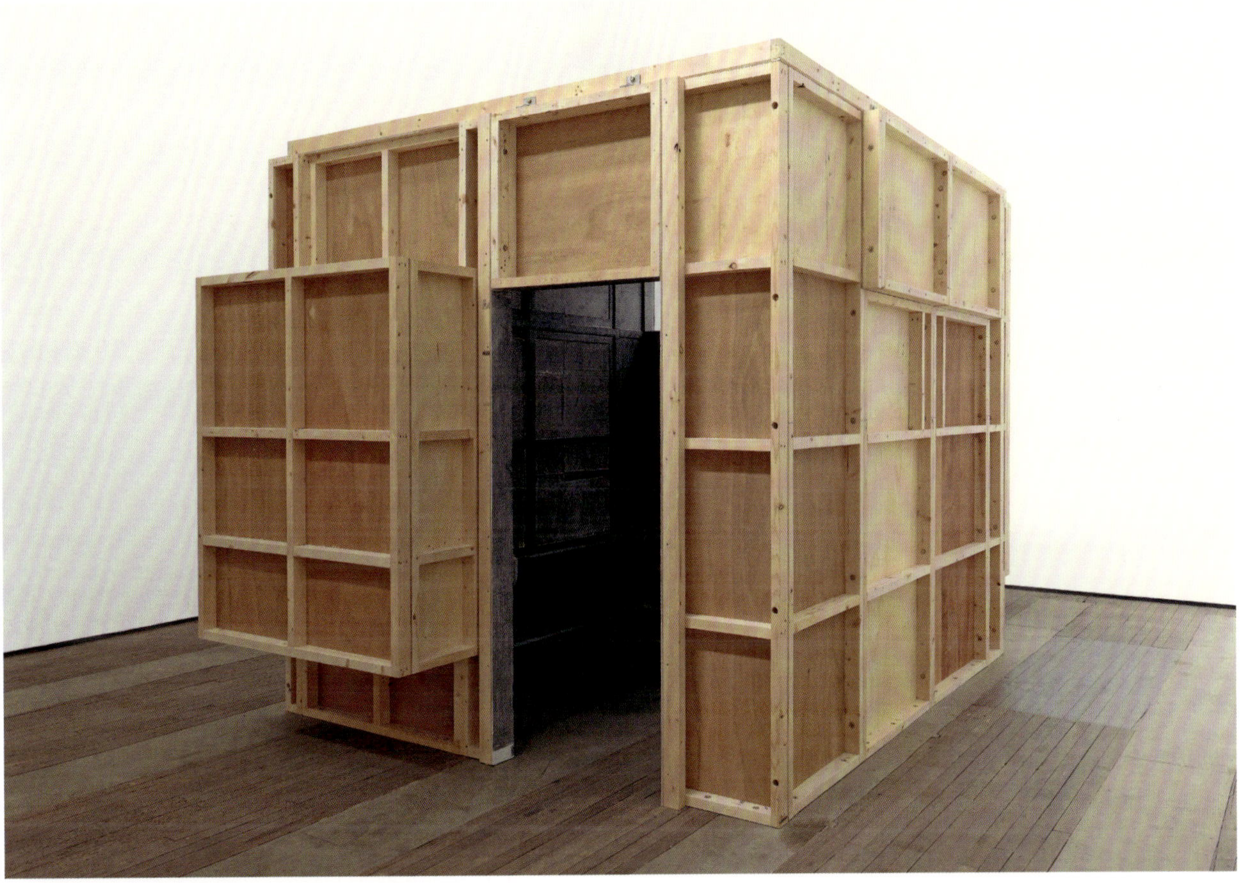

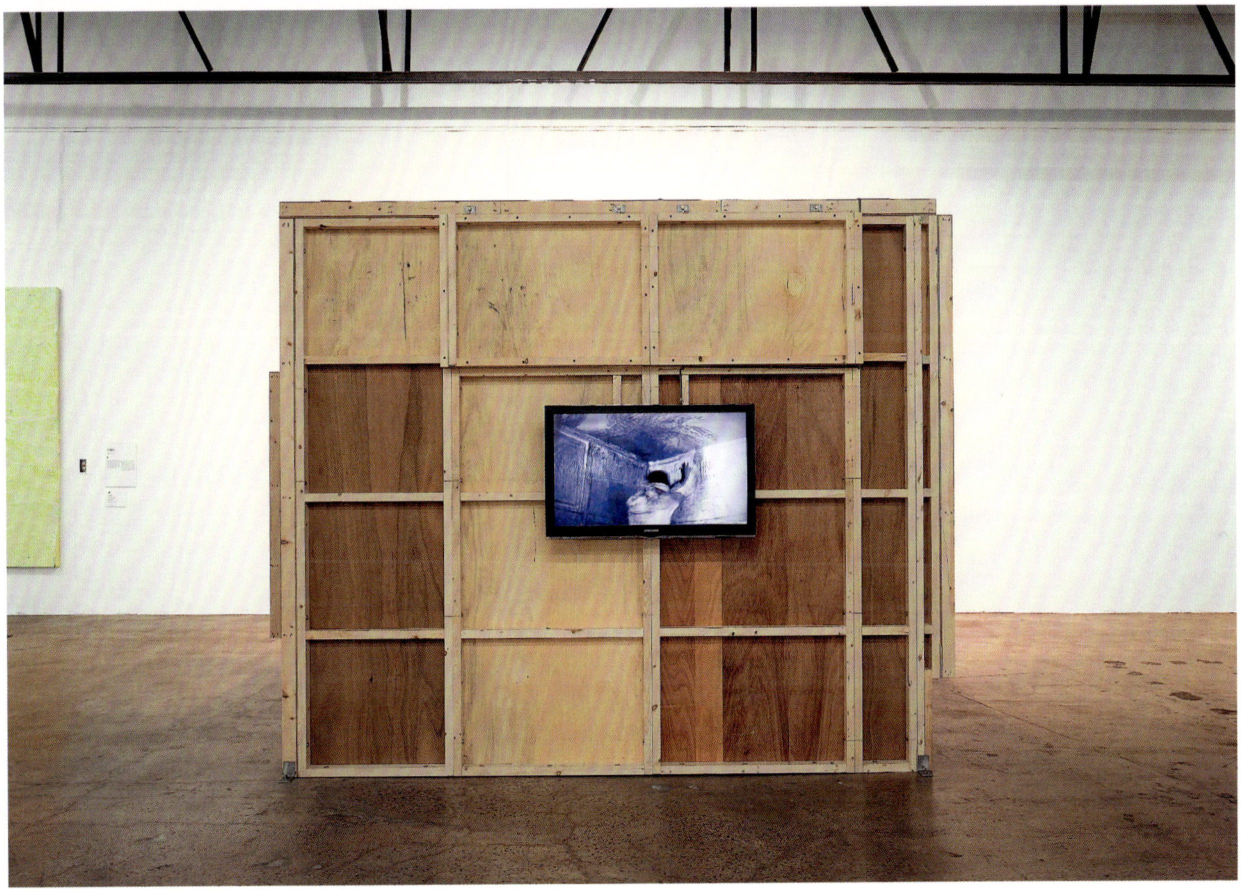

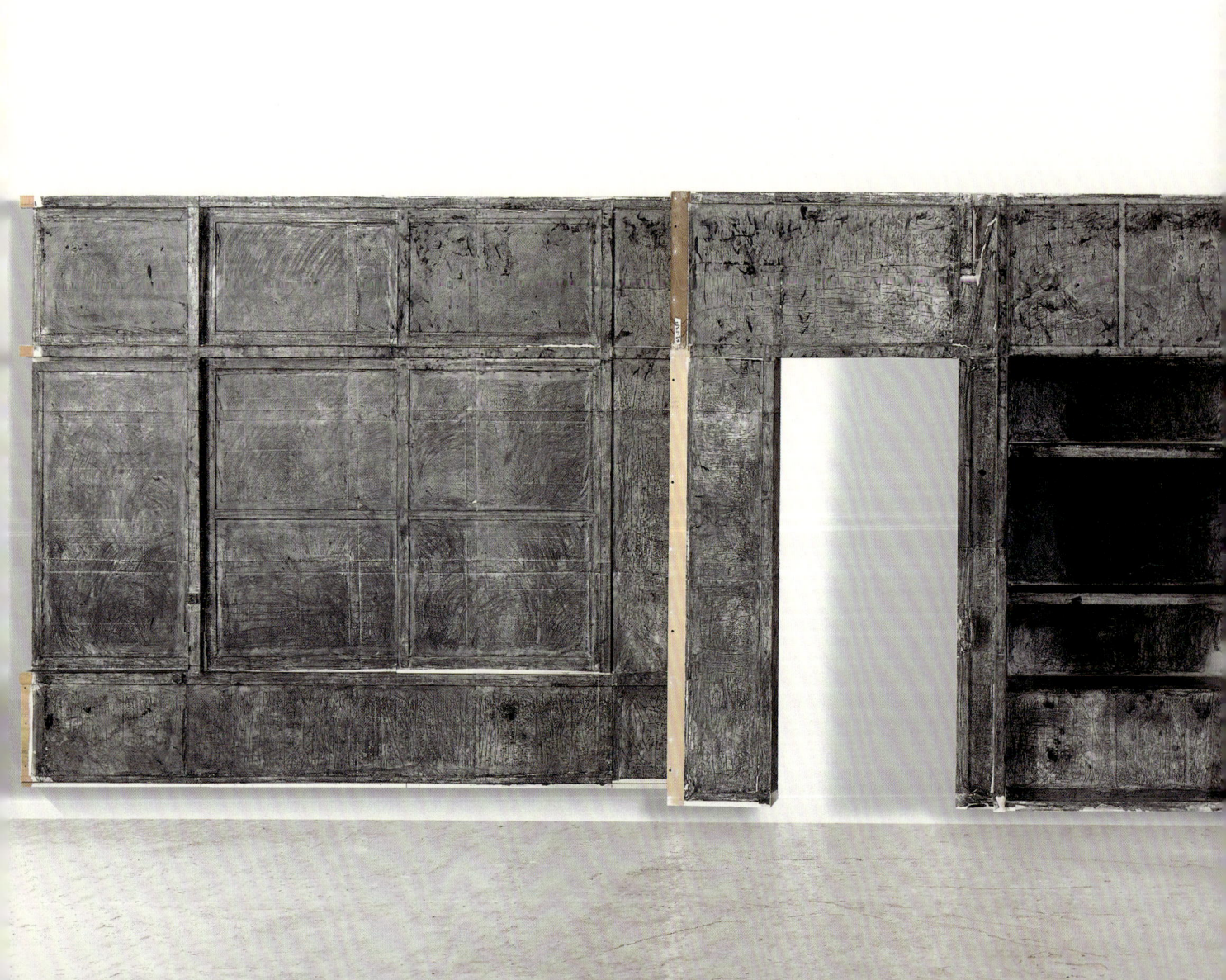

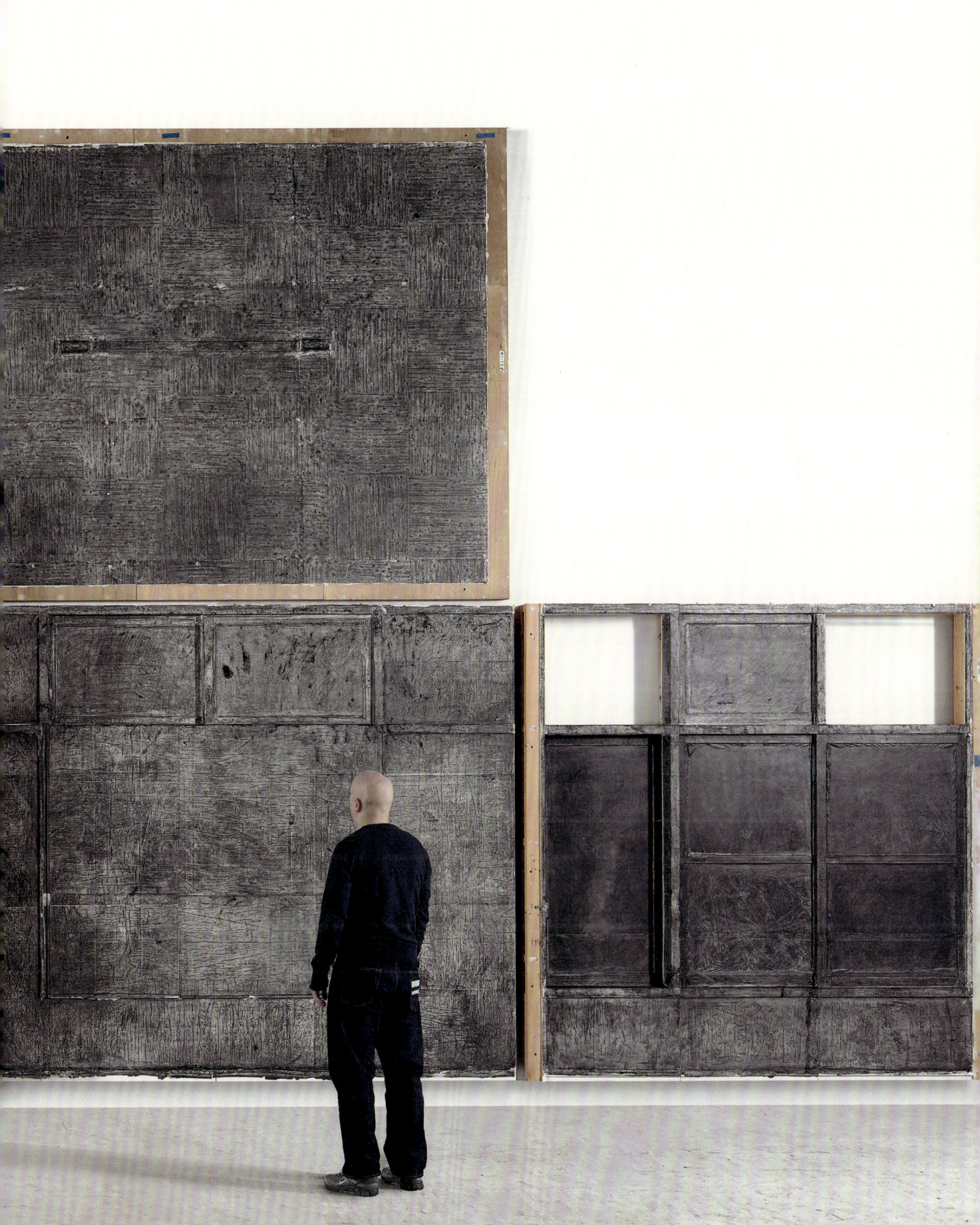

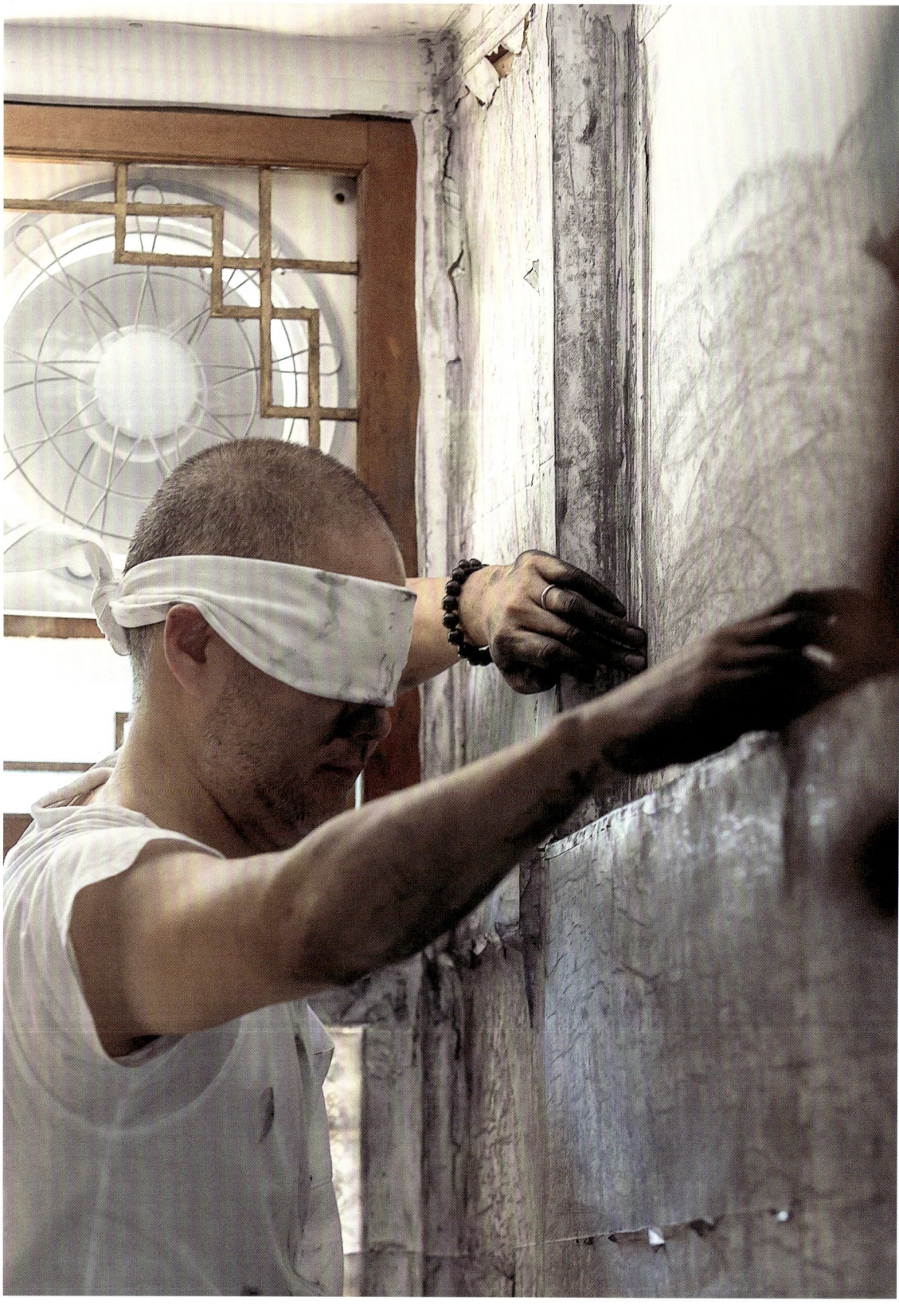

Previous pages: *Rubbing/Loving: Company Housing of Gwangju Theater* 2012,
reconfigured for Tate Modern, 2025
Above and opposite: Do Ho Suh rubbing *Company Housing of Gwangju Theater* 2012

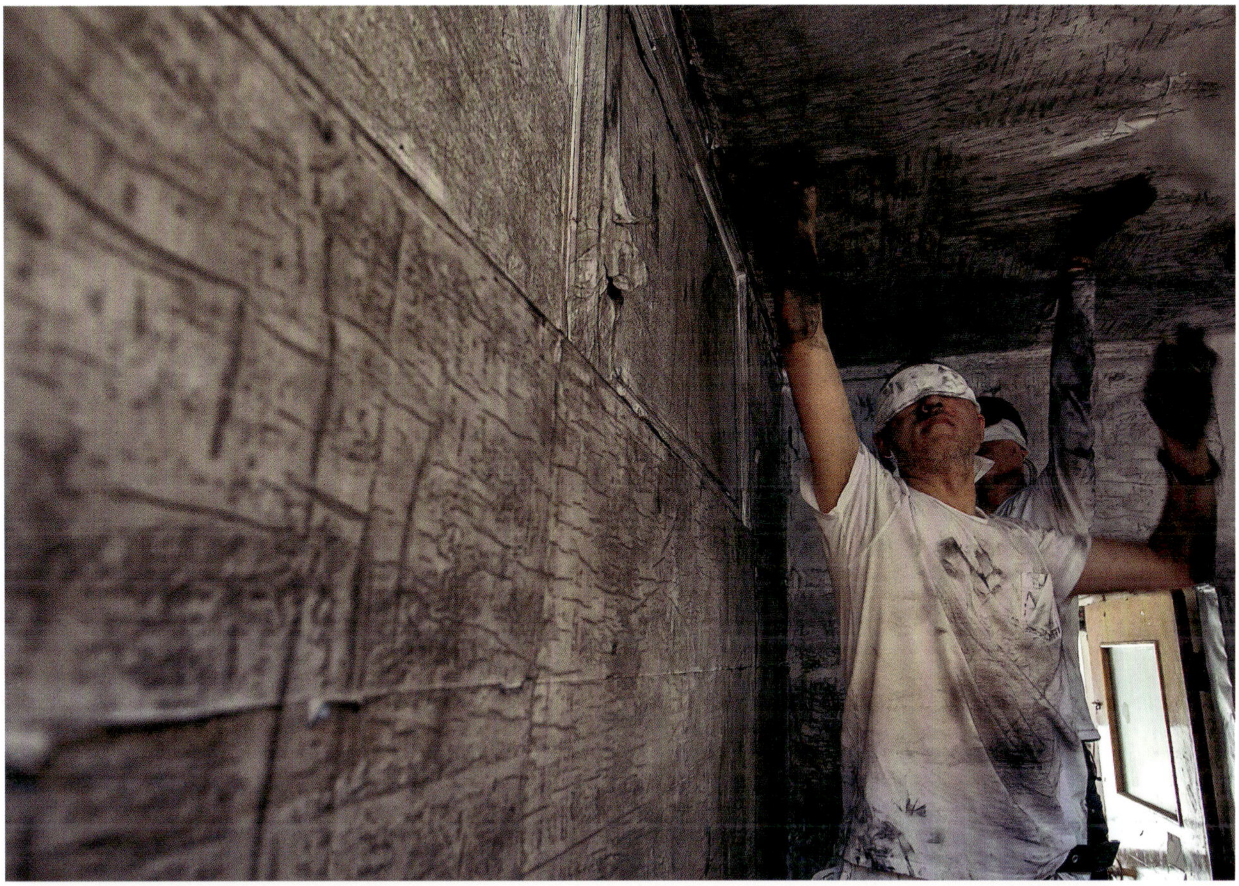

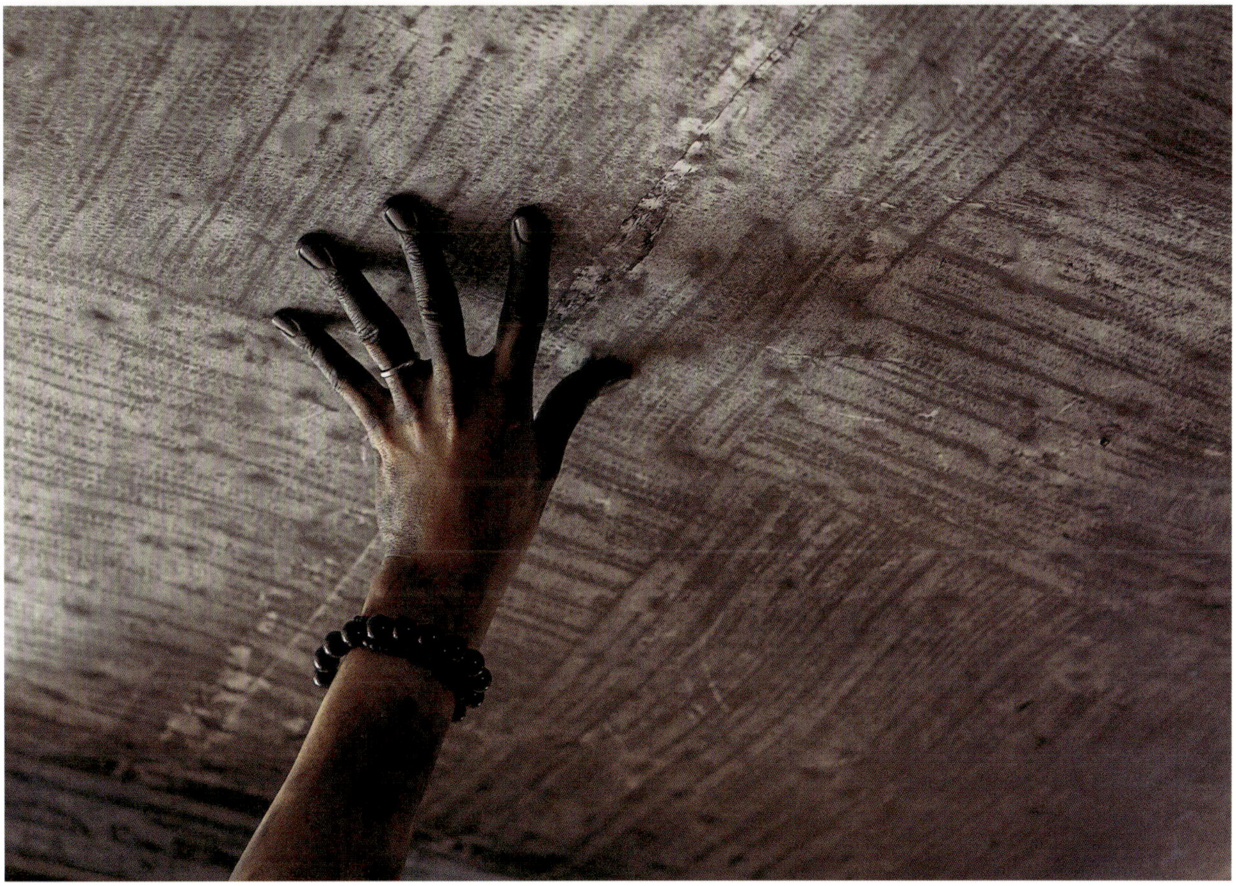

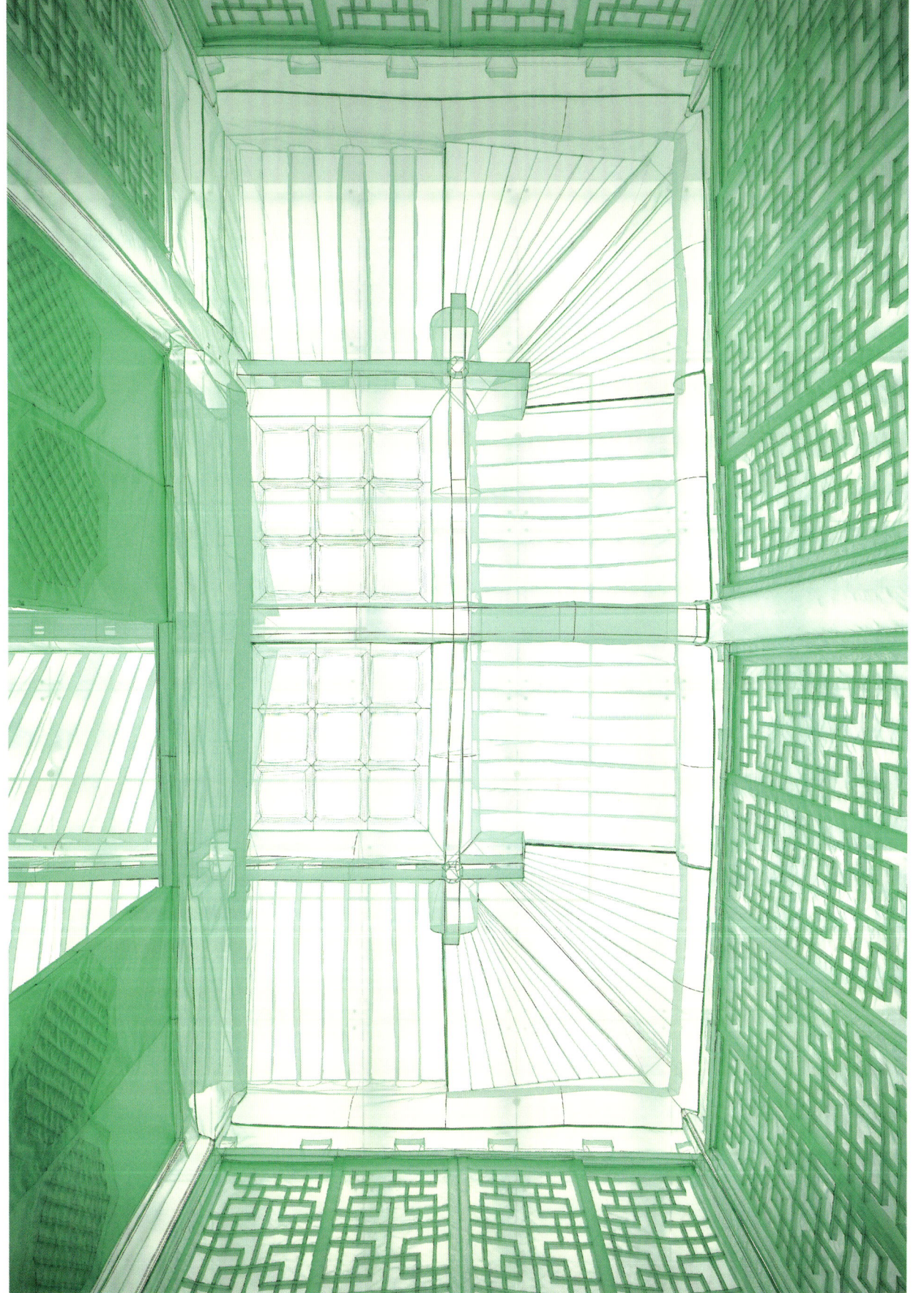

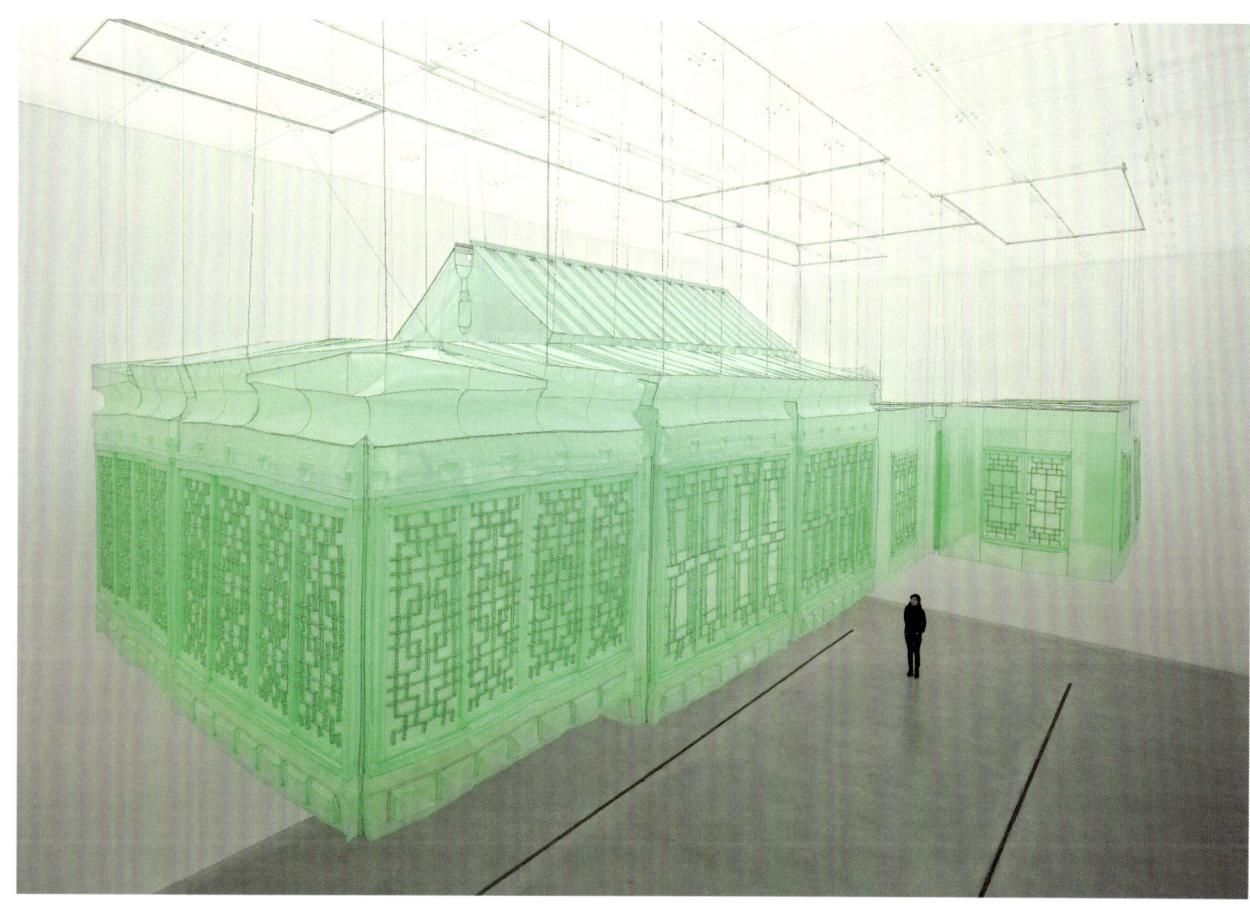

Left, above and overleaf: *Seoul Home / Seoul Home / Kanazawa Home / Beijing Home / Pohang Home / Gwangju Home / Philadelphia Home* 2012, installation views, 21st Century Museum of Contemporary Art, Kanazawa, 2012

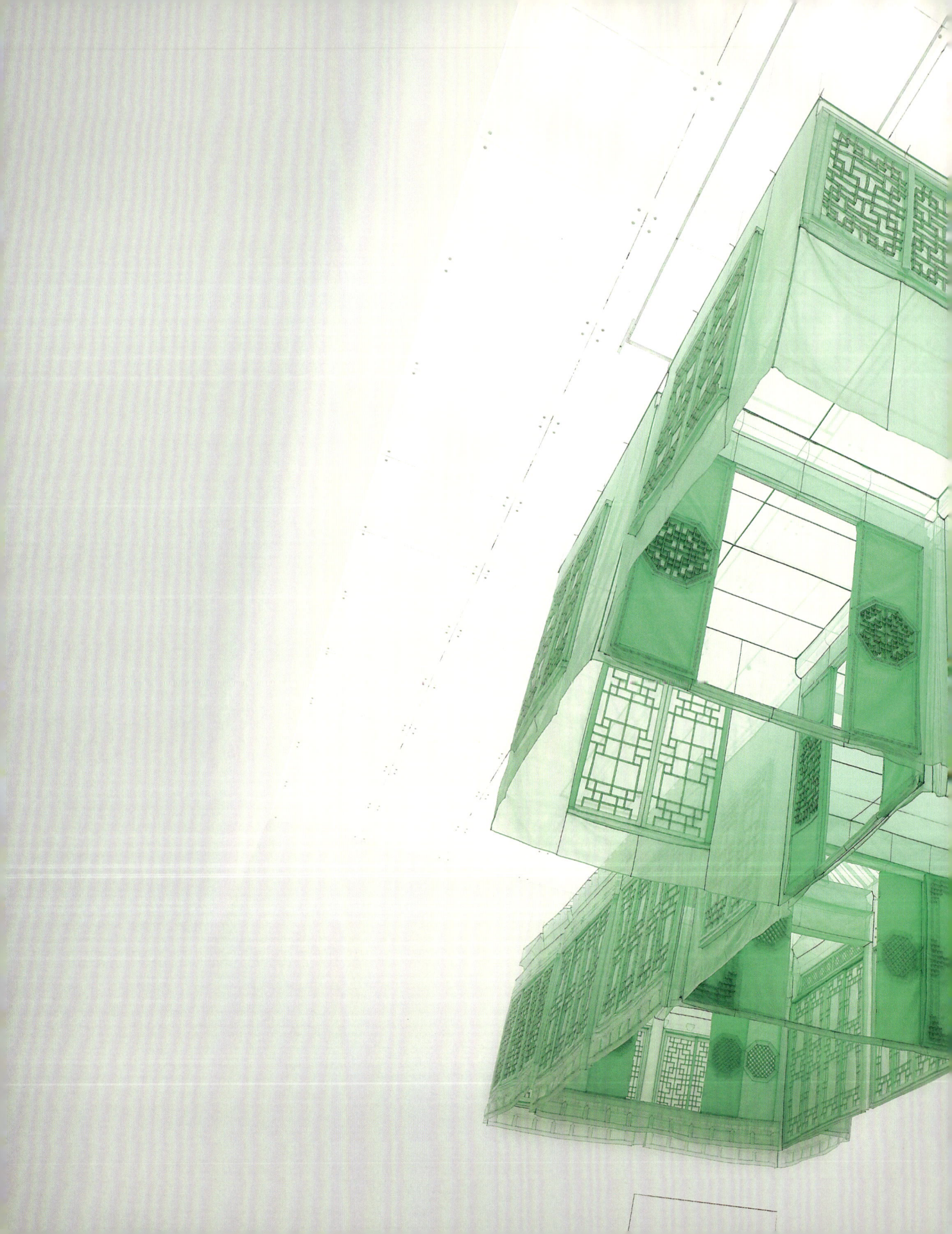

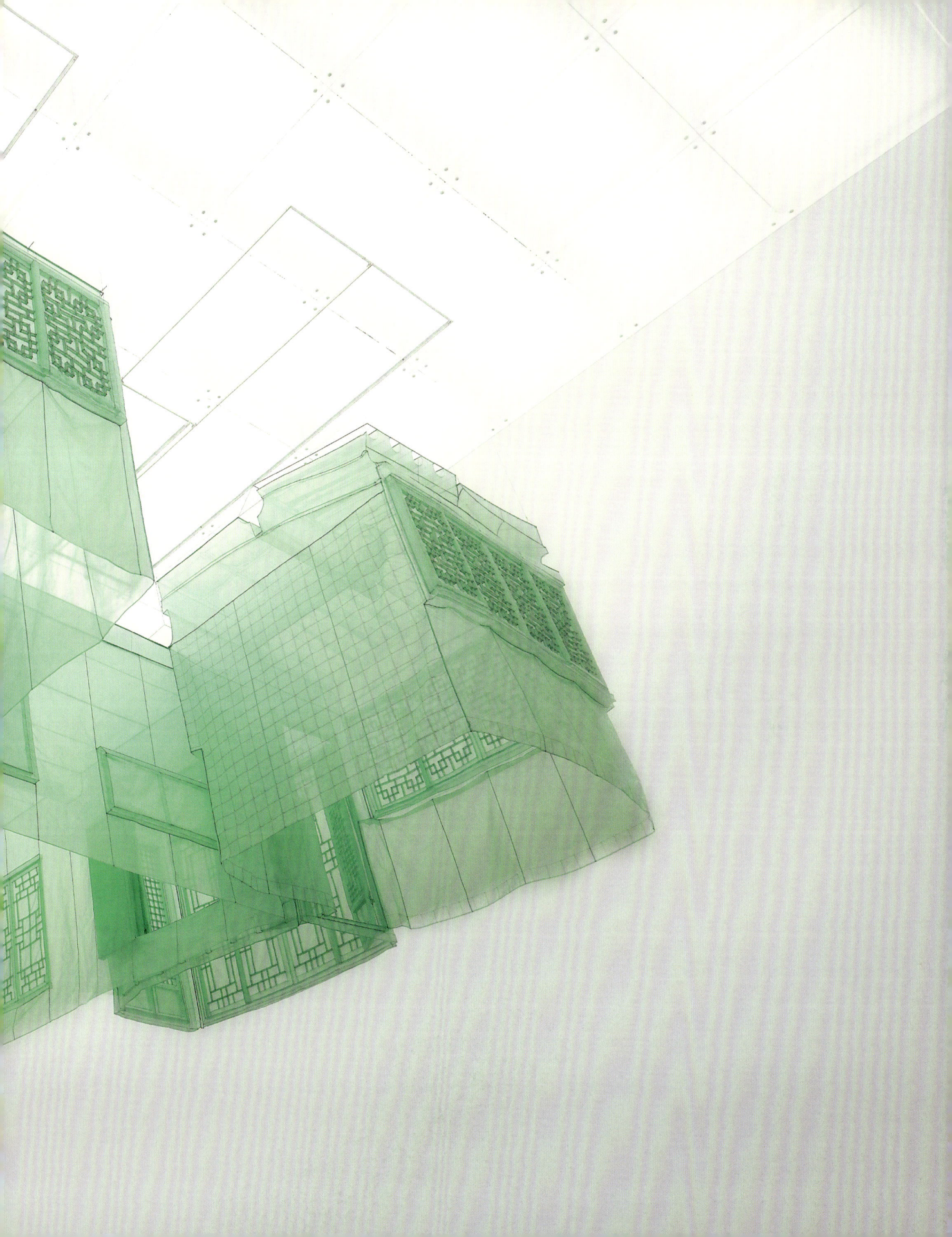

Made decades after Suh moved to the United States, *Rubbing/Loving: Seoul Home* 2013–22 is a 1:1 scale materialisation of the artist's childhood home in Seoul – a house that he says 'has always followed me'. Suh wrapped the entire building in mulberry paper, rubbing over it with graphite to reveal the surface beneath. This laborious process created a portable trace of his home which he could pack up and take with him, 'erecting' it elsewhere on an aluminium armature. Suh's childhood home is itself based on a nineteenth-century house in the grounds of Changdeokgung Palace. These traditional Korean buildings, known as *hanok*, faced widespread destruction during the twentieth century as a result of occupation, war and development. By the time Suh's parents constructed their home in the 1970s, *hanok* were continuing to disappear, this time to make way for apartment blocks. The title of the series from which this work comes, *Rubbing/Loving*, alludes to the intimacy of the rubbing process, which Suh describes as 'a gentle gesture of loving, caring and being attentive', while also playing with the lack of distinction between R and L in the Korean language, which brings these words into proximity with one another when said out loud. (KW)

Rubbing/Loving: Seoul Home

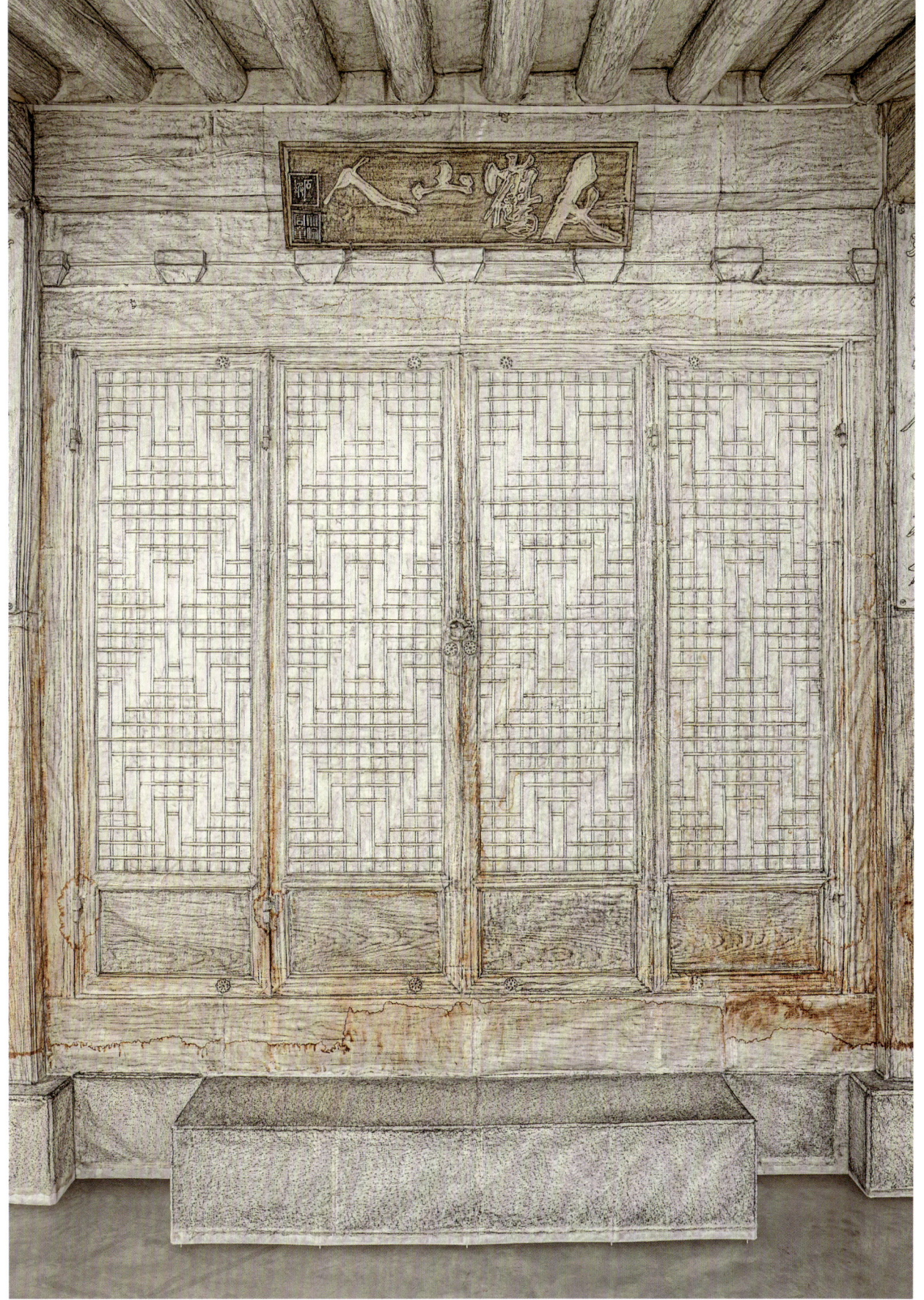

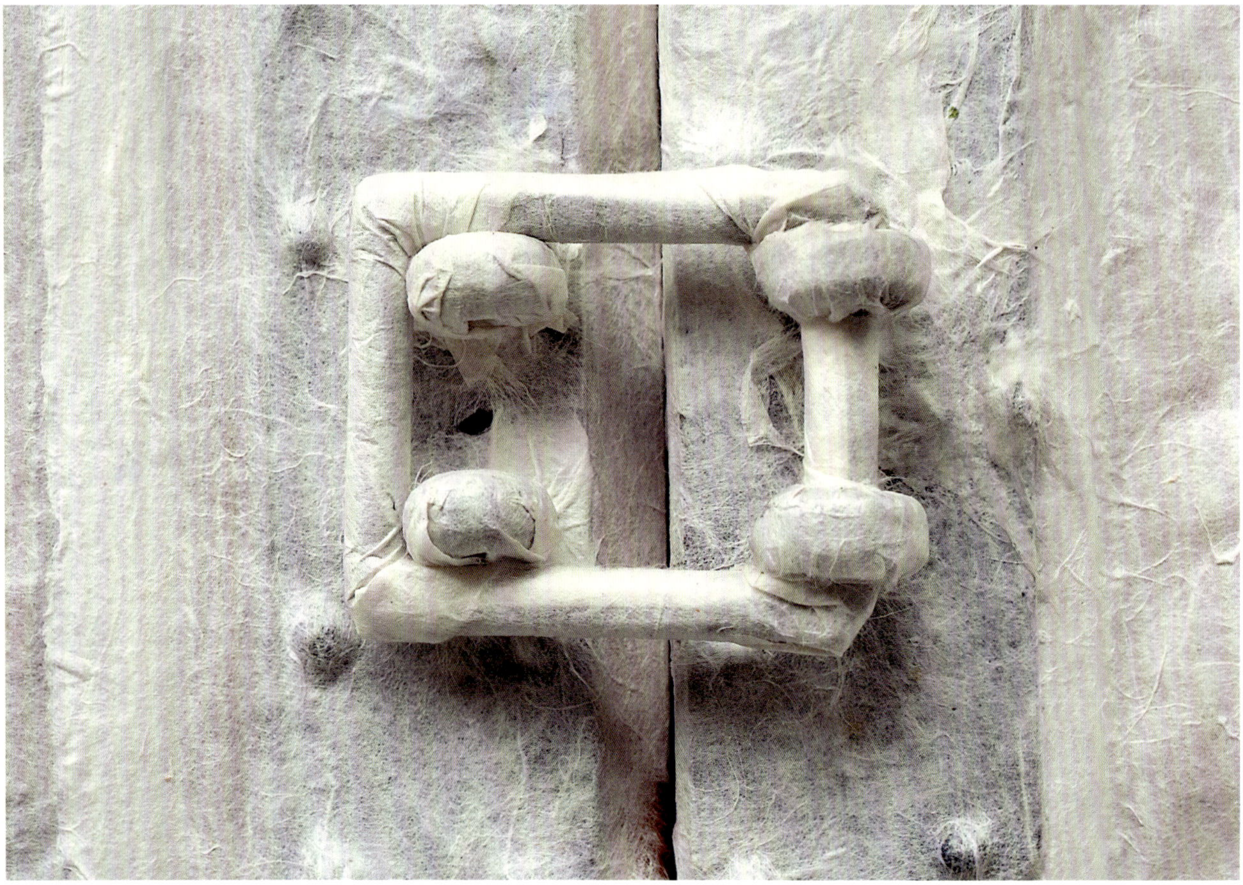

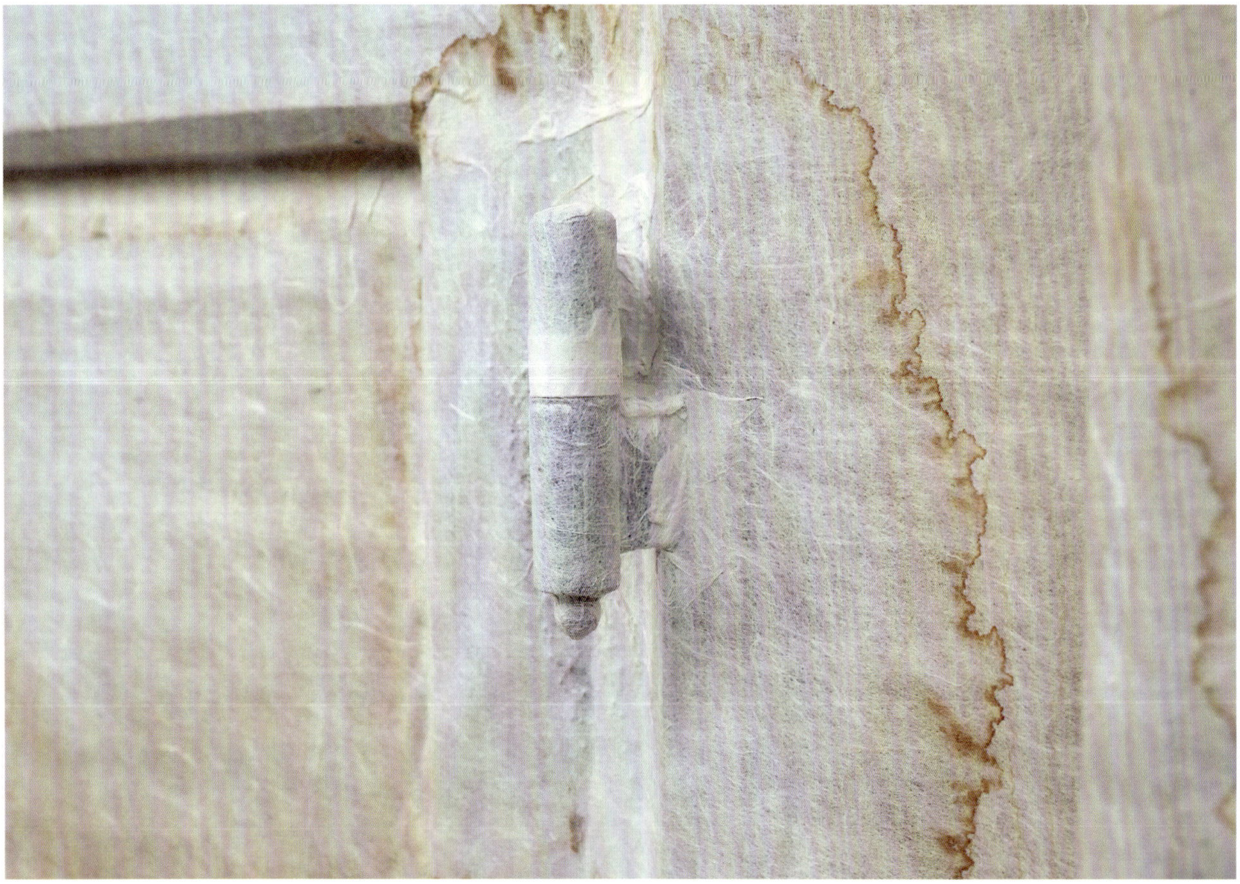

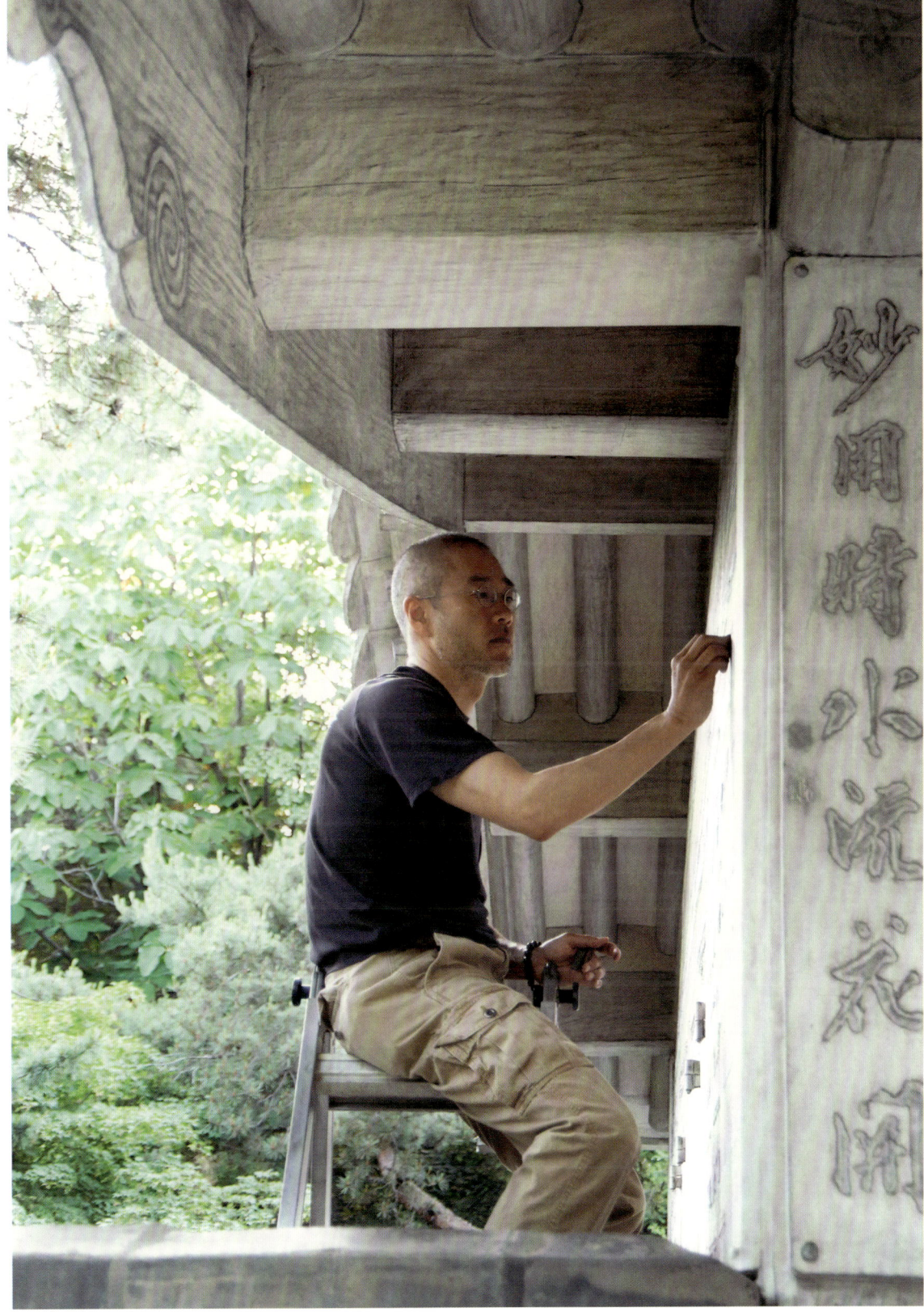

Do Ho Suh at work on the rubbing of his family home in Seoul, 2013

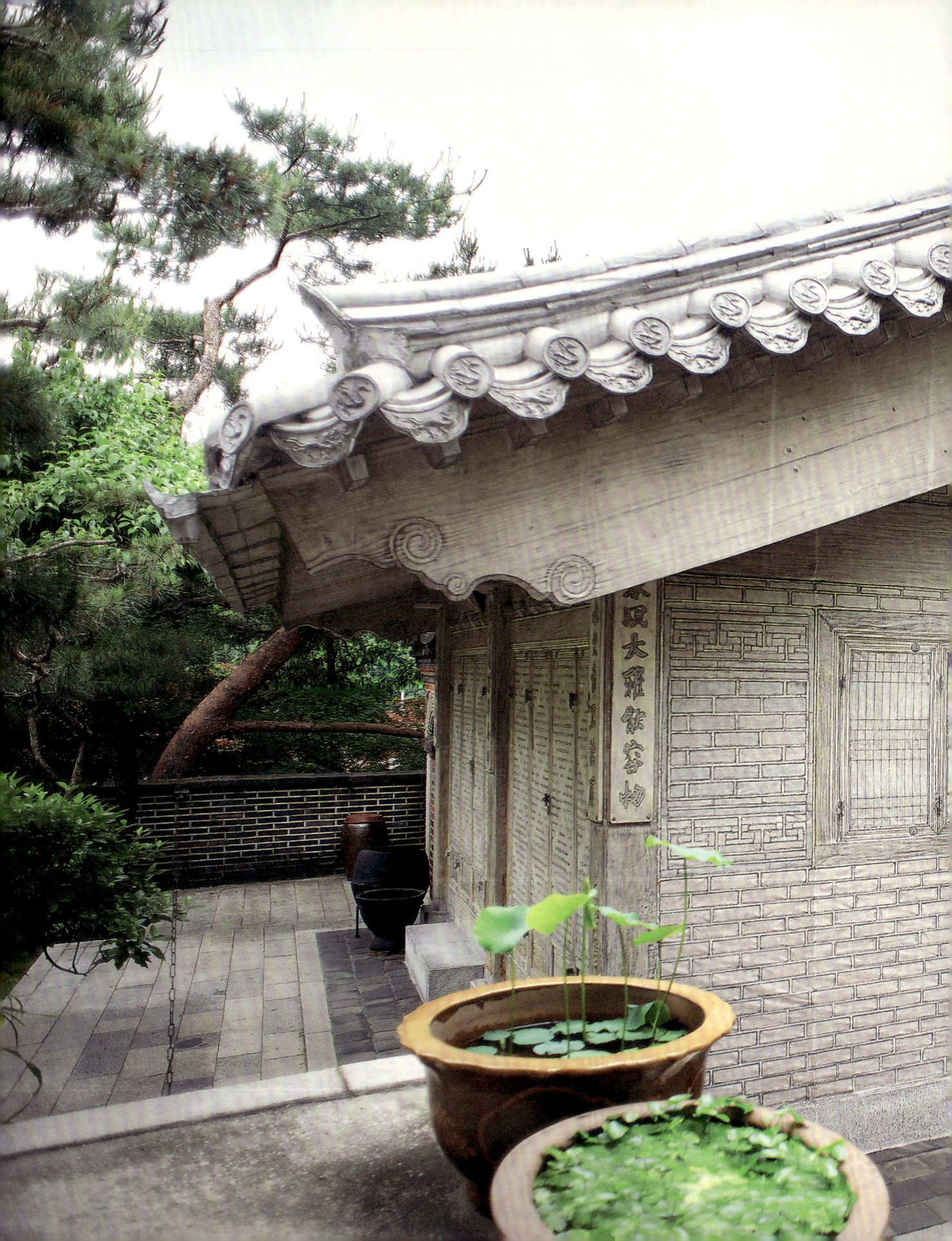

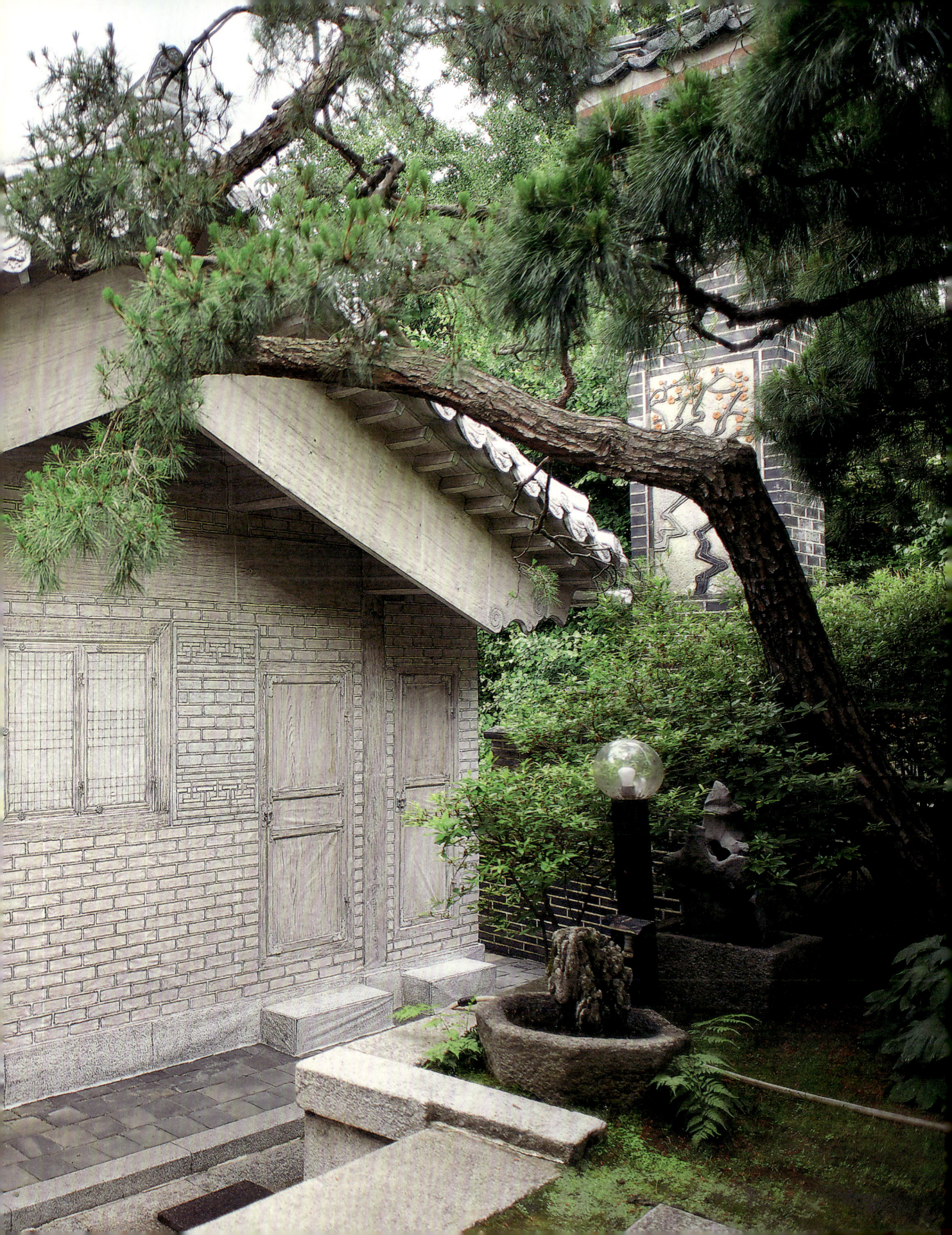

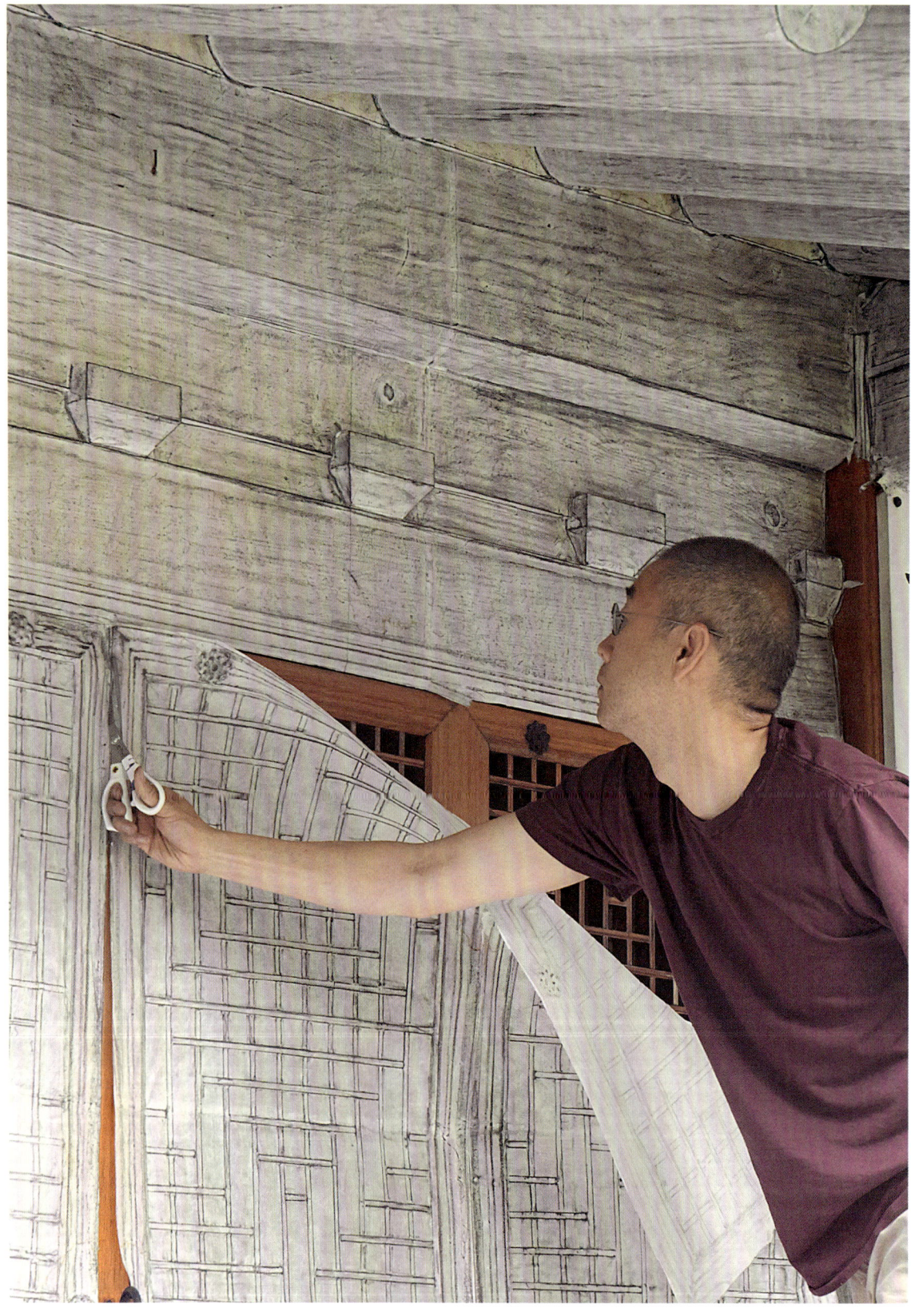

Above: Do Ho Suh at work on the rubbing of his family home in Seoul, 2013
Overleaf: *Rubbing/Loving: Seoul Home* 2013–22, installation view, Museum of Contemporary Art Australia, Sydney, 2022

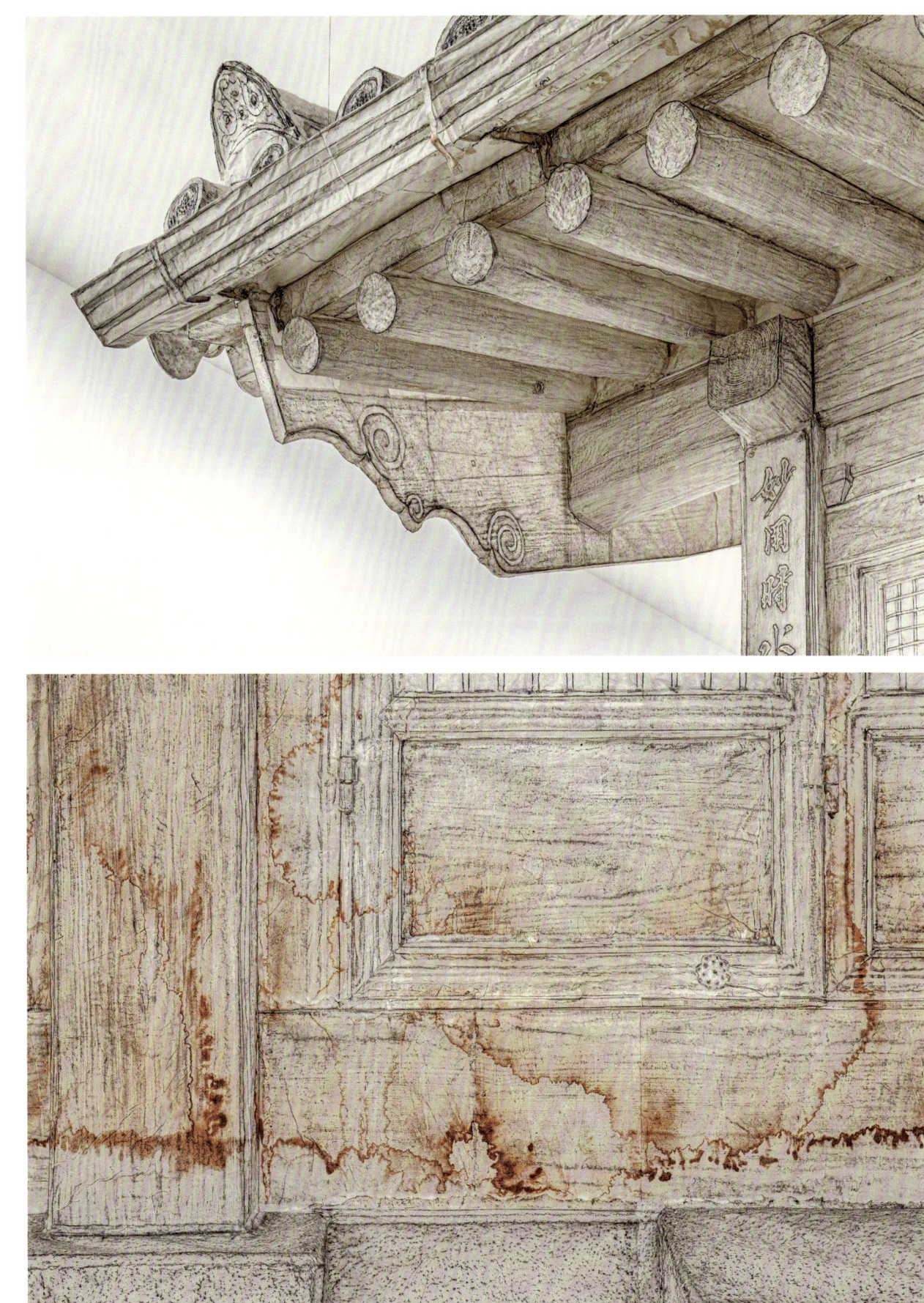

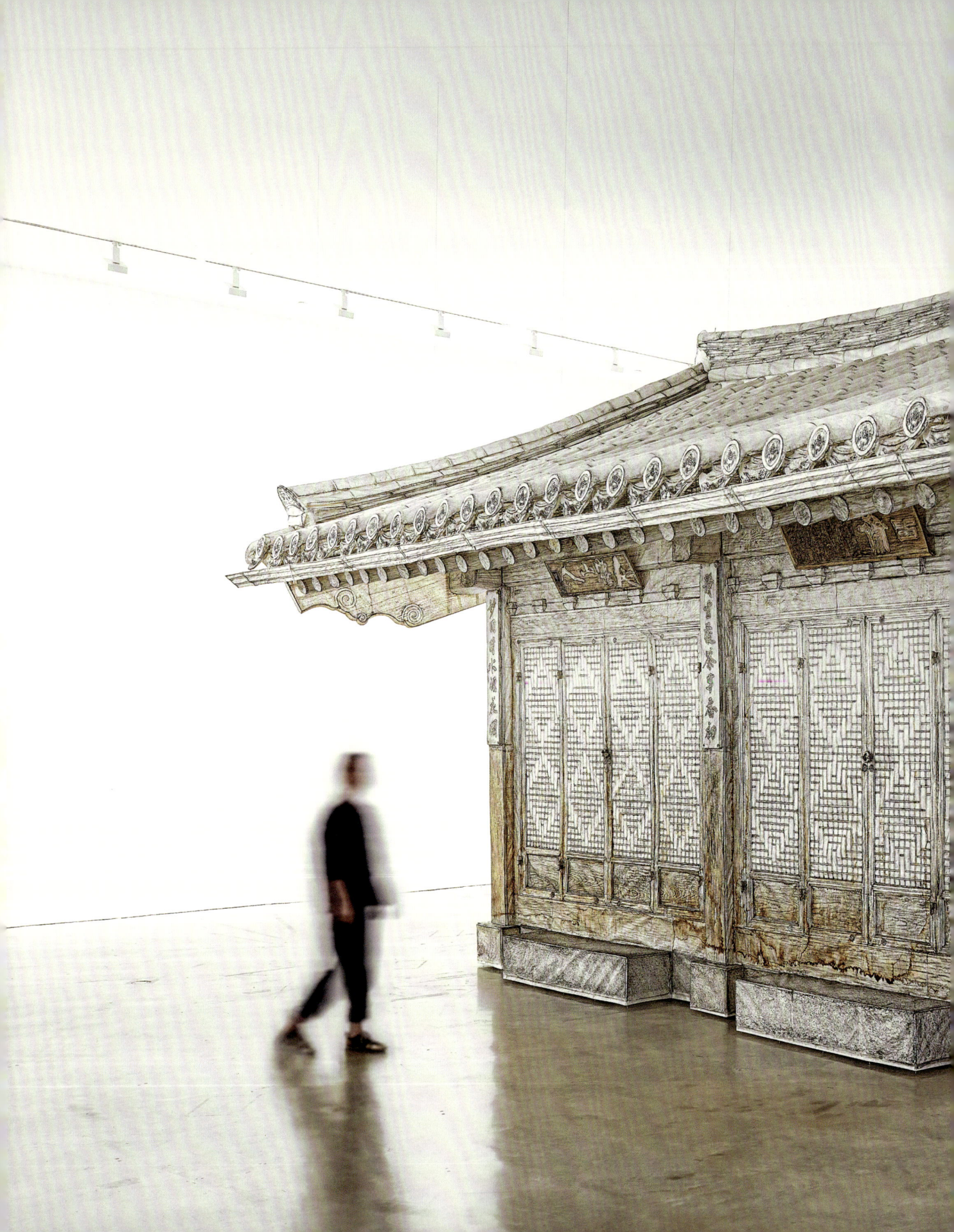

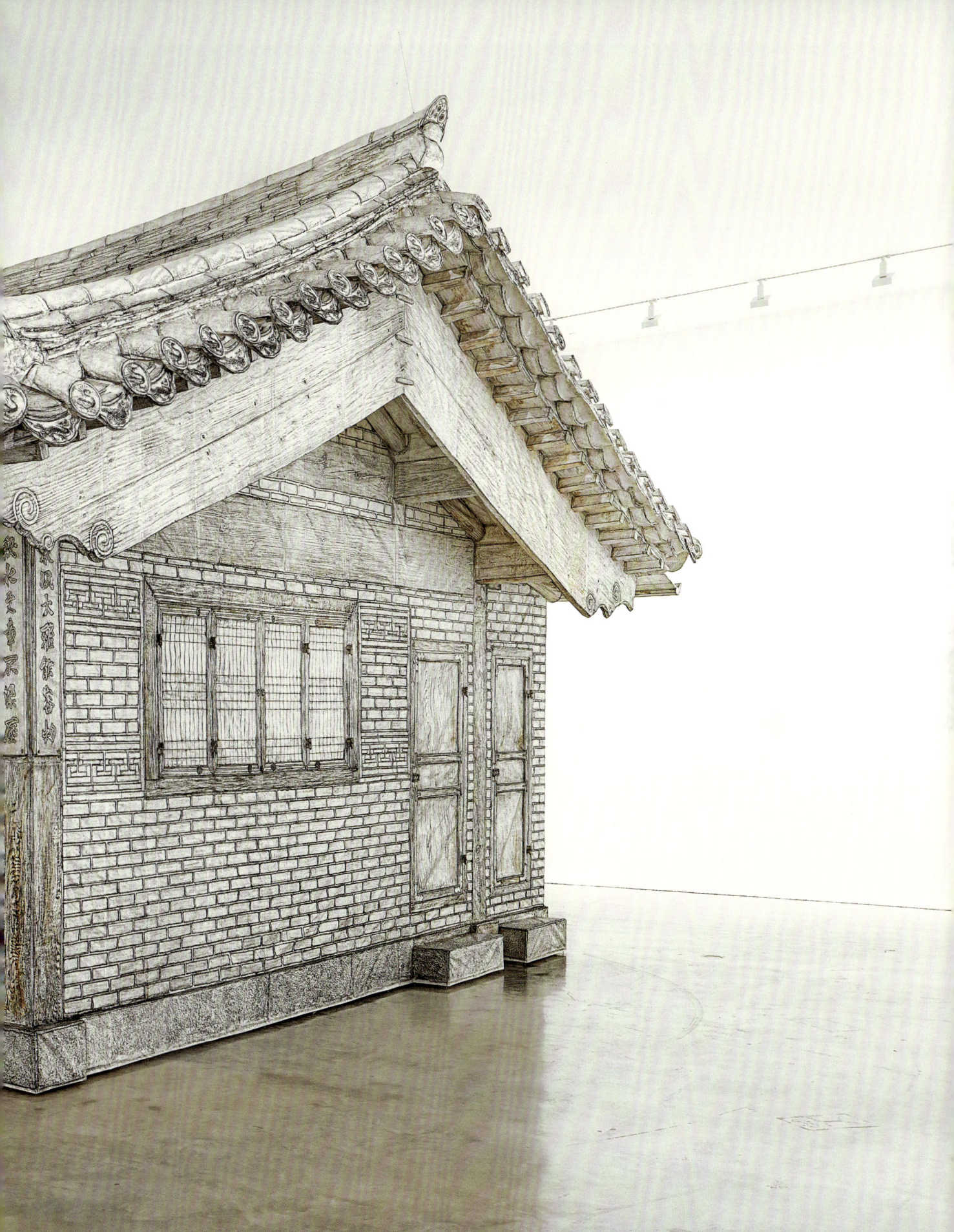

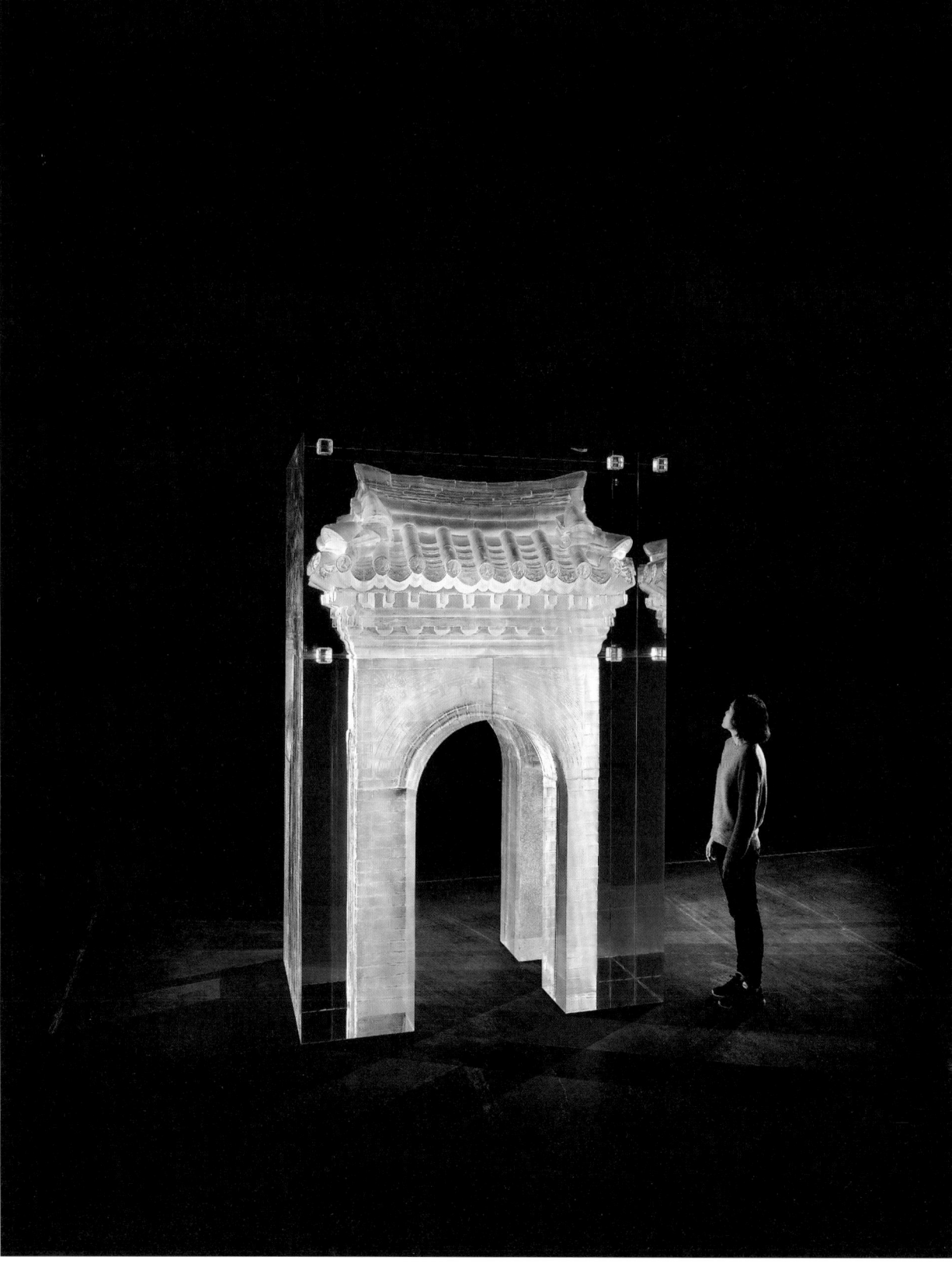

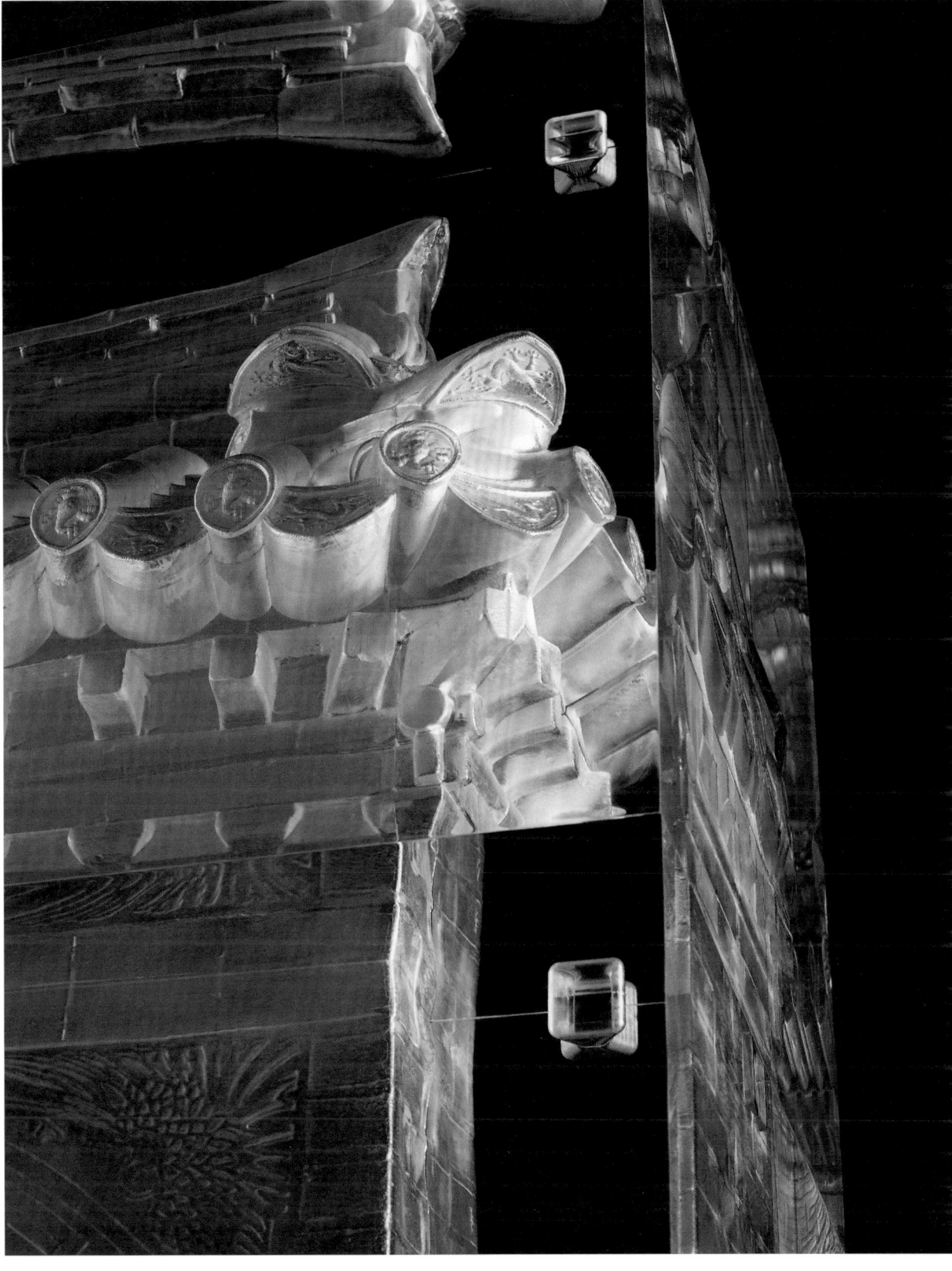

Public Figures consists of a plinth, referencing the visual language of Western monuments in form and colour, held up from below by hundreds of small fibreglass and resin figures. When Suh moved to the United States in 1991, he became preoccupied with the plinth for its embodiment of Western imperialist histories. 'I felt this everywhere,' he has said, 'from the apparently "heroic" male statues that populated civic squares, to the organisation of major museums and their confusing displays of "foreign" objects devoid of context.' Through this work, Suh draws attention to the plinth as a supporting structure that upholds these oppressive narratives and directs patterns of looking: the plinth unfailingly directs the gaze upwards. The plinth here is empty, no person or event being commemorated on its platform; instead, its weight bears down on small-scale figures beneath, who hold it aloft with their legs braced and arms upstretched. This demonstration of collective resilience and renewal likewise engages with Suh's thinking about Korea's histories of oppression. In Korean, the term '*mincho*' refers to the general public or oppressed people, but its literal translation is 'public grass', as Suh explains, 'because it never dies, it continually renews itself'. *Public Figures* was first created in 1998 as a public sculpture for an exhibition in a park in Brooklyn, New York. Suh's original design imagined a kinetic element which would have allowed the work to move independently, inch by inch each day. (KW)

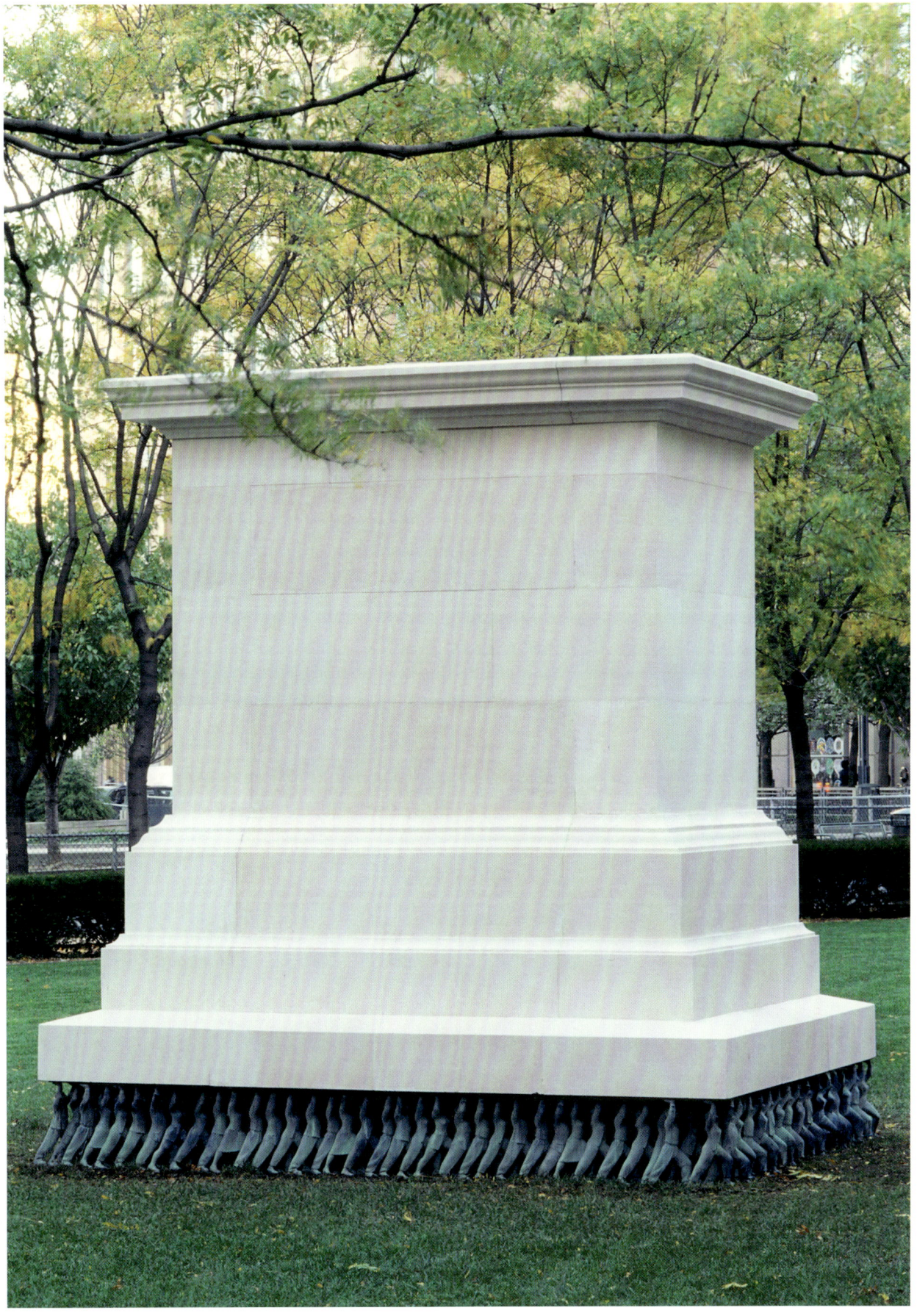

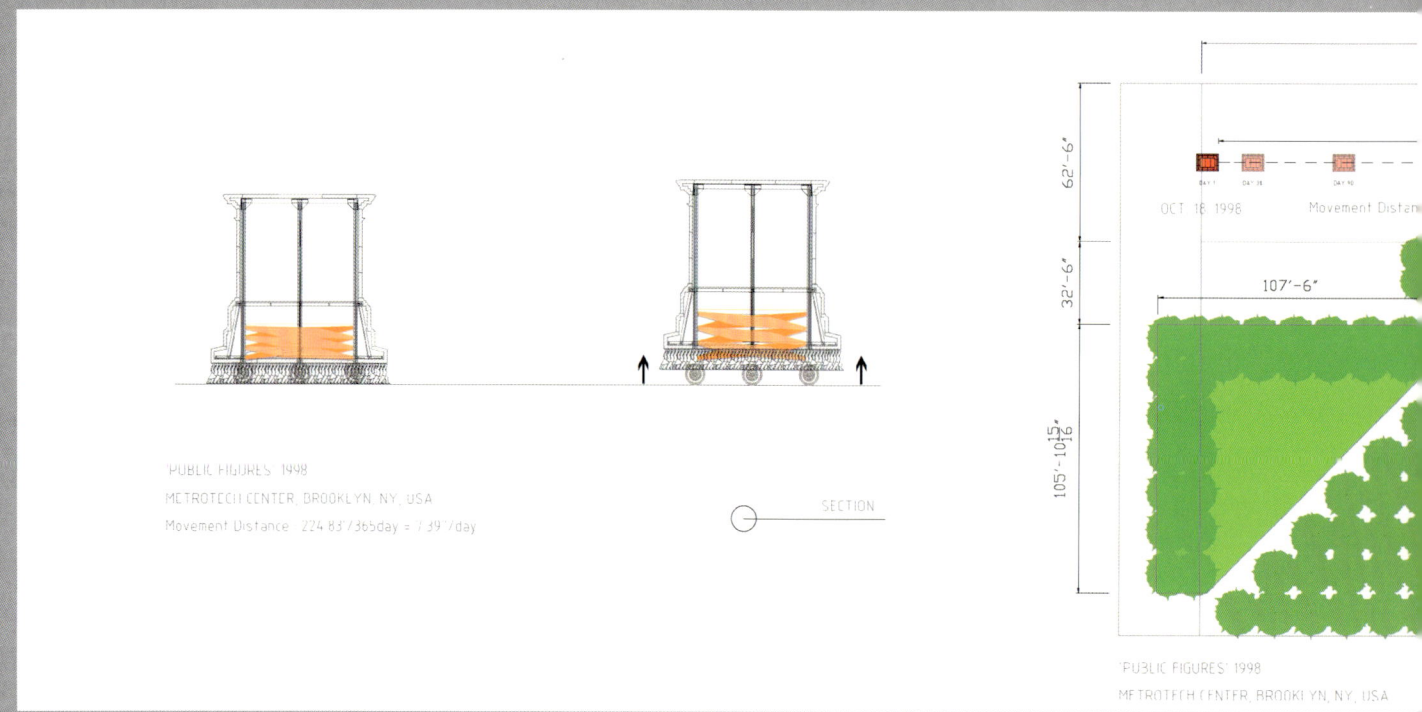

'PUBLIC FIGURES' 1998
METROTECH CENTER, BROOKLYN, NY, USA
Movement Distance 224.83'/365day = 1.39'/day

SECTION

OCT 16 1998   Movement Distance

'PUBLIC FIGURES' 1998
METROTECH CENTER, BROOKLYN, NY, USA

Previous page: *Public Figures* 1998, installation view, Metrotech Center Commons, New York, 1998
Above left and middle: Proposals for the mechanisation and movement of *Public Figures* across
Metrotech Center Commons, New York, 1998

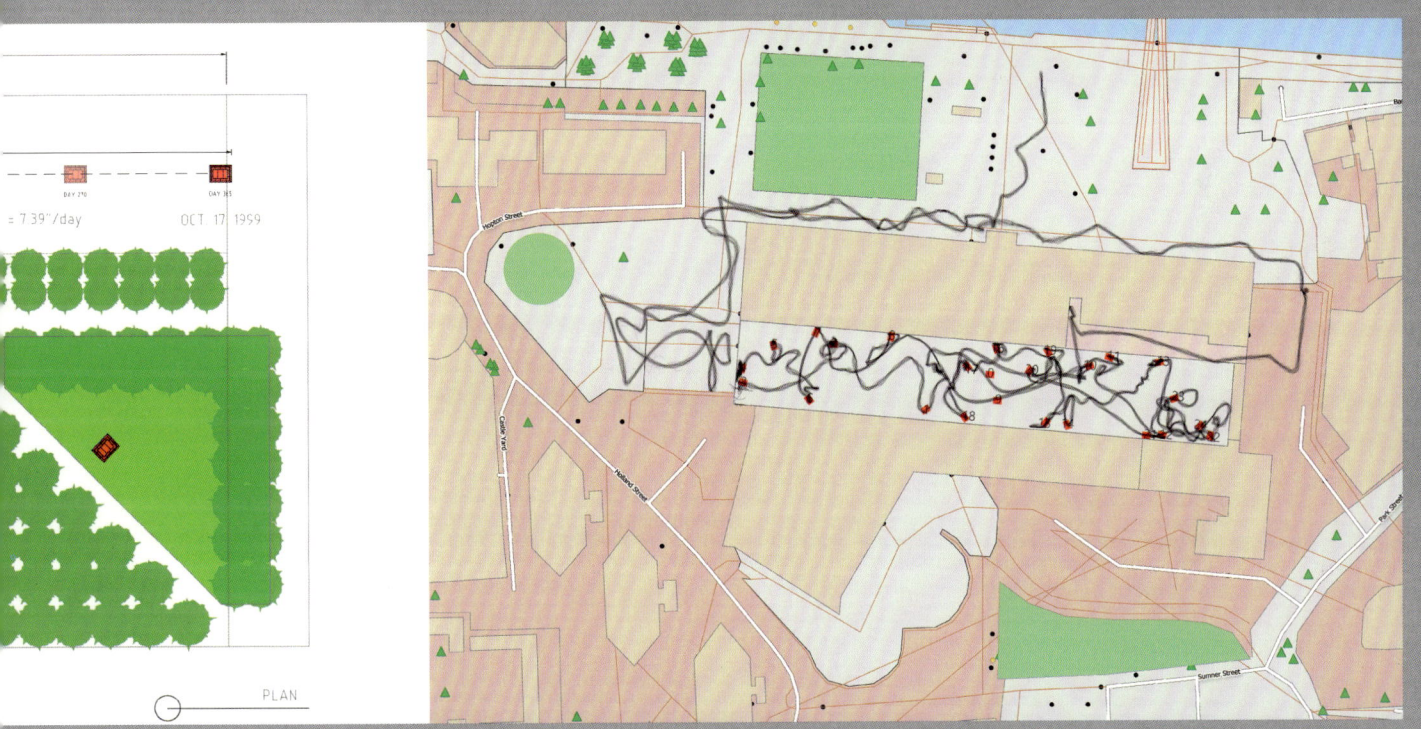

PLAN

Above right: Proposal for the movement of *Public Figures* around Tate Modern, 2024
Overleaf: *Public Figures* 1998 (detail)

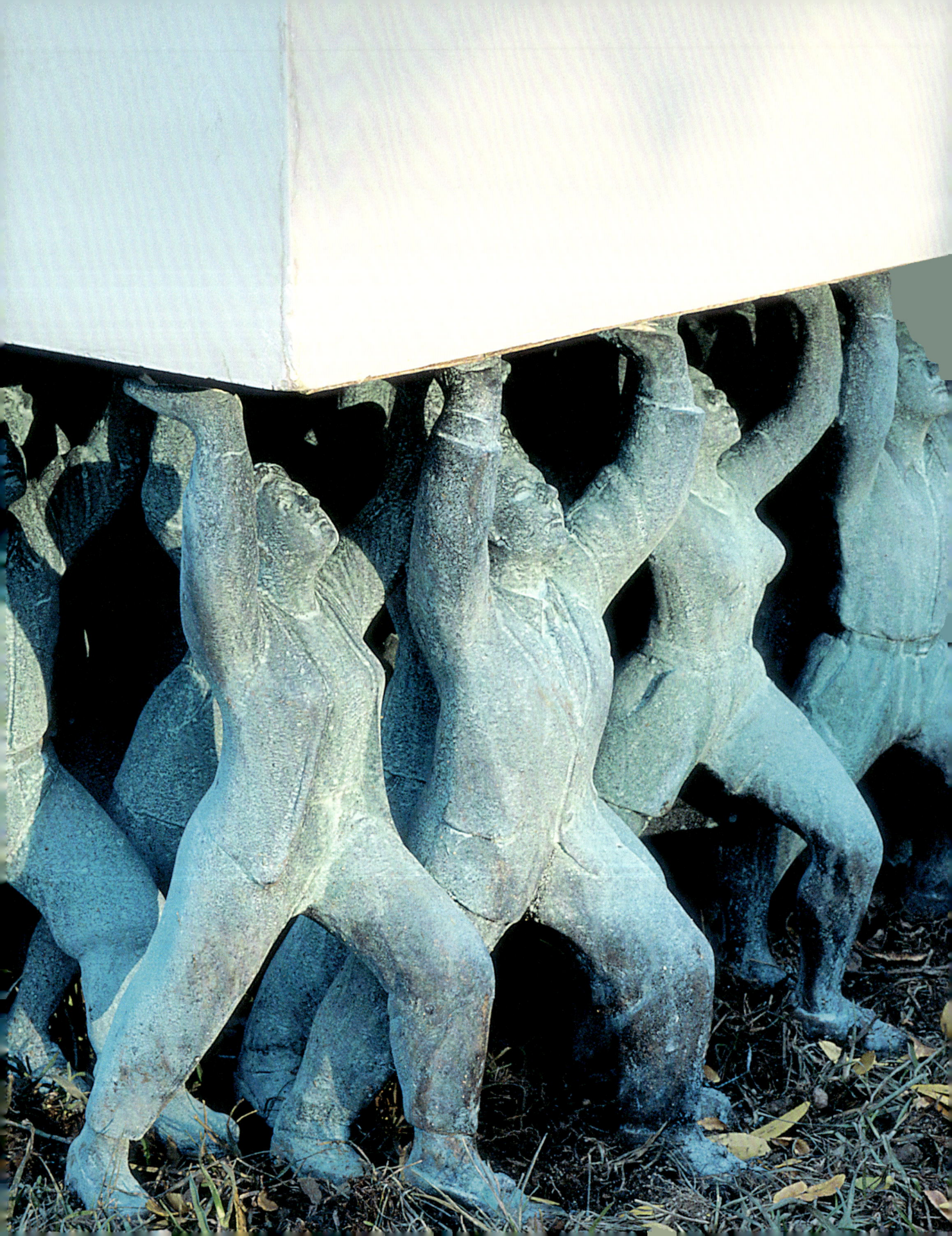

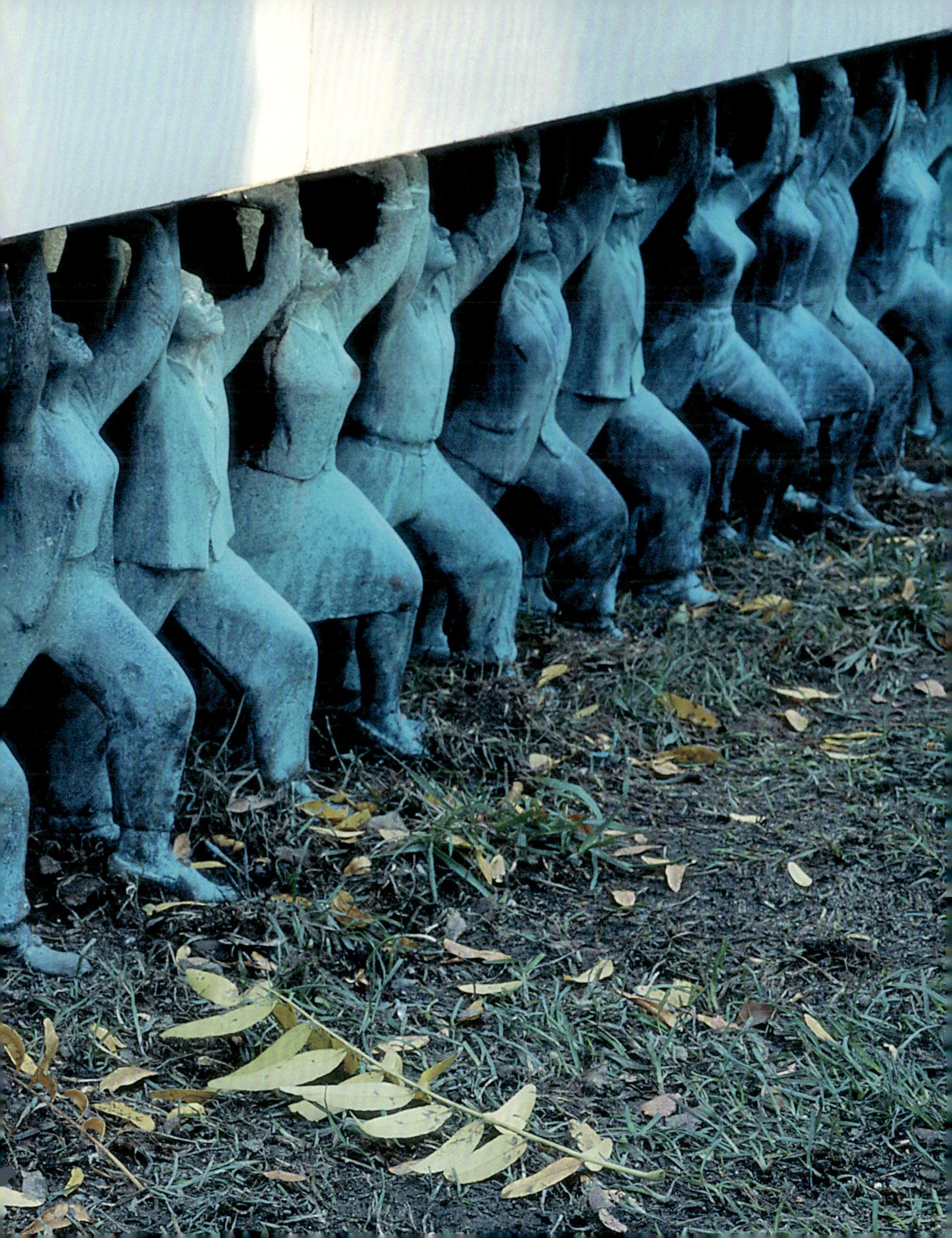

Staircase is part of an ongoing series of works on paper made by Suh since his 2009 residency at STPI – Creative Workshop & Gallery in Singapore, a centre specialising in print and papermaking. During his time there, Suh developed an innovative process using gelatin tissue paper, typically used as a support material for embroidery and designed to dissolve in water. Employing a similar process to his fabric architecture works, Suh uses this gelatin tissue paper and thread to create three-dimensional traces of architectural elements and domestic fixtures such as doors, light switches, sinks and, in this case, a staircase. Working quickly, Suh then places these thread and gelatin tissue sculptures onto large wet sheets of paper, causing the tissue to begin to collapse, shrink, and dissolve into the paper. A vacuum is used to attempt to control the composition, but the form continues to move as the elements dry. Through this process, a three-dimensional space is translated onto a two-dimensional surface. Evoking the act of folding and packing something away, these works continue the impulse that propelled Suh's fabric architectures, which emerged from his desire 'to fit my childhood home into a suitcase'. KW

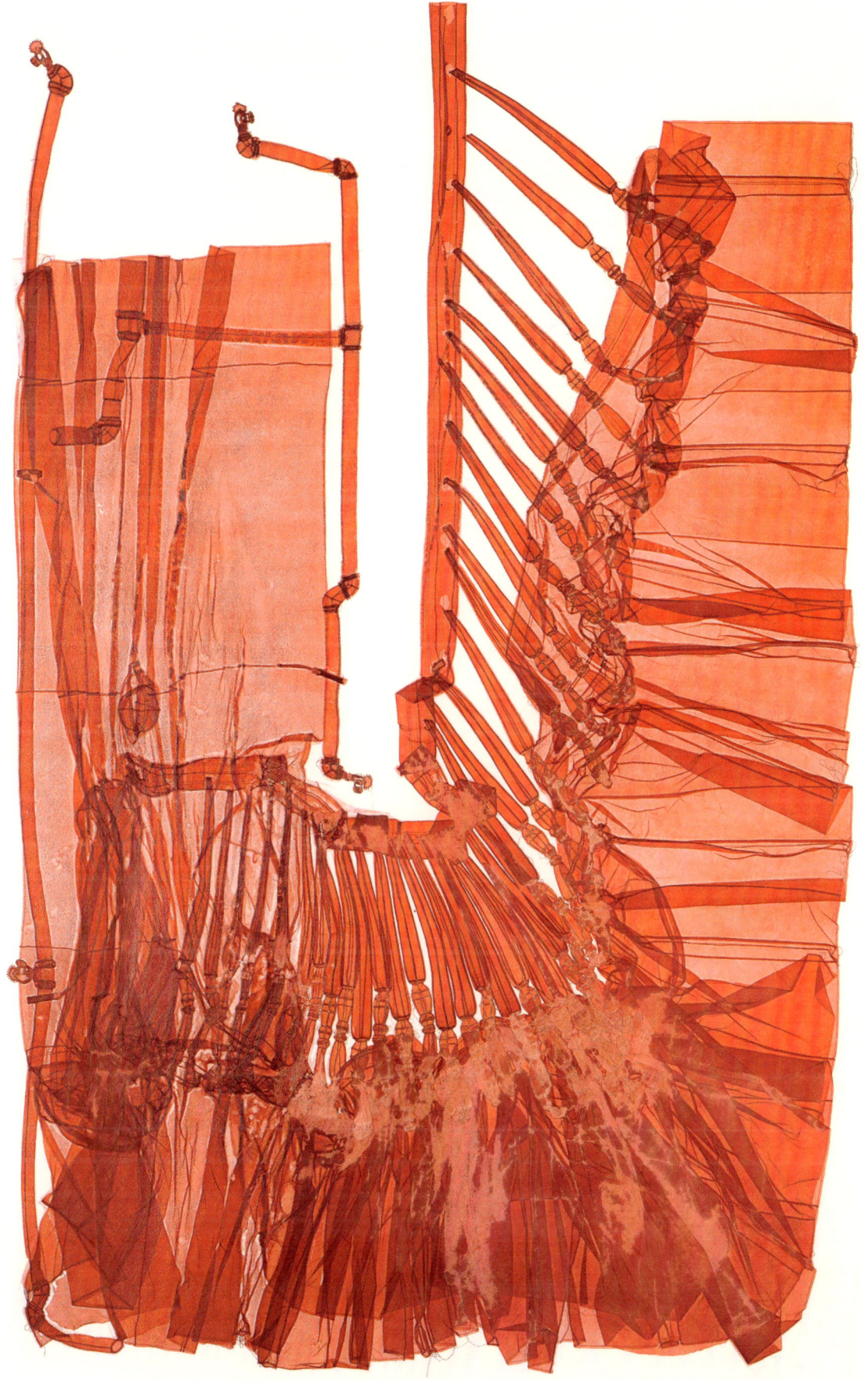

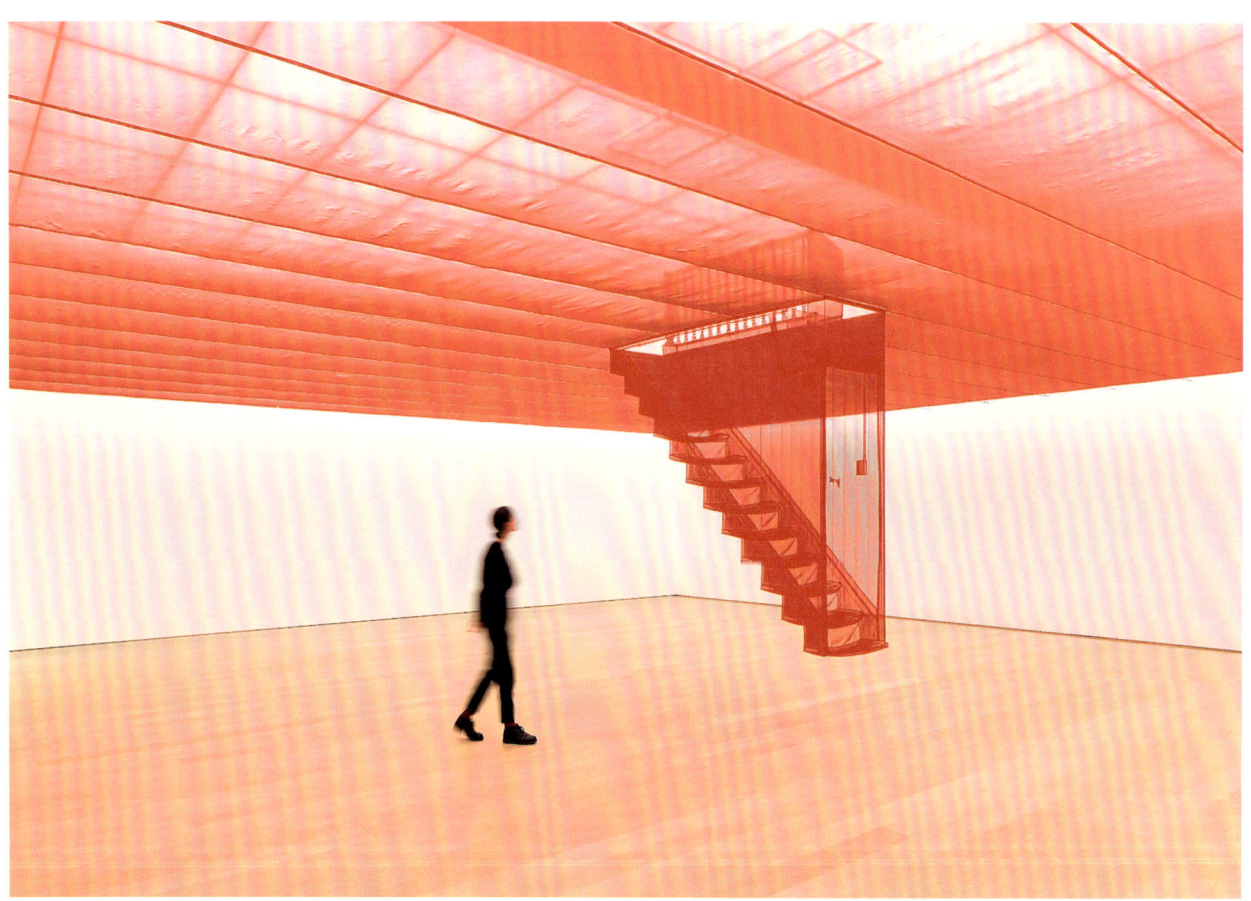

Above: *Staircase-III* 2010, installation view, Museum Voorlinden, 2019
Opposite: *Staircase-III* 2010, installation view, Tate Modern, 2011

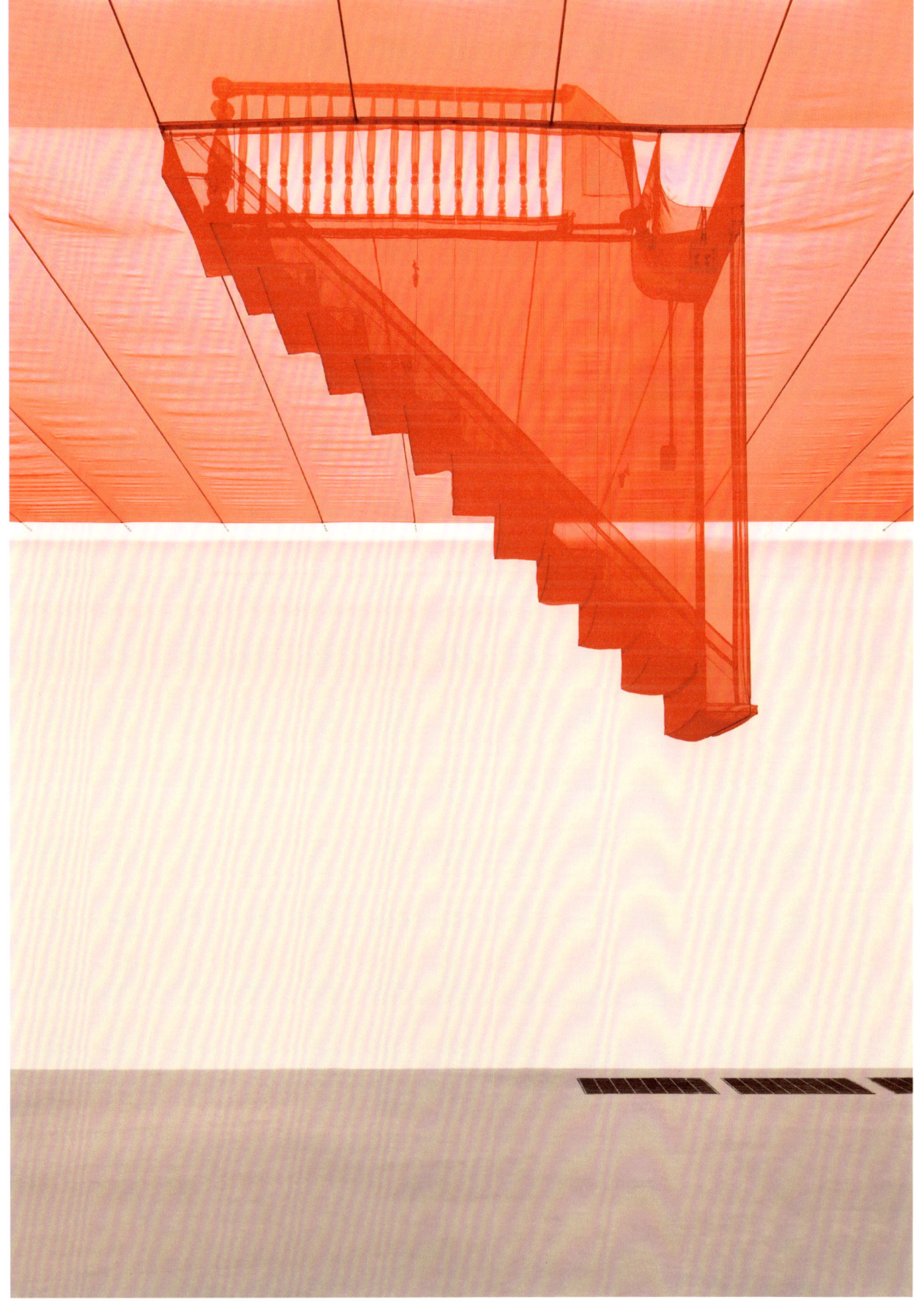

Fallen Star (Scale 1/5) 2008–11

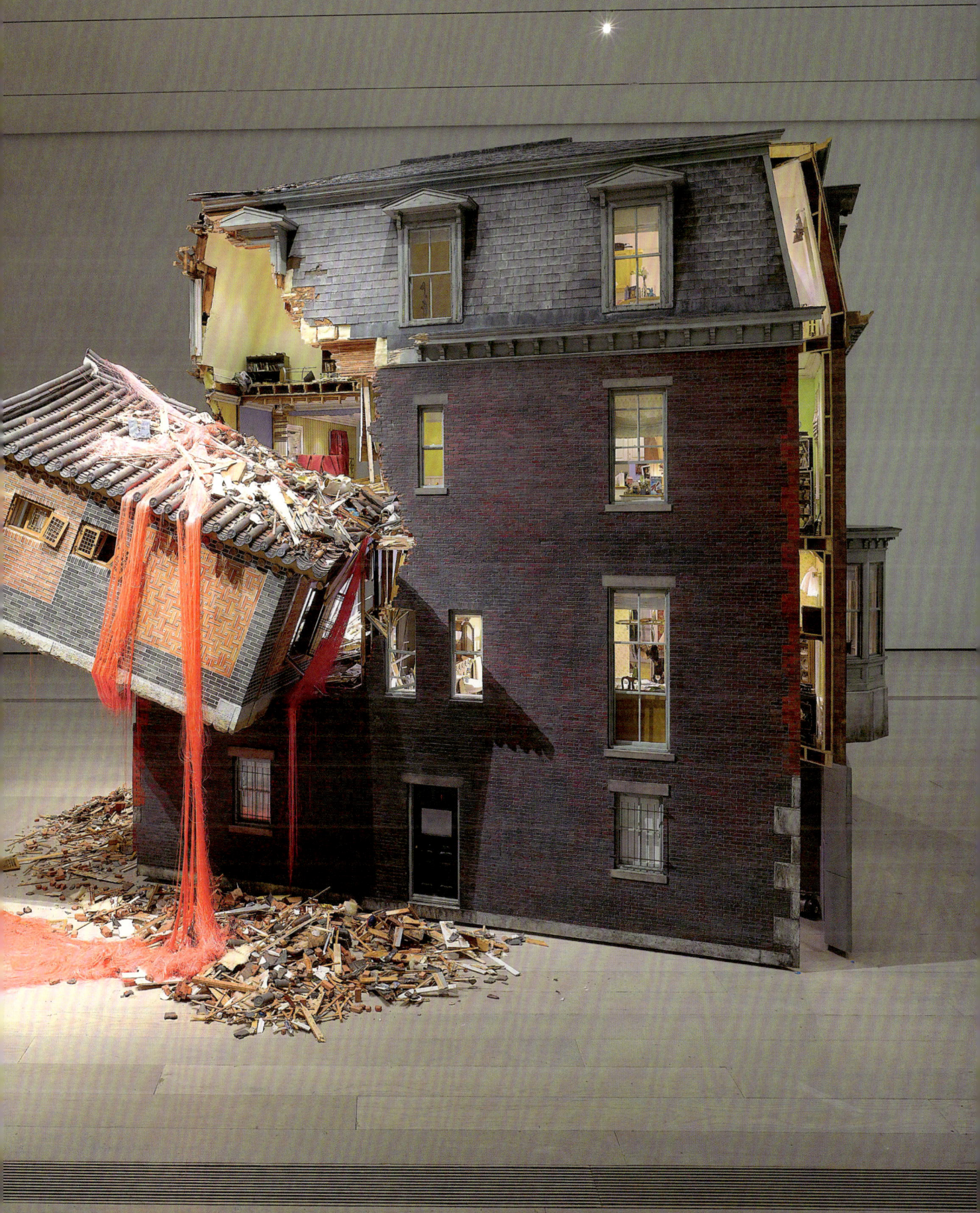

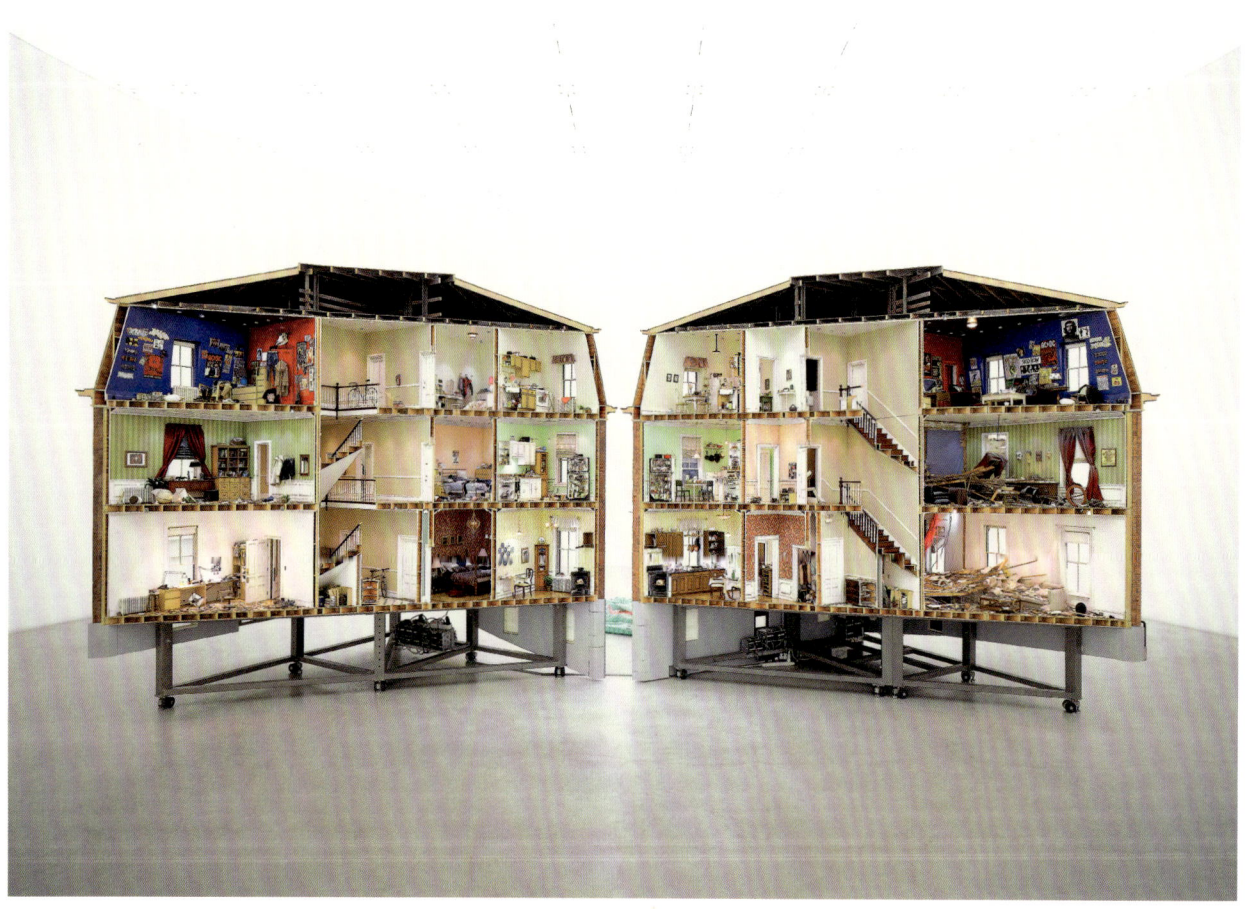

Fallen Star (Scale 1/5) 2008–11

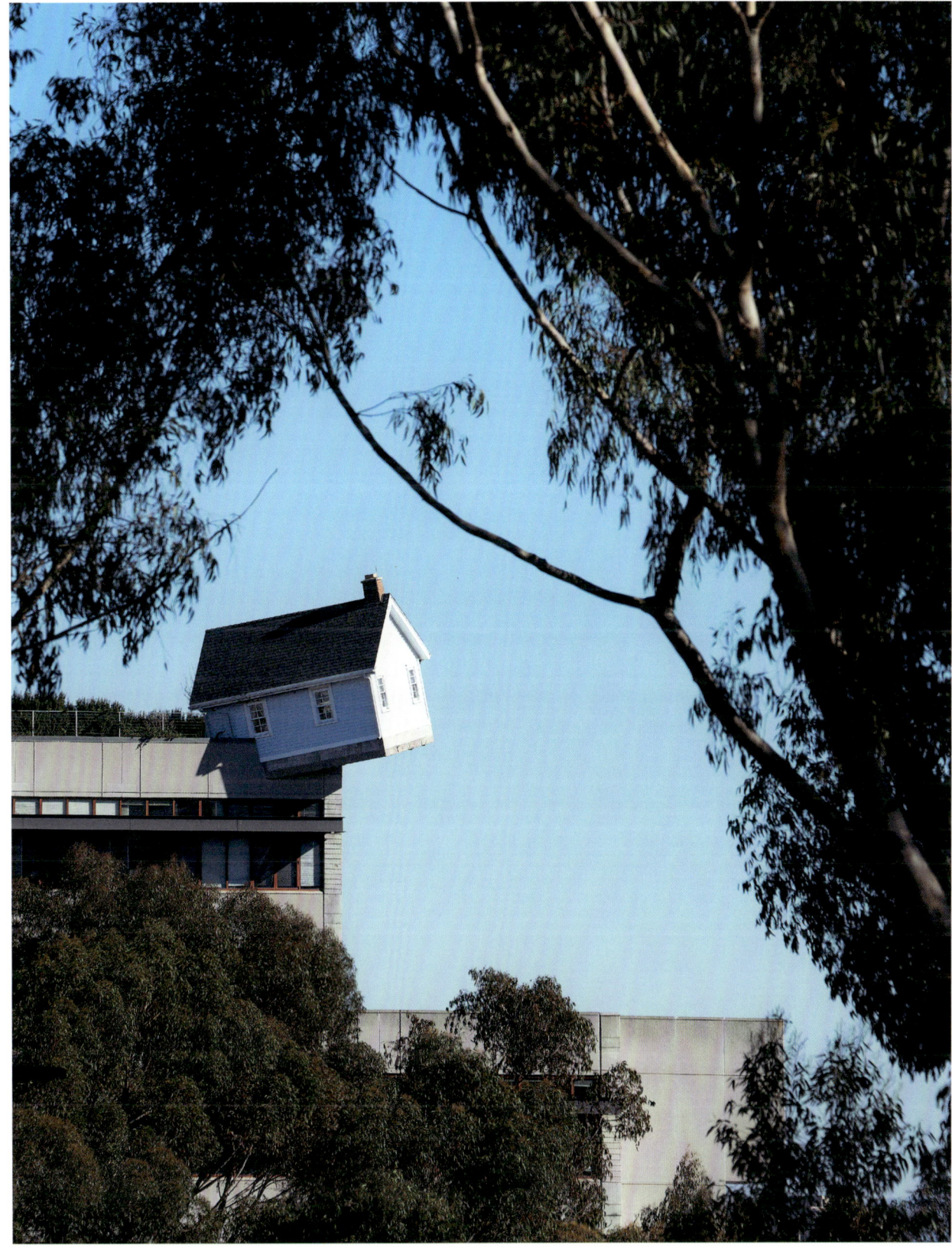

Fallen Star 2012, installation view, University of California San Diego

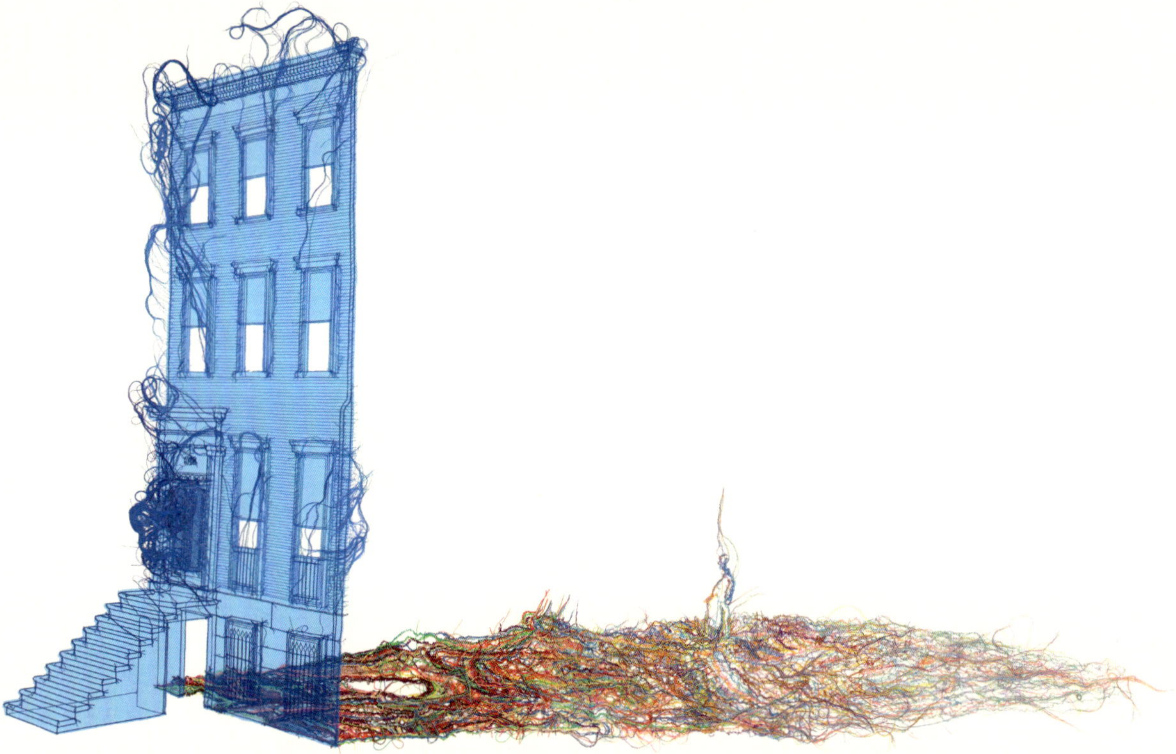

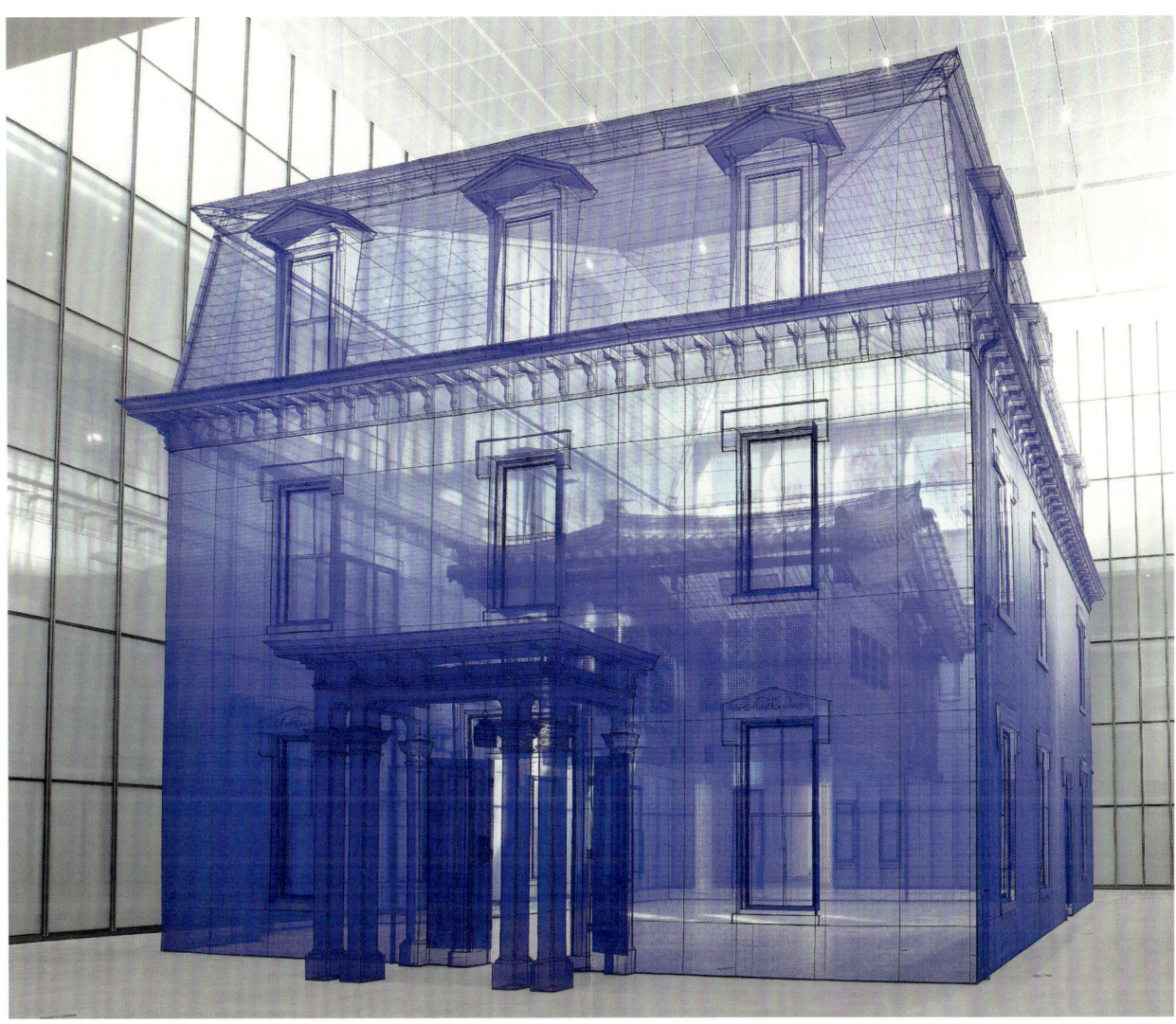

Home Within Home Within Home Within Home Within Home 2013, installation view,
National Museum of Modern and Contemporary Art, Seoul, 2013

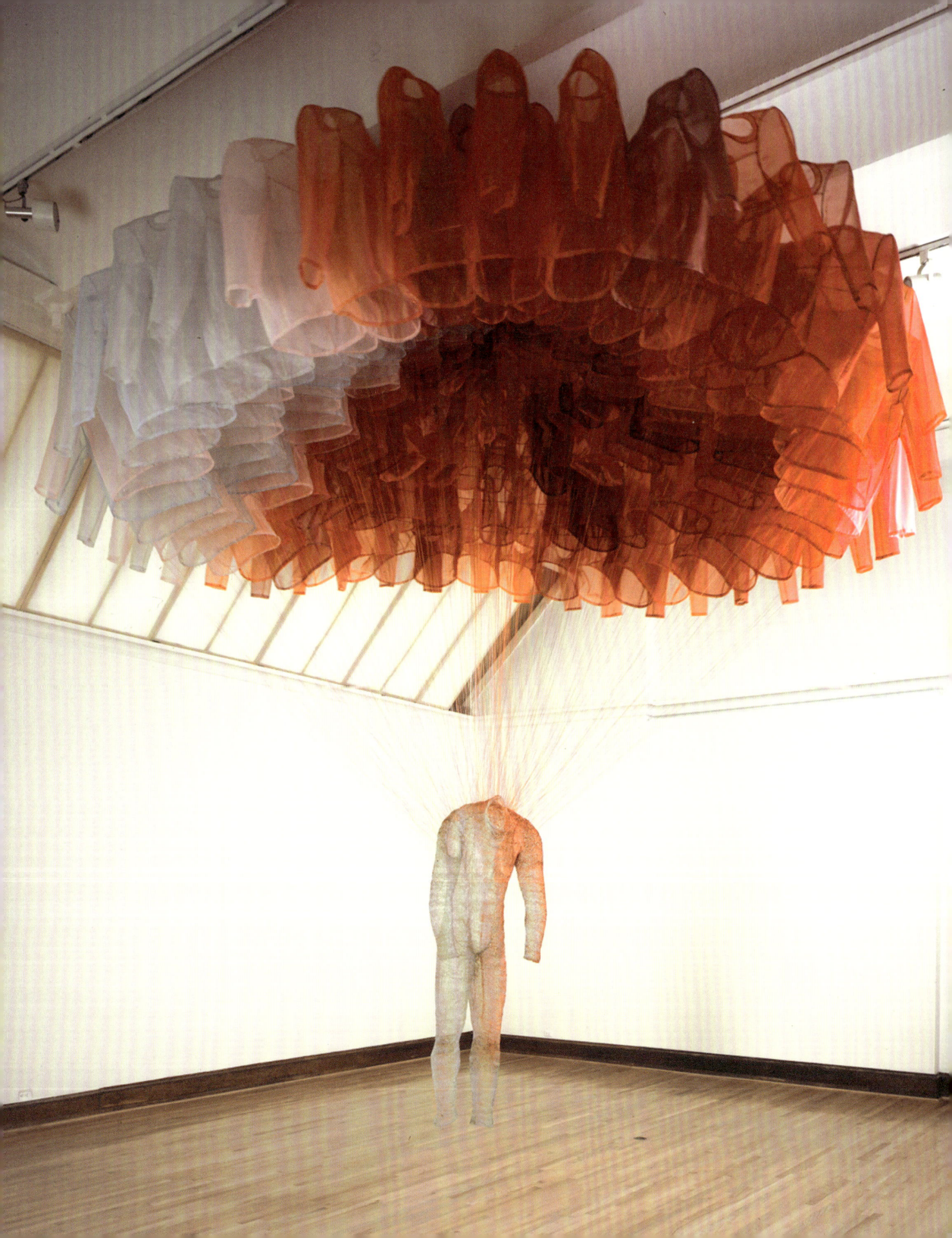

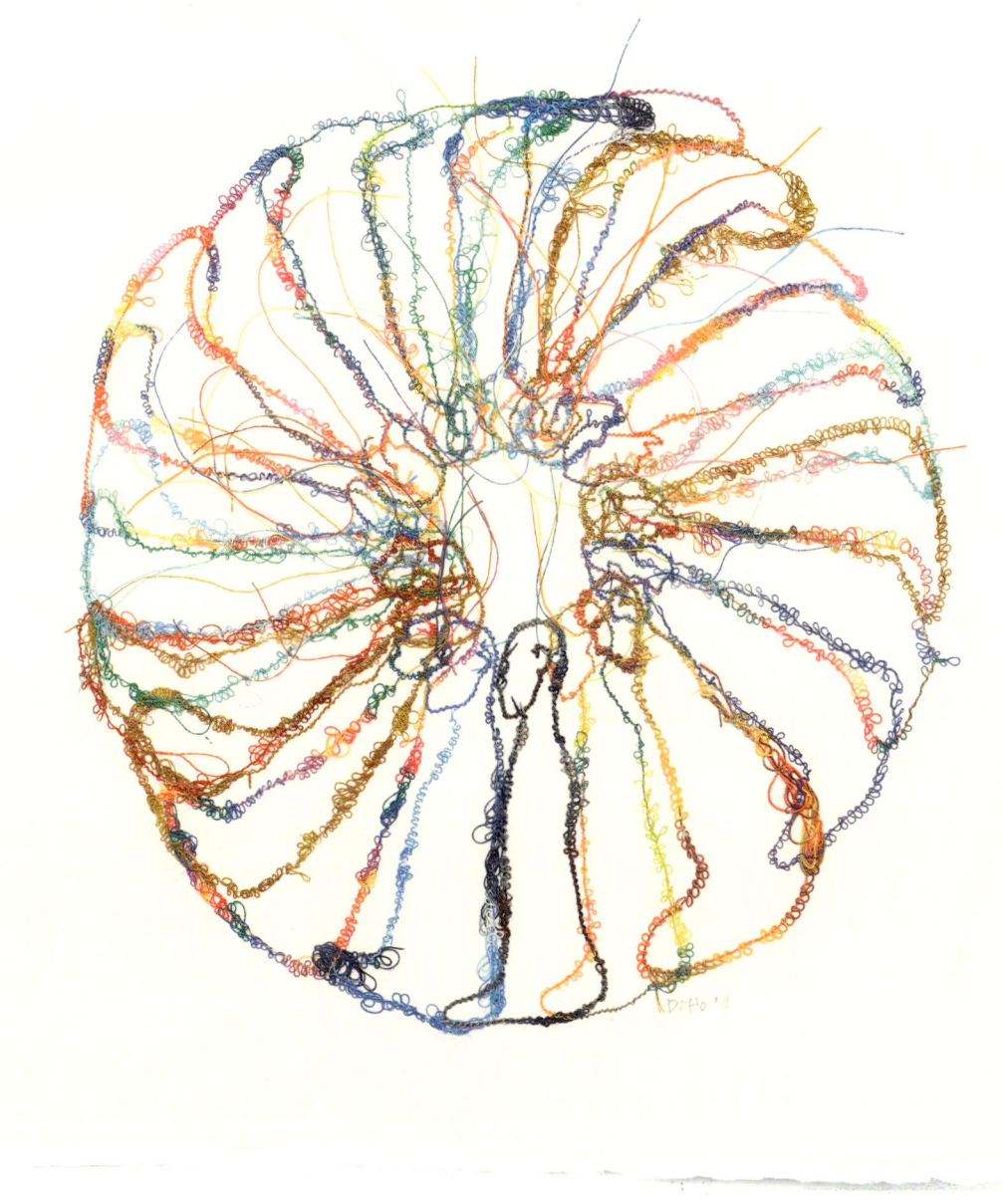

Opposite: *Paratrooper-II* 2005, installation view, The Fabric Workshop and Museum, Philadelphia, 2005
Above: *Facing Myself* 2014

Dylan Trigg

Homeworld(s) in Do Ho Suh

On an empty plot of land on the surface of our planet, a material structure is built from concrete, wood, glass, and cement. These materials are fashioned together to produce a space inside which human beings will dwell. No one has lived here before; this building has no history other than a history of construction.

Other buildings, however, bear witness to a more complex history, their surfaces, alcoves, walls and rooms revealing (or sometimes concealing) layers of experience accumulated over numerous decades, if not centuries. These stories belong to the history of human existence, to the dramas and banalities of any given life, and they all take place within the *home*.

Home is a recurring motif in Do Ho Suh's work, from textile environments such as *Perfect Home: London, Horsham, New York, Berlin, Providence, Seoul* 2024 to moving image works (*Robin Hood Gardens, Woolmore Street, London E14 0HG* 2018, *Dong In Apartments* 2022) and drawings such as *Home Clothing* 2014, *Walking Home* 2014 and *Haunting Home* 2019. Each of these articulations and explorations of home attests to the multifaceted nature of the concept. Suh's work encourages us to approach the idea of home from different angles, literally and figuratively: his homes are displaced, interstitial, transported, miniaturised; they are intimate and personal yet geometrical and topographical; above all, each is the site of a singular biography but also the nexus of a multiplicity of histories. Instead of approaching the home as a beacon of stability and permanence, Suh instead approaches it as malleable and porous.

This conception of home challenges the (Western) view of home as an irreducible presence, unwavering in time. In Suh's work, home is not just temporally but spatially malleable: in the watercolour *Home Within Home* 2010, a home extends from the top of a person's head before multiplying itself time and again. These are homes stacked upon one another, not in separation from each other but forming part of a continuous whole that extends itself in the world. Likewise, in *Walking Home* 2014 the thread home has enmeshed itself in the body of its inhabitant, the two entities fusing into a single structure and walking as one. In *Sleeping Home* 2014, the home presents itself as an entity that extends beyond its own materiality, channelling an aura that reaches into the night sky. 'For me,' Suh has said, '"space" is that which encompasses everything.'[1] How, then, to understand this space 'which encompasses everything' in relation to the home? One way we might think about it is in terms of an *atmosphere*.

Atmospheres of Home

In a general sense, the notion of 'atmosphere' is a constitutive aspect of everyday life. Be it the enchanted

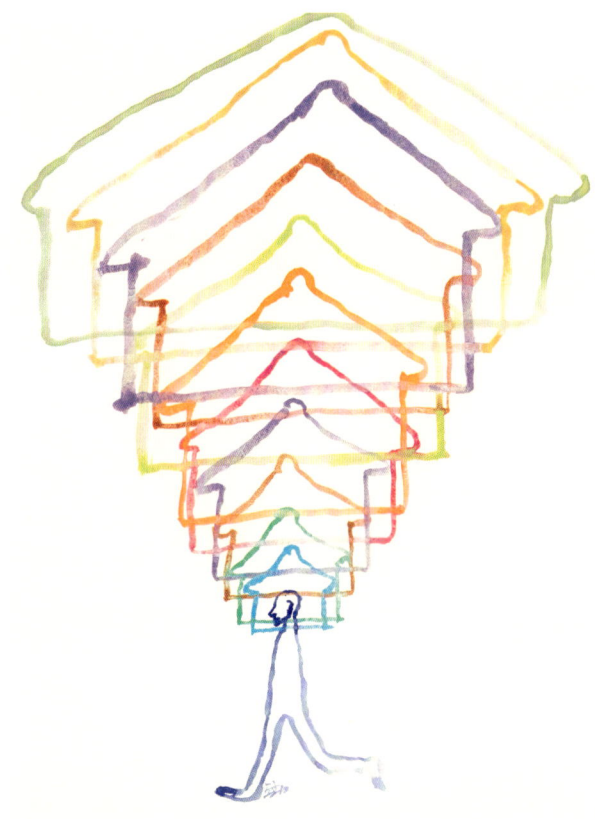

Home Within Home 2010

atmosphere of a cottage nestled deep in a forest or the humdrum atmosphere of commuting, atmospheres confront us on all sides and at all times. Sometimes they are subtle and refined, and we have to be attuned in order to discern them. On other occasions an atmosphere presses down upon us in an invasive way such that it is felt as a mode of oppression. In each case, atmospheres can be both diffused in the air but also expressed in singular objects (aisles lit by fluorescence, empty hallways, ancient ruins, flickering curtains) without ever being reducible to those objects. Indeed, a strong atmosphere seems to dissolve boundaries, lingering in the air before getting under our skin. It is no wonder, then, that in the rich literature on the subject, philosophers will often invoke the language of an atmosphere as *pouring over* space, as being indeterminate and being between materiality and the body. As the philosopher Gernot Böhme writes:

Atmospheres are indeterminate, above all, in regard to their ontological status. One does not quite know whether to attribute them to the objects or environments from which they emanate or to the subjects who experience them. One also does not quite know where they are. They seem to fill the space with a *Gefühlston* (feeling-tone), like a haze, as it were.[2]

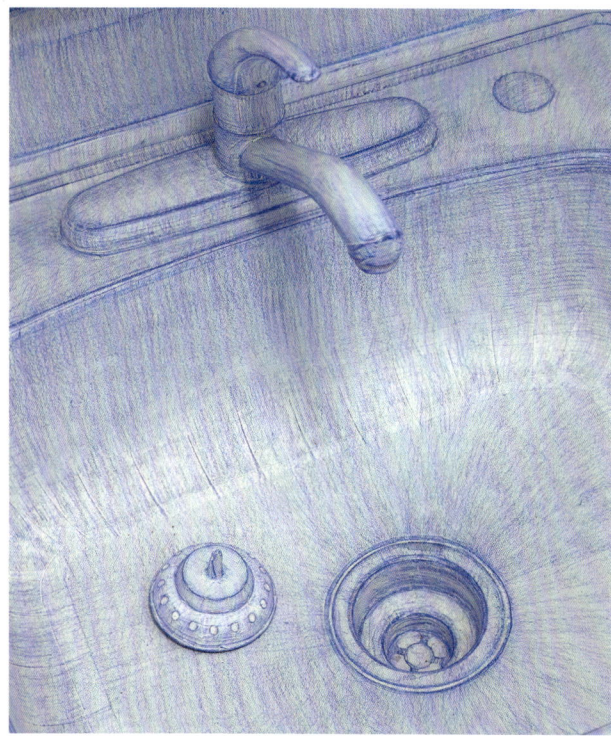

*Rubbing/Loving: Apartment A, 348 West 22nd Street, New York,
NY 10011, USA* 2014 (detail)

This notion of filling space 'like a haze' returns us to Suh's description of space as 'that which encompasses everything'. Perhaps nowhere is this all-encompassing haze more evident than in the case of the home. To think of the home in terms of an atmosphere is to contend with the way its presence is diffused through a given environment while also being expressed in specific local things. This is especially clear in the case of returning to one's home: in the return, the home is not only a material site that is charged with an amplified sense of presence, but also the region in which the home is situated. Returning, we can often 'sense' the home in advance of actually being there; it pours over and 'encompasses everything' within its sphere of influence.

Here, a question emerges: from where does the atmosphere of home derive? Or, to put it another way, how does a home come into existence in the first place? Clearly materiality is not in itself sufficient to generate home, otherwise home would be an interchangeable site. Nor, however, is home simply a property that is projected onto a space by a living subject. Rather, home takes place in a dynamic relationship between a living body and a material world, each of them sculptured by time and memory and by tangible and intangible aspects. This notion of home as a complex nexus of materiality, temporality and embodiment is not lost on Suh: the presentation

of home within his work as an all-encompassing notion incorporates multiple temporalities and histories as well as divergent articulations of temporality, from spaces of comfort to sites of conflict, which spread out into neighbouring regions.

This sense of the home as being diffused into everything is offset by the way in which an atmosphere can be expressed – if not distilled – in specific objects and artefacts. A relic that was once a part of the home is not simply an object in itself but also embodies an entire world. Take the paper objects – three-dimensional artefacts constructed from rubbings made from every surface of the household items they depict – displayed like specimens in *Rubbing/Loving: Unit 2, 348 West 22nd Street, New York, NY 10011, USA* 2014–23. Here, the viewer is faced with the uniqueness of the artist's subjective existence, which is placed in a specific time and place and which implicates singular objects. Displaced and decontextualised, these rubbings of faucets, light switches, locks, stoves seem to exceed their material status, signalling an entire life that is told through the medium of domestic artefacts. Suh's work is operating on a hyper-phenomenological level: transplanted into the gallery space, these objects are renewed, their prosaic everydayness revealed to be imbued with an amplified meaning which we often overlook. Suh has spoken of his desire to fit his childhood home into a suit-

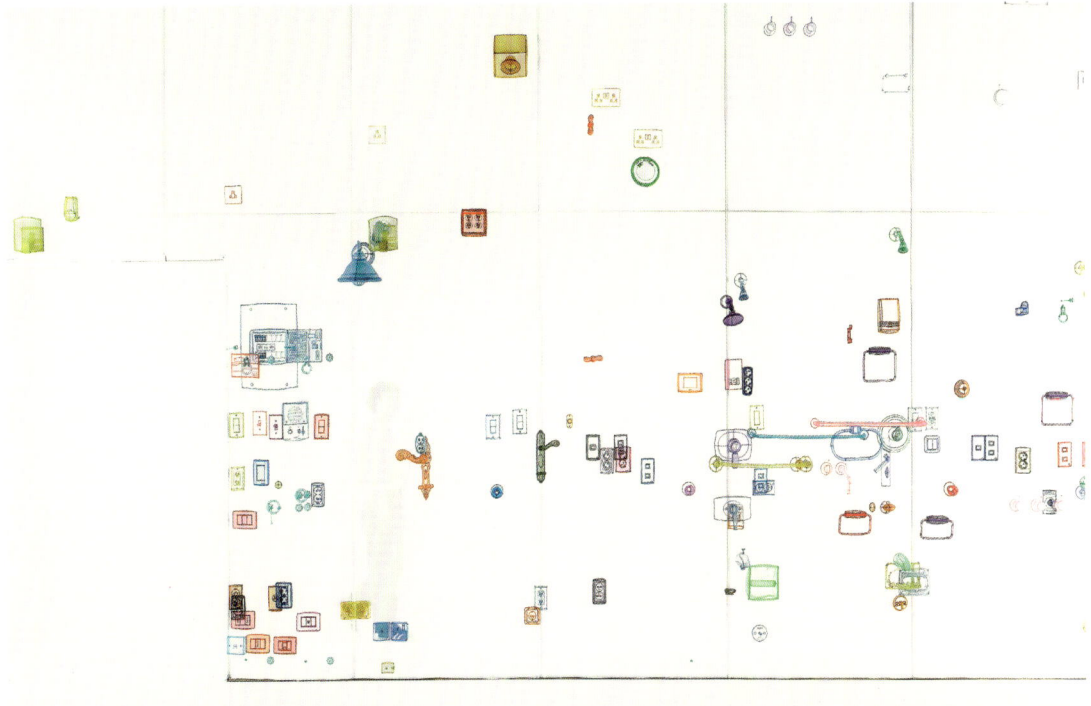

Perfect Home: London, Horsham, New York, Berlin, Providence, Seoul 2024

case that follows him, and while such an aim is a challenge logistically (although his first fabric architecture work, *Seoul Home/L.A. Home/New York Home/Baltimore Home/London Home/Seattle Home/L.A. Home* 1999, was indeed transported from Seoul to Los Angeles in two suitcases), atmospherically the desire remains viable given that things of the (home)world – light switches, stoves or otherwise – have the potential to express an entire world, effectively rendering home a (trans)portable concept.

Lived Geometry

That objects can attest to an entire world is only possible because those objects function as a microcosm of that world. In *Rubbing/Loving: Seoul Home* 2013–22 Suh again employs a process of rubbing in order to recreate and retrace a home, covering every aspect of it in paper then using pastel and crayon to rub the surface so that each texture is archived. This is a devoted methodology, one bearing witness to a subtle interplay between geometry and lived spatiality that blurs the distinction between abstraction and experience.

This methodology issues a challenge to a certain current of thinking about spatiality – evident not least in phenomenology – which evinces a suspicion of measuring and geometry as a mode of disembodied abstraction. One dramatic articulation of this suspicion is to be found in the

work of Gaston Bachelard who writes, in a passage typical of this approach: 'A house that has been experienced is not an inert box. Inhabited space transcends geometrical space.'[3] What to make of this conflation of geometrical space and abstraction? While a distinction between geometrical and lived space is useful in terms of distinguishing different ways of understanding spatiality, to establish a fixed division between these aspects is problematic because it precludes the idea of geometrical and measured space being meaningfully if not sensually experienced.

Suh's *Rubbing/Loving* works introduce us to precisely the idea of measurement as *topophilic* in orientation. Far from leading the viewer towards a formal structure of space, his precise methodology instead embeds and embodies us in the thick texture of place as it is lived (and loved), memorialised and represented. Indeed, Suh has remarked time and again that for him, the gesture of rubbing and measuring is interwoven with a sense of loving that implicates a sense of mourning.[4] For the act of measuring is not simply a method of archiving spatial properties; it is also a recognition of the finitude of lived space, a space that has enmeshed itself in the body of the artist and which will in turn become irretrievable. The result of this methodology is a movement of emplacement – of getting placed – especially within the context of a broader narrative of displacement and loss.

When is Home?

In and through time, the spaces we move into become sites of familiarity. Without thinking about it, we move through these rooms accumulating sense impressions of the surrounding world until those impressions embed themselves in our skin. Even the strange elements of the space – the ticking in the walls, the cold passage between rooms, the light without an origin – become emblematic of an irreducible yet elusive sense of home. In turn, the home gets under our skin: the latch on a window, the smell of the cupboards and the habitual movement of flicking a light switch all become integrated into a sense of self, such that we carry the home with us.

Suh's *Perfect Home: London, Horsham, New York, Berlin, Providence, Seoul* 2024 attests to the microhistories and intimate spatialities embedded in the home. Within the fabric footprint of Suh's London apartment, hundreds of wall-based objects converge: sockets, handles, bells, keypads, switches and more, all reprised from spaces he previously inhabited. Constructing this multi-layered home proved to be a complex process, involving placing rooms within spaces, then rotating these spaces upon themselves. *Perfect Home* problematises the idea of past places belonging in a zone of time behind us by exploring how pastness is accumulative in the present. Fashioned from polyester fabric and steel, it is an oneiric space, at once precise and diffused, both materially dense and ineffably incorporeal. It is a space frozen in time – in Suh's time – before the place undergoes modification, either through the arrival of new tenants or through potential structural changes.

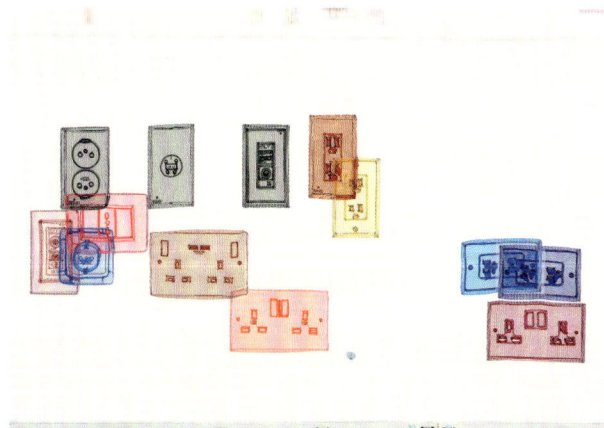

Perfect Home: London, Horsham, New York, Berlin, Providence, Seoul 2024 (detail)

Suh's domestic dwellings have been subjected to a displacement both spatial – in this case, by being transplanted to Tate Modern – and temporal. As such, the question of *where* is home is compounded with the issue of *when* is home. In the space of Tate Modern home is both absent and present, both tangible and intangible. Yet while it would

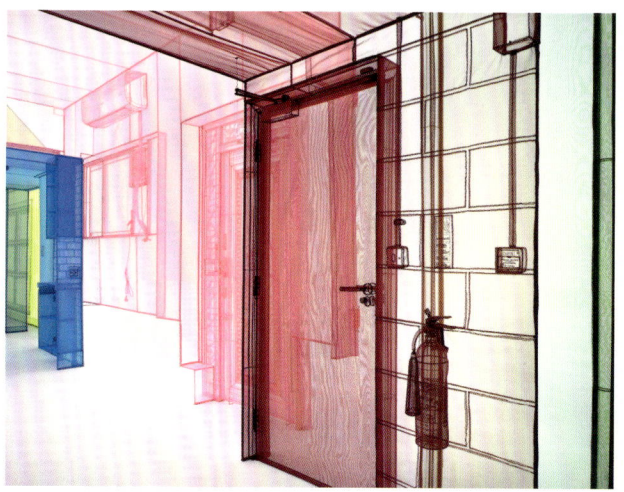

Nest/s 2024

be tempting to assign the status of 'uncanniness' or 'spectrality' to spaces reassigned from one context to another, there is no such sense of the eerie in Suh's work: rather, the affective and perceptual presentation is at once dreamlike and playful, marked by a sense of tenderness and love for the places that enacted an impression upon the artist. Despite that, we find little nostalgic melancholy here. The tonality is an affirmation of pastness that at the same time recognises and accepts the irretrievability of the past.

Suh has spoken of trying to understand his life as a movement through different spaces. *Perfect Home*, like the 'hubs' that populate his work, is a close study of such a movement. In Bachelard's terms, this work embodies a topoanalytical reading of space, one which indexes 'the systematic psychological study of the sites of our intimate lives'.[5] While Suh's sculptures are indeed rooted in a singular and intimate life, thereby revealing the ways in which spatiality constitutes selfhood, his work nevertheless sheds light on the relationship between dwelling, memory and home more generally.

In recent work such as *Nest/s* 2024 and *Home Within Home* 2025, the home is presented as having permeable boundaries, one home dissolving into another. The result is a layering of divergent temporalities, each of which decentres the notion of home as either past/present or here/there. The question of when is home is thus an invitation to think about the ways spaces enact their presence upon us, volitionally or otherwise. After all, just as we live in, remember and dream about places, so too do those same places live within us. Often this inhabitation of places within us is grasped as the realisation that the home that once provided a shelter for us is no longer present. Nevertheless, even the absent home is perceived as an atmospheric force that continues to exert a hold upon us.

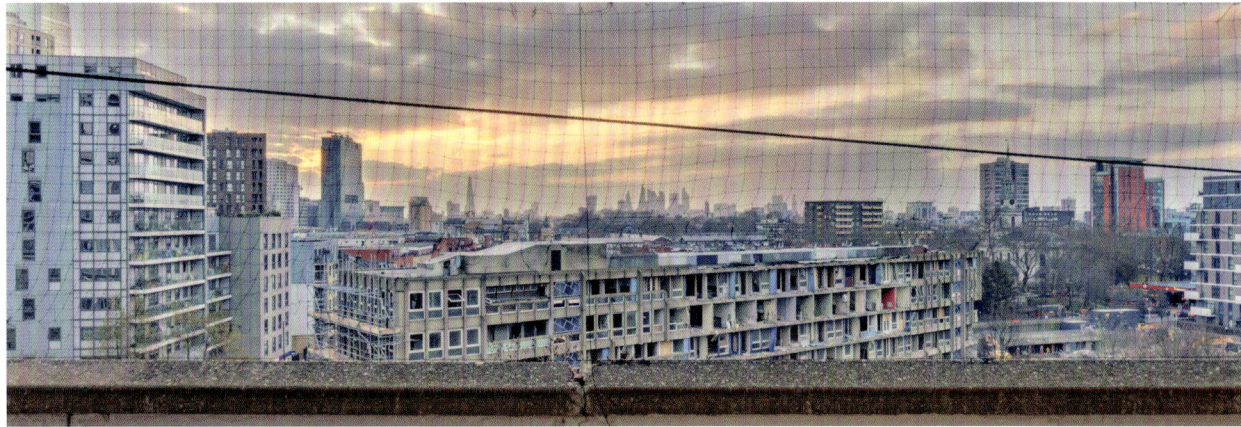

Robin Hood Gardens, Woolmore Street, London E14 0HG 2018

Homeworld(s)

As much as Suh's works have their origins in the life of an individual, they point at all times to the way space is situated in a social and societal context: who we are is who we are with *others*. The concept of 'home' is thus far from an autonomous notion, but instead exposed, transparent, porous. In certain moments, home reinforces and reminds us who we are, engineering a sense of continuity that is otherwise precarious. At other times, home can present itself as a site of multiple identities, each of which converge in the same space and contest one another. In moving image works such as *Robin Hood Gardens, Woolmore Street, London E14 0HG* as well as the moving image installation *Dong In Apartments*, Suh explores these tensions, focusing on how private and public memories unfold in tandem with one another, and in doing so reveal the ways in which memories of home are invariably tied up with histories outside one's own lived experience. *Robin Hood Gardens*, which focuses on a social housing project in London, lays bare the compression of time in domestic space, addressing and archiving how affective forces are built into spaces themselves, even (especially) when these spaces are being torn down. The same is no less true of *Dong In Apartments,* which plays with the relationship between memory and monumentalisation in a modernist apartment block in the South Korean city of Daegu prior to its planned demolition. In each case, Suh's vision makes the boundary line between public and private space porous, such that each aspect bleeds into the other.

The German philosopher Edmund Husserl conceived the terms 'homeworld' and 'alienworld' to designate how our perceptual experience of the world tends to involve a sense of the world as either taken-for-granted and comfortable or, in the case of the alienworld, strange, other, foreign. What is beneficial about this concept is that both of these formulations of how the world is experienced and perceived operate within a social rather than individual context. To have the very experience of a 'homeworld' is in some fundamental sense a privilege, available to those of us who live within a community of people with a shared set of values. This privileging is also evident in a certain formulation of home as a source of protection, a barrier against the world; as Bachelard has it: 'Memories of the outside world will never have the same tonality as those of home'.[6] This elevation of home as barrier against the world, however, risks generating a divisive relationship to the outside and, more problematically, to *outsiders*: what appears as 'alien' is thus that which destabilises a habitual sense of (homely) normality. By contrast, Do Ho Suh's work is a lesson in being attentive to the alien within the home. Through his working and reworking of memory and identity, Suh carefully explicates how the homeworld with which we often intimately identify is co-constituted by an alienworld determined by displacement, loss and otherness, and which resides precisely in the heart of the home.

Notes

1 Quoted in Nan Jie Yun, 'A Conversation with Do-Ho Suh', in Sun Jung Kim and Kyunghwa Ahn (eds.), *Do Ho Suh*, exh. cat., Art Sonje Center, Seoul 2003, p.98.

2 Gernot Böhme, *Atmospheric Architectures*, trans. A.C. Engels-Schwarzpaul, New York 2018, p.14.

3 Gaston Bachelard, *The Poetics of Space*, trans. Maria Jolas, New York 2014, p.67.

4 'Vivian Li In Conversation with Do Ho Suh, May 2020', https://blog.dma.org/tag/for-a-dreamer-of-houses/, accessed 11 Dec. 2024.

5 Bachelard 2014, p.30.

6 Ibid., p.28.

Monica Juneja

Moving Through the World: Art
Making as Transcultural Praxis

[The migrant's] attempt ... to involve himself in the everydayness of being with others ... is fraught inevitably with all the difficulties of translation between accents, inflexions, syntaxes and lexicons ... All that is creole about a culture is indeed nothing other than evidence of its creative overcoming of such difficulty. Ranajit Guha[1]

Today, some three decades after Ranajit Guha mused over questions of belonging both as a spatial problem following geographical displacement and a temporal disjunction between past and present, studies of migration and mobility – and their implications for the production of art – have grown into an expansive, contested field. The incessant passage of contemporary art and artists through global circuits has led to a consensus of sorts, one stating that mobility indeed constitutes a new prism for making sense of art of the present. Describing the unprecedented visibility of art from distant corners of the world in European and North American metropolitan centres today, Miwon Kwon observes a tension between a curatorial projection of contemporary art as a shared 'global language' that transcends national boundaries, and the constraints imposed by national labels when they are used to peg identities to the works.[2]

Such contrary expectations have informed responses to the art of Do Ho Suh, whose works handle many of the themes art critical writing associates with an exilic sensibility – home, migration and memory, all captured within the flux of spatial and temporal conditions. Yet while Suh's explorations are refracted through the lens of his personal trajectories and memories, anchored in the different places he has called home – Seoul, New York, London – the insights enabled by his work take us far beyond individual places and border crossings, leading us to ask: what is the work that art can do? How does the sense of space, time, labour and materiality we experience as we traverse the eerily serene, translucent spaces created by Suh's installations metamorphose into meditations on the terms that routinely inform our lives and languages – notions such as globalism, nomadism, cosmopolitanism, diaspora and, not least, culture?

In his manifesto for mobility studies, Stephen Greenblatt reminds us of the paradox that 'one of the characteristic powers of culture is its ability to hide the mobility that is its enabling condition'.[3] Following from this observation, transcultural theory – a distinct ontology of culture that attends to how the cultural is radically made and remade in processes of interaction with other units, not by necessity contained within the territorial fixtures of the nation state – provides a basis for analysis of Do Ho Suh's work. Transculturation, understood as process rather than essence, describes those long-term transformative relationships that arise from encounters between cultural entities and are formative for the actors, practices and epistemic configurations implicated.[4] The enabling force of the transcultural allows us to examine the ways in which the prolific imagery of deracination, portable homes and movement within Suh's art invariably signal to the instability of a single nation as a normative location from which to speak of people and their relationship to place and culture. Yet these works also exist in tension with the art institutions in which they are exhibited, which are overwhelmingly national bodies and harness their possessions to the tasks of manufacturing ideas of authenticity and consensus that rest on closed or proprietary conceptions of language or ethnicity.

Suh's creations in silk, wood, paper and polyester draw on the communicative power of materials and of spaces, of presence and absence, of the weightless and the transient, to speak to these dilemmas – at times directly, more often obliquely. Suh eschews the labels (diasporic, autobiographical, Korean, global) by which commentators seek to categorise him and his art in terms that conceal the turbulences that go into the making of all culture. Instead, his works explore strategies of uncovering the historical conditions of the transcultural; what Suh calls his 'experiments with coexistence' engage with the challenge of reassembling the past in order to assert its presence within the contemporary.[5] The work of art – and the work it does – itself becomes a site of transcultural practice: an 'undisciplined' constellation of materials, knowledge, subjectivities and temporalities that both clash and conjoin,[6] Suh's art acquires an unpredictable, implosive force that evades the traps of a facile globalism conceived as ahistorical and non-situated.

The well-worn categories of the local and the global do not pre-exist for the artist as fixed entities that then come together in a fashionable hybrid. Rather, Suh's art unfolds in a process of transculturation which transforms materials and spatial coordinates to bring forth a language that is made and remade through recursive iterations of so many of his projects. Aptly described as 'un-built art', Suh's architectural constructions play with inversion: houses and staircases hang from the ceiling or hover in midair; walls appear flimsy and weightless; the home, a place meant to spell permanence, security and comfort, is exposed to the public gaze.[7] Indeed, each work is activated through the movement of the viewer as they walk beneath and look up into its spaces: its language is contingent on the visitor's experience of space and texture, which shifts from place to place, and from iteration to iteration of each project. Additionally, the diaphanous properties of Suh's materials – the gossamer-like silk or translucent polyester – weave their own lines of becoming into the life worlds of those who, in Tim Ingold's words, 'follow the materials'.[8] While

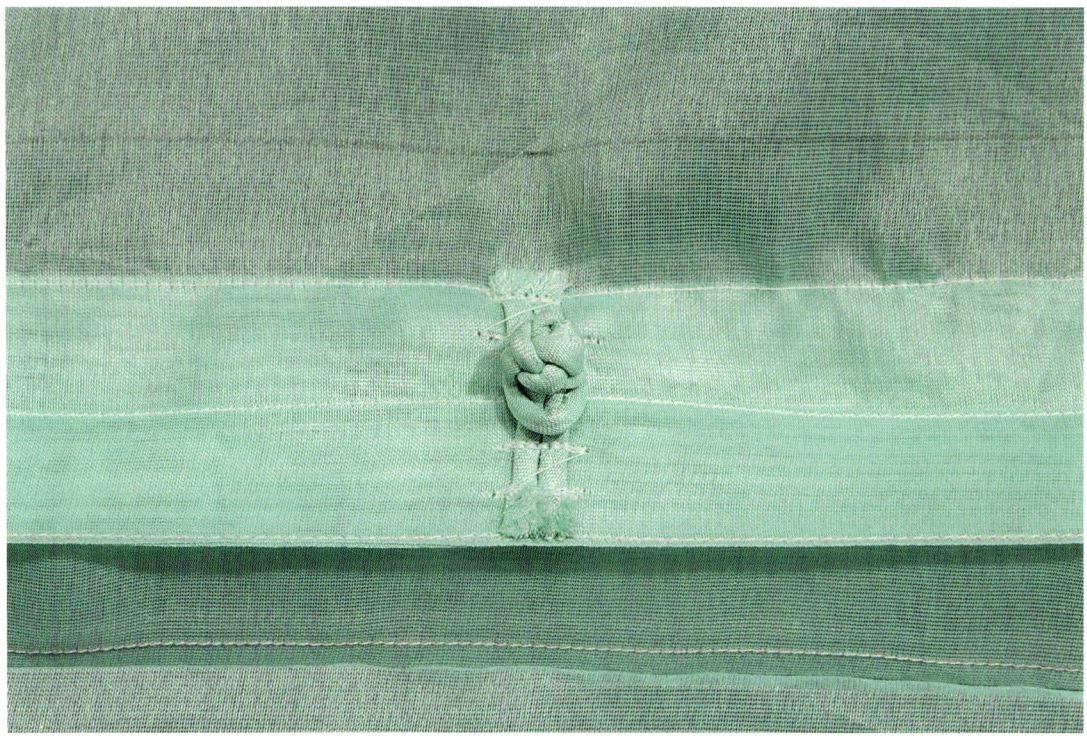

Seoul Home / L.A. Home / New York Home / Baltimore Home / London Home / Seattle Home /
L. A. Home 1999 (detail)

culture as processual assigns primacy to the dynamics of making as against the final product, in this logic of things, reading creativity does not begin with a finished object to take us back to the initial intention of the artist, but lends itself equally to reading in the opposite direction, in an ongoing movement that is both improvisatory and rhythmic, generated through the properties of materials and acknowledging the unfinishedness of the work.

The slippage between home and homeland has been a favourite trope of artists who have lived through relocation, dislocation or forced migration. Though Suh avows that his interest in built structures transmits 'memory and subjectivity', the reach of his work extends beyond the personal to mediate the aesthetic with the historical.[9] A close look at Suh's fabric installations reveals a polyester fabric used to make traditional Korean clothing for summer, as well as finely woven silk in a small number of the early fabric architecture works such as *Seoul Home/L.A. Home/New York Home/Baltimore Home/London Home/Seattle Home/L.A. Home* 1999. Both kinds of fabric have been exquisitely embroidered and sewn with help from specialist artisans in Korea using techniques passed across many generations. They evoke historical memories, some of which go as far back as the Silk Road – the first trade route to connect Europe and Asia, established in the second century BCE. This was also the path followed by the Buddhist monks

who were actors in the proliferation of texts, images and objects across Asia in the early centuries of the Christian era. Suh's art does not simply reference early historical transculturalism in a nostalgic vein, however: it equally signals towards contemporary global production processes that draw on highly skilled labour and traditional knowledge to produce commodities meant to satisfy diverse consumer demands in the Global North as well as the needs of a growing market of local users. An inextricably connected world both enables the movement of privileged artists and curators, who enjoy untrammelled mobility, and transforms domestic labour into a nomadic product even as the bodies performing this work are subject to the myriad barriers regulating the movement of particular peoples across the globe.

Textiles, both as materials and as products of human labour, render transcultural processes haptic. Because fabric has a 'rhizomatic' structure that can extend infinitely in different directions[10] – it can be draped over the human body, spread out or hung, or used as construction material, as in Suh's fabric architecture – it has come to serve as a metaphor for flexibility. Similarly, textiles conjoin the aesthetics of manual work with knowledge and technology, although the rise of global capitalism referenced by Suh has also entailed a destabilising of sites of production and consumption. Today's global intersections have meant that old codes have been scrambled: commodities once associated with European tradition, such as the Bavarian Lederhosen, to take one example, are now mass-produced in factories in Sri Lanka, while brightly coloured batik fabrics long associated in public perception with 'Africa' were, as Yinka Shonibare has demonstrated with eloquent irony, designed and machine-made in Manchester before being exported to Africa. Suh's textile architectures – mutable and portable – exude no whiff of nostalgia for dying tradition, but rather urge us to think with the works through their multiple locations to challenge notions of origin and authenticity built into present understandings of multiculturalism, and to view the ascription of identities as an artificial construct. Such identities, these works seem to say, are no less transcultured than the fabric from which these foldable structures are made.

Both belonging and histories are tethered to national frames. Practices of memorialising – fostered by imposing, putatively enduring monuments erected in public spaces – have grown out of nationalism and nation-building on sites across the globe. Such visual icons in the making of identity in nations old and young alike are more often than not imbued with an ethnocentric and masculinist ethos: they carry a host of assumptions about heroism, history and time, which then find their way into other bodies of knowledge transmitted through institutions – the university, the museum, the archive, the heritage industry. Stone, bronze and concrete – the privileged materials of commemorative sculpture – have historically been used to fabricate 'monumental' repositories of the deepest sentiments and emotions of an 'imagined community'.[11] At a time when monuments and memorials of all sorts (statues especially) are troubled as well as troublesome, the fact that such materialised matter can become vulnerable to shifts in politics and engender changes in our ethical relationship to the past as well as the future becomes palpable through the tension generated by Suh's work. With *Public Figures* 2025 Suh sets out to disrupt the nexus between cultures of belonging and the nation-state and offer a 'model of memorialisation beyond the pedestal'.[12] The emptied white stone plinth of *Public Figures* enjoins us to acknowledge the historically contingent and therefore unstable nature of both the monument and official memory: the symbolic plinth that presents a void plays absence against presence, functioning as a rhetorical device that enlists the beholder's imagination to fill the absence created by art – or to leave it unfilled. It can equally stand for an afterimage that evokes the idea of removal while remaining a phantasm of power that endures long after the formal disappearance of an authoritarian presence.

In this work Suh plays on inversions as well as contradictions: the vacant pedestal of *Public Figures* reverses the conditions of viewing so that, instead of the customary

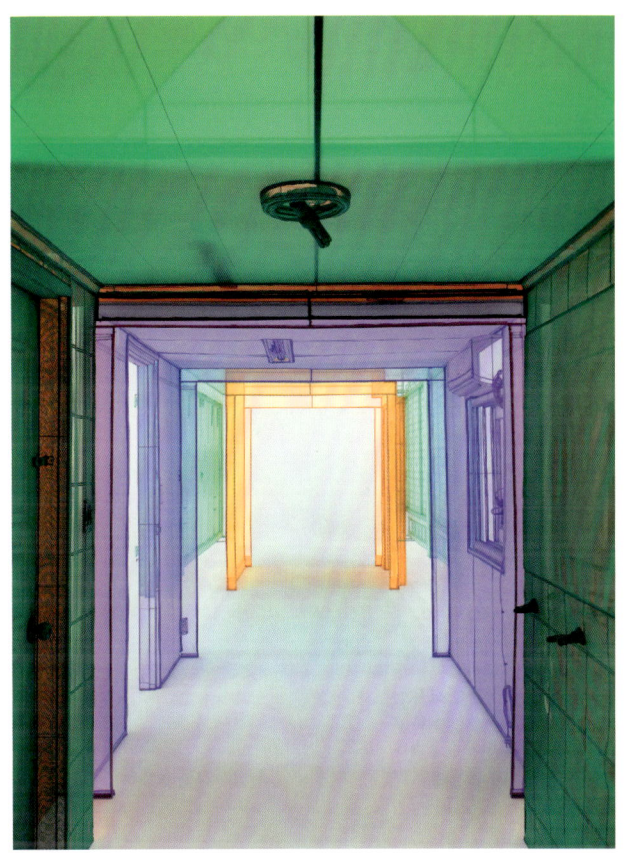

Nest/s 2024

reverent upward gaze, visitors are called upon to direct their attention to the base, to crouch downwards in order to make sense of the hundreds of tiny figures that support the edifice with their outstretched arms and upturned palms. The Korean word for 'public', *mincho*, the artist informs us, could be translated as 'public grass', suggesting a form of life that constantly renews itself and embodies a collective turbulence,[13] while the motif of a mass of miniature bodies holding up a built structure recurs in many of Suh's works, such as *Floor* 1997–2000, in which they support panels of glass, or in *Unsung Founders Memorial* 2004, located in the grounds of the University of North Carolina at Chapel Hill, where the figures seem to emerge from the earth.

The iteration of *Public Figures* shown at Tate is mobile for the first time, journeying into the context of the museum building to activate a contradiction between a stable, powerful monument and a strange, mobile constellation. While monumental statues continue to be built – and indeed seem to be growing bigger and ever more assertive in their presence on landscapes across the world[14] – *Public Figures* points to the process of potential destabilisation within which all entrenched power remains caught.

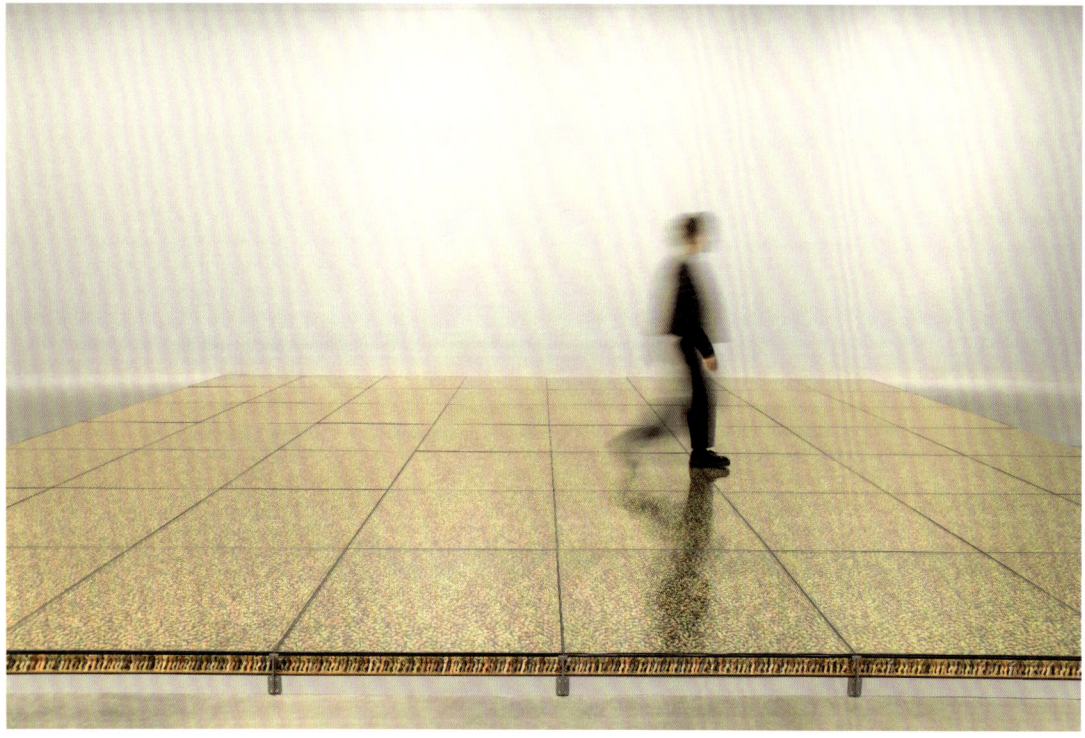

Floor 1997–2000, installation view, Museum of Contemporary Art, Australia, 2022

Do Ho Suh describes his practice as a meditation on 'how we move through the world'; 'As a Buddhist,' he continues, 'I don't believe that anything exists in a state of permanence.'[15] His work does not strive, however, towards a place-based locus of memory. Nor can it be reduced to the act of bringing 'something of the local' to a shared global idiom of art.[16] Rather, Suh's work assumes a constant translatability of plural and heterogeneous cultural positions built into processes of transculturation – one such process unfolding in the artist's practice mostly through the efficacy of materials. His is an understanding of art that navigates through and mediates between different fields: it composes, assembles, builds bridges, reconfigures and re-historicises, while never lapsing into an 'authentic' or nativist reflex. For example, Suh's constant recourse to porosity of matter, combined with the spatial configurations of East Asian architecture, to render movement fluid or the boundaries between the inside and the outside permeable, is a way to make the work into a space-time complex. Porosity is not a mere metaphor: it suggests that the world is not simply 'out there', but brought within, and that it exists in reciprocity with the work. This gives art the capacity to encompass diverse modes of situated and perspectival knowledge, a plurality of histories and subjectivities that mark contemporary societies formed by long histories of migration and contact. Similarly, references to a Buddhist tradition that privileges a path – a set of actions that unfold in the world – over belief inscribe the work of art with the ability to transform and act on the world, while Suh's repeated pronouncements rejecting the romantic myth of artistic genius and 'challenging the concept of the "authenticity" of the artist's hand'[17] signal to the life of the work of art as a continuum.

Art-as-making brings together thought, action, material and knowledge; making is not free from hesitation, uncertainty, friction or refusal. Liberated from the search for origins, art-as-thought can open up new spaces and times, with unexpected results. The work of art thus becomes an extended process rather than an object to be merely displayed and contemplated, and in consequence our connection to it is deeply relational and mutually constitutive. Looking at Do Ho Suh's practice through the lens of transculturation allows us to grasp how it brings different traditions of thought across time and cultural settings into encounter and engagement, thereby rendering them contemporary. This mode can only proceed by suspending the very idea of linear time. The work done by art is to render haptic the ways different pasts, presents and even futures can be brought together to make and remake the contemporary.

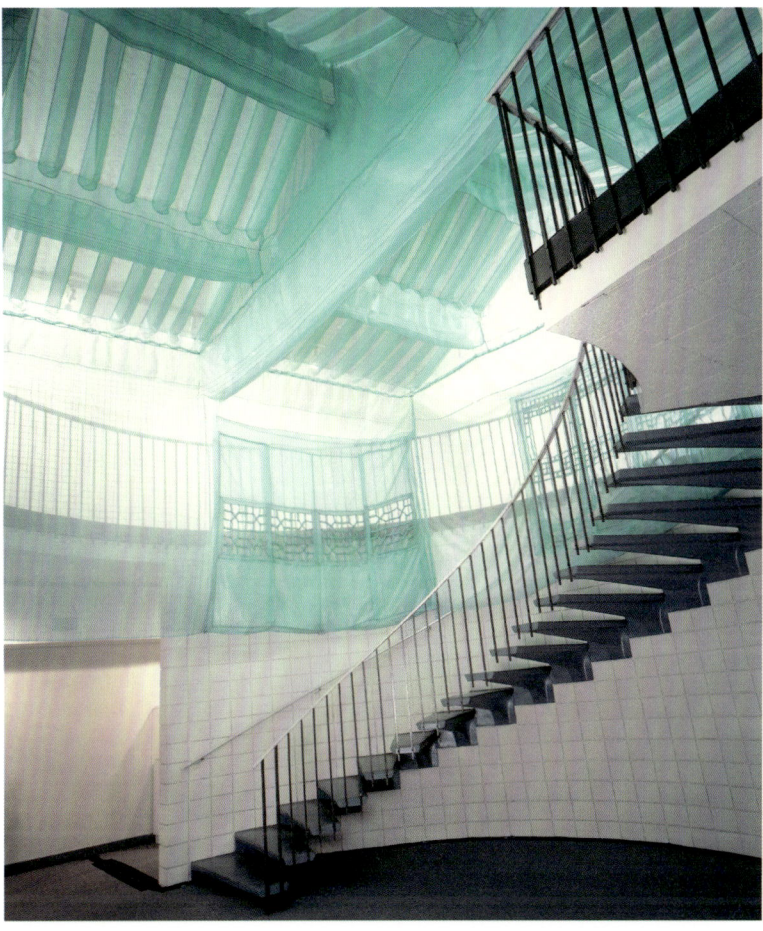

Seoul Home / L.A. Home / New York Home / Baltimore Home / London Home / Seattle Home / L. A. Home 1999, installation view, Korean Cultural Center, Los Angeles, 1999

Notes

1   Ranajit Guha, 'The Migrant's Time', *Postcolonial Studies*, vol.1, no.2, 1998, pp.155–60 (158–9).

2   Miwon Kwon, 'Flash in the East, Flash in the West', in Saloni Mathur (ed.), *The Migrant's Time: Rethinking Art History and Diaspora*, London and New Haven 2011, pp.196–205 (201).

3   Stephen Greenblatt, 'A Mobility Studies Manifesto', in Stephen Greenblatt et al, *Cultural Mobility: A Manifesto*, Cambridge 2010, pp.250–3 (252).

4   For an extensive discussion see Monica Juneja, *Can Art History be Made Global?: Meditations from the Periphery*, Berlin 2023, pp.23–39.

5   Quoted in Christopher Turner, 'For Do Ho Suh there is no place like home', *Apollo*, 3 Dec. 2016, www.apollo-magazine.com/ho-suh-theres-no-place-like-home, accessed 21 May 2024.

6   The term is borrowed from Irit Rogoff: see Hammad Nasar, 'Interview with Irit Rogoff', in Iftikhar Dadi and Hammad Nasar (eds.), *Lines of Control: Partition as Productive Space*, London 2012, pp.101–10 (108).

7   Francesca Romana Forlini, 'Do Ho Suh. Un-built Art and the Impossibility of Permanence', *koozArch*, 8 Feb. 2023, https://www.koozarch.com/interviews/do-ho-suh-un-built-art-and-the-impossibility-of-permanence, accessed 21 May 2024.

8   Tim Ingold, 'The Textility of Making', *Cambridge Journal of Economics*, vol.34, no.1, Jan. 2010, pp.91–102 (94).

9   Forlini 2023.

10   The term appears in Gilles Deleuze and Félix Guattari, *A Thousand Plateaus: Capitalism and Schizophrenia*, Minneapolis 1987.

11   Benedict Anderson, *Imagined Communities: Reflections on the Origin and Spread of Nationalism*, London 1983.

12   Do Ho Suh, *Counter-Monument*, unpublished writing, 2021: 2.

13   Ibid: 4.

14   See, for example, Kajri Jain, *Gods in the Time of Democracy*, Durham, NC 2021.

15   Forlini 2023.

16   Kwon 2011, p.205.

17   'In the studio with … Do Ho Suh', *Apollo*, 12 July 2021, https://www.apollo-magazine.com/in-the-studio-with-do-ho-suh, accessed 21 May 2024.

Do Ho Suh and Janice Kerbel in Conversation

Janice Kerbel: Do Ho, our connection goes back to 1993, when we both attended the summer residency at Skowhegan School of Painting, Maine. Something we've both been interested in over the years are forms that are somehow transitional – in your case, passageways, hallways and the spaces that connect other places. I know we both try to consider these forms on their own terms, instead of what they might lead on to or become. I've been thinking that home is also a kind of transitional space – the place from which we enter the world.

We'll come to the importance of home to your work, but I wanted to start with the birthday cakes of paint you made at Skowhegan. In my experience, cakes always relate to memories of home. I remember you talking about the wish to make something that one could not consume. Or that's how I understood it.

Do Ho Suh: I can't believe you remember those! I very rarely, if ever, show that body of work. I was coming from a background in traditional painting in Korea, and my interests were in painting and the problem of seeing – I was interested in the slippage between meaning and form. So, the birthday cakes were kind of an experiment: when you saw one, you knew it was not a real birthday cake but a lookalike made out of acrylic paint. They were so inviting visually, but if they'd been too successful as sculptures then the beholder would have wanted to consume them. Then again, the three-dimensionality confused the ability to consume them as just an image. I was absorbed with semiotics then – I wanted to avoid readability in a painting, to query the transparency and opacity of language.

The Korean painting I'd been instructed in comes from a completely different tradition to Western painting and I was wrestling with that. In Eastern traditional painting, you use either ink or watercolour pigment on rice paper, which is made up of multiple layers of fibre. Because it's highly absorbent, as soon as you touch the tip of the brush to the paper, the ink starts to bleed into the paper. If you try to make a mark that's one centimetre in diameter, it will end up being two centimetres or three centimetres. There's always this delay – the first mark that you put on the surface is not what you're going to see, and that mark is made up of fibre *and* ink. Basically, in Eastern traditional painting, you don't have full control. And I think that's probably what I was getting into: questioning the ontological condition of the painting, trying to see the contradictions.

It's interesting that you associated the birthday cakes with the idea of home, because it was that process of questioning that led to the idea of transporting architectural space to other places – an idea that started forming because of my experiences at Skowhegan and RISD [Rhode Island School of Design], which I don't think has changed since.

I read something recently by the critic James Wood that I thought was really beautiful. He said: 'I couldn't go back home, because I wouldn't know how to anymore.' I've been thinking a lot about the idea of homecoming, which is part of our cultural and literary hardwiring: in *The Odyssey*, for instance, getting home is the whole objective. The houses you make – your fabric architectures, your rubbing works – aren't exactly replicas of homes, but they embody both a departure from home and a sense of return.

Yes, there's sort of a two-directional thing going on. When I talk about my architectural work I always say that the concept of home didn't exist when I was living in Seoul: it only started to exist when I left home and went elsewhere. That was when I started to wonder where home existed. How much of my former space did I carry into my current space? What was home before then? There's a notion in sociology that I've always found helpful, 'marginal man', which describes the position of people who are displaced or who are immigrants in a society, who cannot be fully part of the mainstream yet at the same time no longer belong to where they came from. I think about that a lot.

I should also say that when I talk about feeling homeless myself, I don't mean it literally, it's metaphorical. I'm mindful that we are seeing an ever-deepening global crisis of forced displacement, and I want to be very clear that my experience of movement was not forced but voluntary.

Yes, I think what your work does very successfully is exist between states. At the beginning of *The Odyssey*, the question is asked, 'Where did this story take place?' and the answer is: 'Somewhere between sunset and dawn.' Which doesn't really answer the question, but it indicates that the question has to be considered on two planes. The collapse of time and space is often happening, but not always obvious.

Another aspect of this in-betweenness in making new work is the tension between a present moment and a projection into the future that's necessary. A lot of your more complex architecture works take a lot of planning, and learning new techniques, such as pattern-cutting. There is often a process of anticipation in making new works.

Anticipation is interesting. Anticipating means a future, but again, it is impossible to anticipate without previous experience …

… and without a future outcome in mind. For all artists, I think, that outcome is a result of what they did before.

Absolutely. My work is not really about replicating a physical

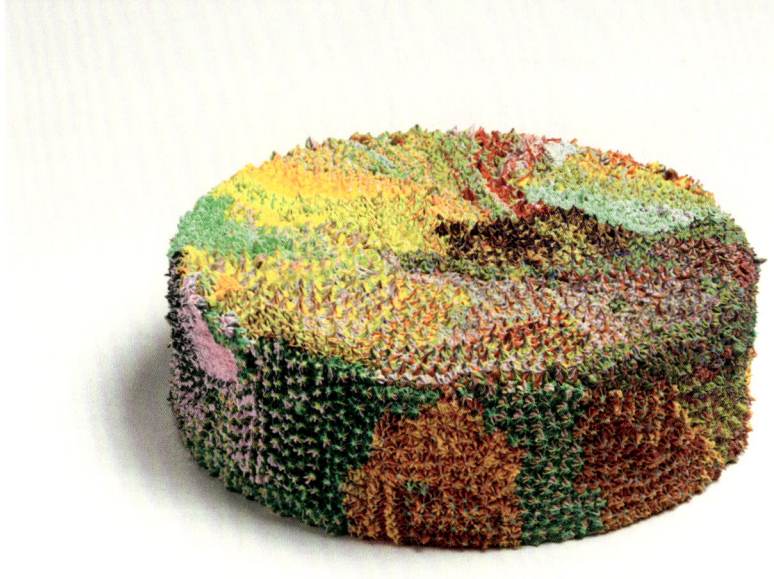

Birthday Cake 1993

space in a physical material. I've actually dreamed, literally dreamed, of making something out of smoke – out of nothingness. But we live in a three-dimensional world, and I quickly learned that I had to work with gravity and materiality. Still, these are works that are about memory, about feelings, about energy. And actually what I have been trying to do with my sculpture is not just to transport these spaces into different places, but also to incorporate time in a physical piece. When you think of the medium of film, you immediately think that there's a narrative in it because it's a temporal medium. So, for me, introducing that dimension of time in my sculptures wasn't that different from working with film – it's a different medium, but it seemed a totally natural continuation.

I never think artworks are 'about' something. Rather they are something. Your works remind me of this. They are neither about home, nor are they homes themselves.

That really resonates with me, yes. About ten years ago, I tried to make a drawing of every room I'd ever lived in. For it to be complete would have meant revisiting my first home after I was born, which I only vaguely remembered, but that building no longer exists. It was demolished. So, I asked my family, my parents and my brother, to draw the house where we'd all lived. And of course we each remembered parts – highly personalised spaces – so differently.

I have a vivid memory, for instance, of one dark corner in the house where I used to hide, yet my mother, who was able to draw whole floorplans, couldn't remember this corner at all. And my brother remembers different things again. I found that fascinating.

Your rubbing works seem to be reaching towards something that is outside of language, beyond memory. They exist somewhere between sculpture, drawing and print. Whenever I go back to my parents' house I am always surprised how something as simple as touching the table in the hall instantly connects me with what is past.

And that touch triggers all sorts of memories. It's actually the opposite of what happens with my rubbing pieces, where I cover entire surfaces with paper, so I become blind to colour and detail. The instant I've masked that surface, I can no longer remember what's exactly behind it. It's like a form of dementia, almost: I'm aware that I know what's under the paper, but I don't have access to the memory. And when I start rubbing, things rush back. When I was rubbing my old apartment in New York, I found two holes in the wall that I'd completely forgotten existed. But as soon as they started to emerge, I knew exactly what they were, why they were there, the fact I'd once made them for a coat rack so I could hang more clothes. Then I remembered

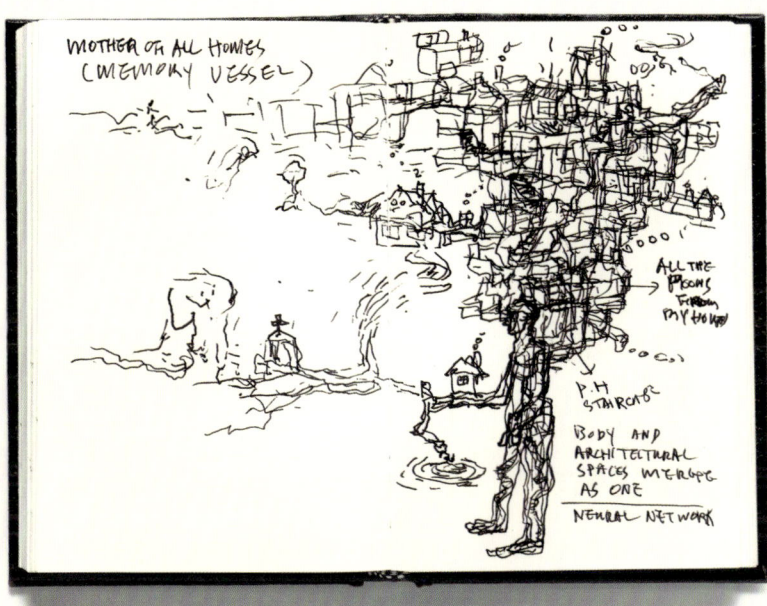

Suh's sketchbook, 2023

even more – the journey from my apartment to Bed Bath & Beyond on Sixth Avenue and back, the temperature that day, the light. It wasn't even a significant day. That made me wonder about memory's mechanisms – why did these thoughts resurface as I was rubbing, when at some point I'd got rid of that rack and completely forgotten the whole thing? When I eventually had the opportunity to rub the entire brownstone that housed my apartment, as it was going to be sold, I thought continually about that because the landlord, Arthur, who I'd become close friends with, had died with dementia.

Can you describe the rubbing process?

I have to use a very precise pressure throughout the entire rubbing. Too light and you cannot depict the texture of what's beneath the paper. Press too hard, you obliterate that texture. It has to be a certain pressure, and also very constant. It's a bit erotic, actually. More than a bit! It's like caressing a lover's body, staying very attentive and sensitive to their reaction. And if it is the right pressure, the right touch or caress, then the paper or the building starts to emerge.

It's such a simple gesture, but when you're dealing with a much larger space it ends up being a really intensive process, both labour-intensive and psychologically draining. By the end of a project, I have literally consumed the

space that I've rubbed or measured and turned it into a *Rubbing/Loving* or fabric architecture work. That's when I feel I can leave that space behind, that I can't do it again, because I am completely exhausted. Yet after a while, I forget that exhaustion.

And you find your way back to other parts that were unresolved.

Yes, I keep doing it over and over again. And I think it's the same with how I make drawings. In Eastern painting, each mark is like the equivalent of a breath. The stroke needs to contain life and it can't be withdrawn. You lay a mark on the paper and that's it – you can't correct a mistake, you'd need to start afresh. It's so different to using oils and having the ability to go over things. It requires a very physical level of focus – if I'm drawing faces, for instance, unless I really concentrate, my hand moves automatically and I end up repeating the same sort of shape. But if I don't like a shape, I have to keep going and try it again. I can't go backwards. I have to constantly remind myself that I want to make each individual face different, whether that's different faces or one person in different times and different spaces. But there has to be a connection at the image level as well, so, with work like the *Spectators* series, what I do is try to draw a line in one breath. When my breath is out, I have to stop, so it is a kind of breathing exercise.

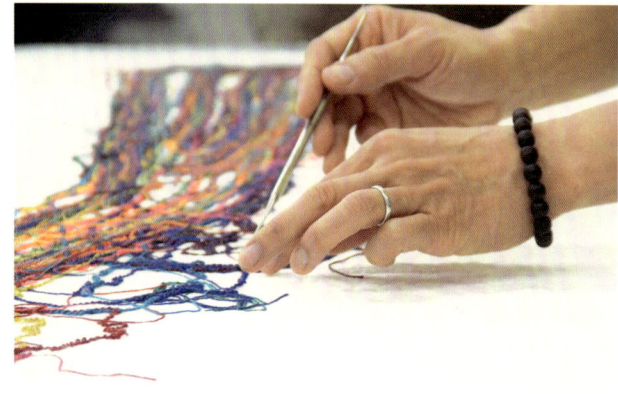

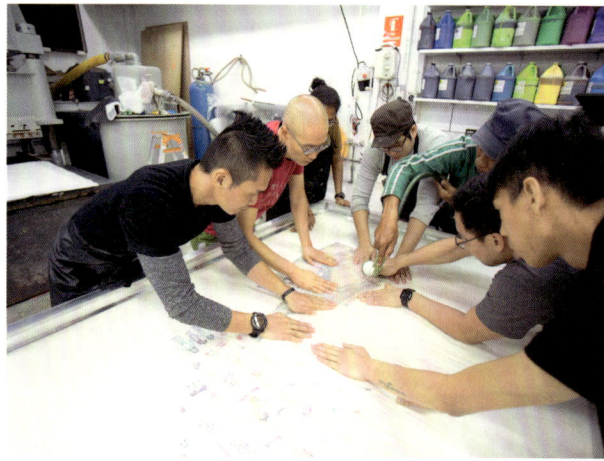

Do Ho Suh and team at work on a thread drawing, STPI –
Creative Workshop & Gallery, Singapore, 2019

I'm relieved to hear you say that! It's similar for me. I always assumed that you worked very much like a painter, but you also work collectively with a lot of people to produce many of your works.

The fact is, I can't make art without other people's help. My current team in London includes several professional architects and a designer with a fashion background. We have a lot of group discussions, and what's interesting – I only started to realise this recently, when I was building this new team – is that my ideas evolve as I'm explaining them to my team and in turn I get new ideas from their responses. I really value that type of collaboration. I think that if I locked myself alone in the studio those ideas might not progress.

I think a lot about ideas around hospitality and reciprocity, and I wonder if the studio model you're describing is a bit like that. Everybody has to feel connected to the process in order for a work – and your collaborators – to evolve. I am wondering if the studio, or the work itself, starts to feel like a home?

Yes. At the same time, I'm fundamentally an extremely introverted person. I do need separation – I cannot really function or think if I don't have my own quiet space and time. It's a bit paradoxical.

I guess it demands both. Some things happens in the studio practically, materially, while other things happens in the space of reflection when you're alone. Sometimes things don't work out as imagined.

That's interesting. One of the reasons I didn't pursue painting was that I think it relies too much on decision making – not decisions based on calculation, it's just that you have to make constant, spontaneous decisions, and I wasn't good at that. My attitude with my work is that I often try to defer those decisions and not to define things too much. I guess that the thread drawings allow me to accept accidents into my more programmatic work. During my residency at the STPI Creative Workshop, which specialises in print and papermaking, when the STPI team suggested using thread to make my drawings, I couldn't immediately see that connection but then I saw what they did. The thread has the same thickness and quality of line as my pen drawings, so it's a close translation. There are decisions made along the way in the thread drawings – steps I figure out in advance, so it's still quite process-oriented – but the making is very temporal and spontaneous, like ink painting.

The major difference, it seems to me, is that the drawn line doesn't want to do anything in particular – it's just what you do with it – whereas the thread has a certain materiality that dictates what it will and will not do.

Thinking about your drawing, how do you get from working in the space of notebooks – where you have always made drawings using the same pen and black ink – to working with colour? I really admire your use of colour, but I don't understand it.

A lot of people ask about this, and I have to confess: for *Spectators*, I just bought a set of pastels and started to use them, in order, starting from the top left corner. That way I didn't actually have to choose the colour. The actual colours themselves don't mean anything to me. With the fabric work, there were some conceptual decisions – I chose jade green for *Seoul Home* because it's a colour traditionally used on wallpapered ceilings in Korea, and a deep blue for the New York work because there was an association with concrete for me, but again, I really just worked through the shades. I always apply some sort of logic, as I also do with the breathing for *Spectators*, so these aren't absolutely free gestures – there's always some other element. I don't know whether that is a good thing or not, but that's how I make things.

It's like catching an eel in a river – I literally have to use the water to control or at least try to control it. The thread has its own life, its own tension, and it doesn't want to move as I want it. That can be frustrating, but it's exciting, too – I like the spontaneity of the sensation. It's immediate, or present. Because actually, when you're drawing, there's a kind of blindness that occurs when you're making a mark on the paper. This is something Derrida talks about: when your pencil nib touches the paper, it *covers* the mark that you are making, so you're blind to the mark on the paper at the moment of its creation, meaning the mark is always in the past.

In the same way, we think of ourselves as living in the present, but in reality we're living in the past, and therefore we can probably talk about the future, too. We believe we're controlling time and this present moment, but we're not. Even now, when you're formulating a thought, it's worth thinking about how much is new. Ninety-nine percent is from memory. I think we're bound to always go back to the past, to the same areas of interest, the same kinds of thoughts.

Because something is still not resolved? Or maybe because it's familiar?

I think it's because it's unresolved, although the reason I keep asking the same question in many different ways is probably that I've known from the beginning that there is no answer.

You recently exhibited your sketchbooks for the first time [at National Galleries of Scotland, Edinburgh], and to me that feels like another aspect of this two-directional flow, this deliberate collapsing of past and present.

Those drawings were never meant to be shown – they were just part of my journal, so I had no intentions for them. I just drew and moved on. Mostly they're technical, trying to resolve details of my sculpture. They're black and white line drawings, made with the same pens and in the same sketchbooks I've used since I was a student. And then suddenly they became the basis for the thread drawings.

The thread introduces difference while the line is always the same … That makes me think of something the poet Elizabeth Bishop said about letters: 'Once detached from the moment and circumstance of composition, there is something impersonal and strange about any piece of correspondence. On that level, every letter is a letter found on the street.' I think something similar applies to drawings: when they're in the sketchbook, they're part of a whole world – but rip the page out and it suddenly becomes its own thing.

It's interesting that you relate it to letters, to words and language. When you look at a sentence in English, I think you have an idea of what it is before it is formed into words. There's something similar going on with these drawings: they are not abstract, but they are a mix of the recognisable and the imaginative or speculative. There'll be a realistic figure, but it will be situated in this unrealistic realm. There's a rawness to the drawings, a directness and an urgency, because they're based on fundamental questions about our existence, but I haven't yet formed a sentence to describe the image.

As visual artists we deal with visual signs and symbols, but I'm also interested in semiotics. I took courses in linguistics when I first arrived in the US, and I realised that the domain of language is actually inseparable from visual art. That made me really think about transparency and opacity, both in language and the visual arts, at a time when I was having difficulty engaging or clearly explaining my work in English. My frustration with the language barrier allowed me to think more about the function or purpose of language in conveying the meaning of the artwork, and that led me to decide to make my work as clear as possible – to cut out everything unnecessary and strip it back to its core – so that I wouldn't really need to talk about it. Subconsciously, I think I was also trying to remove my fingerprints, which in turn relates to the collaborative nature of my practice now – using a robot to create drawings, or making work with a lot of people even though I'm not that social a person.

That's something I'm always challenged by – this question of how to be rigorous and free at the same time.

Are you intentionally trying to be rigorous in your work?

Actually, I'm trying intentionally to be a little bit less rigorous! I remember talking to Ann Hamilton when we were at Skowhegan about how difficult I was finding a certain thing, and she said – you know how sometimes a colleague or a friend or a teacher says something that really burns a hole in your mind – things that present themselves as obstacles can become positive qualities of your work, rather than things you need to change or avoid.

Right! I was so pleased to meet Ann because her very large-scale, very labour-intensive site-specific work chimed with my own interest in site specificity. She and I talked a lot about language, about text and context and history, and the language difficulties of coming from a different culture. But I think what she inspired in me most was the idea that art doesn't have to stay in the white cube, this completely isolated space that cuts out all the surrounding context.

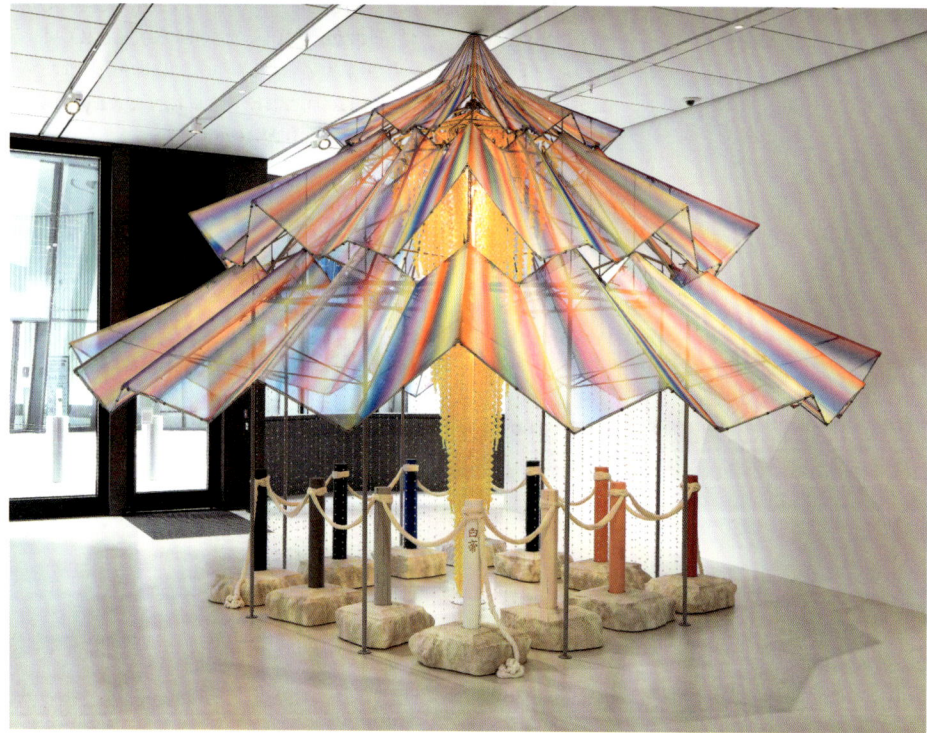

Proposal for Sach'onwang-sa (Four Heavenly Kings Monastery) 2019–21

What are your thoughts on working in the context of the museum as opposed to working outside of it? I know you've had experience of both.

The museum as we know it is a relatively recent invention, a product of modernity, and has all the attendant problems of modernity. Because of that, it's impossible for me to see the museum as a purely physical space – I'm always considering the context around it. And within it, too, which is why I began to question the plinth. If you go to the Korean gallery of a Western encyclopaedic museum you'll see a statue of Buddha made in 400 BCE right next to this eighteenth-century ceramic bowl that was probably used for drinks at the pub. They're from completely different times and contexts, yet they're both inside a case, on a pedestal, juxtaposed, made equivalent. I have a huge problem with that. That's why my freestanding sculptures touch the floor.

In terms of the museum – I chose fabric for the architectural pieces because the translucency means that you can bring the surrounding space into the piece, blurring the boundary between the artwork and the visitors' bodies. If the works weren't translucent, they'd be no different from a modernistic sculpture on a pedestal, but I want visitors to see the architecture of the museum through my work – that it's not just this white space for art. If you're inside a fabric architecture piece, you're actually part of the piece,

you activate it, in that other visitors see the artwork and you inside it simultaneously.

At the same time as doing everything they are meant to do in terms of architecture and detail, the fact the homes are made of fabric renders them totally dysfunctional. They wouldn't keep you dry or warm, for instance, and so they remind us that to have a home is also to be vulnerable, to have something that can be taken away from you.

I think once you leave your first home, your original home – which most people will, because by nature we're an animal that doesn't really settle in one place – then a perpetual sense of displacement and vulnerability sets in, even within the solid walls that protect you physically. The fabric architecture obviously amplifies that feeling of vulnerability.

For instance, my old apartment in New York was a half-basement studio, streetside, with two big bay windows and my bed was right next to one of them, meaning I could hear everything from the street. There were metal bars on the windows for security, but sometimes I dreamt that people were looking in my window – hundreds of them. Sometimes within the dream they got into my room through the window, and then there would be hundreds of them inside a four-hundred-square-foot apartment.

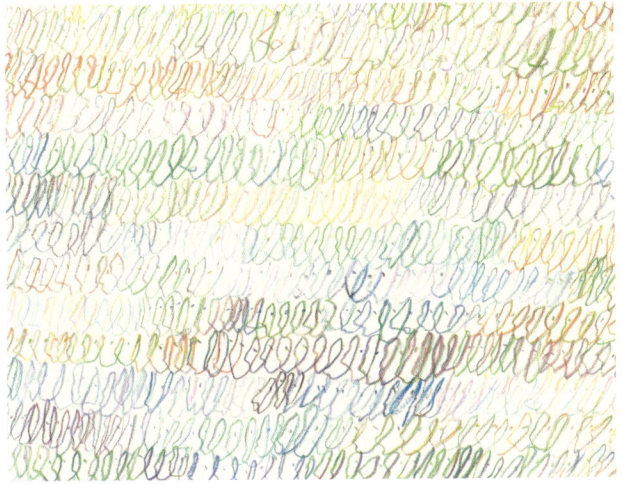

Spectators 2023 (detail)

I think that's also related to memory. At least in my mind, things from the past overlap with the space I'm occupying right now. My London apartment constantly reminds me of spaces from the past. Physically I may have left New York, but I never *left* New York. I've moved around so much in my life that the notion of home has become very complicated and cumulative. Although again, I want to stress that reflecting on voluntary movement is a privilege.

I was also thinking about ruins.

Yes! I find ruins fascinating, because so much information is missing. I've done a few projects dealing with archaeological sites. In one, I worked from a couple of sentences from *Samguk Yusa*, a twelfth-century book written by a Korean monk. The events he describes are highly questionable, but it's a really important historical text. The story is that the Korean king learned of an imminent Chinese invasion, and none of his advisors could come up with a defensive strategy, so instead he consulted a monk who told him to build a temporary temple out of silk, and to pray. These twelve monks prayed day and night, and summoned a typhoon which sank the Chinese ships and foiled the invasion. Afterwards the king ordered a Buddhist temple to be built on the site of the temporary silk temple. Nobody knew the temple site was there, though, until its ruins were found during the Japanese occupation. I've planned my own interpretation of that temple, which could be installed at the archaeological site as a temporary structure. In 2021 I showed a model of it at Bloomberg Space in London, which occupies the space above the ruins of a Roman temple.

There is a sense of accumulation in your more recent works. It's as if the most recent memory is no longer the one that has to be prioritised – it's like you're asking what one memory is in relation to all the others.

The timeline gets confused. In *Perfect Home: London, Horsham, New York, Berlin, Providence, Seoul* 2024, you're no longer working with the whole but with fragments, bringing elements together in such a way that the attachment to the real is fractured.

For a long time, my thinking about time and space was really linear. I was trying to find the 'perfect home', a search I'd been carrying out for thirty years without ever finding it – or rather, discovering along the way that there is no one perfect home, but many different versions. When I began making *Perfect Home*, I realised it was impossible to think linearly about those things and that if I wanted to get closer to the notion of the perfect home, I would have to embrace an element of chance.

So, although every artefact in *Perfect Home* comes from an actual space and has been measured, modelled and stitched, they are arranged according to a computerised process almost like the *I Ching*, where each actual outcome is just one of a million different combinations. I wouldn't say it's arrived at entirely by chance – I had to set the rules for the selection process and choose a certain combination from hundreds of thousands of options, so there is some subjectivity involved, but only a little. What you get then is thirty different rooms superimposed on each other, thirty sets of objects all converging, sometimes losing their shape where they blur together.

It's kind of like a hybrid memory. This seems especially apt at a moment when to have a home at all begins to feel like a luxury.

Absolutely. Today I would say that I don't have a perfect home, but I think I'm still on that quest for the perfect home, the perfect world. The *Bridge Project* (1999– ongoing) started out as another attempt to find the perfect home. Currently, there are three different cities in my life that I've called home – London, New York and Seoul – and if you triangulate the place that's equidistant from all three, it's actually right next to the North Pole. So, in trying to find the site of my perfect home, I end up in one of the most environmentally challenging places in the world. How am I to get there? I would need a bridge. One question follows another: how am I going to handle all these extreme climates? What would I eat? Whose waters and land would the bridge infringe on? What would it destroy? How would I overcome the violence and bureaucracy of borders? Wouldn't I be so isolated that any notion of perfection would be rendered obsolete? It's more epic than I originally intended. Again, I just followed this thread of thought and this is how it's turned out. I guess the perfect home is a much broader, more complex idea than I'd originally thought. It's not a small, cute house in a field. It's not something that can be easily imagined.

Sean Anderson

Ghosts

What is called a ghost is no more than this: an image of memory that has found in the air – in the atmosphere of the house, in the shadow of the rooms, in the dirt of the walls, in the falling dust that falls – its most effective fingerprint holder.
Georges Didi-Huberman[1]

Images never rest. Dynamic, percussive, revelatory, the image and its sometime elusive companions, including language and medium, speak across temporalities and contexts. The image confronts and may also diminish, decay, fall into memory, only to resurface in other forms. While an image can turn towards melancholy, its shadow, the ghost, is an agent of the past waiting to evince a shared present. Making visible the topologies of collectivity as well as the limits of an individual, a ghost is a presencing of an empire of spirits that structure and inform worlds. The ghost is a marker of time and yet does not belong to it. Spaces hold ghosts as much as amplify them. And yet, the image-ghost also constructs, making time visible, revealing the capacity for one to seek and feel and belong.

For more than thirty years, the nurturing and disappearance of the image – while especially referencing the elasticity of home(s), of an ephemeral architecture to capture and collect a genealogy of atmospheres – has been an unbroken narrative running through Do Ho Suh's work, revealing the presence of an absence that each of us as viewers possesses. That this absence is one which many seek to redress but do not achieve, build but never inhabit, speaks to the ways in which the illusory qualities of the quotidian establish mutual longing – desires that supersede us in and through time. For Suh, the image-ghost is embodied across sculptures, installations, public art, video and drawings. Such are a cultivation of intimacies that are recognised by viewers and by Suh himself, yet rendered by the various spaces and objects his works configure and simultaneously dislocate. It is through one's encounters with the multiple scales conjured by these works and their traces that our own antecedents, our own self-defined mythologies, are refashioned, made whole, even for a moment.

Phantoms
Deriving in part from the Greek term *phaínein*, meaning 'to show', and the verb *phantazein*, 'to present to the mind' or 'to reveal', the phantom – or, as rendered in Anglo-French, the *fantasme* – is one of a collection of imaginary occupations that, while existing in one reality, may not in another. These provisos suggest one's relationships with an imaginary, with the influence of logic, departing from meanings that are ghostly but not necessarily haunting. Additional utterances such as 'phantasmagoria' and 'diaphanous' materialise ancient voices as mobile images. Within Homeric metaphysics, the phantom, while lacking voice, or a skeleton upon which to carry its assemblage of

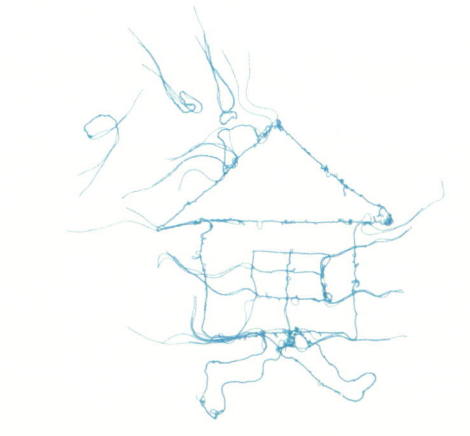

Walking Home 2014

stories, moves in and out of bodies sustaining reciprocities with environments, an unbecoming in the built world that is fugitive, fleeting.

In the Korean language, by comparison, similar connotations bridge multiple realities and historical times, offering bodily and sometimes gendered conditions that may generate fear, but also actively engage the present in modes both didactic and natural. Within Korean folklore, the phantom and its imagining are enlivened by multiple customs, including music, rituals and poetry, from which personal agency is derived to inform broader societal conditions. The multiple locative states within which one inhabits in death are understood as transient and are accompanied by cycles of liminality, between pasts and futures. Korean Buddhism places emphasis on ancient belief systems linked with rituals including Cheondojae (천도재). These practices ensure one's soul travels to 'Sukhavati' (translated from Sanskrit as 'Land of Bliss' or 'Pure Land') where it awaits judgement following such transitional periods. Since a soul without a body is understood as moving closer to enlightenment, the rituals are spatiotemporal guides that accompany long journeys. Ghosts (*gwishin*, 귀신), by comparison, are derived typically from the forces of inanimate domestic objects rather than from the loss of a human being. The appearance of such energies, however, departs from ideas of their occurrence as materially grounded: instead, both rituals alongside a ghost's furtive presencing are part of structured temporal processes that reveal ways forward for individuals as well as society.

Outlines of the human body appear among Suh's two-dimensional works as excavations of the self. In each, a line, a room, skin, a body is activated by indeterminate actions enacted upon them, outwardly expressed as openings into which meanings enter, filling both the body and the space of the paper. While potentially autobiographical, ghost-like plural bodies are loosely drawn as amorphous yet inter-dependent – in *Family Cuddle* 2020 – or as vibrational, in *Myselves* 2013/2016 and *Karma Juggler* 2022. In earlier drawings such as *My Homes* 2013 and the series *Walking Home* 2014, the personification of a conventional house form with legs or wheels is caught in movement, during a voyage of unknown proportions. These images reference Korean verbal expressions that refer to the portability of the house, the possibility of dismantling it and reassem-bling it in another location. In other works, Suh shows the house subsumed or captured by the body: as an exten-sion of both head and mind in *Home Clothing* 2014 and internalised in two *Self-Portraits* of 2006 and 2015. The forging of home and body are thus congruent. In their multiplicity, we identify a return to congruent subjects that evokes Suh's desire to pack his childhood home in a suitcase, which he realised with his earliest experiments with fabric architecture. The 2003 and 2010 drawings of the contained and uncontainable, entitled *Home Within Home*, prefigure sculptural works of the same name while also expressing figurative aspects of home as both built construct and subversive metaphor.

For the ongoing conceptual *Bridge Project* (begun in 1999) Do Ho Suh envisions a series of bridges linking the cities he has called home – Seoul, London and New York – while traversing the land- and seascapes that evoke through their dissonance an uncertain temporal linearity. Eschew-ing dialectics for an unlimited stretching of presence, the series captures a hopeful longing to be in more than one place at the same time. These works suggest that one always is *in* and *of* more than one place. Initially envisioned as an inhabitable bridge, the *Bridge Project* remains one of postulation that is enduring. The work reflects Suh's continuing interest in spaces of displacement while also examining the conflicting technologies, patterns and struc-tures associated with the migratory movements of people. Each drawing in the series reflects unintended aspects through the impossibility of establishing 'a perfect home': they navigate phantasmatic passages across oceans and continents. Suh's sculptural works translate and magnify these internal cartographic impulses as trajectories of becoming, without end. They are dreamworlds, evanescent.

Apparitions

In his reckonings with the anterior, of those idealised forms found in metaphysics' histories and conceits, of fluctuating capital, Jacques Derrida writes: 'to haunt does not mean to be present, and it is necessary to introduce haunting into the very construction of a concept'.[2] Among both Korean and Western worldviews, the image-ghost circulates among us, carrying value(s) that we inculcate and can challenge, and from which we sometimes seek retreat. Suh's works are thus palpable meditations on the

image-ghosts that extend our bodies into conditions that are too often manifest through the fixity of place, language and function. His works shift a viewer's physicality out of one space and transport them to another. Without con-ventional boundaries that serve to delimit completion, the sculptures present spaces and instruments with which we seek not only reassurance but also knowledge. They are suffused with shared energies.

The (in)determinacy of home is an active element in the authoring of Suh's formation as an artist. Suh acknow-ledges the profound effects of growing up among copies of historic houses (*hanok*, 한옥) some of which were built in the 1970s but used older timber from buildings demol-ished during Korea's occupation. As an artist and erstwhile occupant, he references home as both a physical and an intellectual construct throughout much of his oeuvre. Originating in the fourteenth century, during the Joseon Dynasty, a *hanok* was organised around internal spatial divisions literalised in the physicality of its floors and roof and extended by materialities of class, gender and labour. Designed according to the occupant's seated height within it, a *hanok* was also responsive to the environment through sensitive approaches to the reuse of building materials. Each material performed as an expression of limits that magnified how bodies informed the resolution of interior(s). Rice paper was often coated with bean oil to produce shimmering flooring that, when coupled with its pleasant aroma, augmented the sensorial nature of house evolving into home. The permeability of its walls allowed the *hanok* to sense, breathing with the changing of seasons and accepting the forces of light and air on its exterior structure while also sheltering multiple functions within that contain, protect and erase.

Seoul Home 2012 is a one-to-one scale replica of Suh's family home, itself a copy of a house constructed in the nineteenth century by a king in his gardens of Seoul, thought to have been built so he could experience the life of ordinary people. Gathering in its naming convention all the locations where the work has been shown previously, from 2012 to the present, *Seoul Home/Seoul Home/Kanazawa Home/Beijing Home/Pohang Home/Gwangju Home/Phila-delphia Home* – is a collection of placeholders, of stories, of chimeric potentials that simultaneously hide and disclose the artist in multiple locations. Each condition found within the home is regarded as synecdochal, with individual colours indicating various spaces, then assembled to be seen as part of the whole. Suh's choice of a jade green silk organza in the work doubles aspects of the home: the colour is a reference to his parents' ceiling wallpaper. For the artist to have departed this originary home and remade it as an occupiable nomadic ontology in translucent colour-ful fabric implies an active seeking for rootedness amid the ever-changing contours of internal imagistic transformation.

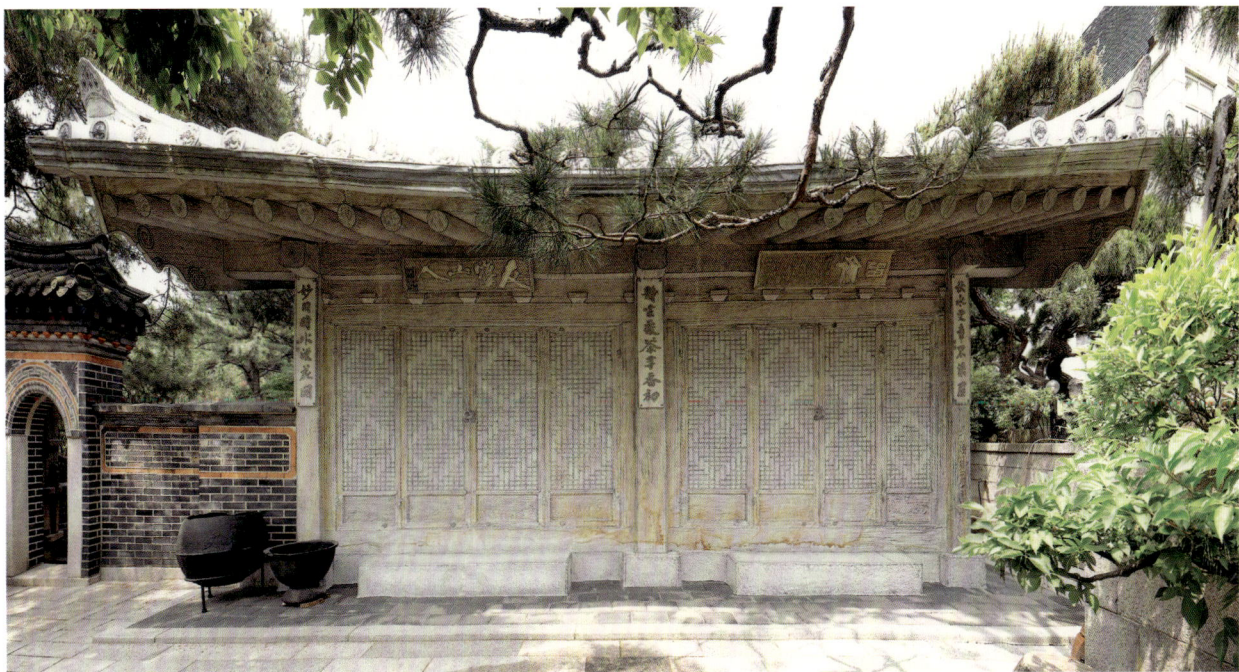

Rubbing / Loving: Seoul Home 2013–22, work in progress, 2013

Contemporaneous with Suh's volumetric remaking of lived spaces is a series of two- and three-dimensional works entitled *Rubbing/Loving*, born from an intensive methodical attention to calculating the measure of spaces. The artist records every aspect and detail of these environments on paper through the act of rubbing with hand and pencil, applying just enough pressure to make visible that which lies beneath the thin paper. Suh began this practice when he first moved to New York City and occupied a half-basement apartment of a brownstone on West 22nd Street (later rubbing the entire interior of the then vacant townhouse before its sale). His first work, *Rubbing/Loving: Company Housing of Gwangju Theater* 2012, was developed for the Gwangju Biennale in 2012, followed by *Rubbing/Loving: Seoul Home* 2013–22. Both works capture in their subtleties not only the rhythms and memories of those who helped produce them, but also of those persons who once inhabited, lived, breathed and dreamed in these buildings. Their rubbing may be understood as a volumetric history writing. An intensive recoding of lived moments; a coalescing of temporalities. These works are as much archaeological as they are commemorative recordings: private choreographies of sound and weight, of bodies, breath and time. 'I think that's how your house gets inside of you', Suh writes. 'For me, time and space are always together, and they are usually collapsed into one other.'[3]

None of these works attempts to replace or reconfigure the artist's experience of living in the spaces. Rather, Suh has stated: 'My desire to guard and carry around my very own intimate space makes me perceive space as infinitely movable. I experience space through, and as the movement of displacement. Space, for me, becomes intrinsically transportable and translatable.'[4] These constructions reify the ways in which home – in its malleability of formation, in its fraught capaciousness as both built space and concept – reacts to and expands who we are as individuals within and among communities, among shared lineages, across invisible lines of territories, amidst journeys, despite the connivances of time.

Spectres

For the philosopher Aby Warburg at the turn of the twentieth century, and more recently through interlocutors including Georges Didi-Huberman, the image can be spectral, intersectional, and the concept of 'image-survival' establishes entanglements of temporalities read through non-linear experience. 'A surviving image,' Didi-Huberman writes, 'is an image that, having lost its original use value and meaning, nonetheless comes back, like a ghost, at a particular historical moment'.[5] Warburg's polymathic efforts to assert the discontinuities of art limn transformations in the world while describing conflicted aspects of humanity found in the commonplace. In 1896, he writes of agency and action: 'Lightning imprisoned in the wire, captive electricity, has created a civilization that does away with paganism. What does it put in its stead? The forces of nature are no longer conceived as anthropomorphic or biomorphic shapes but rather as infinite waves obeying the pressure of the human hand.'[6] Deploying aspects of the image and its transmission of empathic feeling, a signaling of hope and

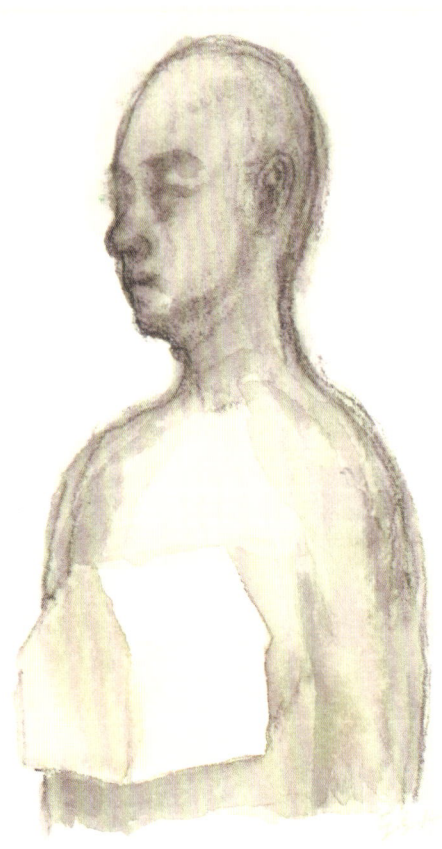

Self-Portrait 2014

architecture first described in words and lines on tracing paper – becomes a repository of lost voices and lost time, deferred generosities activated through our witness. We, perhaps as complicit lenses, are engaged in an ocular 'rubbing' of these containments. In its foregone spectacle of destruction, for which violence is always at the intersection of social and political realms, the political nature of these building(s) evolves into dramatic mediation. The video is a reciprocation of multiple gazes that 'decentre and recentre' the viewer in a matrix of systemic diminishments defined by and embedded within a seemingly failed architecture.[7]

Spirits

It might be said that all buildings contain the possibility for residual hauntings. Spaces, imagined and real, become like batteries, among the fabricated and collected, wherein assembled objects including the walls, the wood and concrete beneath one's feet absorb and enfold energies to be released later. The compact shared between building and occupant is a bargaining among forms of haunting that allow for dust to collect while bearing an imprint of histories, in which traumas prefigure an inhabitation of the present. In its embodiment of 'unconscious contents', the home, in turn, can contain a 'soul'. According to Carl Jung, the 'self' is the unity of psychic processes through which one is individuated, while the 'soul' endows meaning if wholeness were possible.[8] When a house is understood vis-à-vis the making of home, in its outfitting of things, this process suggests an individual does not possess a soul but is rather one part of a soul always being made, never undone.

failure rooted partly in trauma, Warburg's 'ghost stories for grownups' are situational as much as chronicles in their delineation of new ways to understand lapses in interpretation, to return to a grounding found within image making and identification with the body.

In 2018, Suh produced *Robin Hood Gardens, Woolmore Street, London E14 0HG*, shown as a component of a three-part exhibition at the Venice Biennale of Architecture. Suh's panoramic video of an East London housing estate built in 1972 by the iconoclastic British architects Alison and Peter Smithson indexes the pathos of a much-debated building on the eve of its partial demolition, its legacy in architecture histories and among the lives of its former residents. The video was installed as a large wall projection in which the viewer is both consumed by and embedded within slow-moving tracking shots, time-lapse photography and photogrammetry. Segmented, x-ray-like images, deployed as sliding transparencies, invite the viewer to inhabit four apartments and experience the massive exterior façade of endless framed windows. Even though its structures lie inert as the lens passes through and across its surfaces, *Robin Hood Gardens* – as an

Among other large textile works, *Nest/s* 2024 is a further expression of Suh's personal account conjoined with a now. The work complements the invention and revelation of found spaces that – while sometimes hidden within or among others – can be assembled to evoke a nexus of multiple forces, or contrivances, in which the body is itinerant yet encumbered. Beginning as a sketch, the installation that comprises *Home Within Home* 2025 is realised as a generative set of interlocking conveyances in which Suh's multiple embodiments are registered. In these works, our experience of the interior is as a congregation of exteriors turned inside out like memories: estranged from their context, yet decipherable.

Such emanations, when joined with other rooms, recompose one's recollection of a building or house that is not our own, for which possession is never assured. These complicate home as image, myth and mirror, locating where, but not how, memory happens. The home, for Suh, thus invites the making of a soul as that which transgresses boundaries and speaks from within. Yet can we ever occupy a home? In their construction, Suh's sculptures embed material changes that signify a translation of human and non-human experience. Through their visuality, of transference dissolved

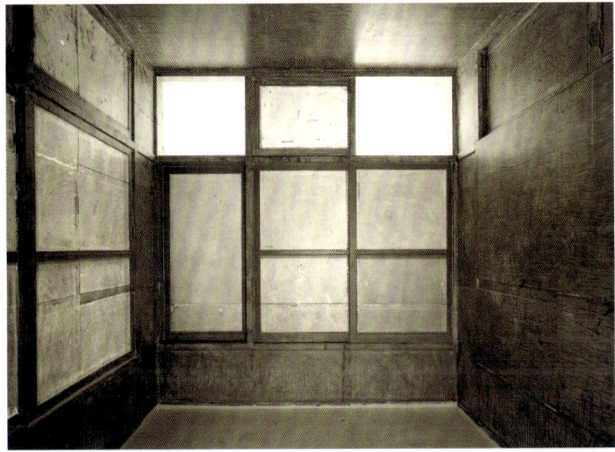

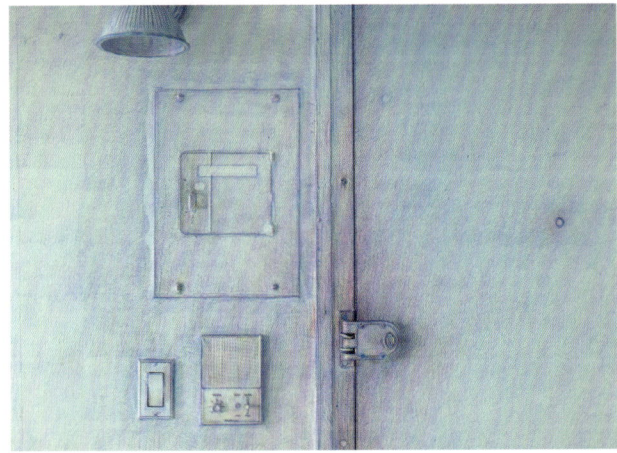

Top: *Rubbing / Loving: Company Housing of Gwangju Theater* 2012
Bottom: *Rubbing / Loving: Apartment A, 348 West 22nd Street, New York, NY 10011, USA* 2014 (detail)

we seek locality, consolation. And in their ultimate disappearance (or our departure) from Suh's resuscitation of his search for home, we too acknowledge our own losses. How and why we choose to build, to collect, is as much a response to absence as it is part of our own unstable self-formation. For the artist, these acts are unceasing and catalytic.

In due time, having been discretely withdrawn from the hooks and wires and weight that ultimately keep them 'in place', the works that comprise this exhibition will be quietly withdrawn from the room. Perhaps on a day like today, they will ceremoniously descend to a table or floor where they will be politely folded, wrapped and covered again, creating an enclosure within another enclosure, collapsible rooms within sealed dark crates. Those who have stood in wonder among the works will be remembered amid edges and folds and cuts and lines that revealed new spaces sometimes challenging the logic of gravity. They will await reassembly alongside an unpacking of their ever-transitioning geographies and meanings. Their voices will carry. Time will be designed. Until exposed once more, Do Ho Suh's architecture – this atlas of ghosts, an archive that each of us bears within ourselves – is at once our own and still may one day be presented with another name or wall label or unfixed date. These home(s) will haunt new lands and spaces while traversing limitless horizons where others might find them again, resonant phantoms waiting to be occupied, seen and measured.

in and among scales of possibility, they hint at ways of inhabitation. In their softness, they evoke quasi-deviance from the rigidity of norms, but also supple bodies, a sloughing-off of immanence and a disregard for gravity in their framing within a gallery space. These constructions do not disembody; rather, they are replete with bodies, living and dead, for their inhabitation is dependent upon the viewer appearing amid their seams, their openings into and out of internally reconfigured domains. The phenomenal is construed among these works as sources for and reflections of the known. Here, the accepted and the acceptable cross from the most private of conditions – the bedroom, the bathroom, the closet – into a realm for which a public can access and restore their own vision of revenance among a collection of discernible objects and spaces.

Among Suh's sewn and video works, it is we who are the ghosts frequenting our own past, present and future. Through our recognition of or at least identification with these spaces and their intrinsic sentience – home-ness is found in their every detail, their unfolding of the uncanny across multiple temporalities and circumstances – while

Notes

1 Georges Didi-Huberman, *Génie de non-lieu: Air, poussière, empreinte, hantise*, Paris 2001, p.113.

2 Jacques Derrida, *Specters of Marx: The State of the Debt, The Work of Mourning and the New International*, trans. by Peggy Kamuf, London 1994, p.202. Derrida writes: 'Is there there, between the thing itself and its simulacrum, an opposition that holds up?': ibid., p.10.

3 Do Ho Suh, unpublished writings, 2023.

4 Hyesoo Woo, 'Building Homes', in *Do Ho Suh: Home Within Home*, exh. cat., Leeum, Samsung Museum of Art, Seoul 2012, p.17.

5 Georges Didi-Huberman, *Confronting Images: Questioning the Ends of a Certain History of Art*, University Park, PA 2005, p.6.

6 Ernst Gombrich, *Aby Warburg: An Intellectual Biography (With a Memoir on the History of the Library by F. Saxl)*, London 1970, p.225.

7 The phrase is taken from Jane Rendell, 'Decentring/Recentring Do Ho Suh', in *Site-Writing: The Architecture of Art Criticism*, London 2010, a revised version of 'Surface Encounters: On being Centred, Decentred and Recentred by the works of Do-Ho Suh' (2002), a text initially written as companion guide to an exhibition at the Serpentine Gallery, London.

8 Carl Jung, *Psychological Types*, Princeton, NJ 2013.

Rirkrit Tiravanija

This is the House that Do Ho Built[1]

True emptiness is like a translucent sea
where the faintest movement makes foam
as soon as we have a body
we worry about food and clothes
with feelings racing past like horses
and delusions as restless as monkeys
until we understand the Master of Emptiness
The Wheel of Rebirth rolls on
Stonehouse, 'Poem Number 68',
The Mountain Poems [2]

I rolled the die and opened the book, as one would with a toss of the *I Ching*, and I found a starting point for this text by reading this poem from *The Mountain Poems of Stonehouse* by the Chinese Zen master and hermit Stonehouse (1272–1352), perhaps a diversion I needed to start, was intended to give myself some thoughts as to how I could begin to think and interpret the ideas of another. Another, in this case, is the life and work of Do Ho Suh. I flipped the book of poems open, thinking about Do Ho, and it opened at page 73, and I came upon poem number 68, the Zen Buddhists' reflection on emptiness. I found the words, images and reflections they conjure to be rather relevant in my relationship to the works of Do Ho Suh.

I met Do Ho in the sculpture studios when he was still in graduate school at Yale University. As a guest visitor, a number of students would sign up for a visit with a visiting lecturer, something I was doing to help sustain myself at the time, but also out of interest to meet, look, hear and think with a lot of people, people who were working with their ideas about art and its possibilities. It was at least twenty-plus years ago, so my recollection isn't as clear and bright, but some things stood out upon reflection.

When thinking back about Do Ho, I remember a young Korean artist who had been working his way around different schools in the US to find his way and purpose but had already matured in process and thought. I didn't feel he needed much of my critique but rather some guidance and reflection about the bigger picture we were both in, the art world. At the time, I had not realised how much closer in age we were, but again, that knowledge would not have really mattered to me and would not have had a bearing on my thoughts and my words.

I think I remember what I saw in the studio that afternoon, but it has probably been filtered by years passing, through which subsequent encounters with Do Ho's works, in person and through images, have made their way into those memories. So, as I recount the images of that studio visit that afternoon, I remember a mass of plastic toy soldiers holding up a sheet of glass, the kind of green vacuum-moulded toy soldiers we would play with when we were nine or ten, but perhaps I saw them on another occa-

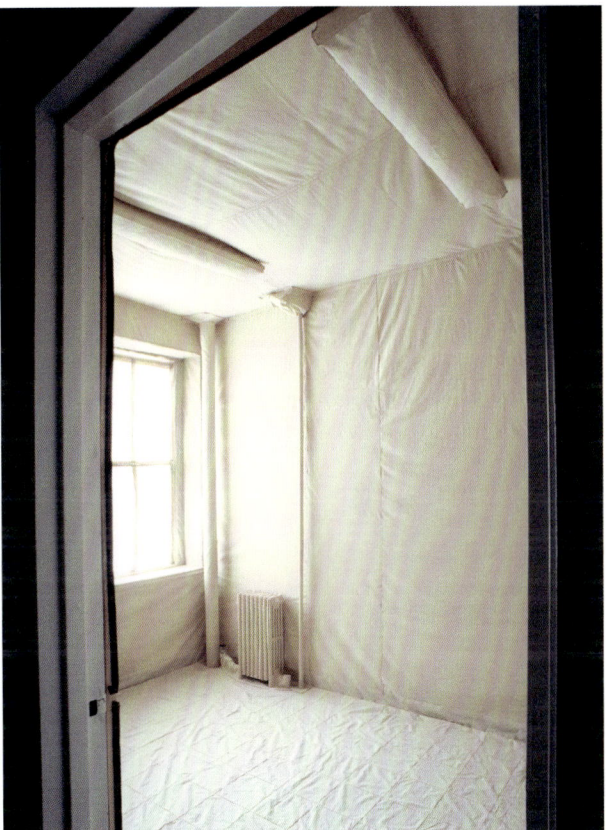

Room 516/516-I/516-II 1994–5

sion later. They seemed to be the kind of readymade that was perhaps too ready, too well, and perhaps too banal. Perhaps I did say something, perhaps not; I generally try to focus on the person and their intentions to get close to the core of the idea, the core of the person, the artist.

I do, however, remember a wallpaper work that gave a first impression of snakeskin from a distance, but upon closer inspection, these tiny ovals, which gave an impression of scales, were hundreds or thousands of images of faces; within each oval, a different person. They all were wearing uniforms, high school uniforms I saw in a Japanese teenage television series that I recall watching when I was growing up in Bangkok. All were consistently uniformed with a haircut cropped to the skin, hundreds of faces, individuals in the sea of sameness, a conformation of self and identity, an idea not surprising coming from a Korean artist. I cannot generalise to another culture, such as the one Do Ho had grown up in (Korea), but from my own experience as a Thai person, the ideas of conformation and respect for the elder (authority) figure were very much ingrained into modernisation. In Thailand, we modelled our institutional foundations on the British constitutional monarchy. Where we were not colonised, we colonised ourselves; a balancing act of traditional nationalism and modernised democracy, at odds and in conflict, down

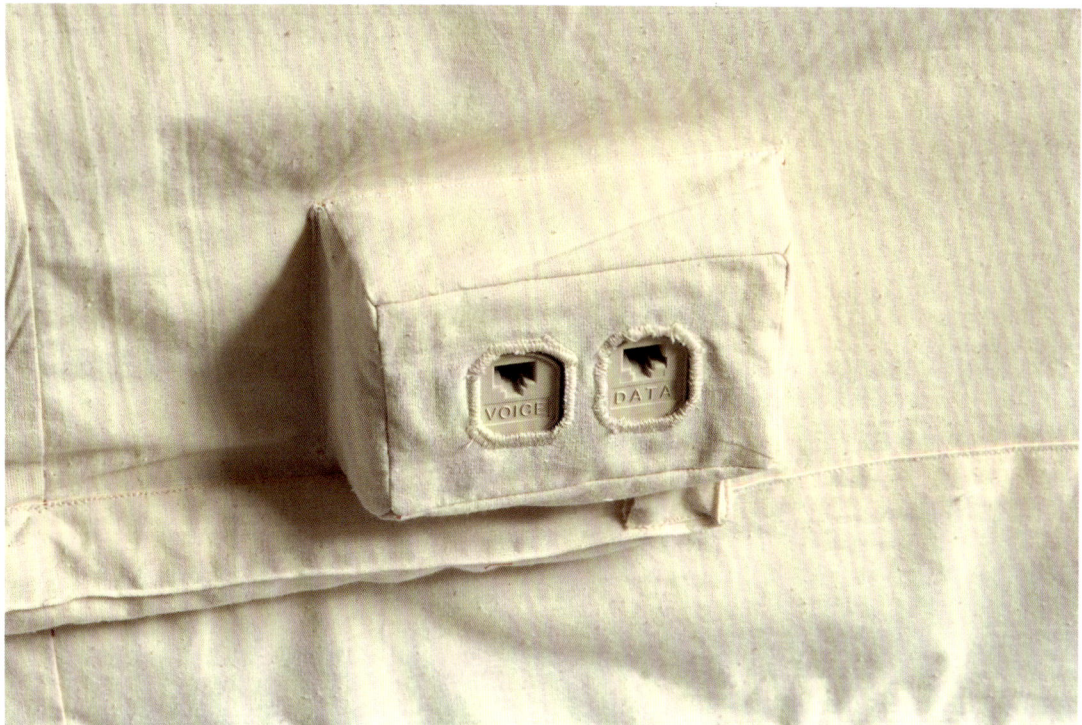

Room 516/516-I/516-II 1994–5 (detail)

to our identity formation. The masses acted uniformly in unison to uphold the institutions; perhaps one could see the same coming through in the early works of Do Ho. Coming from such a mindset, he perhaps thought about how to reconcile oneself, to be set free in the sculpture class he attended at the Rhode Island School of Design; he forewent his own family heritage, first of ink painting and painting in general, to become a sculptor. Do Ho addressed his anxieties in his work, as he was then and perhaps still is now.

When Do Ho spoke briefly about his father, I understood that his father was an established figure in the arts back in Korea. Perhaps I did feel a slight tinge of Do Ho's anxieties about his obligations to such a heritage.

The other work I recalled in that day's studio visit was a fabric sculpture, or, rather, the start of such an idea. Do Ho told me about the house his father lived and worked in, a reconstructed traditional Korean house, but the house was modelled from a palace library. I faintly remember being confused but nonetheless fascinated by the narrative. It was, from my faded memory, an architectural element, made from sheer fabric, which reminded me of mosquito netting, very familiar to us in Thailand. I was drawn, in hindsight, to what would become Do Ho's signature and life project. The scrim-like architectural detail was light blue,

almost green, I felt. Do Ho didn't use that almost-green fabric until 1999, for his now-iconic work *Seoul Home/L.A. Home/New York Home/Baltimore Home/London Home/ Seattle Home/L.A. Home*, a fabric rendering of his home in Korea, and perhaps later recollections or images of it reproduced have made their way into this memory. I recall saying to him that if he was going to do the house, he should go all the way to make the whole house, as it seemed to be the logical move forward, but perhaps such was already his intention, since he had by then clothed the interior of a room in thick muslin a few years earlier, a work that would become known as *Room 516/516-I/516-II* 1994–5.

True emptiness is like a translucent sea where the faintest movement makes foam

It is movement that carries me each day, and I speak of faint memories. These lines from the poem bring me to think that all the motion of passing through things, places, time, space and life, is an accumulation that at the end, defines us individually and even collectively. Such motion defines the time we live in, it defines the humans we become. And for an artist such as myself, it was a question of the self. People would ask me where I lived, and my answer would be, I live where I am standing. The sense of being, or the attachments we define as being, is something perhaps human, and it is a search that doesn't end.

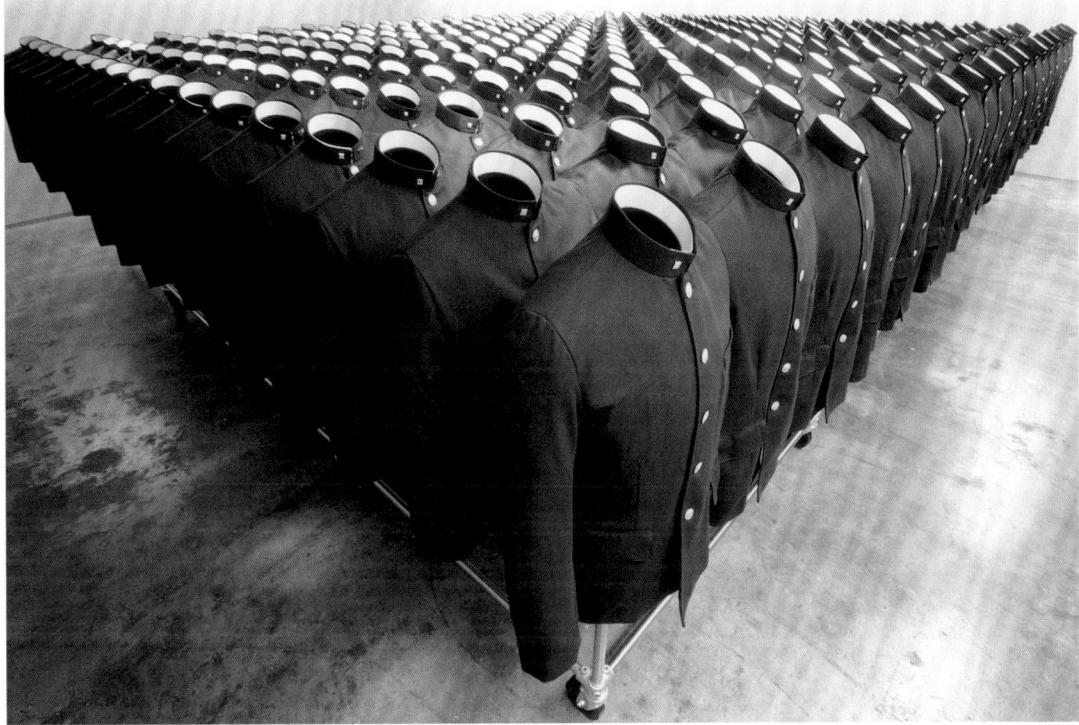

High School Uni-Form 1997

Do Ho is making an index of things he has touched and perhaps has been touched by. They are like the foam of emptiness, but such emptiness isn't lost or a loss; it is layered – layers of space, layers of clothing, layers of shelter, layers which make comfort and discomfort. Happiness is not funny; it is a lot of work – or, rather, layers of work. It is a shell, an emptied outer shell, a void, but a void to be filled by the movement of others, the memories of others, a collection of differences, a collection of different recollections. We have lost our sense of remembrance; we have given all our memories to a small tool, and we are just the vessel that carries the tool from one place of our lives to another.

we worry about food and clothes with feelings racing past like horses and delusions as restless as monkeys

Do Ho wants us to pay attention to the moments we have passed up: the flick of a switch, pressing of a knob, turning of a handle, the things we touch and feel, without senses, without feeling. We are passing through passages, from one room to another, from one house to the next, from large to small, and back again. We don't scale ourselves; we float like an avatar in a virtual game room, and we see the selves beside ourselves but without the soul of the self. In the House that Do Ho built, Do Ho gives us his memory, the places he had lived in, the knobs he had turned, and the light switch he had turned off and on. He is building a house of his memories, memories that informed his soul, his being, and his existence. Today, we ask less and less of existence, of reasons of being, and of nothingness. We don't ask anymore; we just wait for the 'like' thumbs-up to appear, as if that defines one's self-worth and self-being. I find the works of Do Ho resisting those easy notions of existence; he is pushing up against the larger picture, which reduces individuals into one surface. He is pushing against disappearing details that are fading away from our notion of experiences. To find the self, we need to live in chaos; to withstand chaos, we need to know ourselves; and to know the self, we have to understand differences, and I think Do Ho understands.

until we understand the Master of Emptiness The Wheel of Rebirth rolls on

Notes

1   General Editors' note: Embracing the ways in which the haziness of memory functions, Tiravanija's text has deliberately retained and foregrounded encounters with Suh and his works coloured by imperfect recollection. While this entails some factual inaccuracies, these elements have been intentionally kept through the editorial process, in conversation with the author, in accordance with the character of the text.

2   Stonehouse, The Mountain Poems, Copper Canyon Press, 2014, poem no.68, p.73.

Sarah Fine

Bridges, Projects and Bridging Projects

When we encounter people, places, projects and so on, we can't help but bring ourselves to them. I see and experience the world around me as the person I am in that moment. What I perceive and experience in these encounters will be different in some ways from what you perceive and experience.

At the same time, the encounter makes its mark on the people, places and projects involved. Something of the encounter comes with us, and something of us is left behind. That is true in a material sense – we leave behind biological markers and our bodies absorb parts of the environment – and also in an immaterial sense, insofar as the encounter becomes part of memories and narratives for the various parties. Everything is affected in the encounter.

Bridges

This phenomenon comes to mind as I look at Do Ho Suh's designs for the *Bridge Project* (1999–ongoing). The project identifies a location equidistant from Suh's childhood house in Seoul (1970 to 1991), the apartment he rented in New York (1997 to 2016) and his current place of residence in London (from 2010 onwards). It is this site, which lies in the Arctic region, close to the North Pole, at coordinates 77°55'33"N 161°23'49"W, that Suh has called 'The Perfect Home', and the bridge proposals in the piece explore different kinds of structures that connect Suh's past and present homes.

The noun 'bridge' has multiple meanings and uses. One of these meanings is figurative and refers to 'a person or thing which connects, reconciles, or unites different groups, events, periods, etc.'[1] I doubt that meaning escaped Do Ho Suh's attention when he named his project. The idea of a bridge as a connection between entities which would otherwise remain apart invokes a sense of discrete and separable units simply coexisting. Remove the bridge and things become separate once again. However, Suh's bridges interact and intermingle with the environment in ways that make me think more of processes of mutual change through encounters.

Suh is mindful of the interactivity dimension to his work, and it has an ambivalent character for him, appearing both as a design feature and as a cause for concern. At the heart of the *Bridge Project* is the interaction between the Seoul house, the New York apartment and the London flat. The video elements of the project explore how those three different structures might (or might not) meet, mix and merge in 'the Perfect Home'. Interactivity is a core element of 'The Bio-Bubble Bridge', for instance, which is presented as a living organism. It is also central to Suh's investigations into how humans and environments might adapt to accommodate each other. In Phase II of the project, which includes London, one of Suh's questions is how he might reach his Perfect Home. He imagines the possibility of intermediary spaces on route, helping to acclimatise person to new place (and possibly place to new person?). Yet interactivity and its effects are also a worry for Suh. He hopes to avoid or minimise negative impacts on the natural environment and on settled populations in the surrounding areas. In its objectives, this is a project seeking to connect rather than to impose.

There are innumerable barriers to forming interpersonal connections – communicative, psychological, physical, economic and political obstacles, to name but a few. That might explain in part why the feeling of connecting deeply with another person can be so magical and intense. A deep connection has overcome considerable impediments and so is a special kind of achievement.

I feel a deep connection with Suh and his work. I should add that a feeling of connection need not imply understanding, however, which may require different things from feelings of connection. Feelings of connection may involve a kind of humility regarding the challenges inherent to seeking understanding, especially understanding other people. Indeed, what connects me with Suh and his work may rely on some absence of understanding or rest upon productive misunderstandings.

In some respects my feeling of connection with Suh and his work is unremarkable. We share a range of similar interests in themes such as home, movement and displacement. We also share London – my place of birth and his place of residence. That is an important source of connection, involving familiarity with some rhythms, sights, sounds, smells. But in other respects I think the connection itself is noteworthy, as I'll explain.

Projects

Before that, I note that the *Bridge Project* is also a project. 'Project' can mean something like 'scheme' or 'plan' or 'goal', but again the word has multiple meanings and uses. For example, it can mean a collaborative enterprise. That certainly seems to be part of Suh's conception of the *Bridge Project*, as indicated by his ongoing engagement in research and conversation with specialists across diverse disciplines, from anthropology and animation to engineering and philosophy. In effect, the *Bridge Project* is also a *bridging* project. Through this kind of interdisciplinary 'bringing together' approach, Suh is able to achieve something that would not be possible within the confines of a single discipline or medium.

Given my work and educational background, 'project' also has another kind of meaning for me. In some parts of philosophy, people use the word 'project' (and especially 'ground project') to refer to the pursuits and commitments

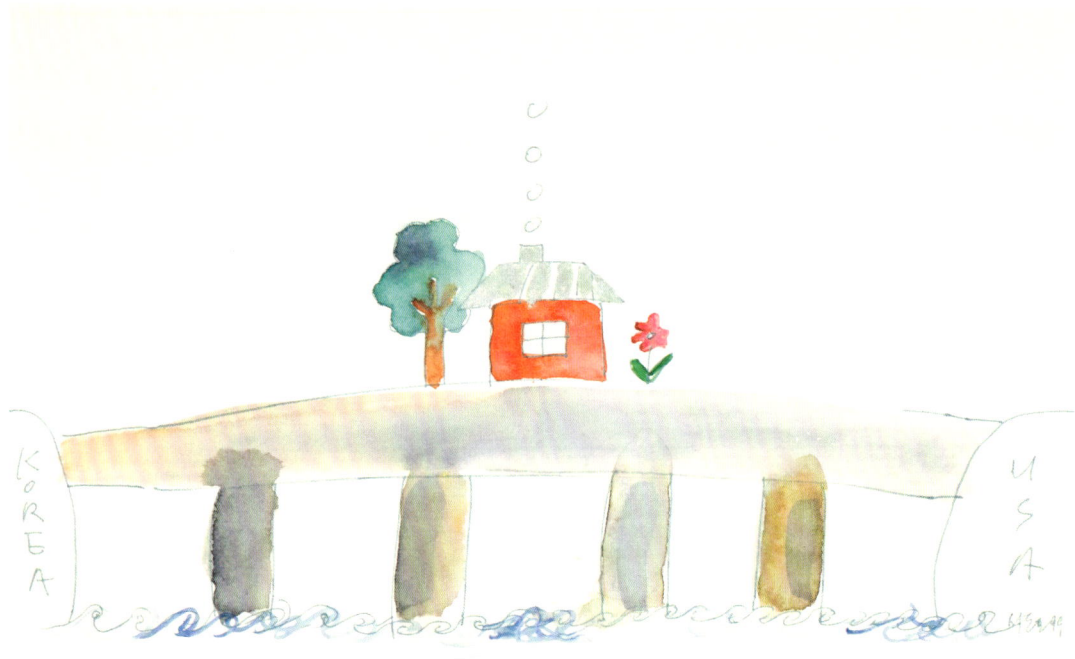

A Perfect Home 1999

that a person deeply cares about, that matter to her, that she relates to in a special kind of way and with which she identifies. Projects of this sort help structure our deliberations and give us reasons for action.[2] I wonder whether the *Bridge Project* might be a project for Suh in this sense, too. In conversation, Suh informed me that there are similarities between his life and the *Bridge Project*. Perhaps there is even an intermingling of the two. Furthermore, Suh and his work are themselves the bridge in his project and in his life, connecting across people, places and traditions. They also form a bridge across time, connecting Suh to his past, present and his future.

So, I come to Suh's work as the person that I am, with my own history, language, conceptual frameworks, modes of communication, location, education and preoccupations. The questions that it occurs to me to ask of a project will reflect things about me, sometimes obviously and sometimes implicitly. Similarly, Suh comes to his work as the person that he is. In our first meeting Suh described his work as emerging from his experience – in particular, his experiences of mobility, crossing boundaries and living in different places. That is something else we share, although my boundary crossings have taken a different form.

I am an academic, specialising primarily in political philosophy and ethics. Anglophone political philosophy has long been gripped by a series of questions about methodology – about how to do political philosophy – focusing mostly on the proper relationship between politics and philosophy in political philosophy. To what extent should political philosophy take account of the messy world of real life politics? How should it deal with questions about practical constraints and feasibility? Some argue that if our work sticks faithfully to the world as it is now, it could be unduly conservative about possibilities and prospects for positive change. Others maintain that if our work deviates too far from the world as it is now – if, say, it strikes readers as utopian and unworkable – it could fail to have purchase or relevance, and so would lack any practical value.

In our first conversation, Suh raised some questions about his work that resonated with me, especially against the backdrop of those methodological debates. The Arctic location of Suh's 'Perfect Home' is fascinating for a host of reasons. As Suh notes, the site is inhospitable and difficult to reach. In addition, the area is subject to a range of rival territorial claims from surrounding countries who want to exert control over its resources.

Suh explained that as soon as he started to explore the idea of a home in this location, the issue of borders arose. Who lays claim to the site? Who has jurisdiction? Who protects the space? Who enforces the rules? Who is allowed to enter? Who decides?

On the one hand, it makes sense that these questions would arise in the course of the project. After all, the world

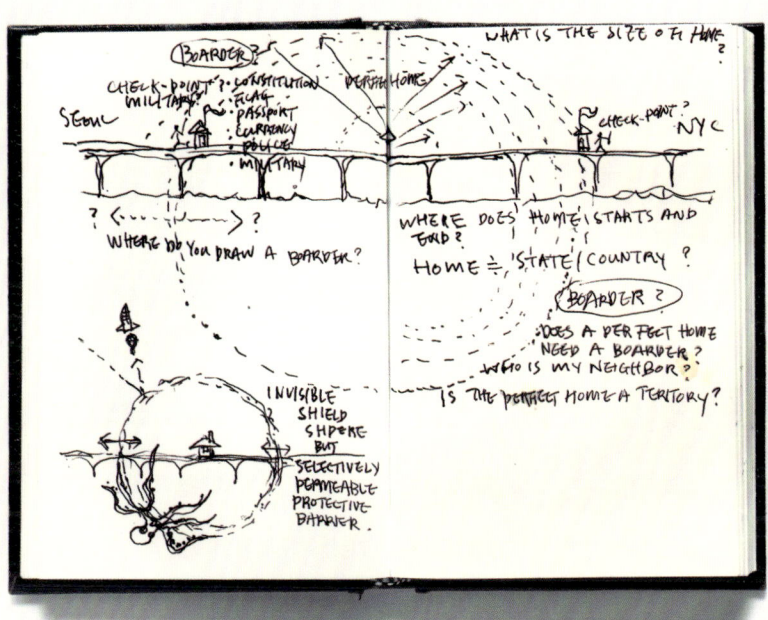

Suh's sketchbook, 2005

in which we live is one that often forces us – sometimes very much against our will – to confront such questions. It is also one that has developed its own violent, practical answers to these questions and has been shaped by the dominant answers. Most people do not have the option of moving and living wherever they please. All sorts of freedoms and unfreedoms, goods and bads, are unevenly distributed in our world, and there are all sorts of historical reasons for those distributions. To have relevance or purchase, perhaps a project like Suh's ought to ask these questions and engage with these issues.

But, then again, why? Why should the *Bridge Project* be constrained by the ways our world has addressed and answered questions about movement and residence and control? Knowledge about how borders and identity documents and territorial disputes and so forth currently operate is knowledge about our actual world, but it seems different from the kind of knowledge involved in some of the other aspects of Suh's project. For example, the design of Suh's 'North Pacific Drift Bridge' draws on knowledge of ocean currents, while his 'Dead Reckoning Bridge' draws on knowledge of mechanical engineering. We might wish for ocean currents and mechanics to work differently, but there isn't much we can do about that. By contrast, states and passports and visas and territorial claims and border guards are all human inventions and interventions. They are contingent features of our world. If we wish them to be otherwise, well, there is a lot that we can do about that.

In fact, as philosopher Jessie Munton argues, it is possible that at least some of our knowledge of the actual world can get in the way of us acquiring 'modal knowledge', which is knowledge of how things *could* be. As Munton explains, 'the worry is … that our imaginative capacities may be *unduly* disciplined by experience'.[3] Munton's discussion of modal knowledge and fictional spaces is instructive here:

> Fictional spaces … can offer us the resources we need to hone our cognitive capacities and concepts in ways that facilitate modal knowledge … The common core to their power lies in their ability to disrupt the disciplinary force of experience on imagination and concept formation, by envisaging alternative ways things could be but are not.[4]

To my mind, the fictional spaces that Suh creates in the *Bridge Project* offer the perfect example of that, and I find it exciting. The work helps us envisage alternative ways things could be but are not. It does this, in part, by showing them to us through a range of media and enabling us to navigate in and around them. In other words, the absence of certain (mostly regrettable) political features of our actual world strikes me as an imaginative virtue rather than a vice of the *Bridge Project*.

Now, someone might reply that the *Bridge Project* without the real world politics is 'unrealistic', just as political philosophy removed from real-world politics is 'unrealistic'.

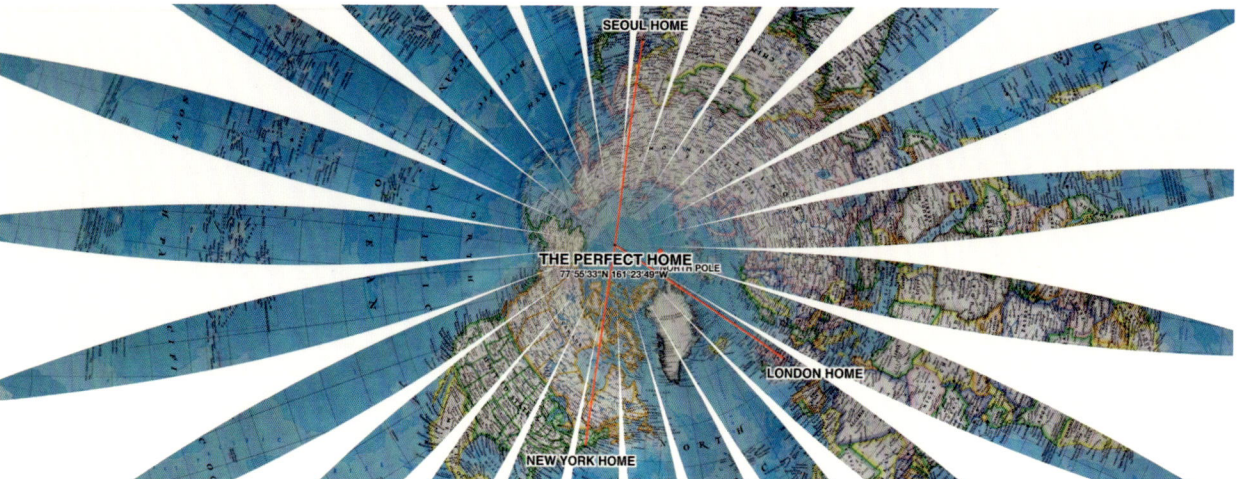

Bridge Project 1999–ongoing

It is worth examining what that charge might imply. Certainly the *Bridge Project* doesn't mirror the actual world (although it still wouldn't mirror the actual world even with the addition of passports and borders). As Suh himself emphasises, this is an 'artist's project'. Does it want to mirror the actual world? Or does it want to present us with just enough of that world to provide a springboard for an imaginative leap?

In this work, Suh deftly bridges the worlds of science and art, revealing what we can learn through playful research and from pushing at disciplinary and methodological (and even psychological) boundaries. A charming example comes in the form of Suh's studies for survival suits, which experiment with the question of how to prepare for the enviromental conditions in that part of the Arctic region. The suits – some made from durable materials suited to the climate, and another, a latex skin – are also explicitly works of art, incorporating the *Bridge Project*'s wider influences and inspirations. Notes for the suit designs make this clear, emphasising that the project combines 'practical problem solving with artistic, speculative thinking'. In my view, however, that characterisation actually underestimates the inventiveness, originality and contribution of the work. It is not simply the combining of practical problem solving with artistic, speculative thinking; rather, the project illuminates the ways in which artistic, speculative thinking *itself* can offer paths toward practical problem solving. This also serves as a reminder that playfulness does not signal the absence of seriousness. If anything, the *Bridge Project* is an exercise in serious playfulness.

Bridging Projects
Let's bring these ideas together. Some knowledge of the actual world can interfere with our ability to acquire knowledge of the world as it could be. And when we encounter the world around us, we encounter it as the situated,

distinctive people we are. There are all sorts of barriers to communicating and connecting with others, and so connection is an important achievement.

Somehow Suh is exploring his own distinctive, specific, often quite personal experiences – what could be more personal than home, or our memories of our childhood? – in a way that can connect with people who occupy entirely different locations, and who perceive and experience his work in their own specificity. One common way of trying to explain this (both in art and in philosophy) would gesture at something like the 'universalism', 'timelessness' and/or 'generality' of the themes and questions, or at the ability of some disciplines to communicate across differences. I am not sure I agree that those quite hit the spot, though.

For me, the important factors are the ways the *Bridge Project* bridges. It is an intermingling of personal experiences, people and places, disciplines and approaches, expertise and experimentation, the material and immaterial, knowledge of the world as it is and ideas about the world as it could be. As a special kind of living and developing project, it helps structure deliberations and generate insights. It interacts sympathetically with the environment, affecting everyone and everything involved in the encounter. Above all, it is able to resonate and connect through that bridging. That is a significant and unusual achievement. And on it goes.

Notes

1 See 'bridge (n.1)', *Oxford English Dictionary*, March 2024, https://doi.org/10.1093/OED/1878290668, accessed 25 June 2024.

2 See, for example, Bernard Williams's contribution in J.J.C. Smart and Bernard Williams, *Utilitarianism: For and Against*, Cambridge 1973.

3 Jessie Munton, 'Lost in (Modal) Space: Demographic Base-Rate Neglect in the Service of Modal Knowledge', *Proceedings of the Aristotelian Society*, vol.123, no.1, 2023, pp.73–96 (81). Author's emphasis.

4 Ibid., p.93.

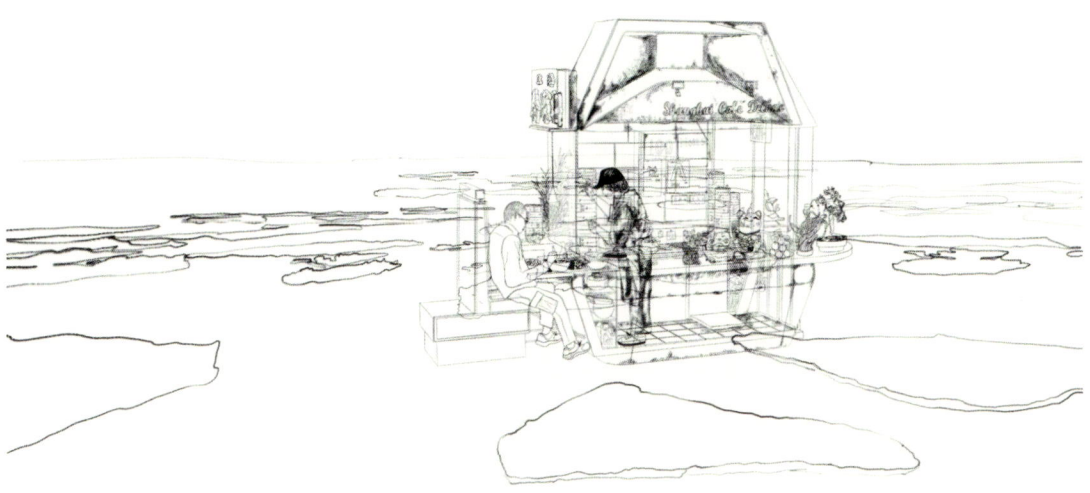

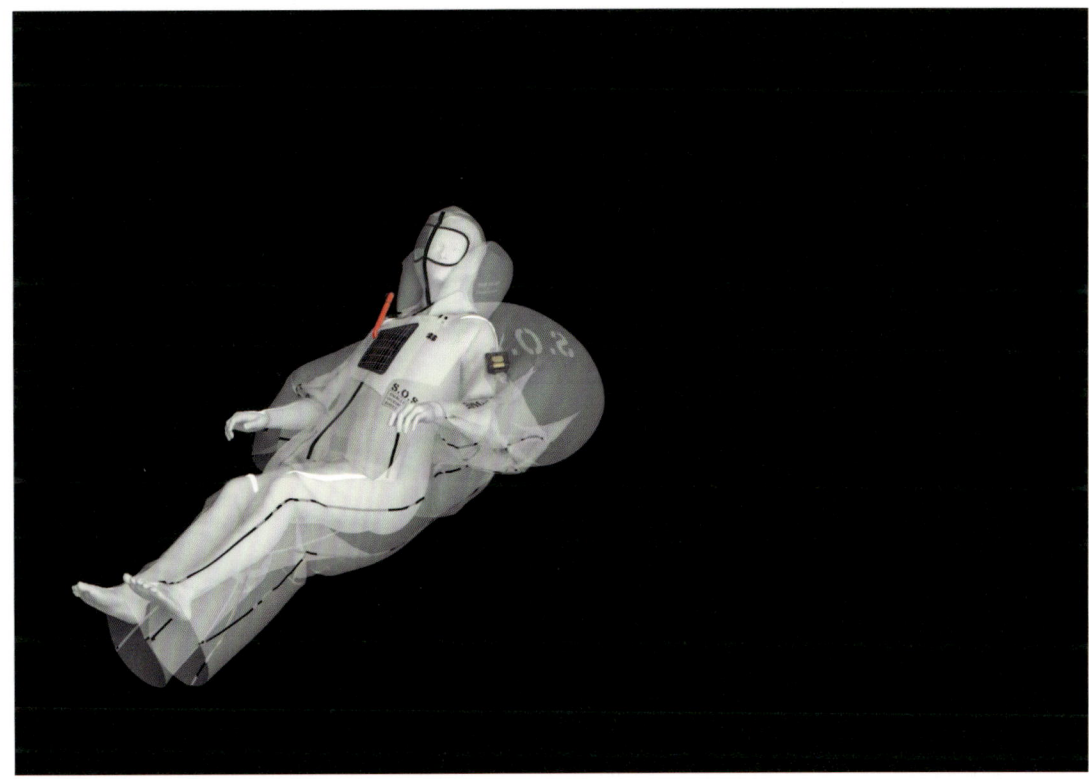

Top: *Bridge Project* 1999–ongoing
Bottom: render of *Perfect Home S.O.S. (Smallest Occupiable Shelter) in collaboration with KOLON Sport* 2024

Rubbing/Loving: Unit 2, 348 West 22nd Street, New York, NY 10011, USA is a collection of rubbings made in 348 West 22nd Street, New York, an address at which Suh lived for twenty years. The house has become a site of repeated return and an ongoing subject within his practice since 2000. Suh rented a half-basement studio apartment in this building, living three floors below the landlord, Arthur, with whom he developed a close relationship. Following Arthur's death, and before the property was vacated and sold, Suh was given permission to rub the surfaces of both his and the other apartments. Each room was covered in paper and rubbed with a different coloured pencil – yellow for one studio apartment, blue for another, and so on. This presentation shows the surface of the rooms broken into modules, including the fixtures and fittings, displayed in cases like specimens in a natural history museum. The original space is packed into cases and becomes transportable, which is a recurring theme in Suh's work. Through the act of rubbing, Suh resurfaces the marks and indentations left behind by the building's inhabitants, connecting the process of tending to the traces of lives lived with the process of mourning. A physically and emotionally exhausting task, carried out over many months, it is a process somewhere between an act of preservation and that of moving on. As Suh recalls, 'It was a really condensed experience of reliving twenty years in that time … Each mark and detail began to trigger memories of events, even conversations that had taken place in the apartment. At times, overtaken by the meditative process of rubbing and the scratching sound of the pencil on paper, I felt as if I was hallucinating.' (KW)

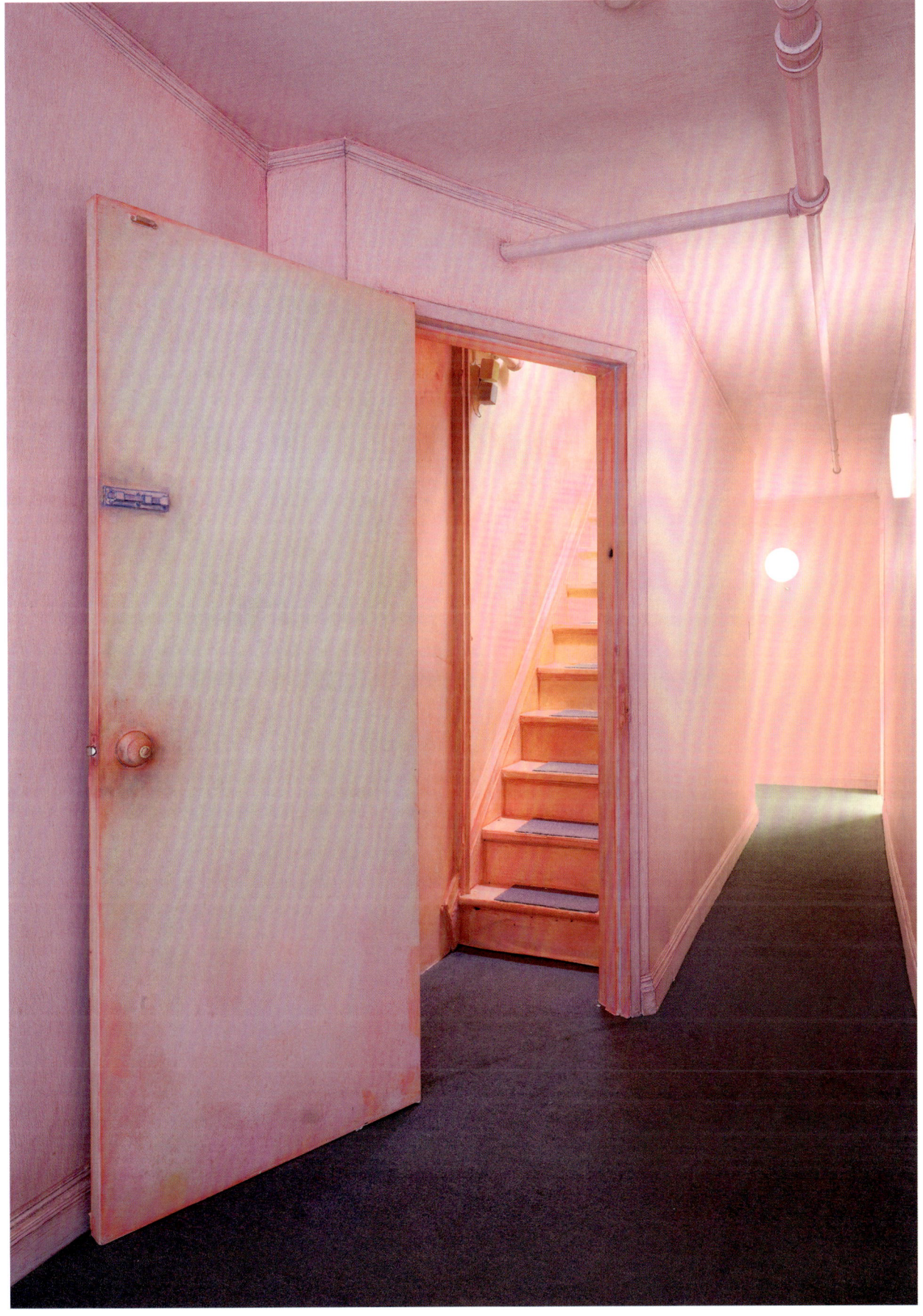

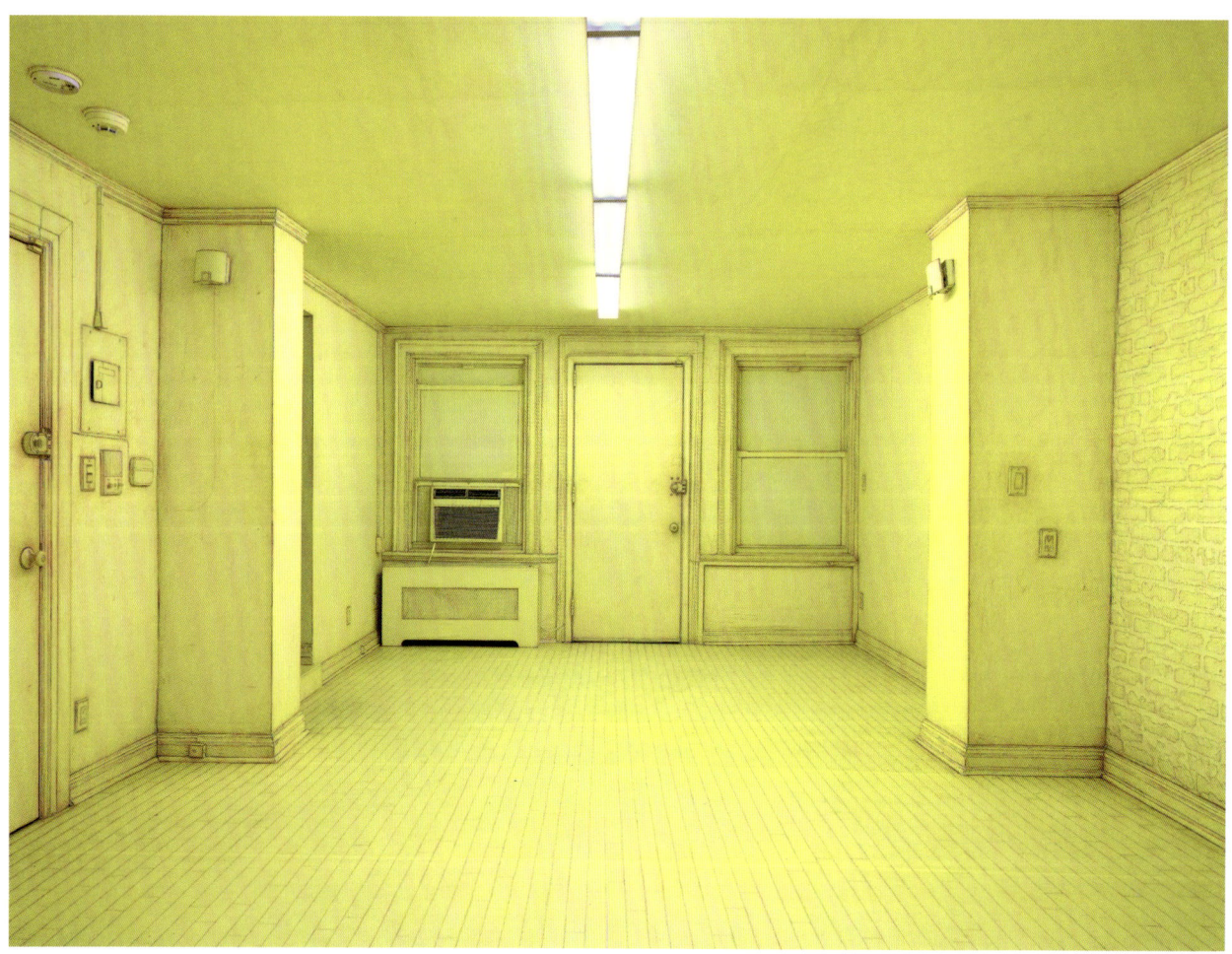

Pages 113–17: *Rubbing / Loving: 348 West 22nd Street, New York, NY 10011, USA* 2014

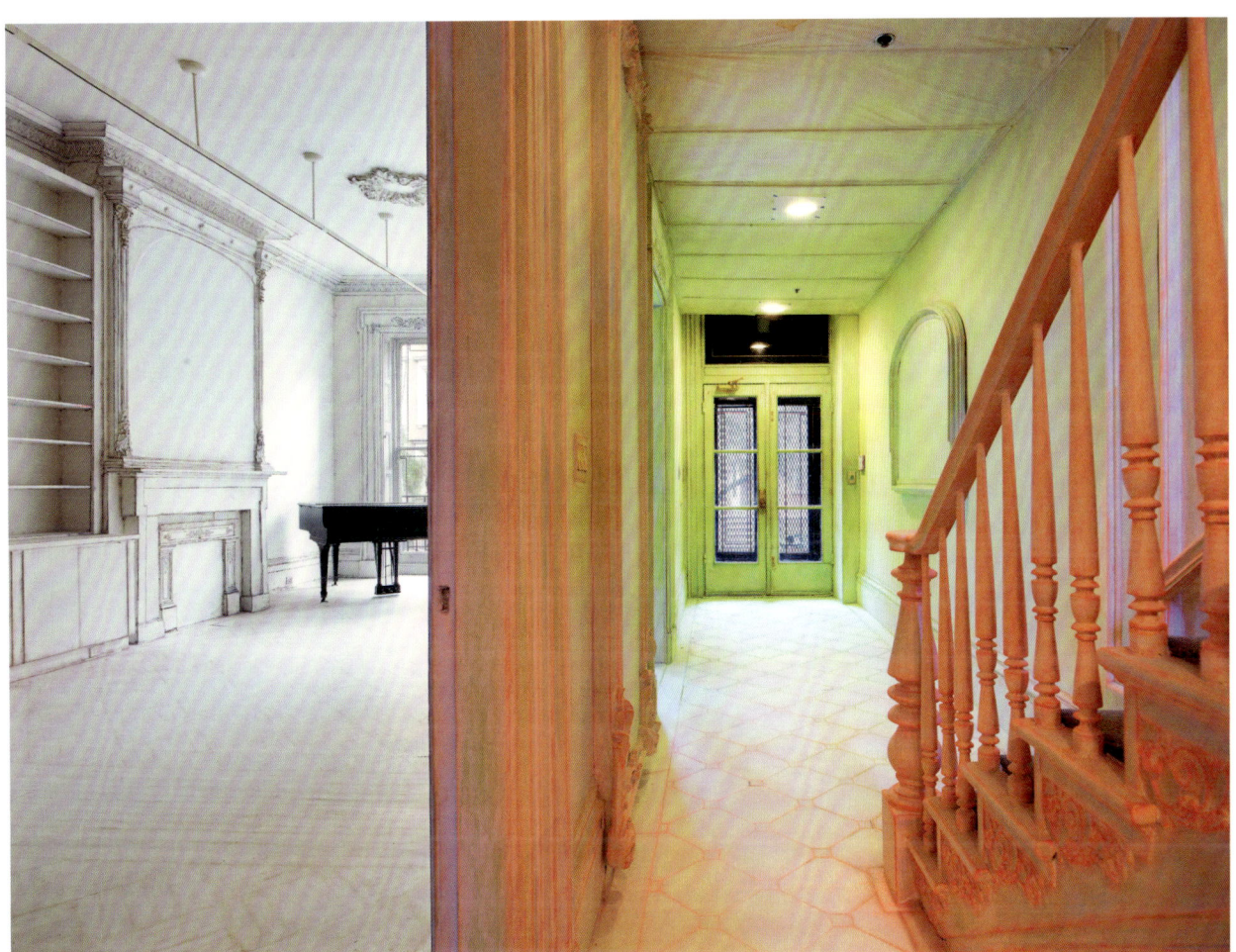

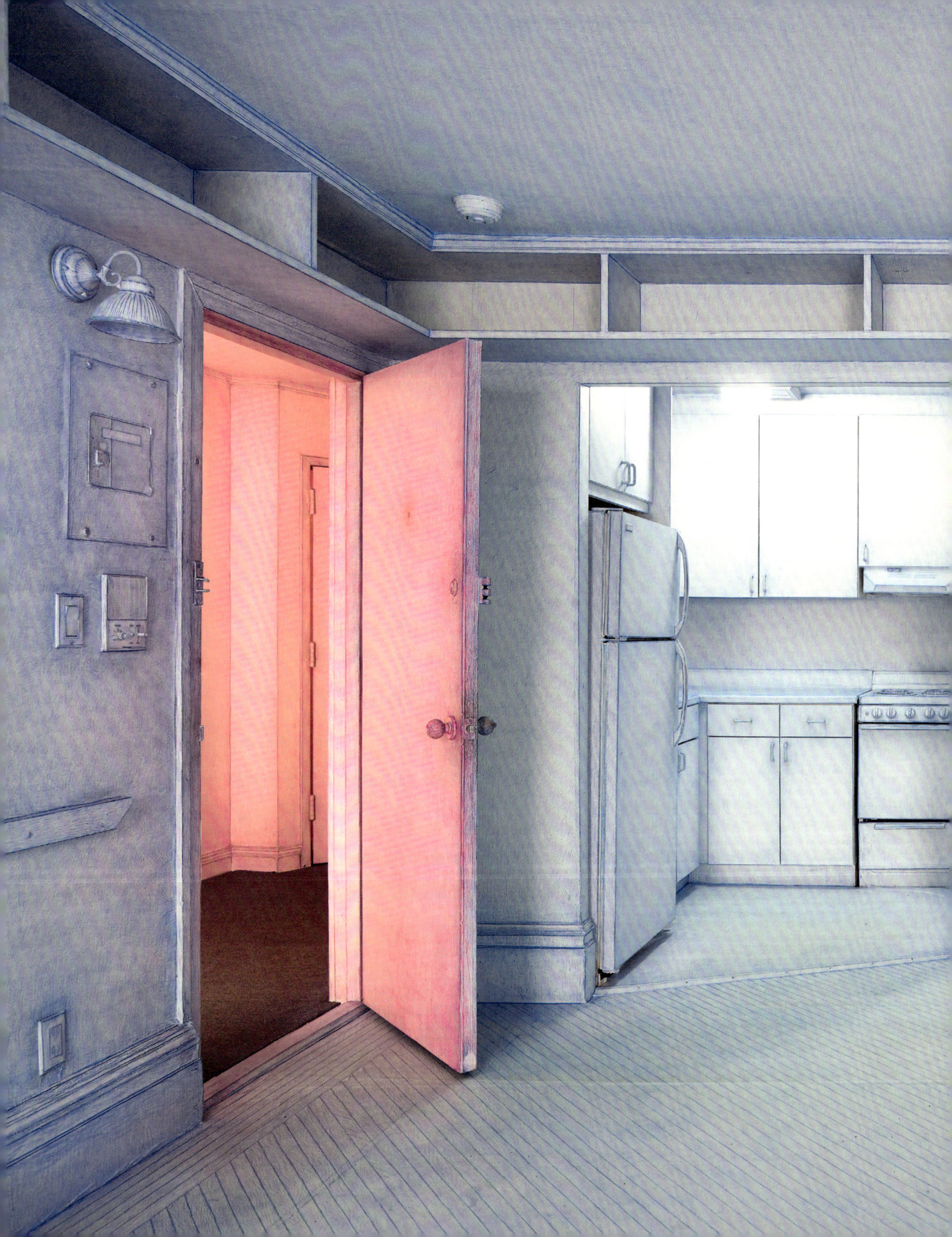

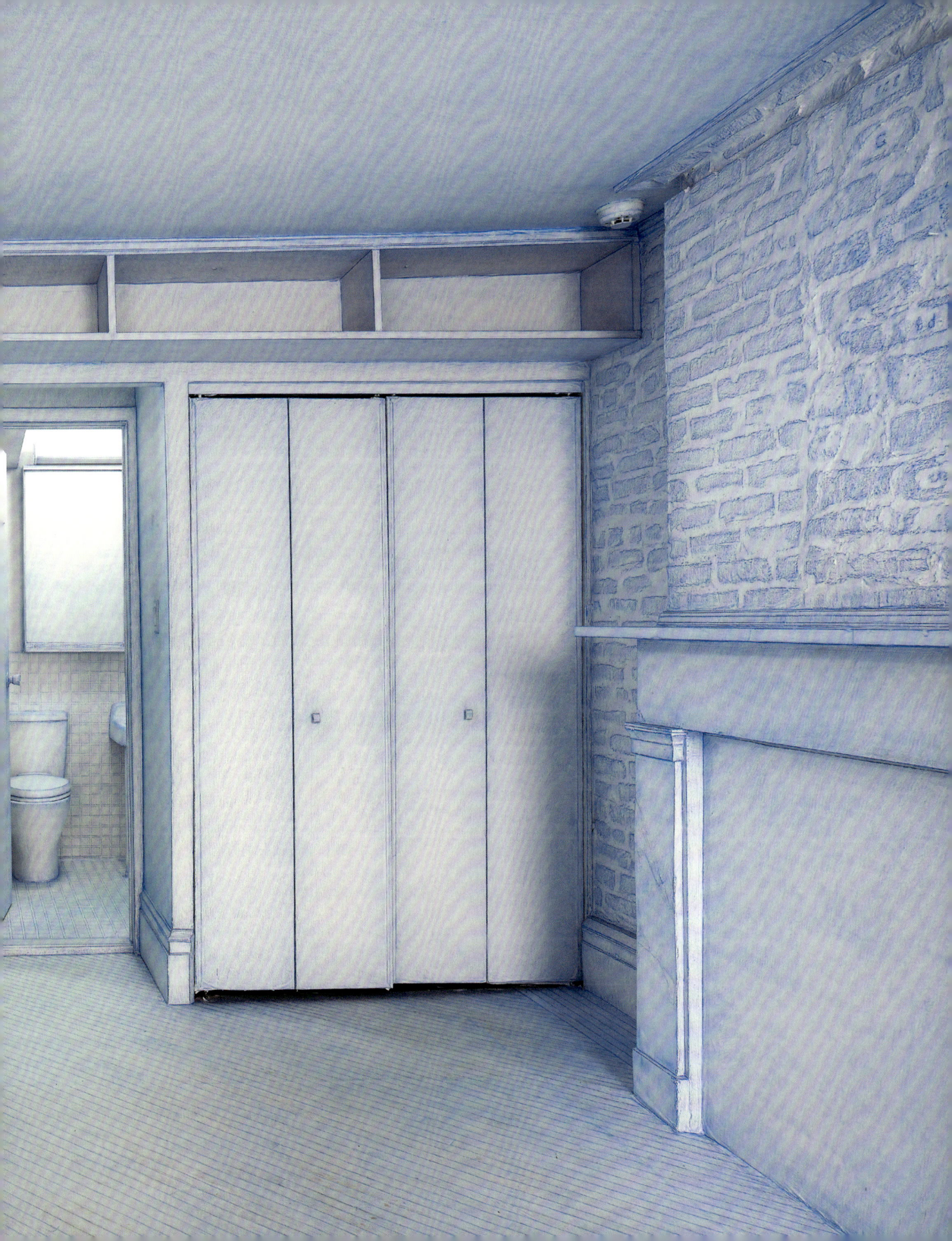

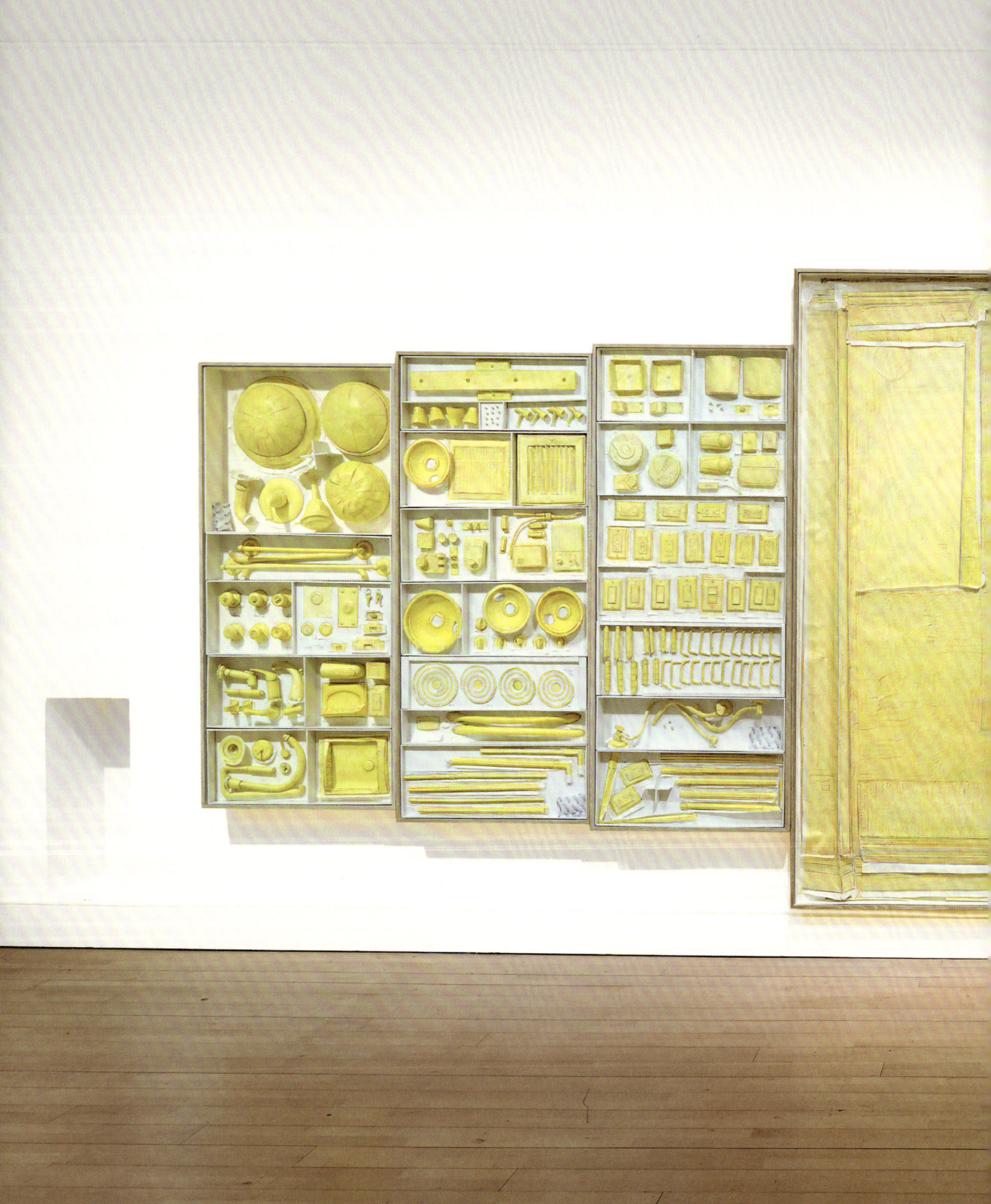

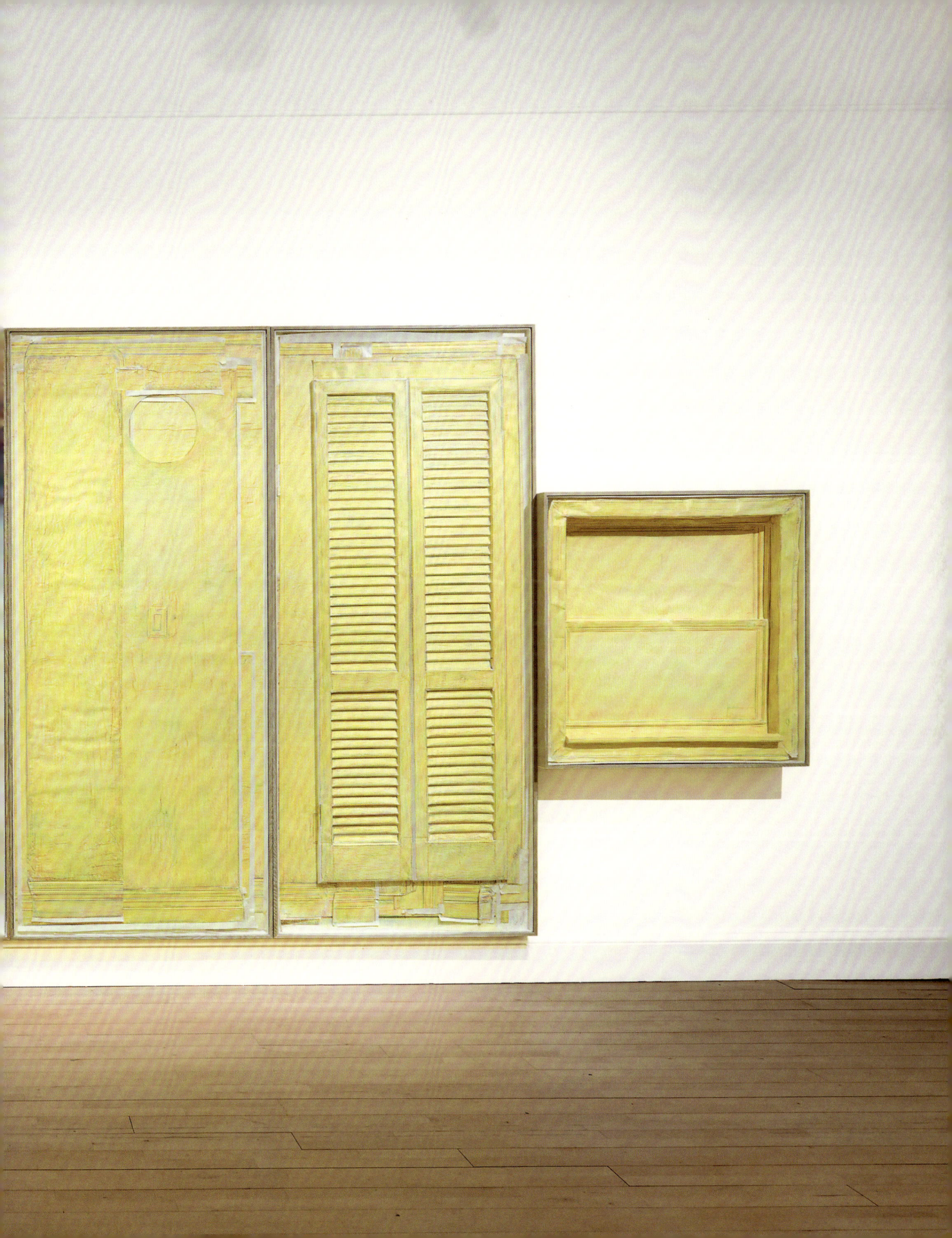

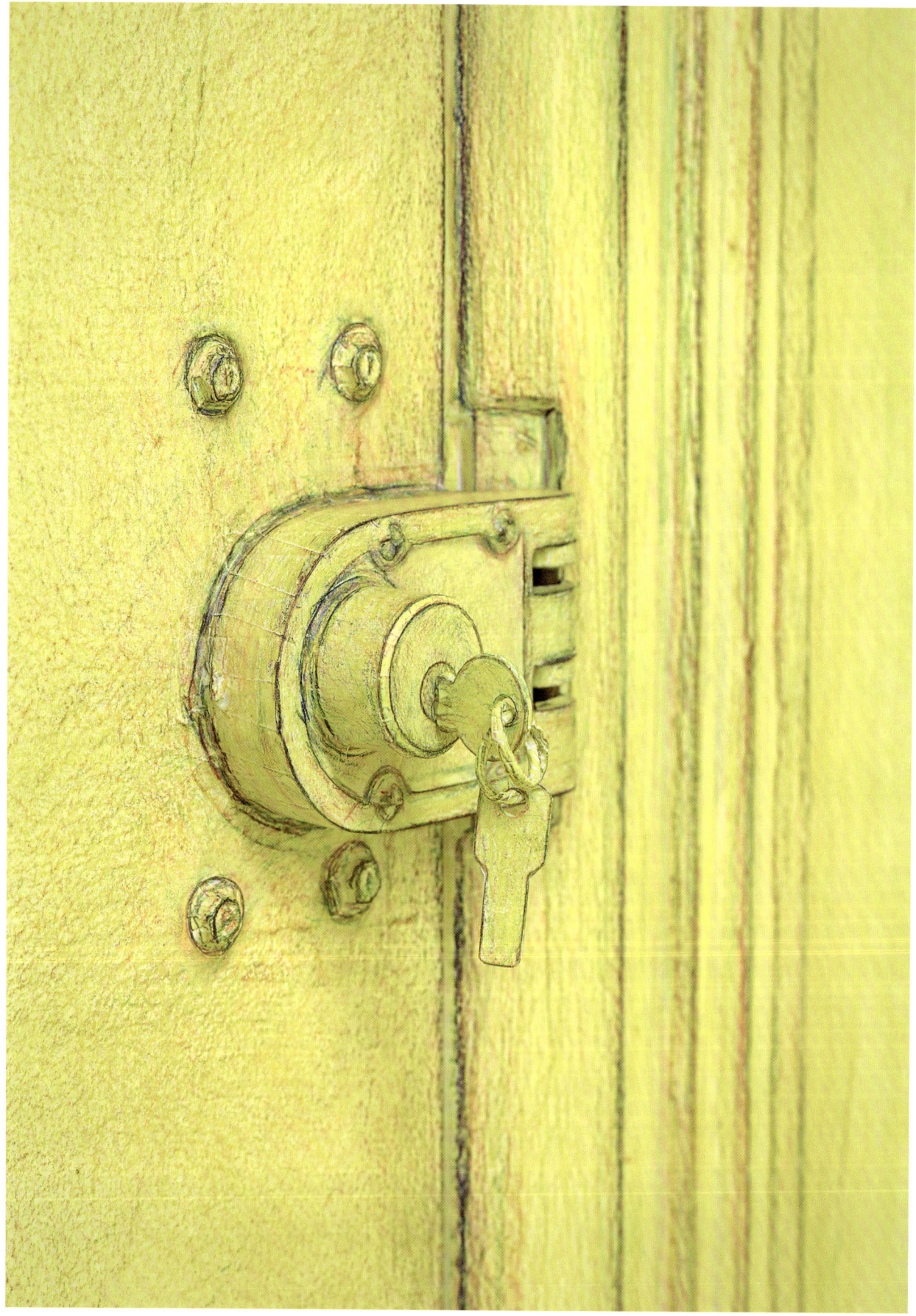

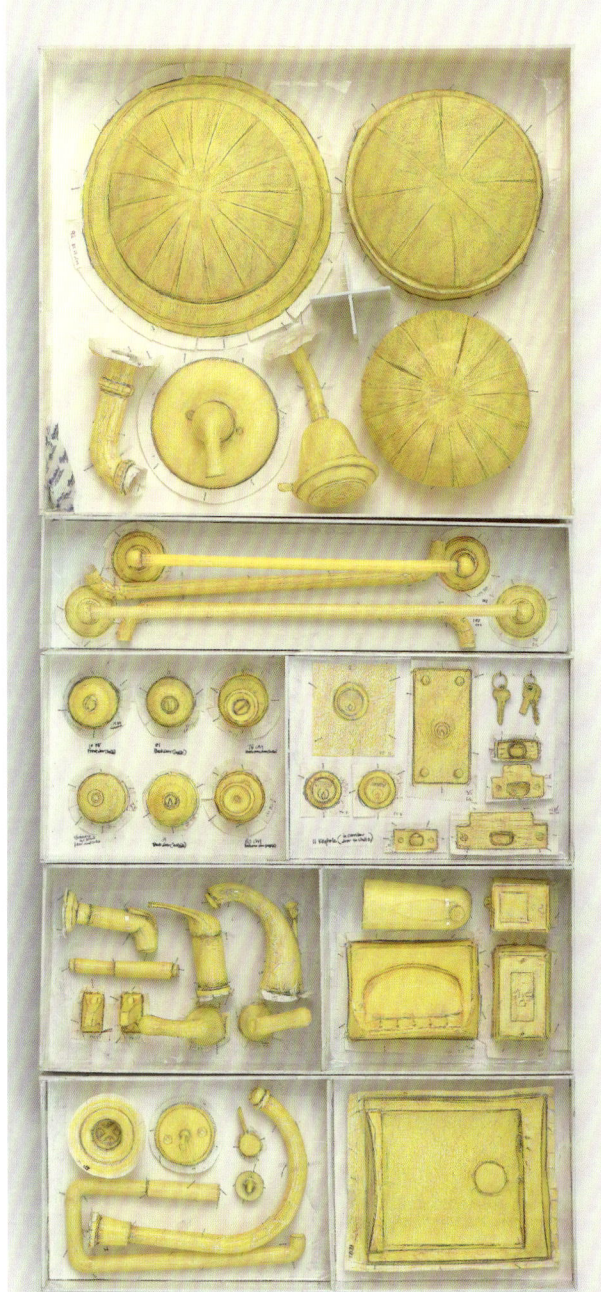
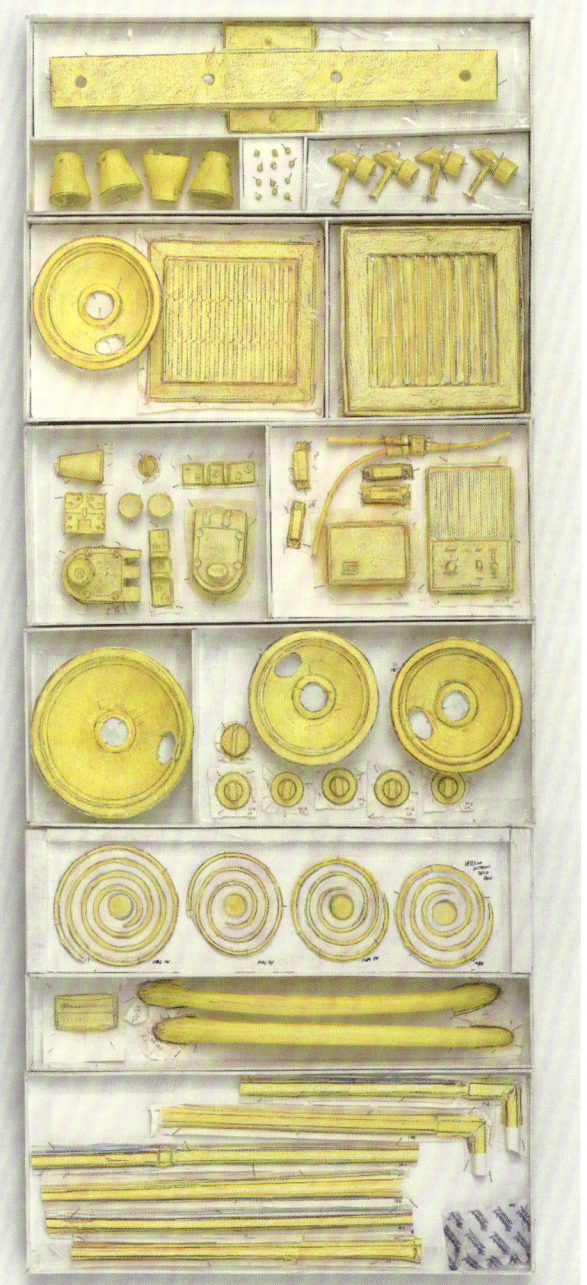

Previous pages: *Rubbing / Loving: Unit 2, 348 West 22nd Street, New York, NY 10011, USA* 2014–23, installation view, National Galleries of Scotland, Edinburgh, 2024
Opposite: *Rubbing / Loving: Apartment A, 348 West 22nd Street, New York, NY 10011, USA* 2014
Above: *Rubbing / Loving: Unit 2, 348 West 22nd Street, New York, NY 10011, USA* 2014–23

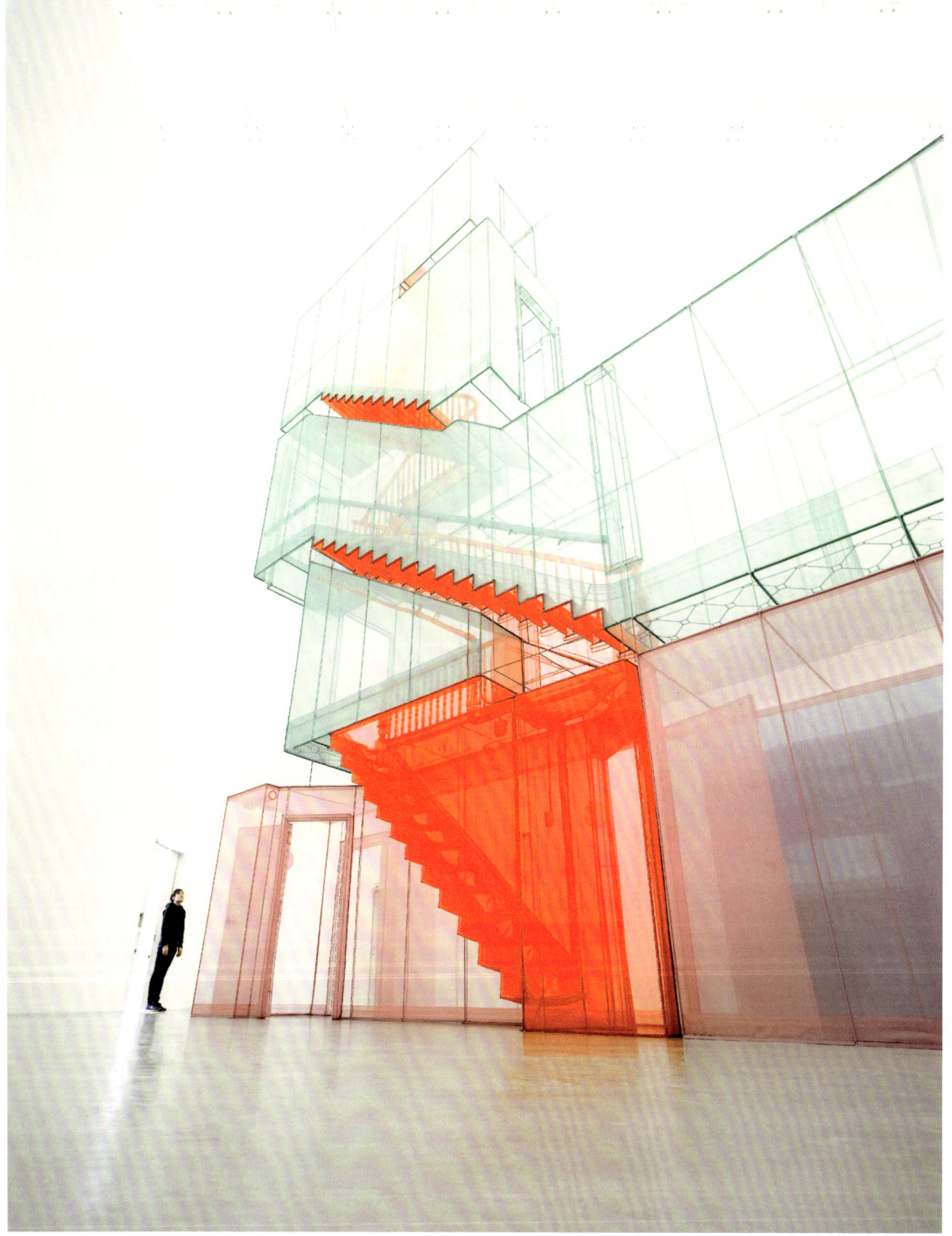

Above and opposite: *Apt. A, Corridors and Staircases, 348 West 22nd Street, New York, NY 10011, USA* 2012, installation view, 21st Century Museum of Contemporary Art, Kanazawa, 2012

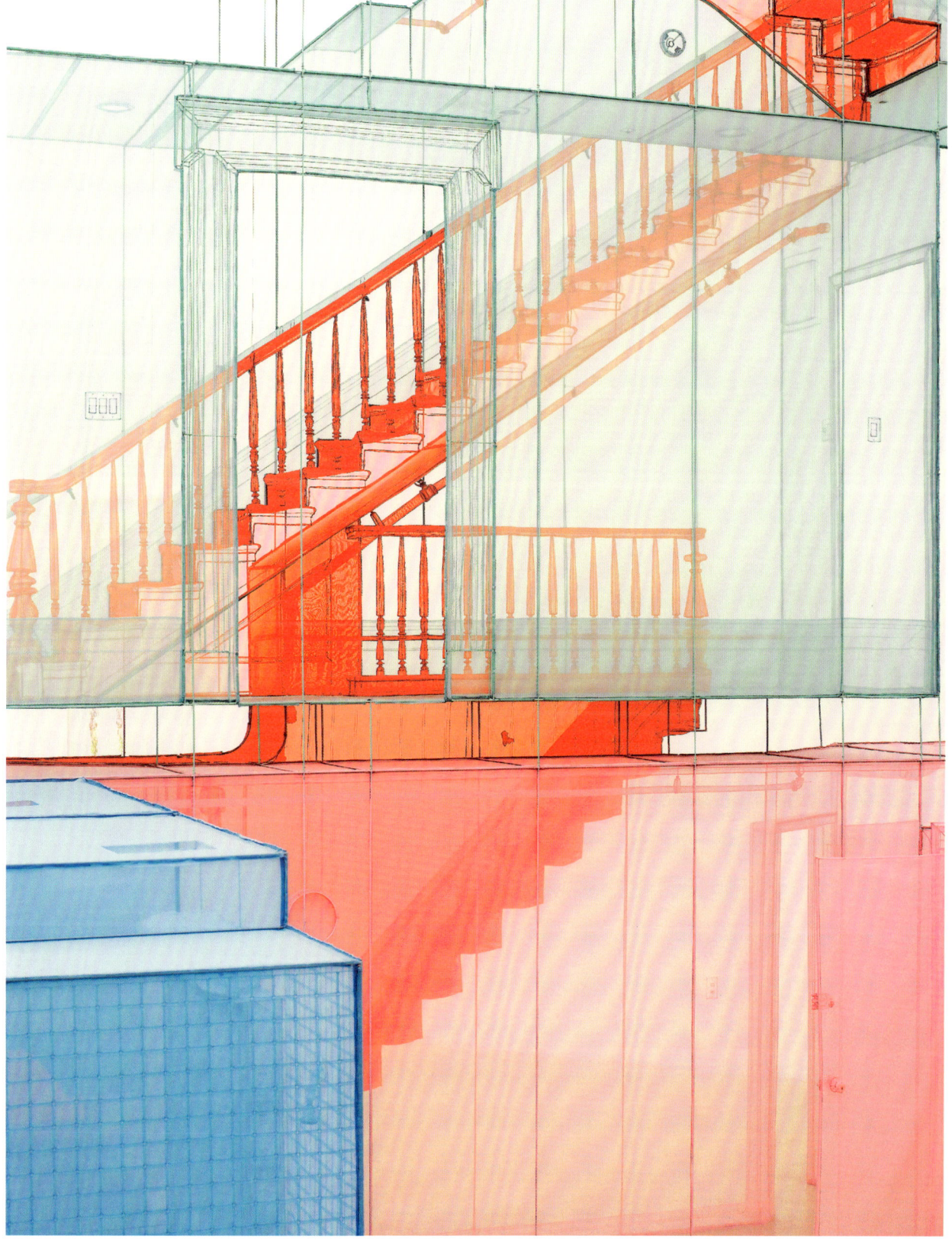

Nest/s builds on an ongoing fabric architecture series Do Ho Suh has called *Hubs*, that form a kind of impossible architecture, a sequence of 'nests' modelled on different spaces which Suh has inhabited throughout his life in Seoul, New York, London and Berlin. They are based on thresholds, such as corridors or entryways – an in-between space to pass through rather than dwell in. *Nest/s* itself is conceived as a passageway allowing visitors to move from one transitional space to another. Suh says: 'I don't see it as a shell or container so much as a passage or portal. Memory amalgamates in these spaces and memories shape our perceptions of them.' Unlike most building materials, the fabric of this work is flexible and has give, making these spaces more akin to a feeling or memory of the original space rather than intending to be a faithful replica. The use of fabric also reveals the relationship between clothing and architecture, which is central to Suh's practice: 'For me, clothing is the smallest intimate inhabitable space you can carry with you, and architecture is an expansion of that.' Using translucent polyester, a readily available fabric now often used to make traditional Korean summer clothing, Suh creates spaces that are breathable and porous, allowing in the surrounding architecture of the museum. (KW)

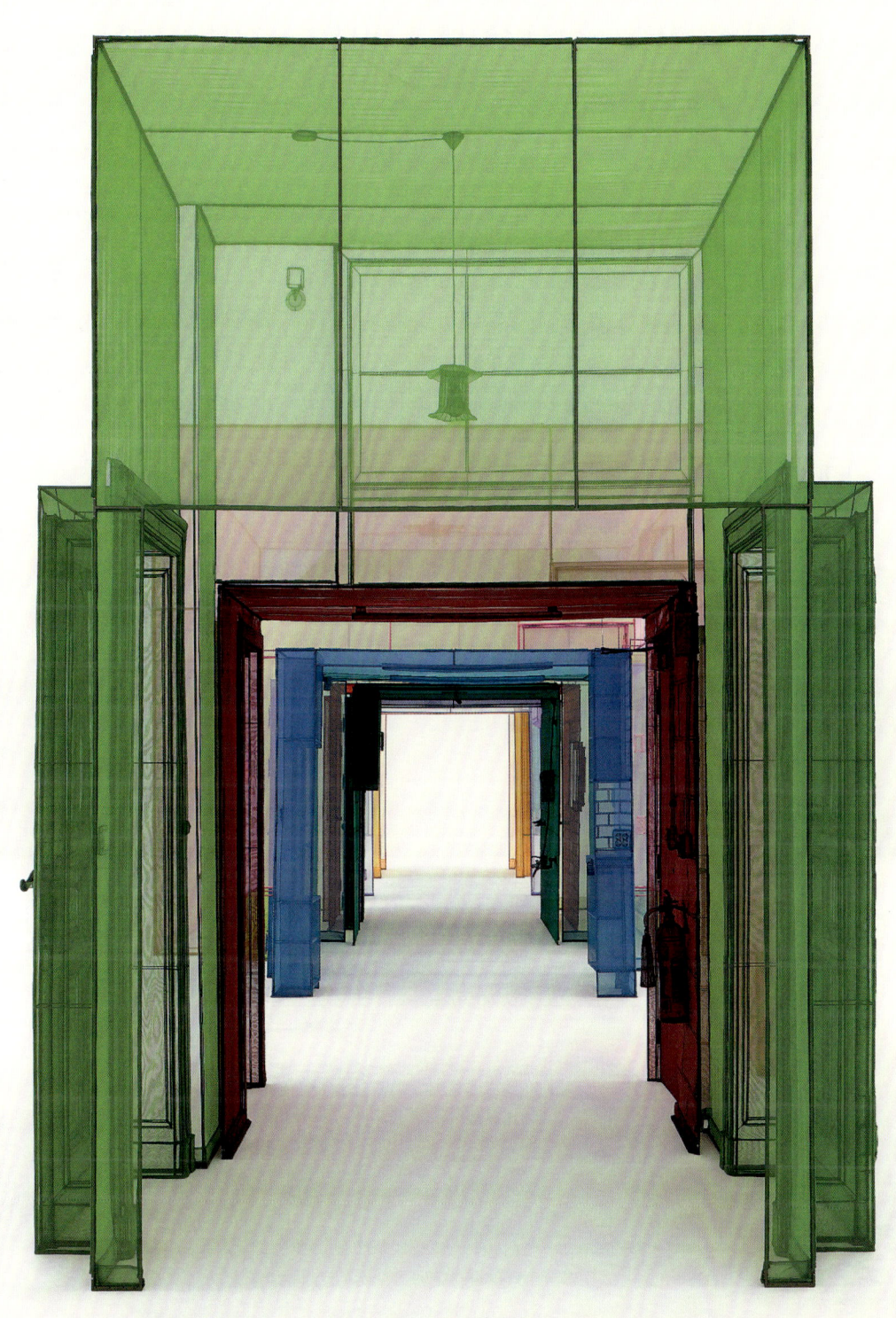

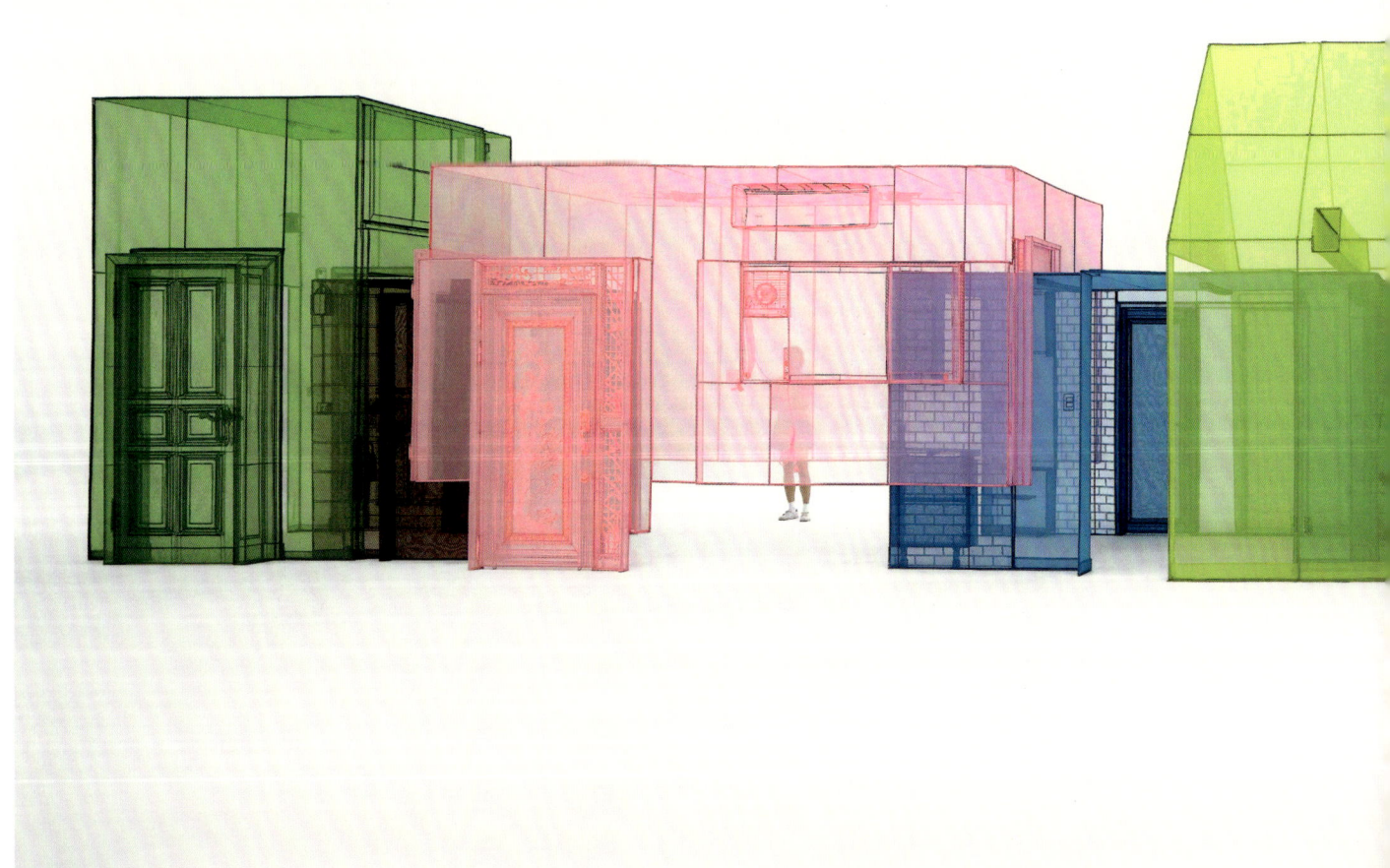

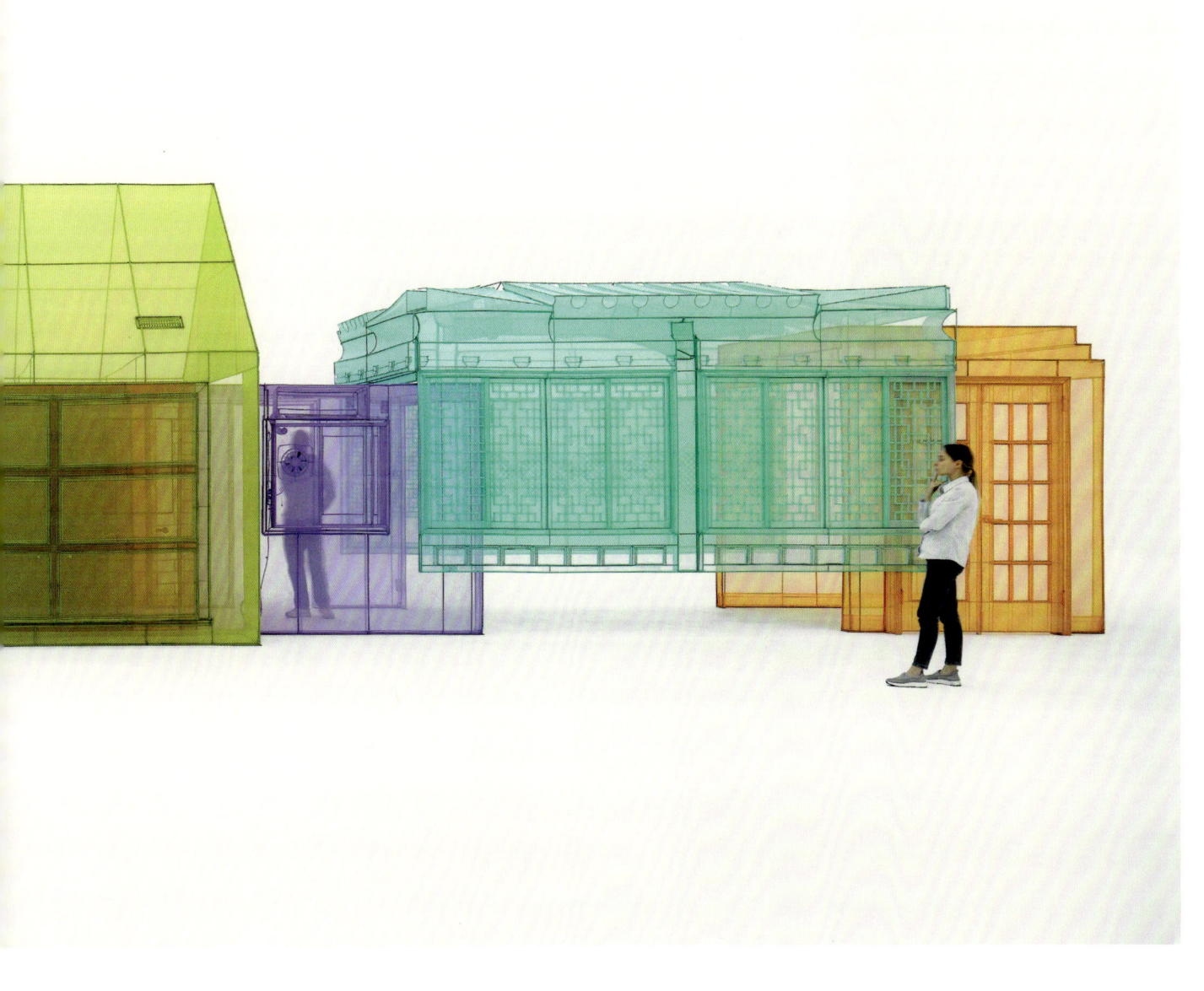

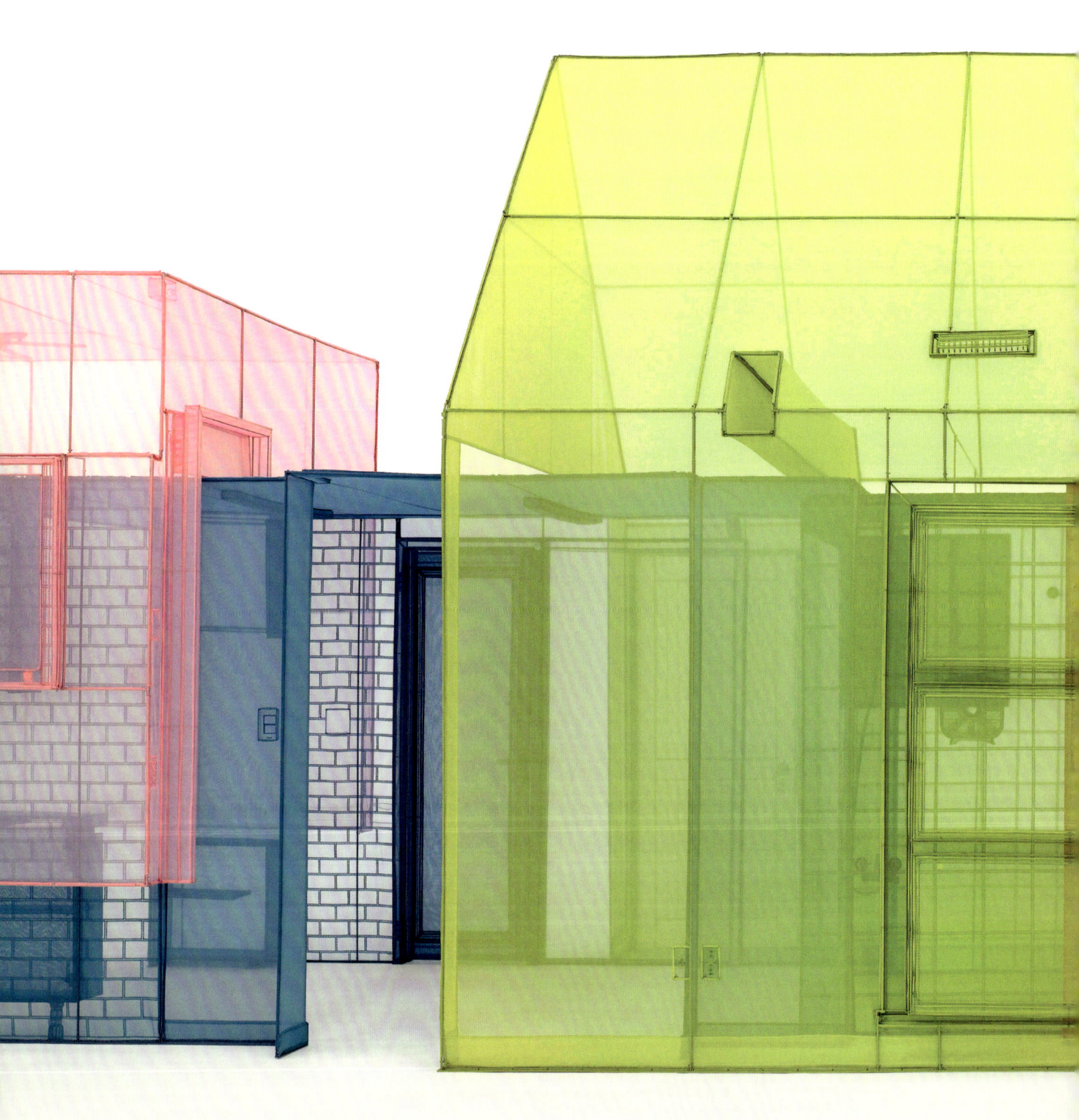

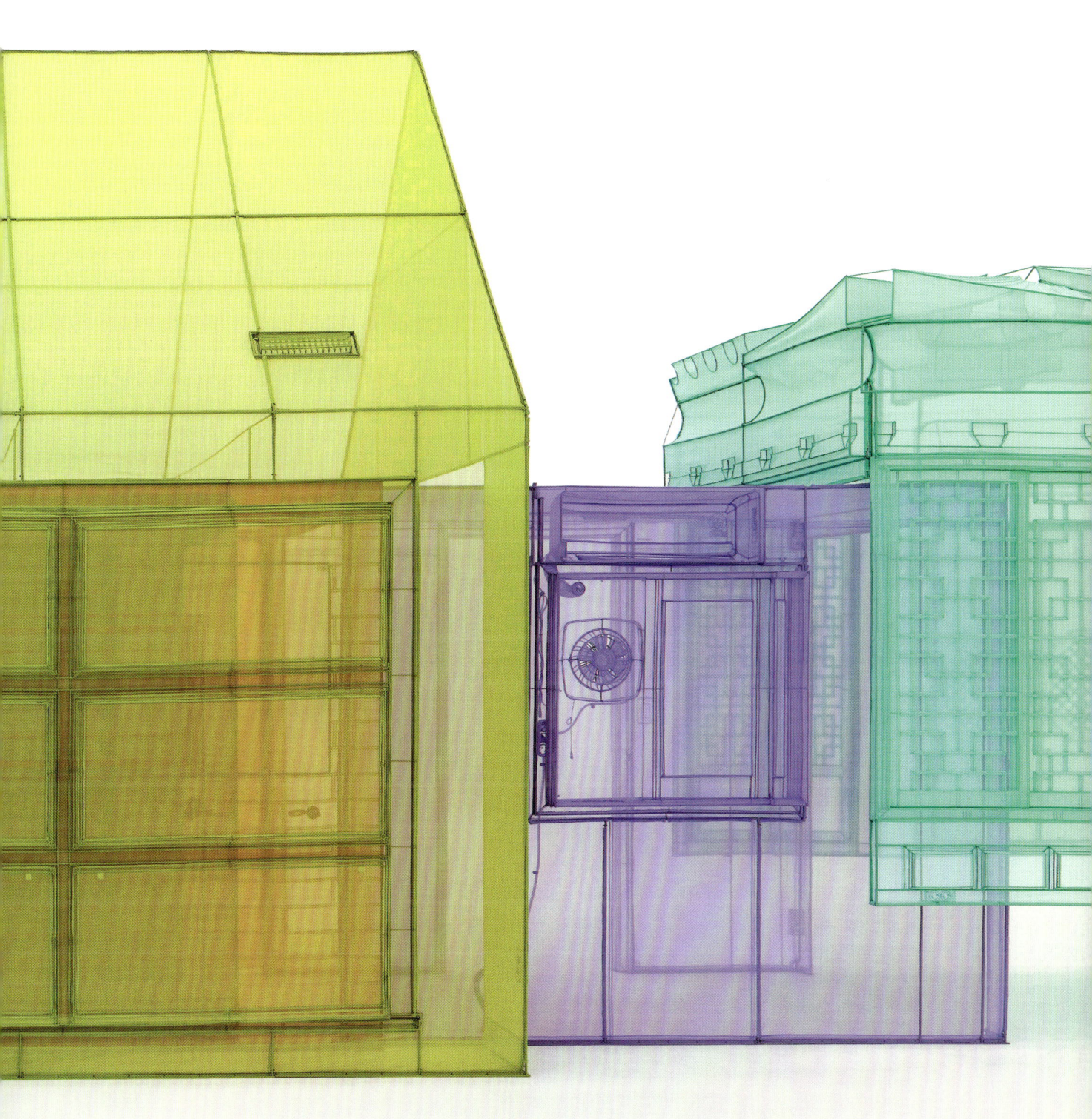

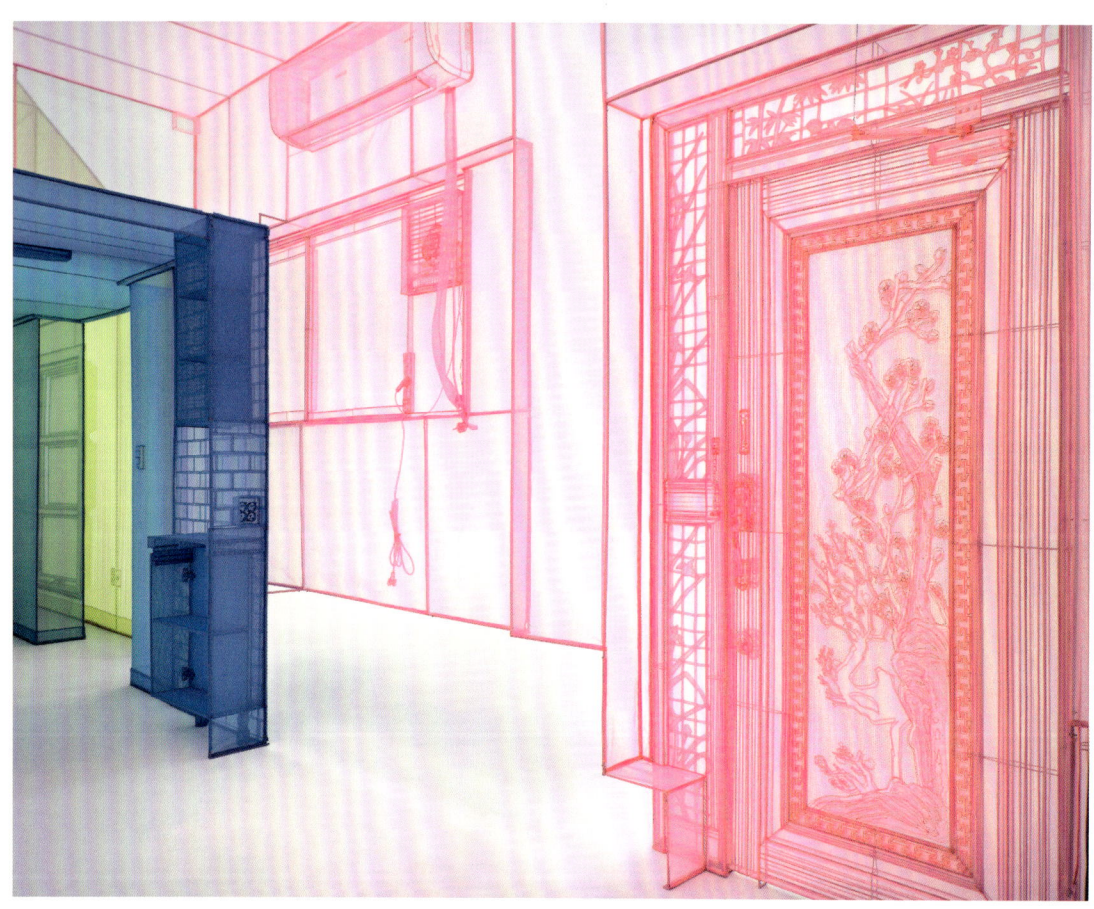

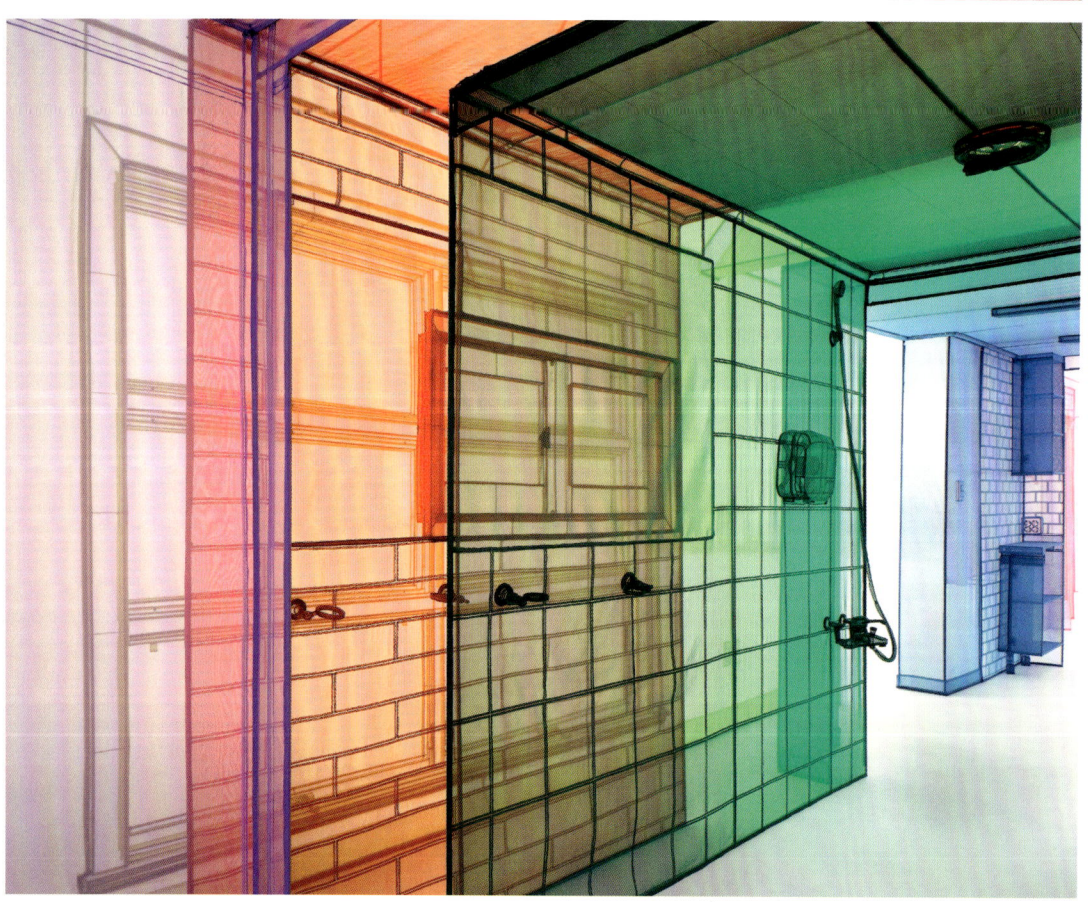

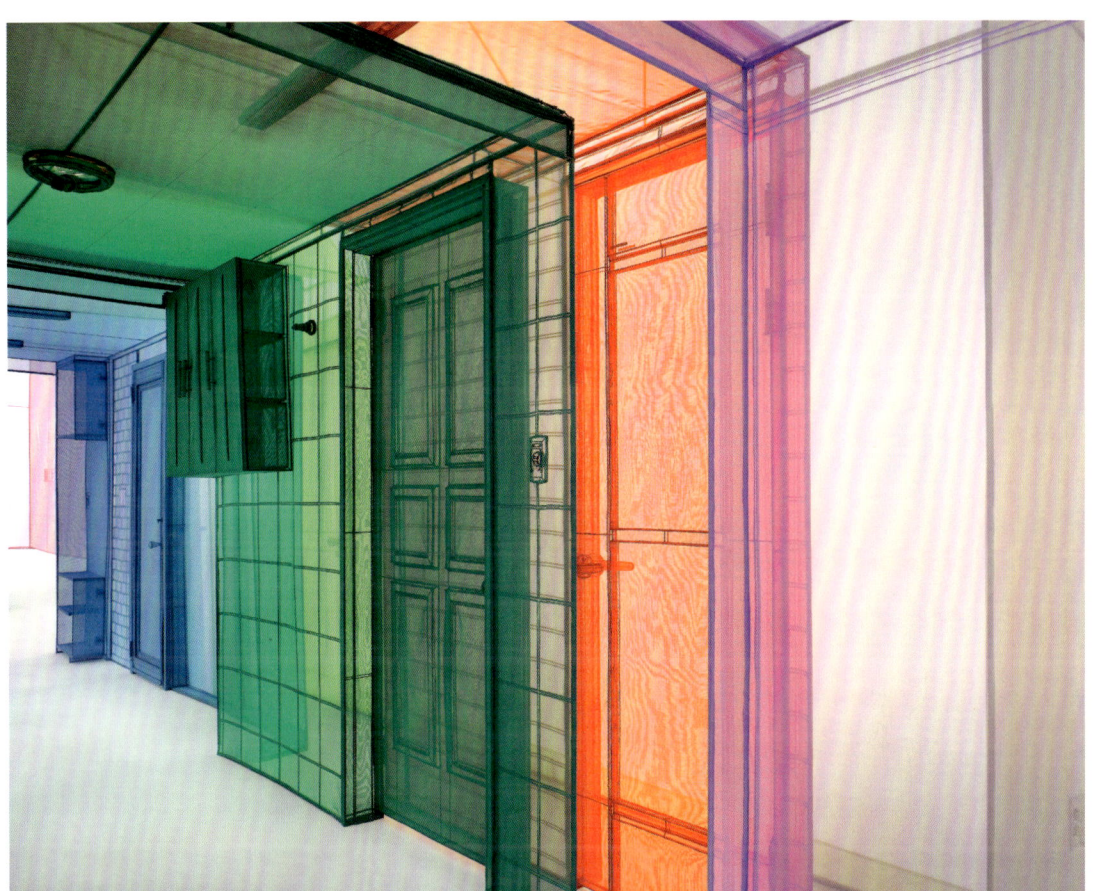

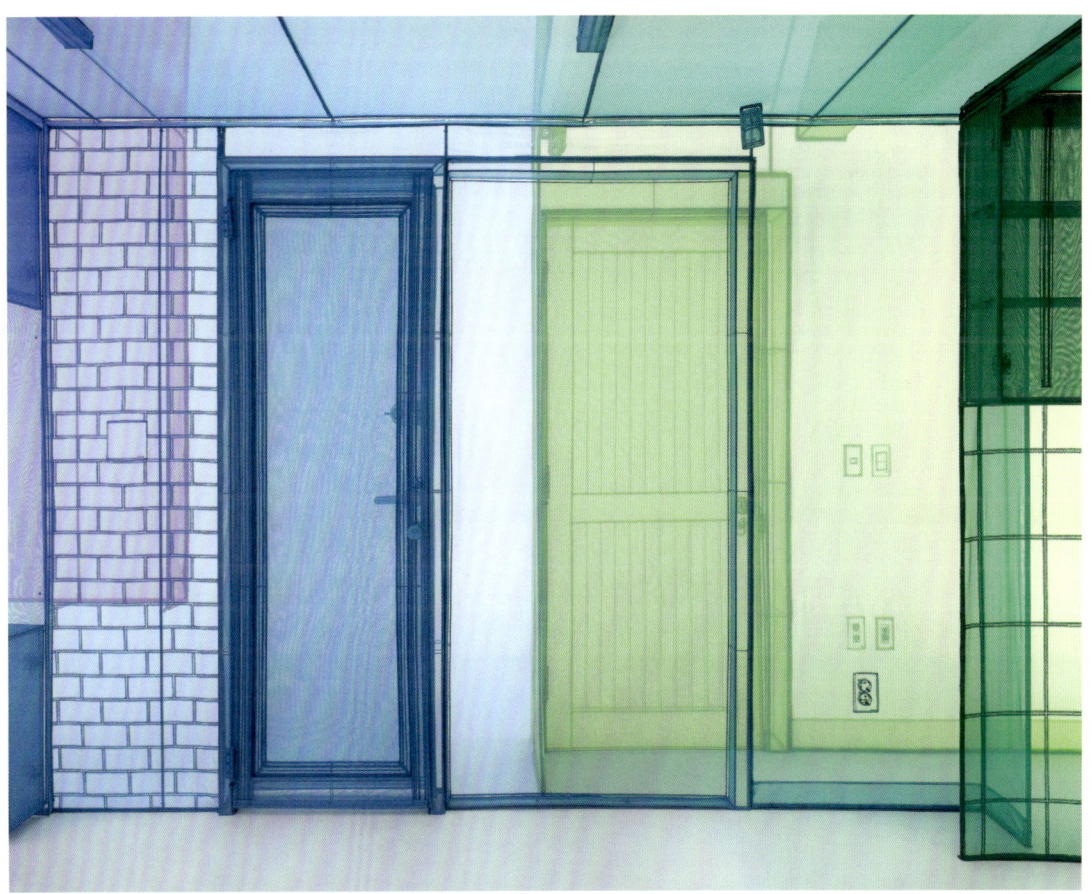

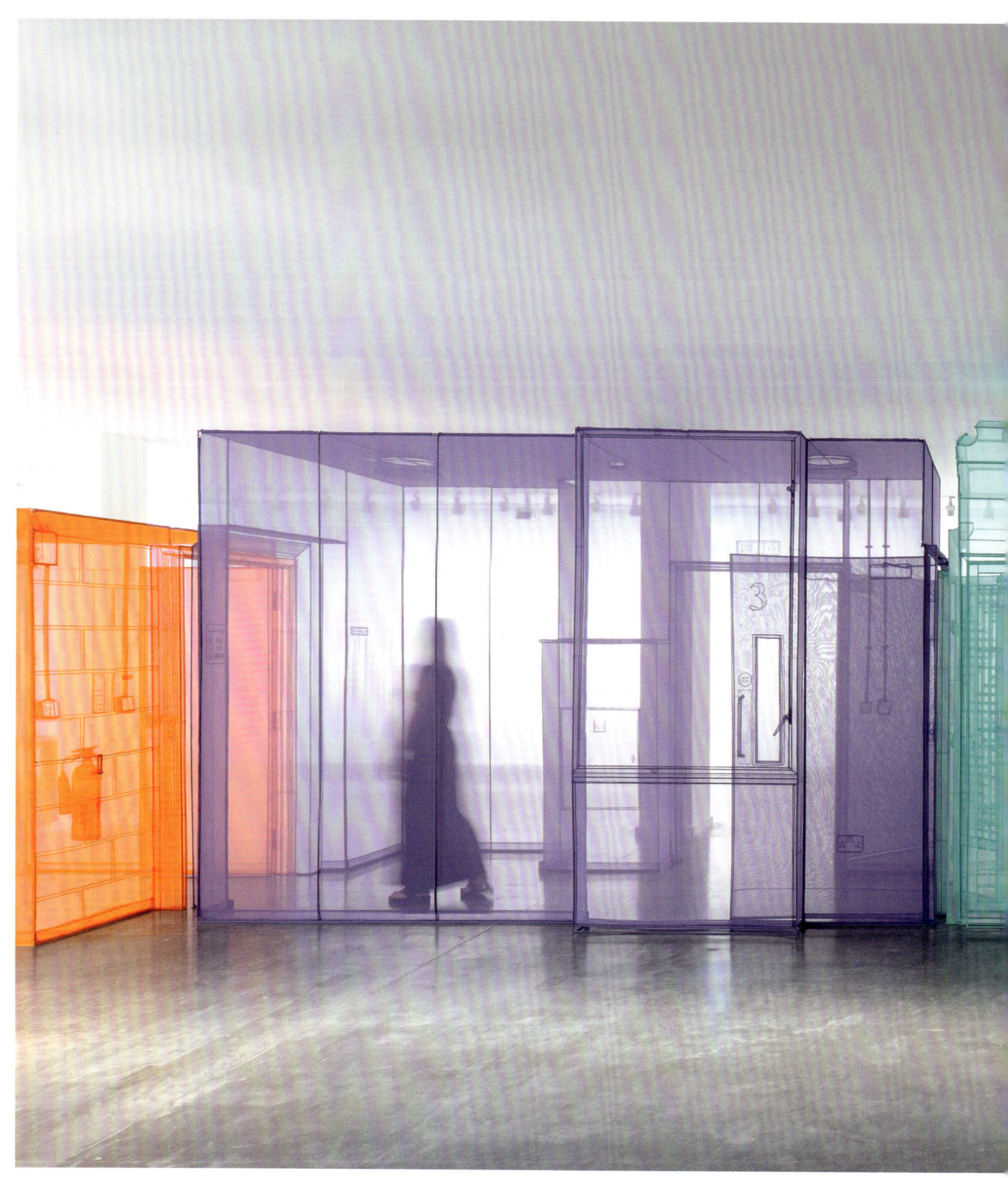

Previous pages 126–31: *Nest/s* 2024
Above: *Hub* series, installation view, Museum of Contemporary Art Australia, Sydney, 2022

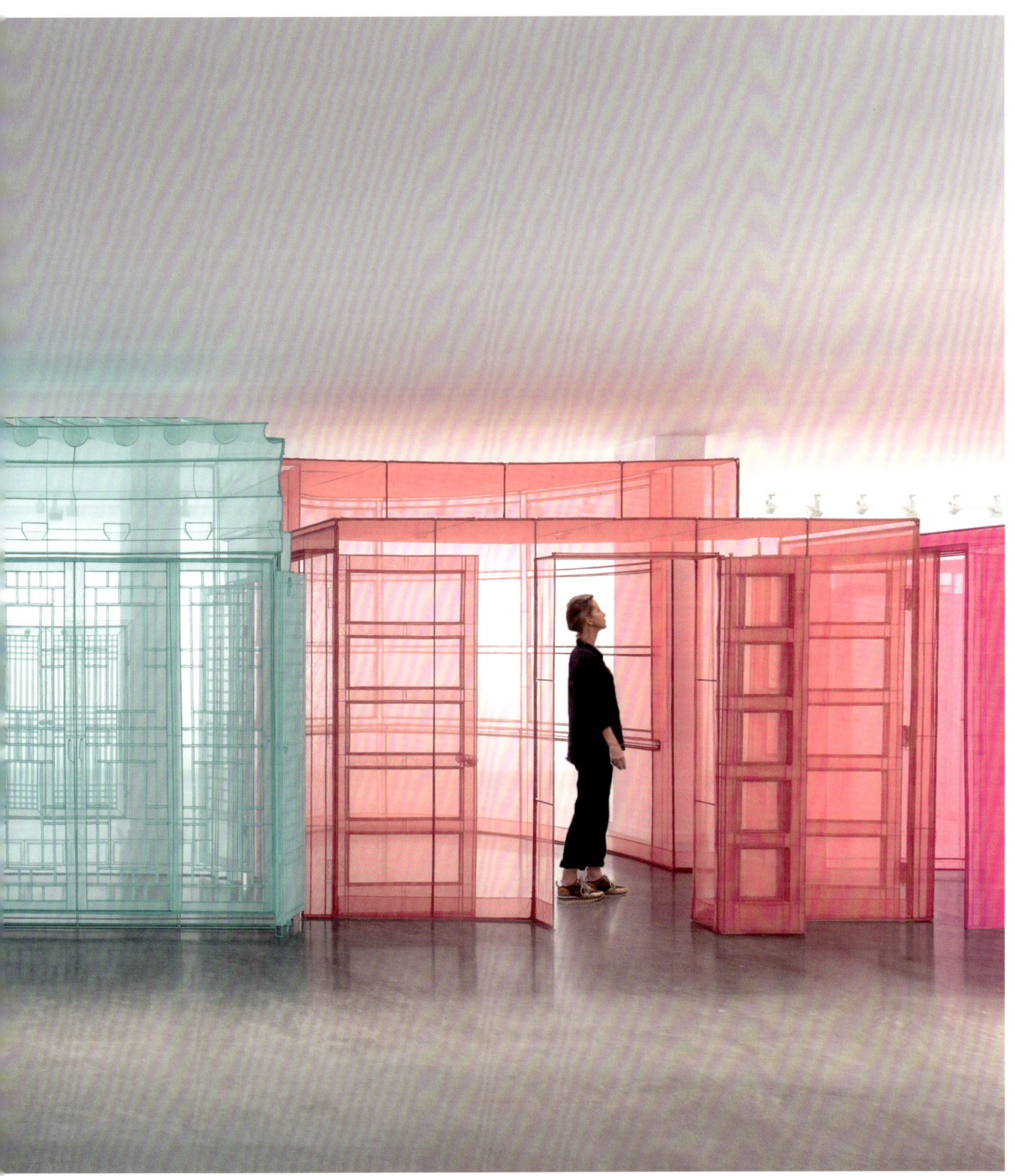

Home Within Home (Scale 1/9) belongs to an ongoing body of works Suh calls 'speculative':works that exist largely in the language and scale of architectural models and plans. Suh originally created *Home Within Home* working with architectural tools, measuring, 3D-scanning, shrinking and combining two existing buildings:his childhood *hanok* home in Seoul and the nineteenth-century building of a housing block near the Rhode Island School of Design in Providence, the first place Suh lived in the US as a student. Created at 1:9 scale for Tate Modern, the work is cut into quarters to reveal the interruptions between these architectures, which have been arranged to allow for passage between and through intersecting doors and windows. The *hanok* is trapped inside the Providence house, unable to be disassembled and moved, while infiltrating and taking up the space of the Providence building, undermining both structures' functionality.

The fantastical, speculative nature of the architecture Suh created for *Home Within Home* is connected to the mental space of a recurring dream Suh had. In it, the *hanok* house in which he grew up flew over the Pacific Ocean and crashed into the Providence building of his student housing trailing an emergency parachute stitched on the journey. While the relationship between these architectures is fraught but not explicitly destructive, it belongs to an ongoing series of projects in which Suh imagines and stages clashes and frictions between the *hanok* and where it 'landed', sometimes appearing to rip through the architecture of the 'host' building in the manner of a meteorite. This has resulted in multiple site-specific projects imagining this landing, including in London in 2010.

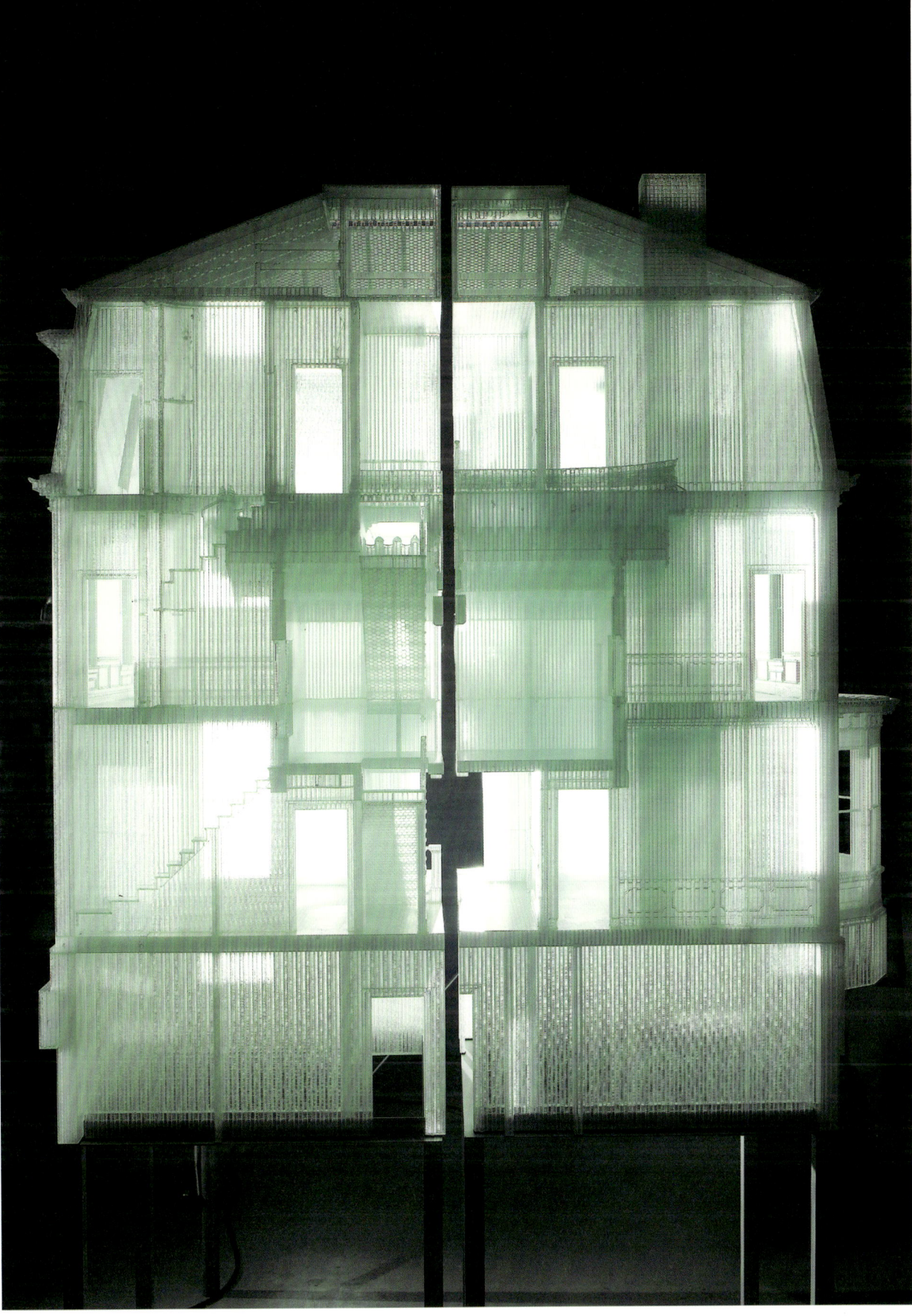

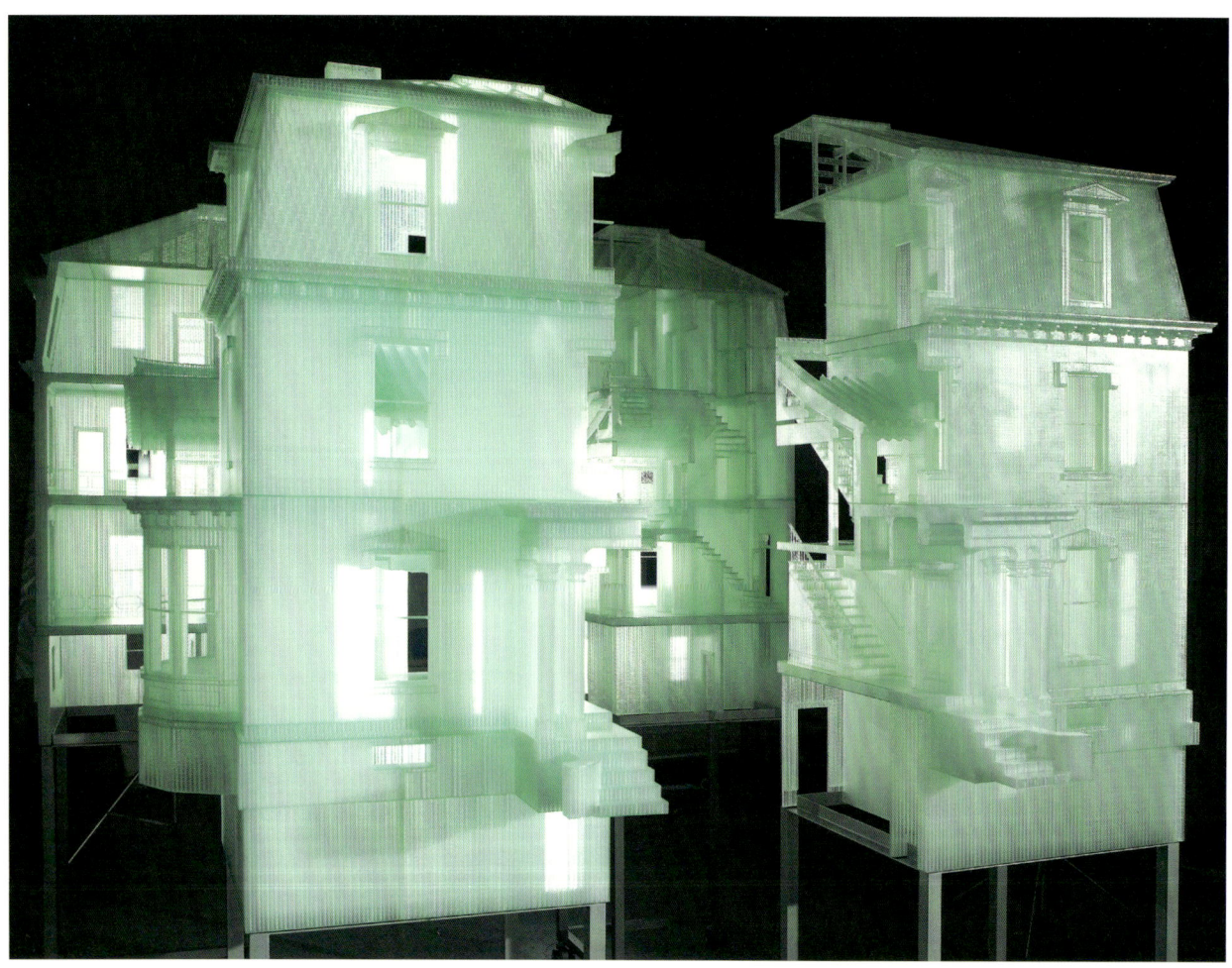

Previous pages, above and opposite: *Home Within Home (Scale 1/11)* 2009–11

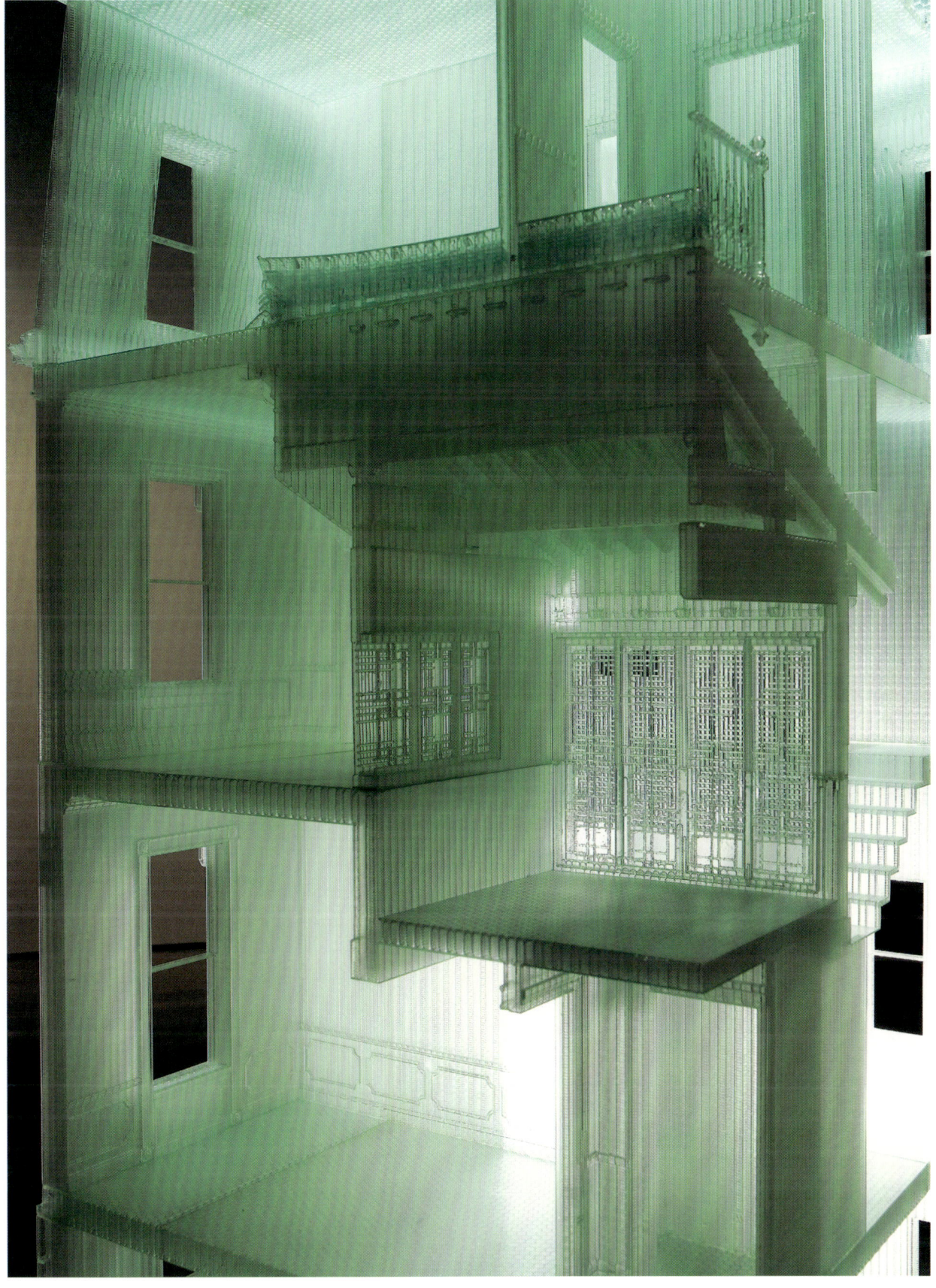

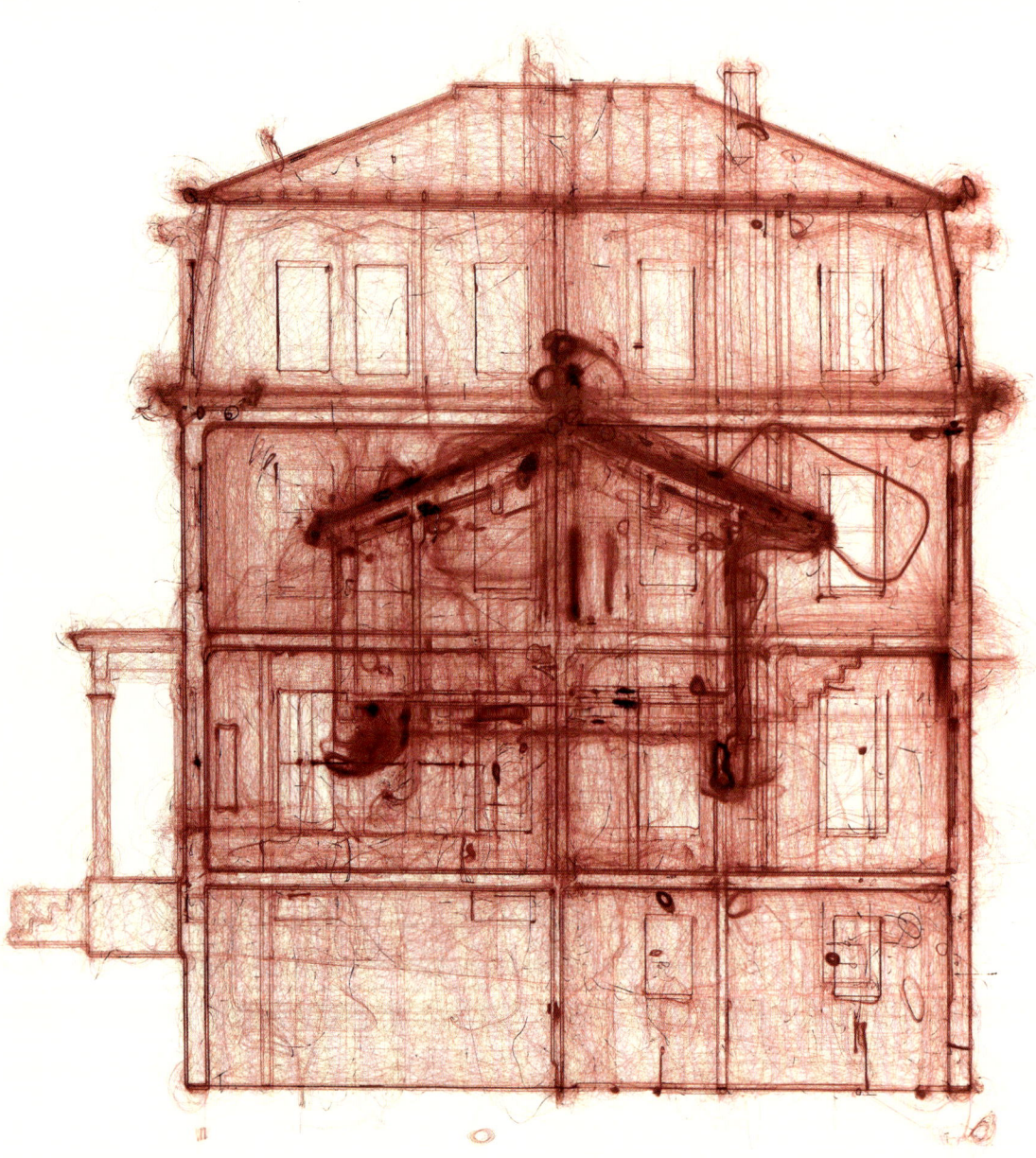

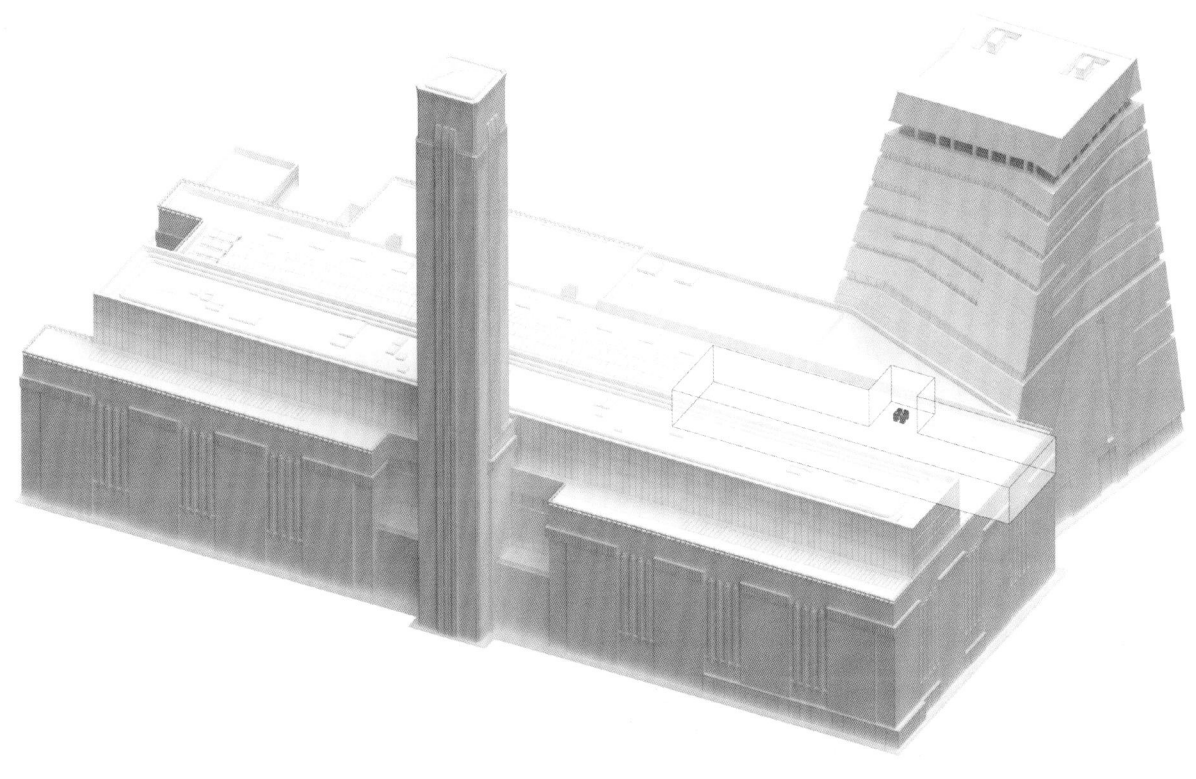

Opposite: *ScaledBehaviour_drawing(HomeWithinHome_elevation_A_02)* 2021
Above: *Home Within Home (Scale 1/9)* 2025 rendered within Tate Modern, London

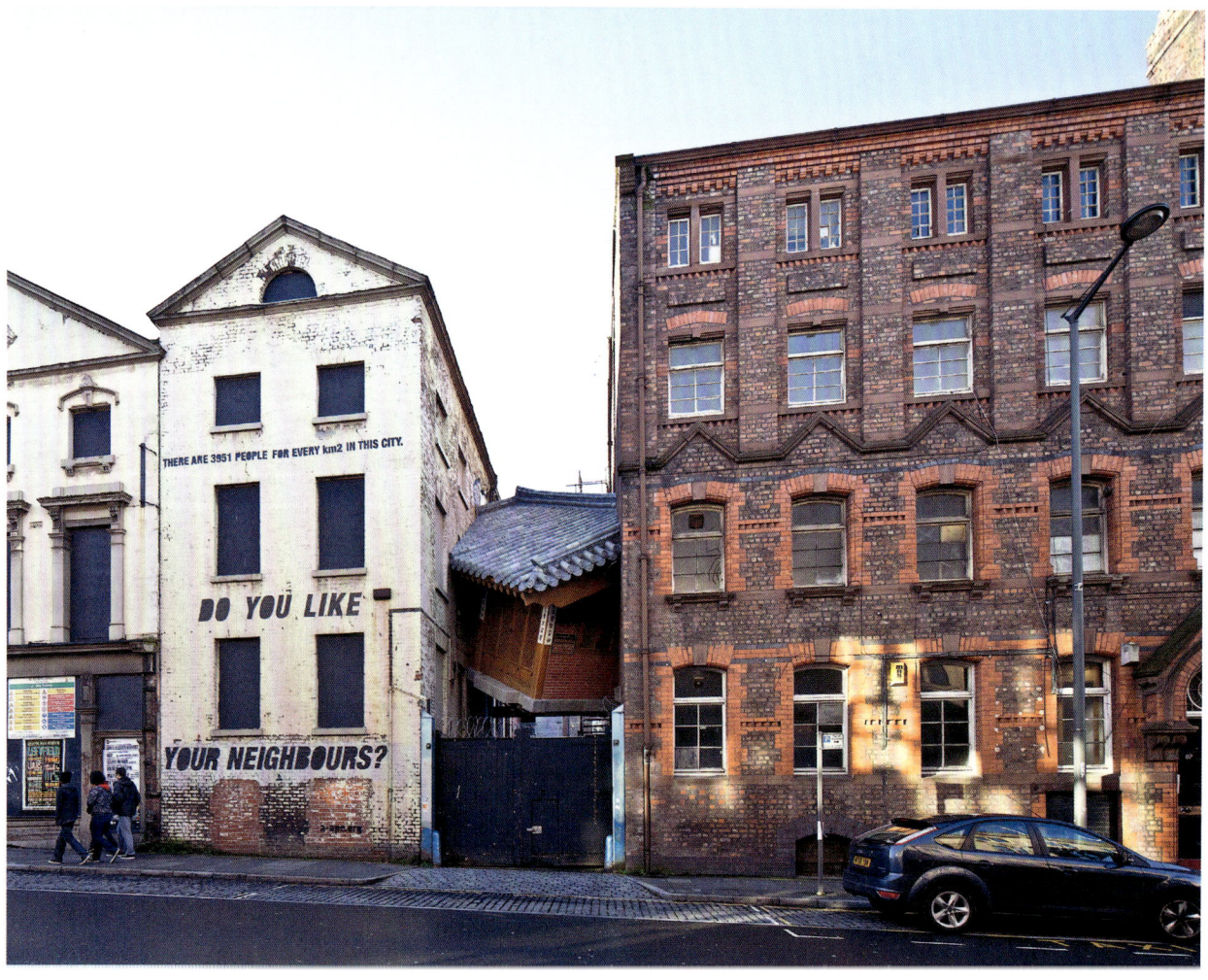

Bridging Home, Liverpool 2010

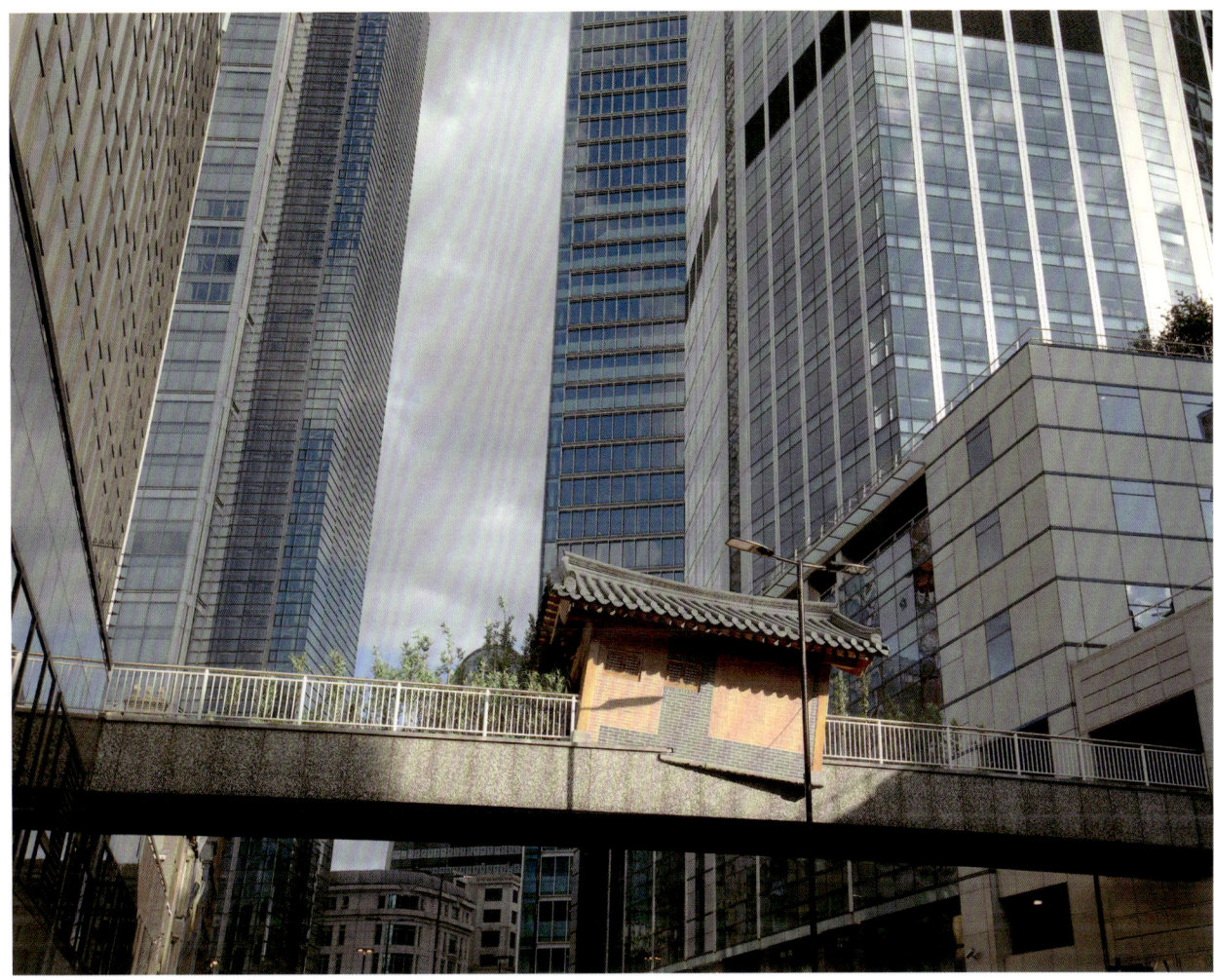

Bridging Home, London 2018

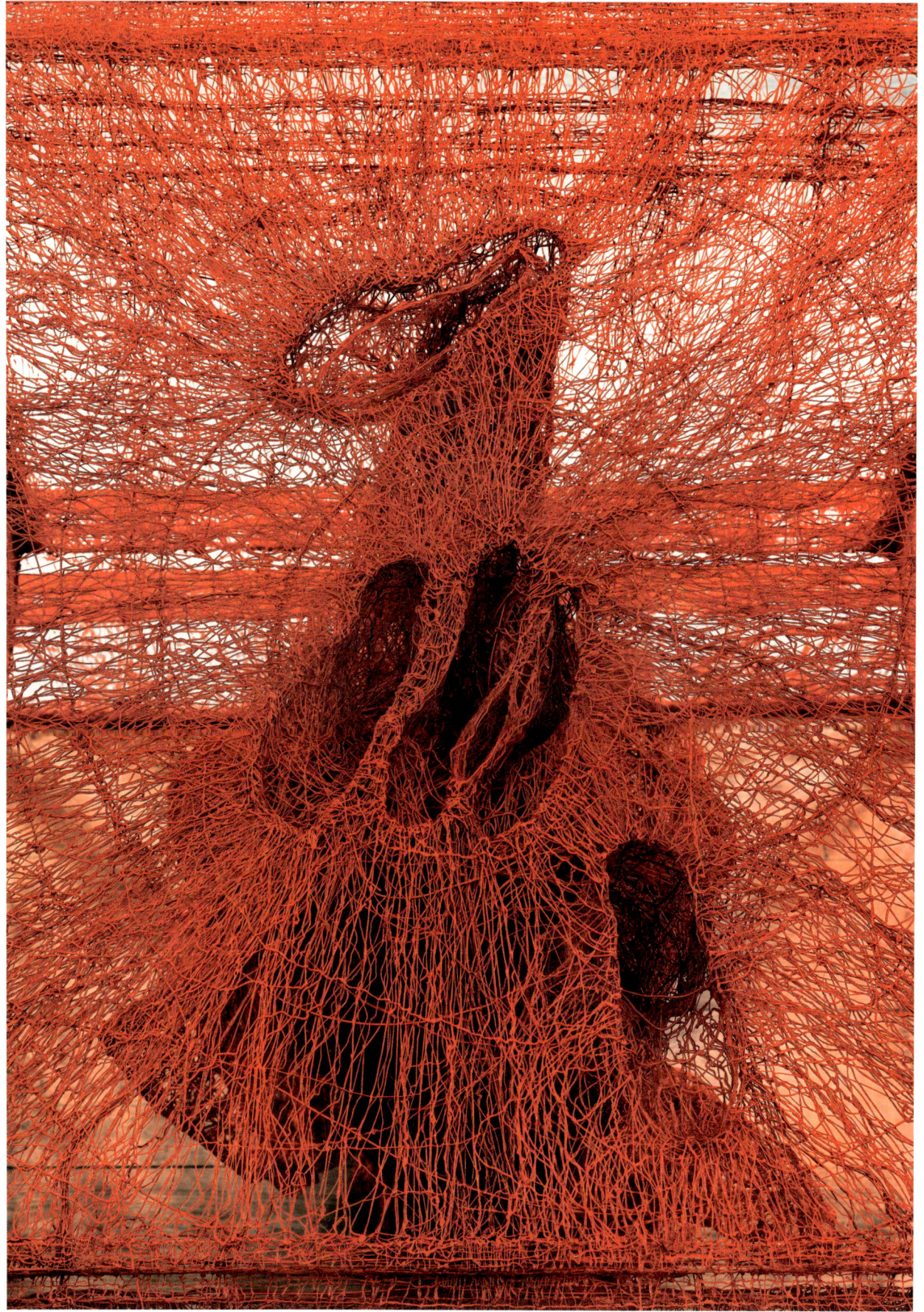

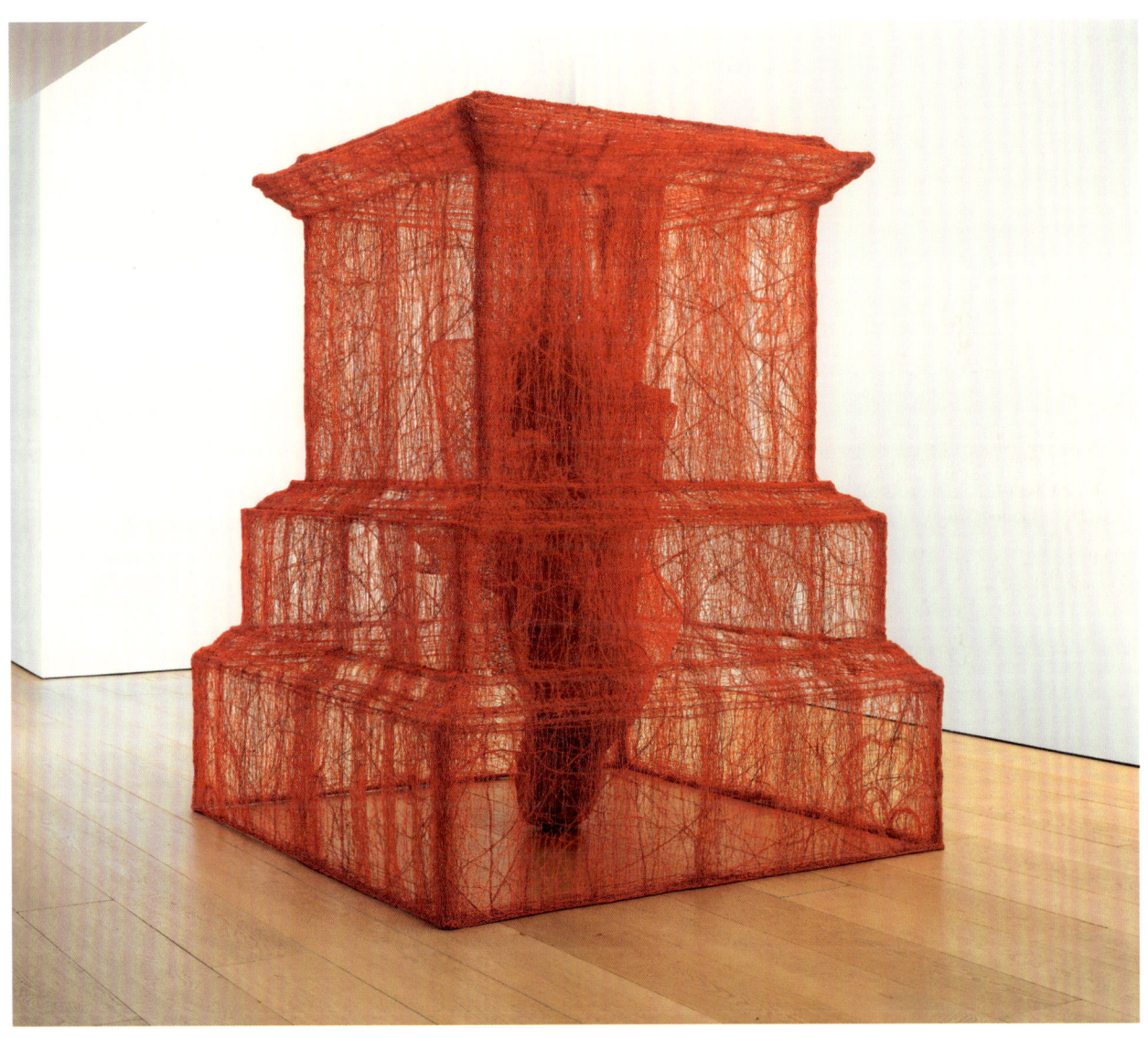

Left and above: *Inverted Monument* 2022

Robin Hood Gardens, Woolmore Street, London E14 0HG

Robin Hood Gardens, Woolmore Street, London E14 0HG is a video work that explores the changing architectural fabric of the city of London and its impact, focusing on Robin Hood Gardens, a Brutalist housing estate in Poplar, East London. Built in 1972 and designed by architects Alison and Peter Smithson, the estate featured external raised walkways that were envisioned as 'streets in the sky', a hallmark of Brutalist design at this time. The local council took the decision to redevelop the area in 2008 and, despite multiple public attempts to preserve the estate, demolition of the western block, Block A, began in 2017. Residents lived in a state of uncertainty until demolition was confirmed. Suh's work combines time-lapse photography, drone footage and photogrammetry (a process of stitching together photographs to create a digital 3D model of a space) to record both the building and traces of the homes it contained before their destruction. The techniques mean the camera remains at a steady, consistent distance from its subjects, limiting the artist's ability to make decisions. Following a series of shots of the exterior building, accompanied by ambient sounds, there is a sudden quietening of the soundtrack as we enter the interior. Although this block was by then almost empty of its inhabitants, the work records traces of those who were still in residence: rooms that remained fully furnished, beds left unmade, oranges in a fruit bowl. We are then shown the first signs of the demolition, the repeated symmetry of the original building interrupted by missing windows and walls that render the architecture open and porous. Finally, some of the last remaining permanent residents are seen sitting alone in their homes, until they too must vacate the building. The demolition took place in stages, and the last residents left the eastern block of Robin Hood Gardens, Block B, in June 2024. (KW)

Opposite: *Robin Hood Gardens, Woolmore Street, London E14 0HG* 2018, installation view, Venice Architecture Biennale, 2018
Pages 146–51: *Robin Hood Gardens, Woolmore Street, London E14 0HG* 2018, stills

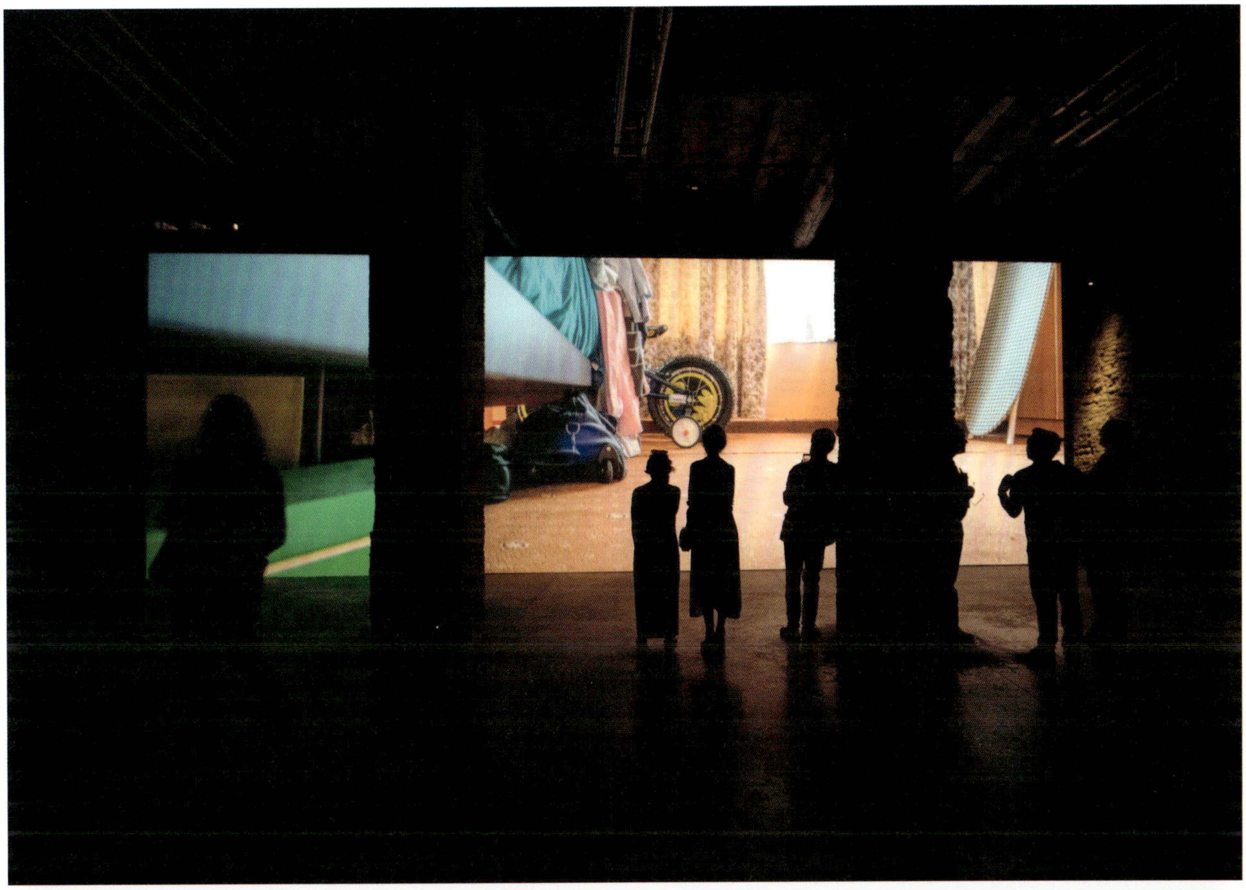

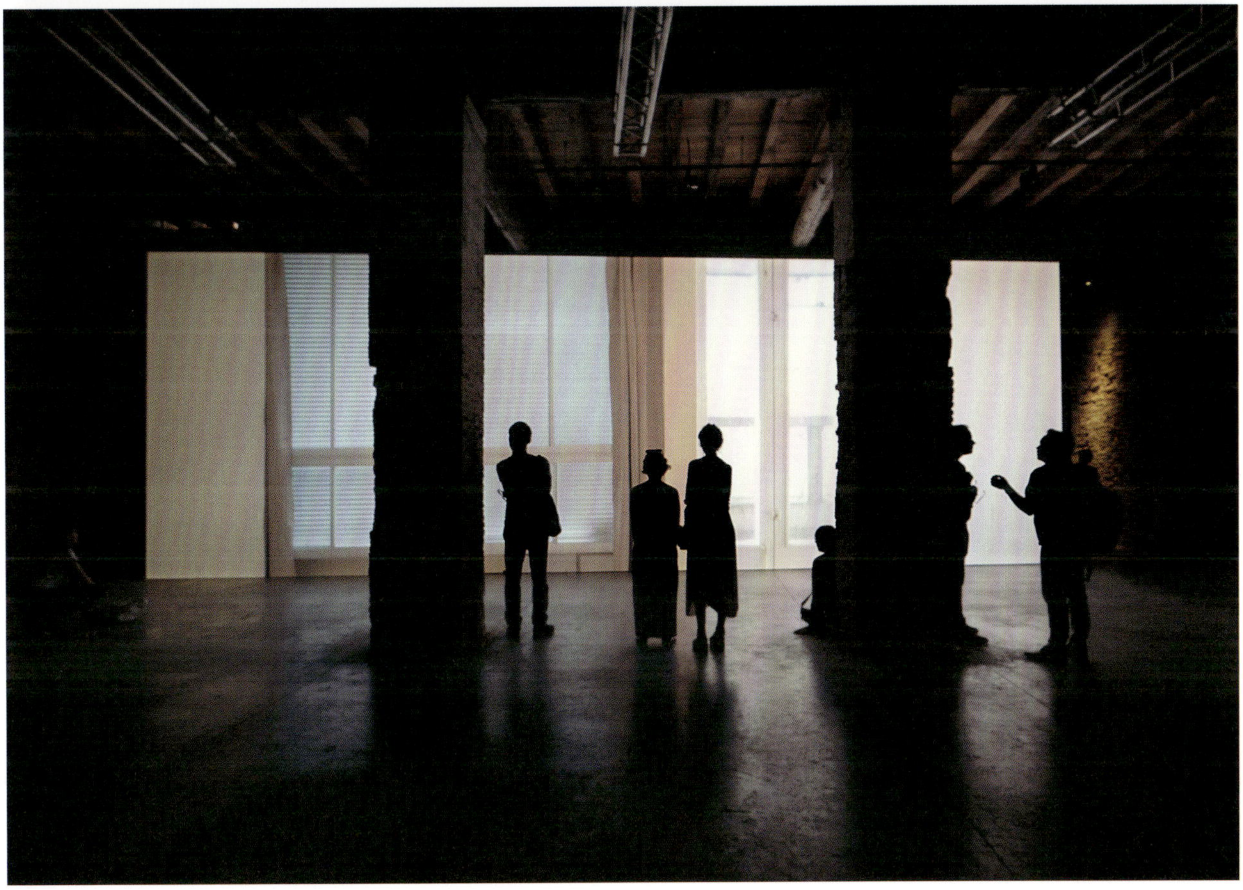

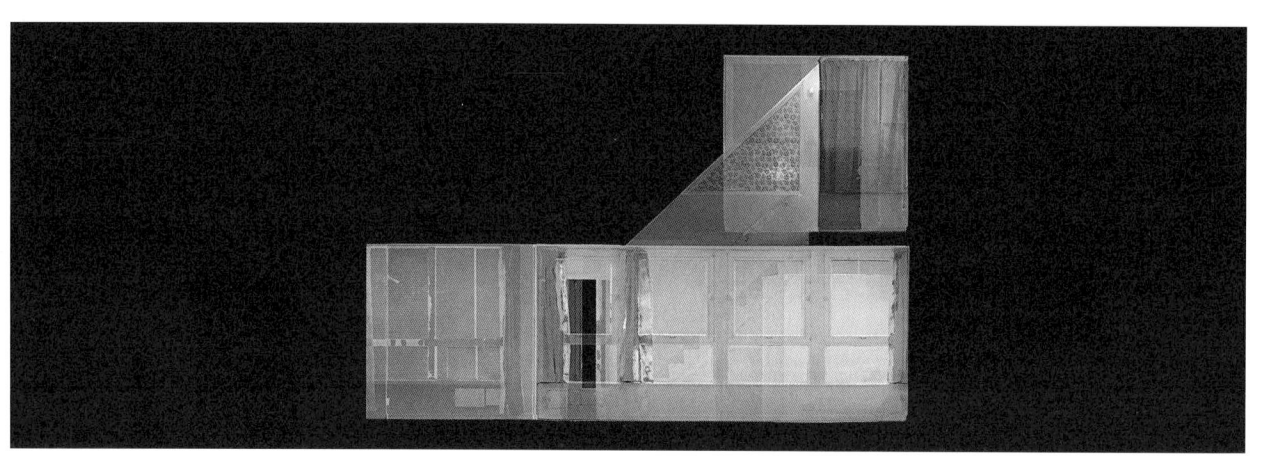

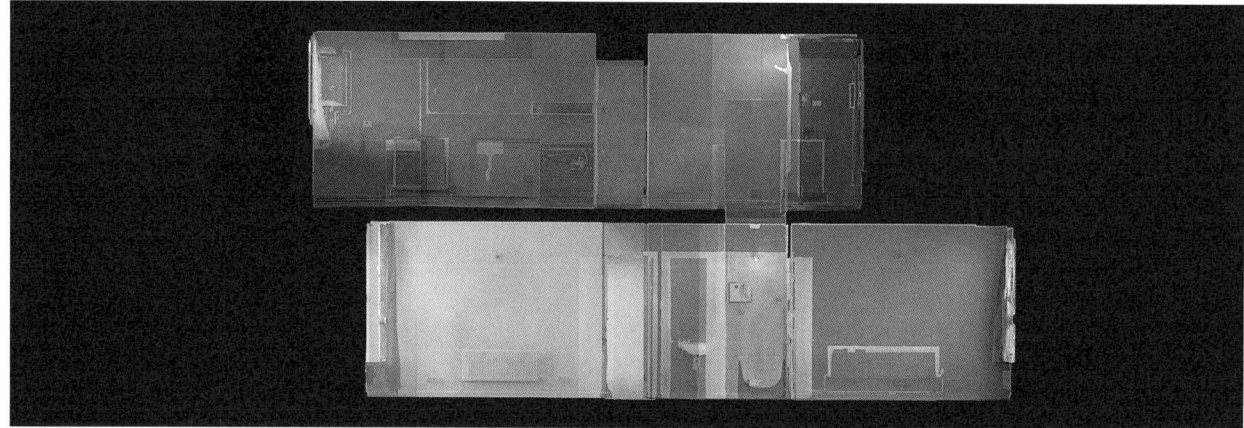

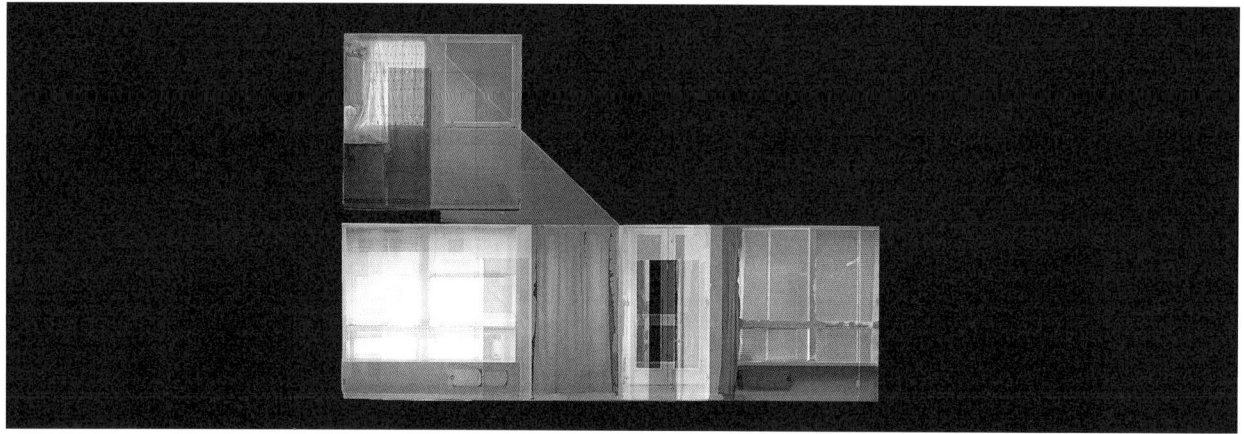

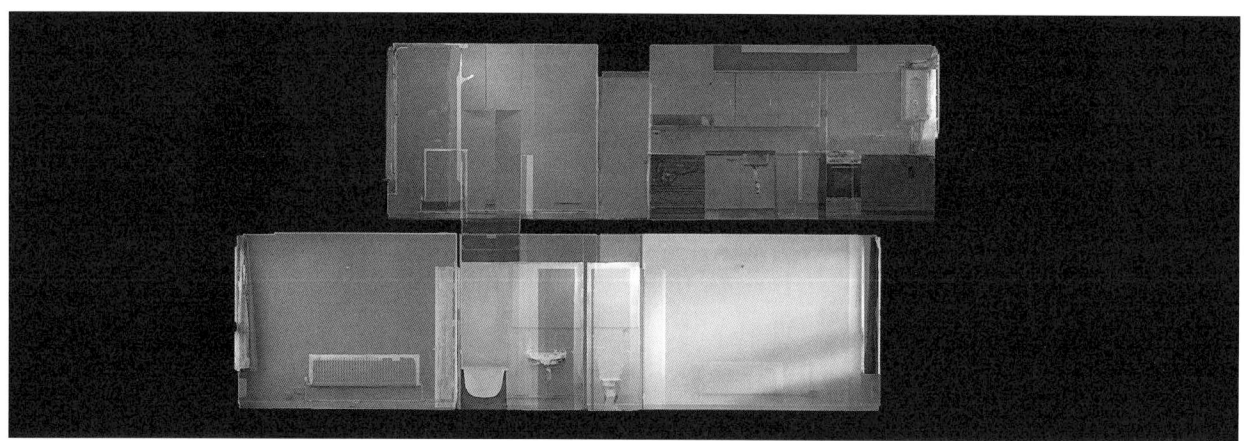

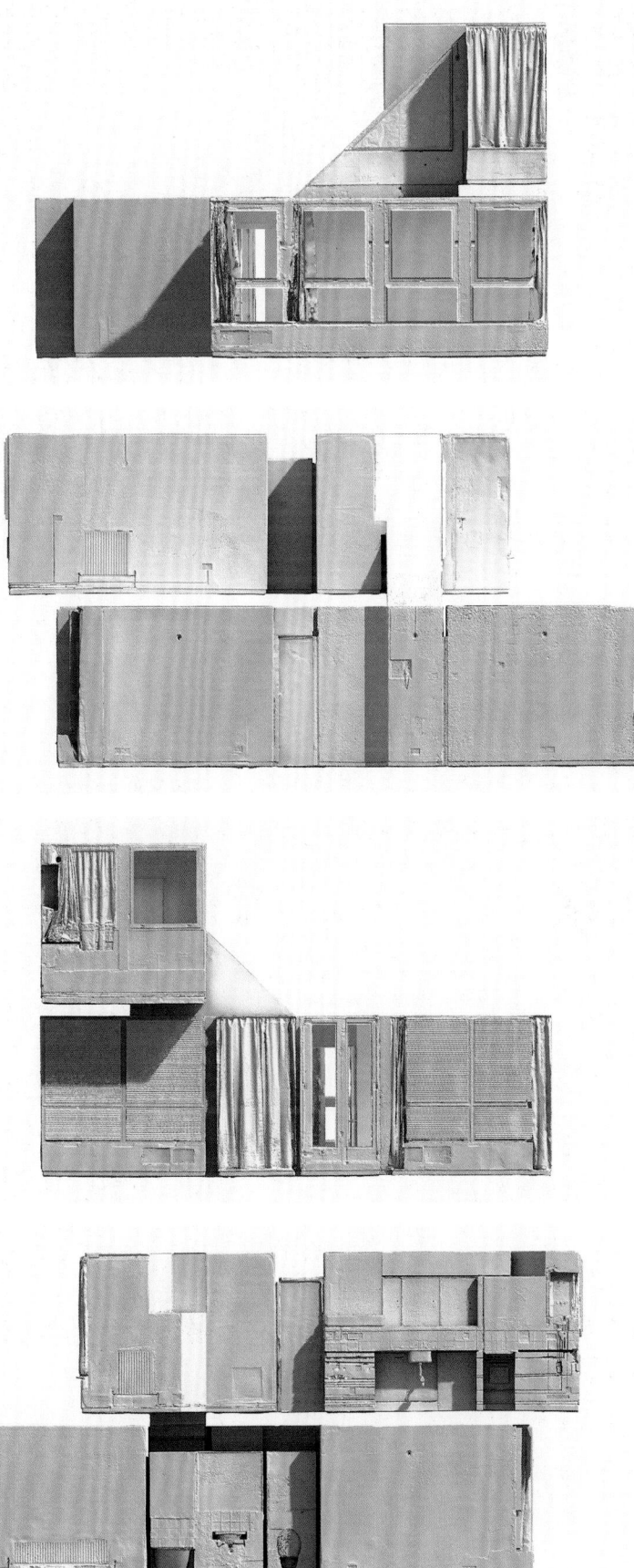

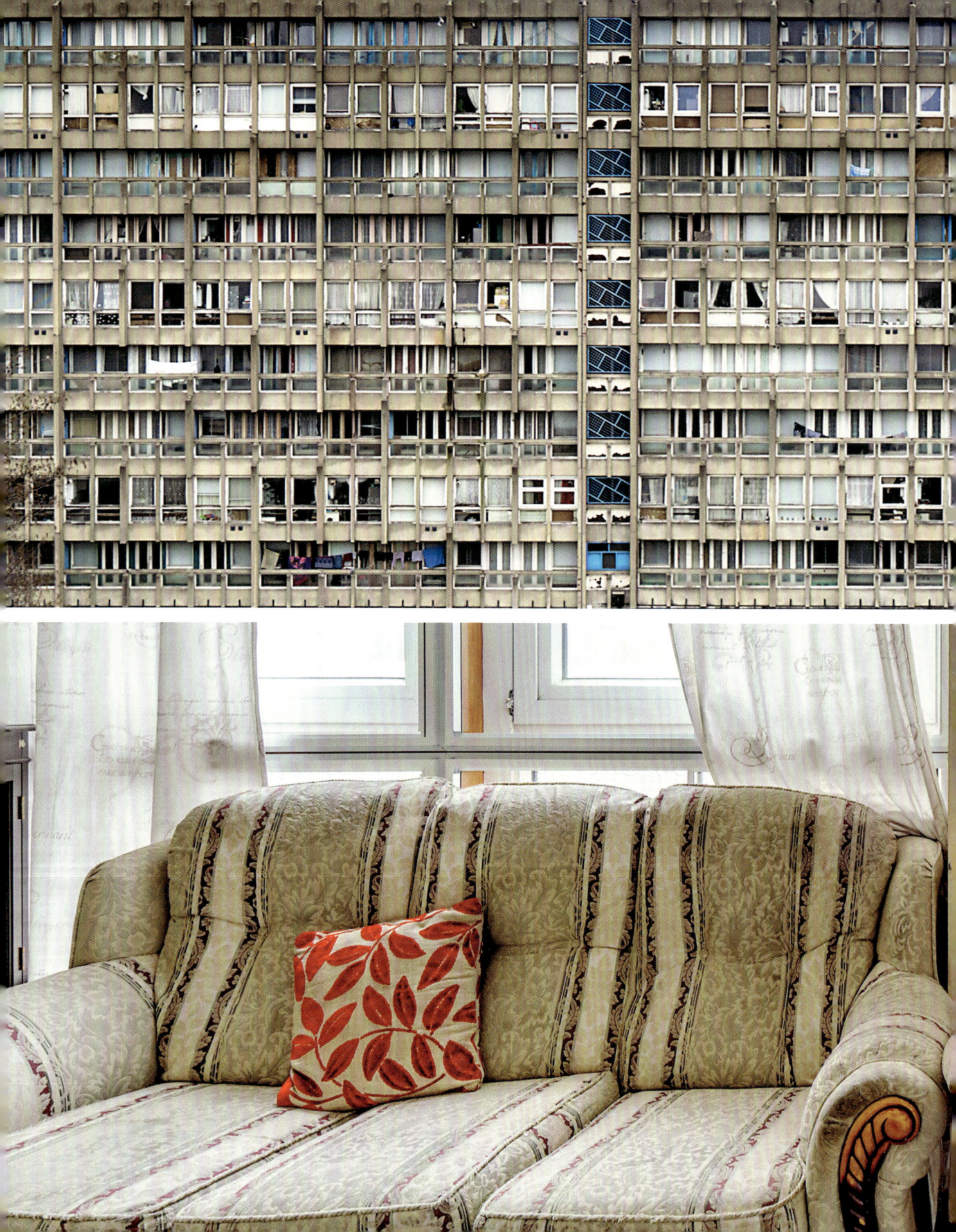

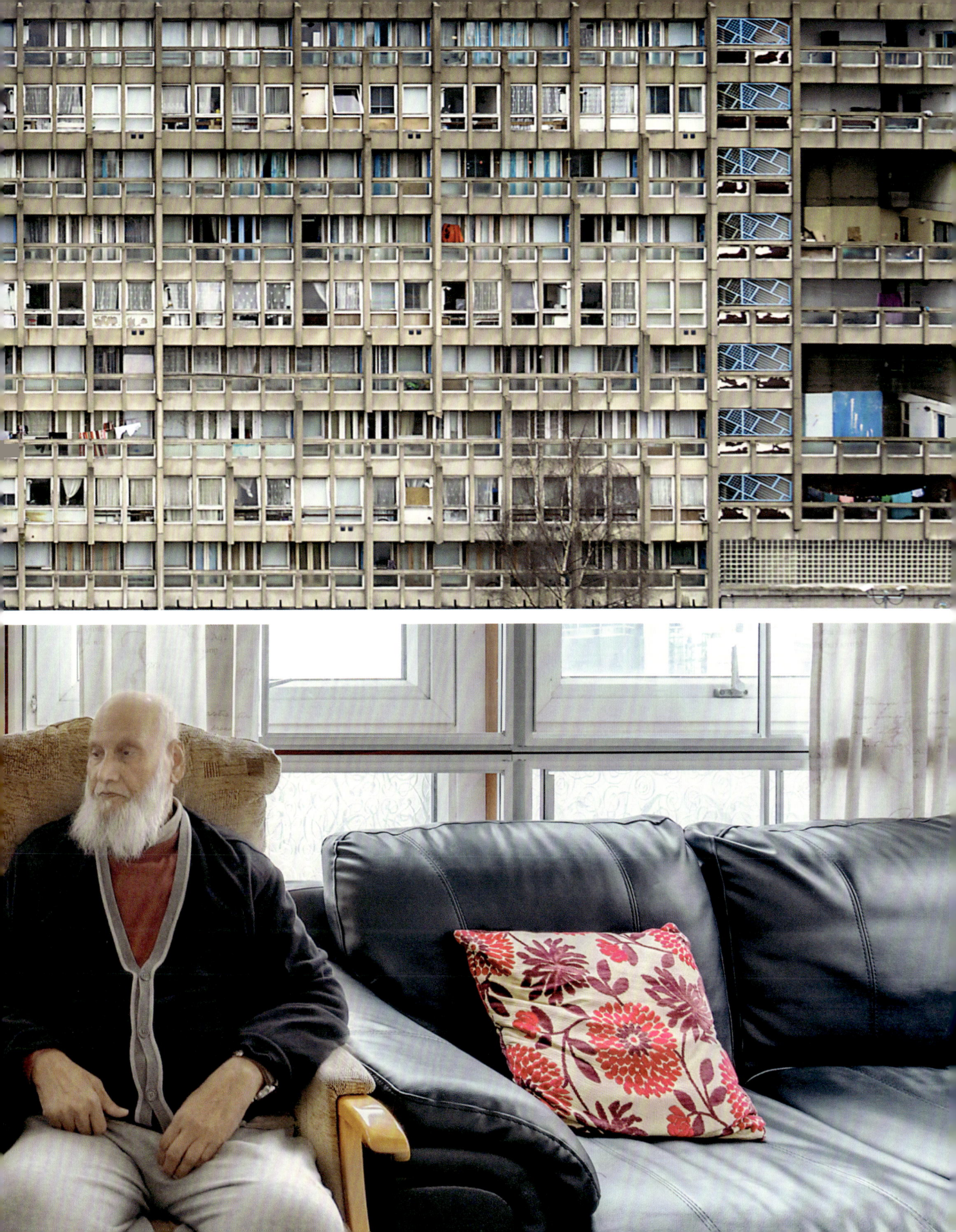

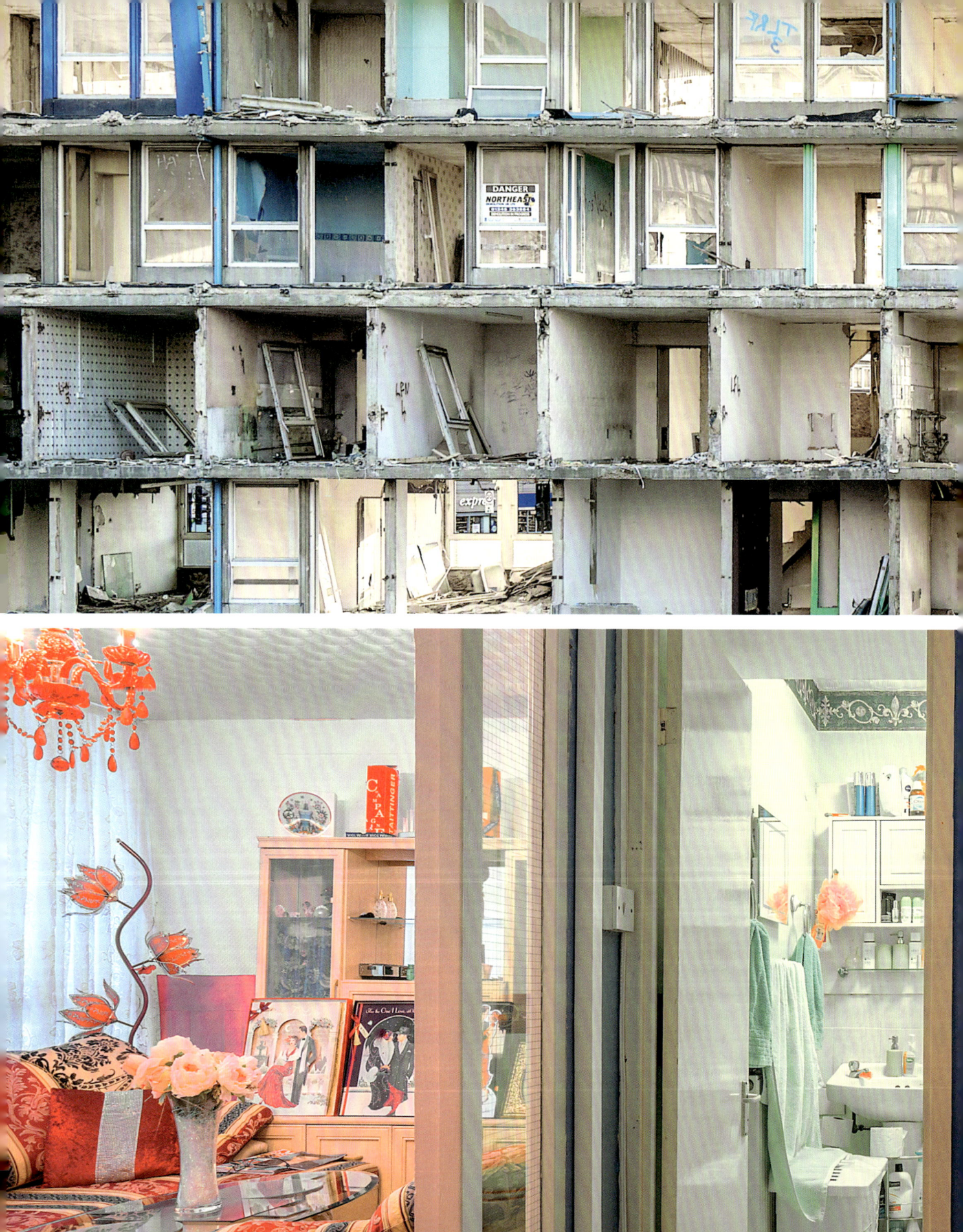

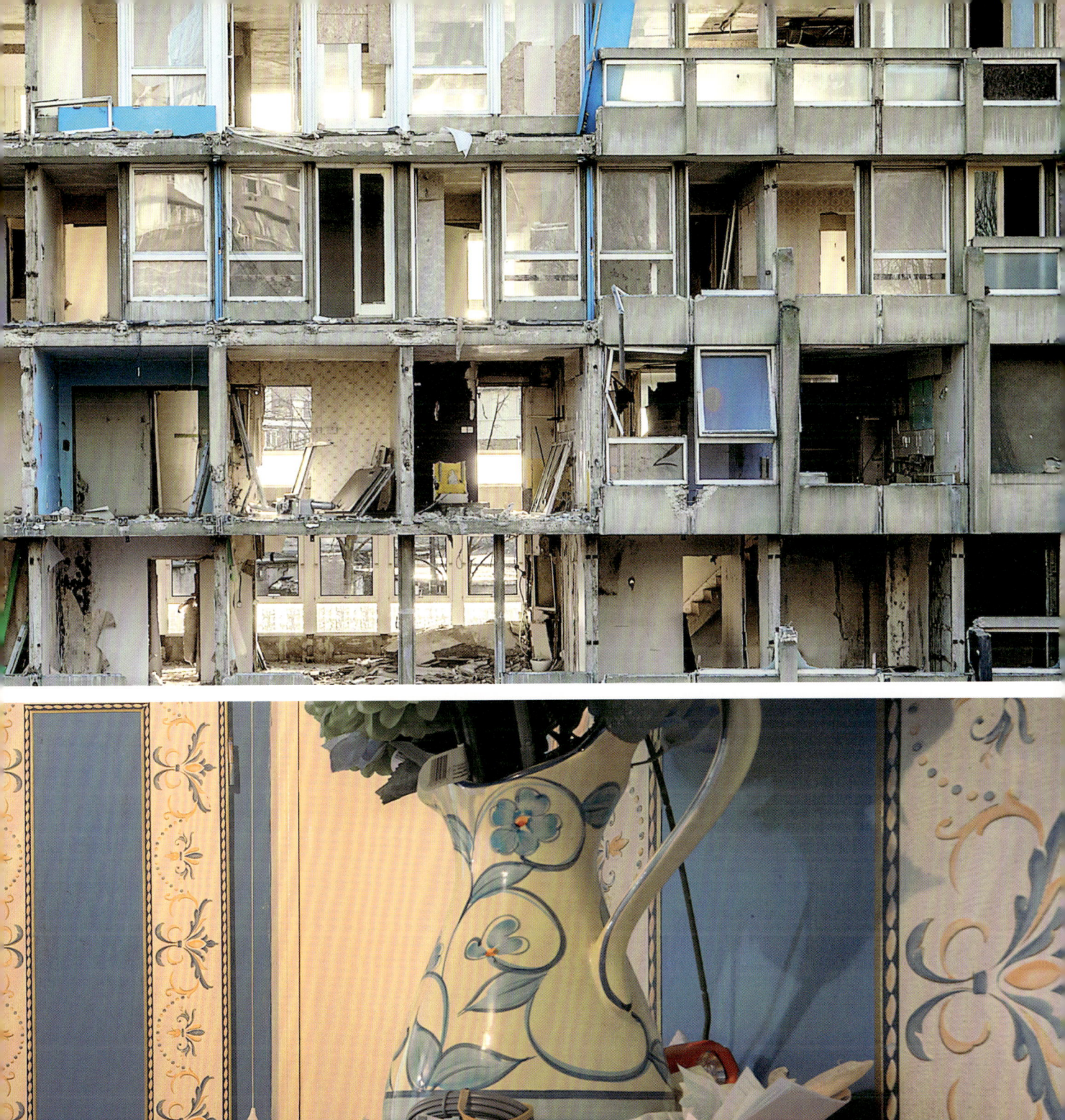

Dong In Apartments builds on Suh's exploration of cycles of urban development and its impact through the moving image that he began with *Robin Hood Gardens, Woolmore Street, London E14 0HG* 2018, and focuses on Daegu, South Korea. Apartment blocks like Dong In were built from the late 1960s onwards to serve a growing need for housing, replacing the single-floor traditional Korean *hanok* buildings such as the one in which Suh grew up. Once towering above the rest of the city, these apartment blocks were overshadowed in subsequent decades by even newer high-rise developments in the ongoing reshaping of the city's architectural fabric. With Dong In (completed in 1969) slated for demolition in the 2020s, Suh's work documents the near-empty block. Unlike in *Robin Hood Gardens*, most of these apartments have already been cleared of furniture and possessions. Instead, the traces of life here are more subtle: a nail that once held up a picture frame, discarded litter, floral wallpaper covering an empty room. While we do not see the eventual demolition of Dong In, its architecture is revealed as porous through Suh's use of flythroughs, in which the camera moves seamlessly between the building's exterior and interior, traversing the boundaries between public and private space, and the shift between a building and a home. (KW)

Dong In Apartments

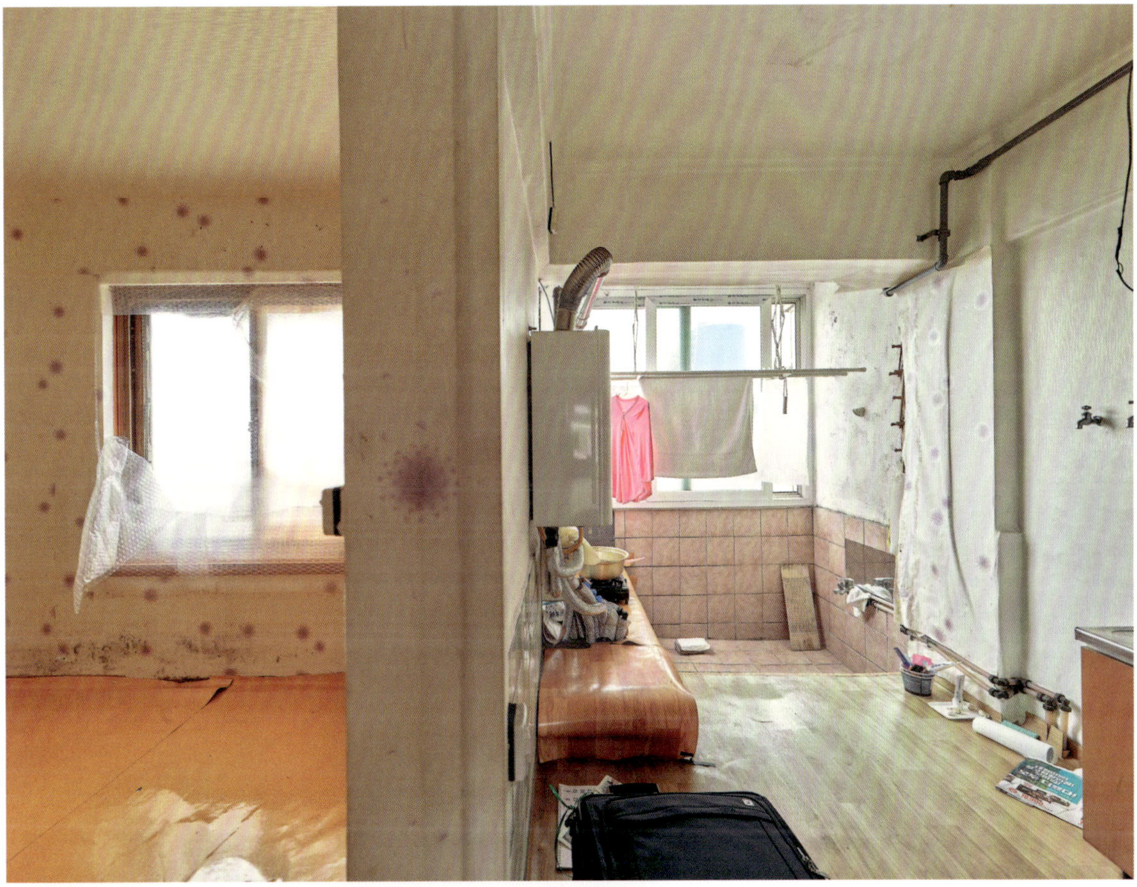

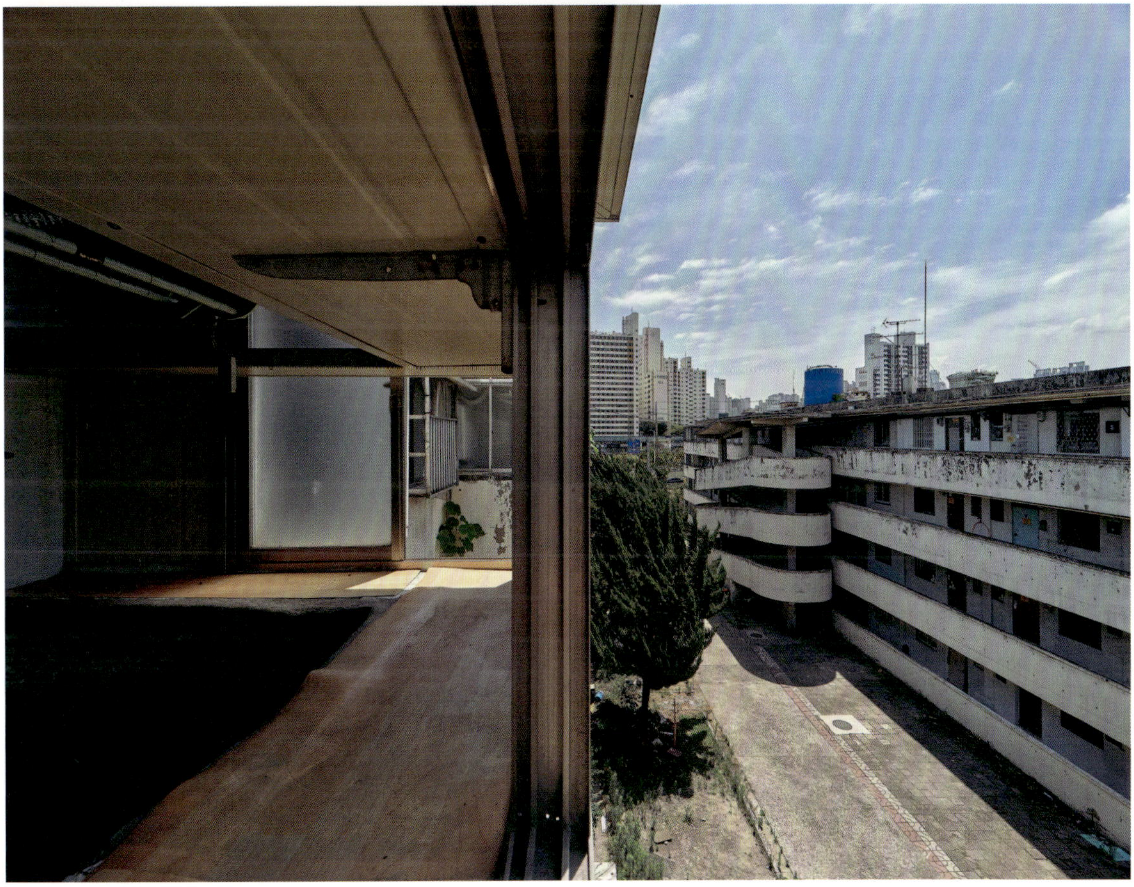

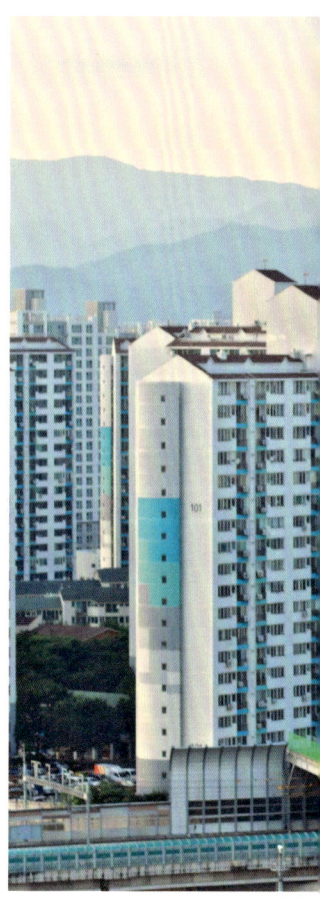

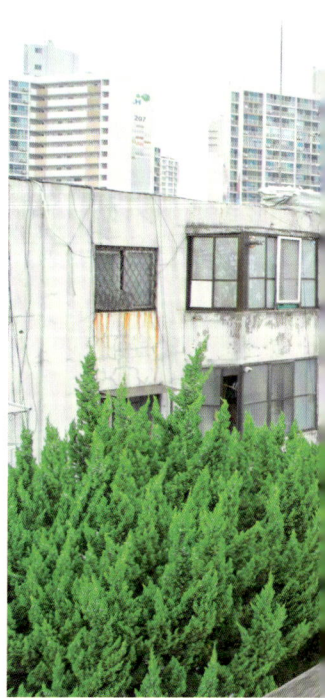

Previous page and opposite: *Dong In Apartments* 2022

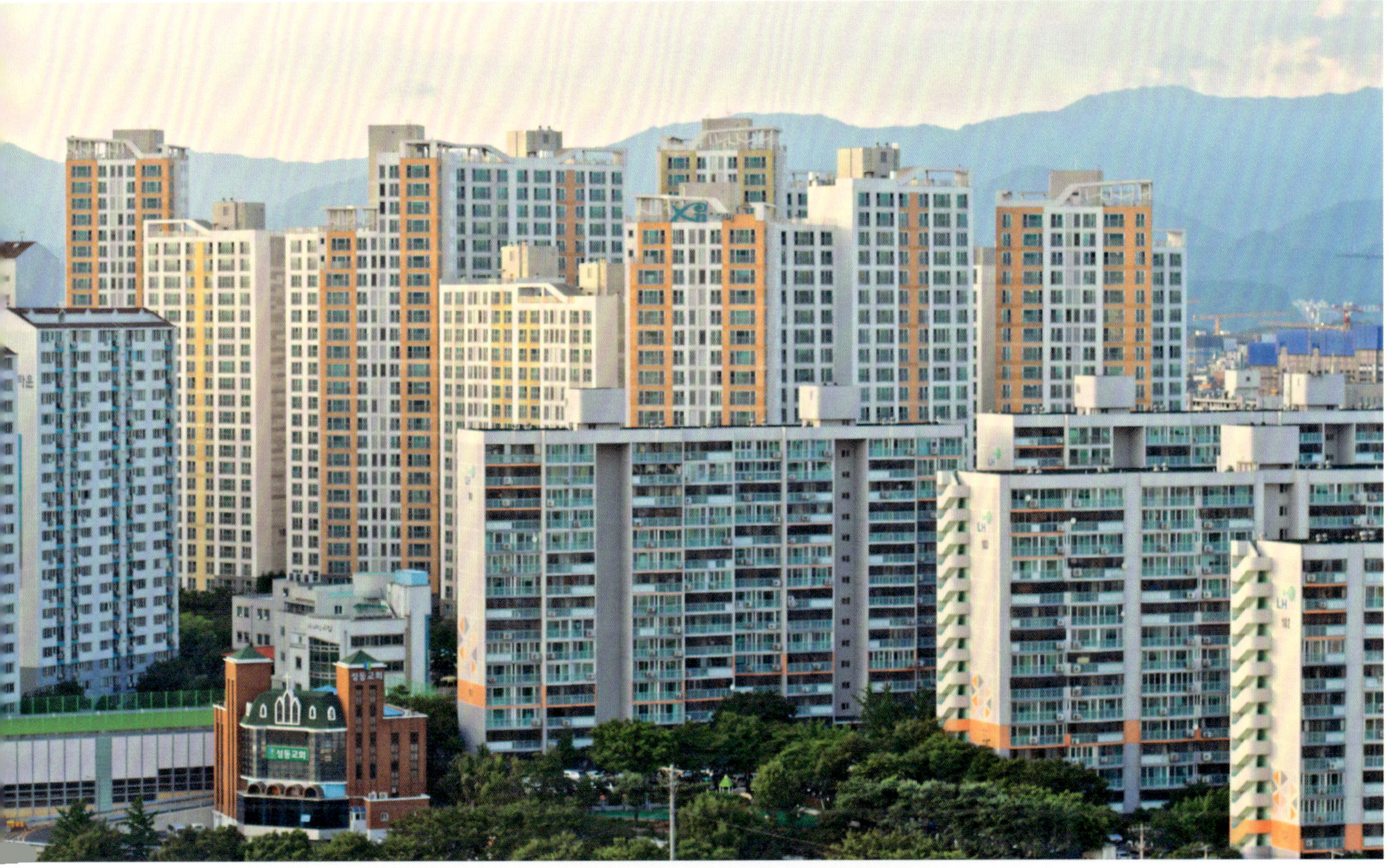
성동교회
성동교회

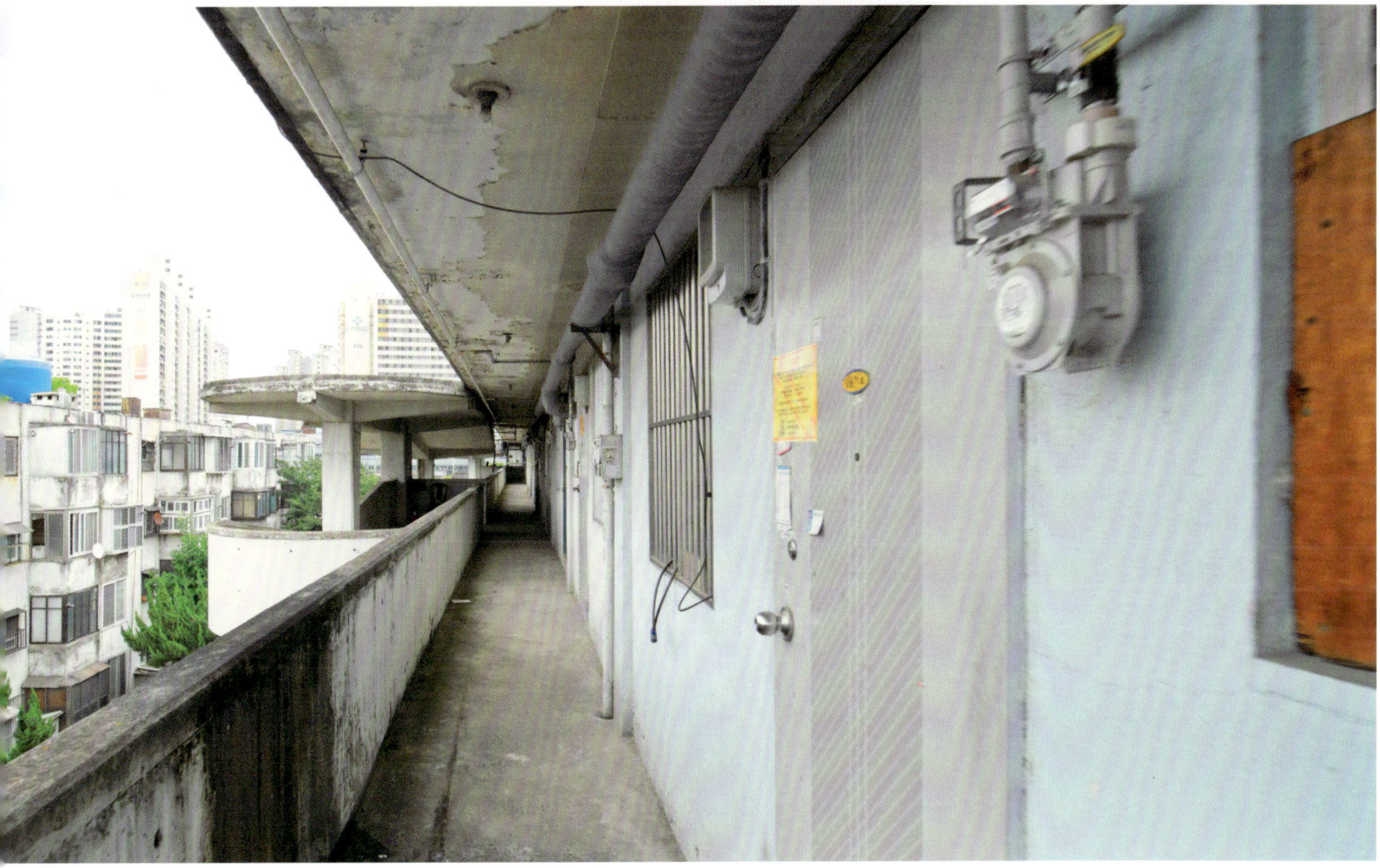

Perfect Home: London, Horsham, New York, Berlin, Providence, Seoul is Suh's most recent fabric architecture work. Its translucent outline takes the form of his present home in London, following his migration to the city in 2016. Inside, the structure is empty of the details of that space, filled instead with the architectural details, fixtures and appliances from past and present spaces Suh and his family have inhabited throughout their lives, folding multiple spaces, times and geographies into one. The walls are filled with objects such as light switches, doorknobs, telephones and plug sockets – seemingly negligible elements of our dwelling spaces which, over time, almost subconsciously, come to furnish our understanding of home. Suh refers to these wall-based objects as 'specimens', and colours them based on their location of origin, creating a cacophony of hues against the ghostly outline of his current home. The position of each specimen is painstakingly established through a digital process of placing rooms within the footprint of the London apartment and 'projecting' the specimens back on the fabric shell, creating horizontal patterns reminiscent of musical scores. Minute differences between the objects and their height variations, which Suh kept faithful to their original positions in those former spaces, give clues to their geographic origins. Suh has likened the disorienting effects of adjusting to these physical variations to the experience of jet lag. (KW)

Perfect Home: London, Horsham, New York, Berlin, Providence, Seoul

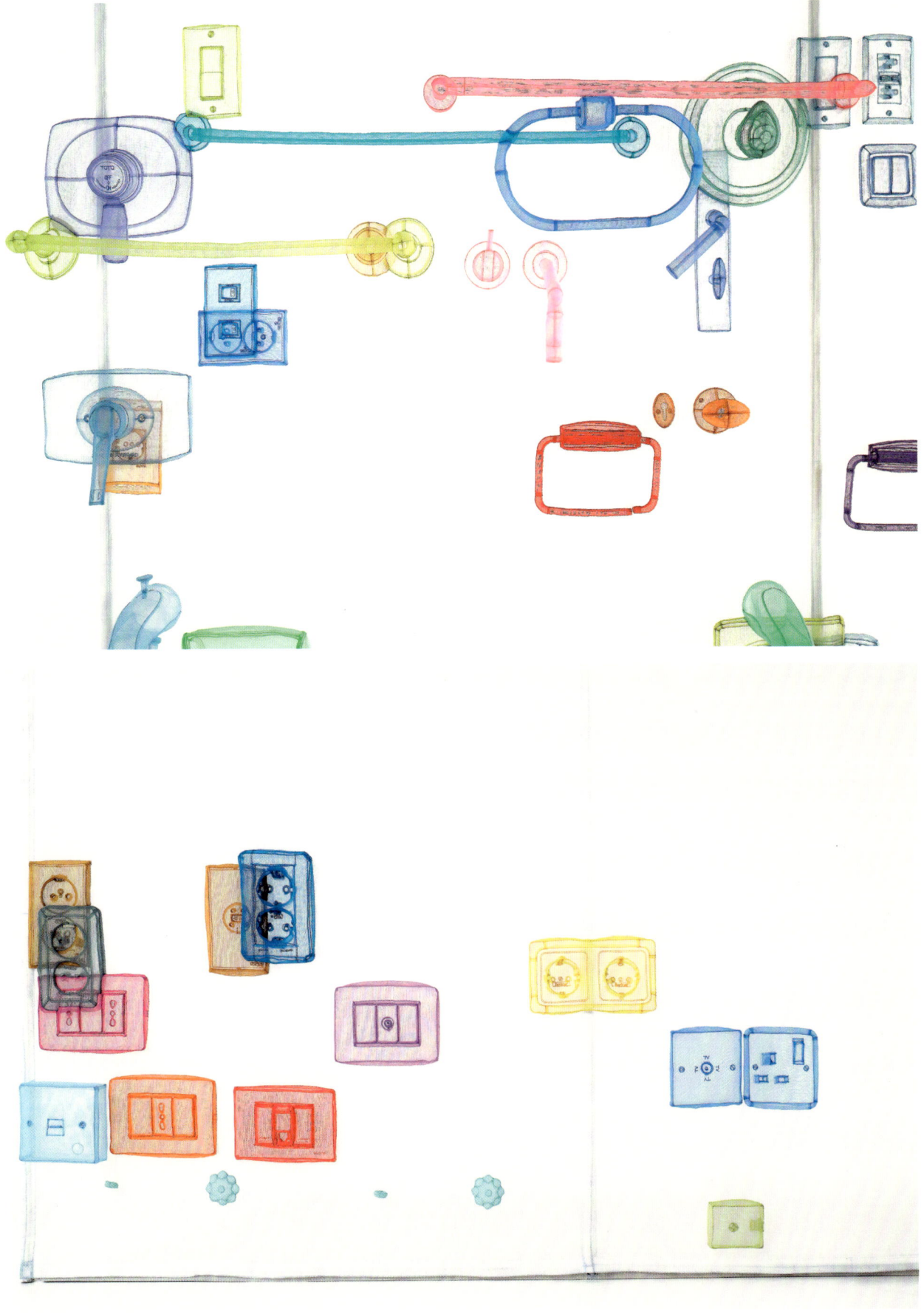

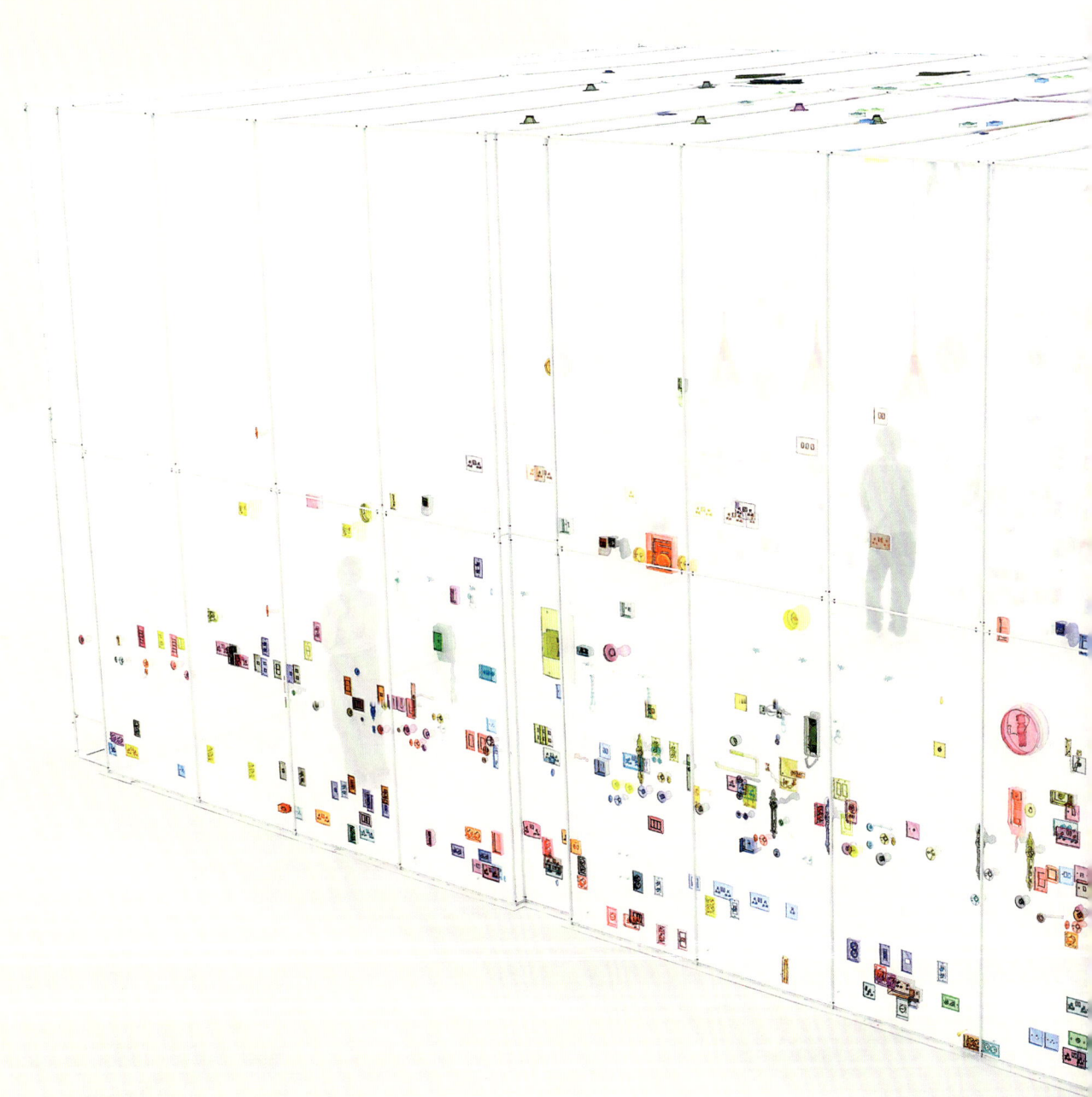

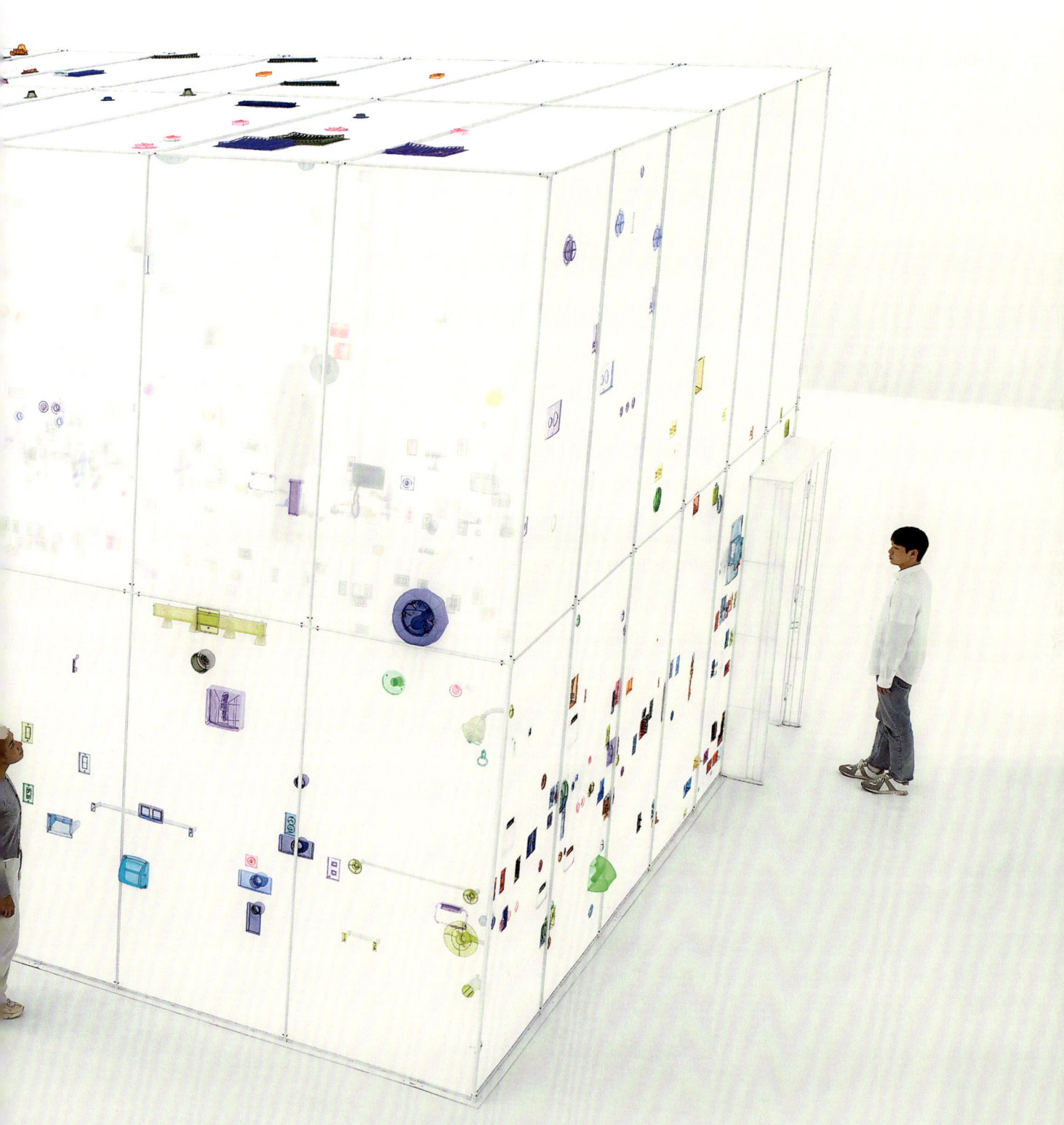

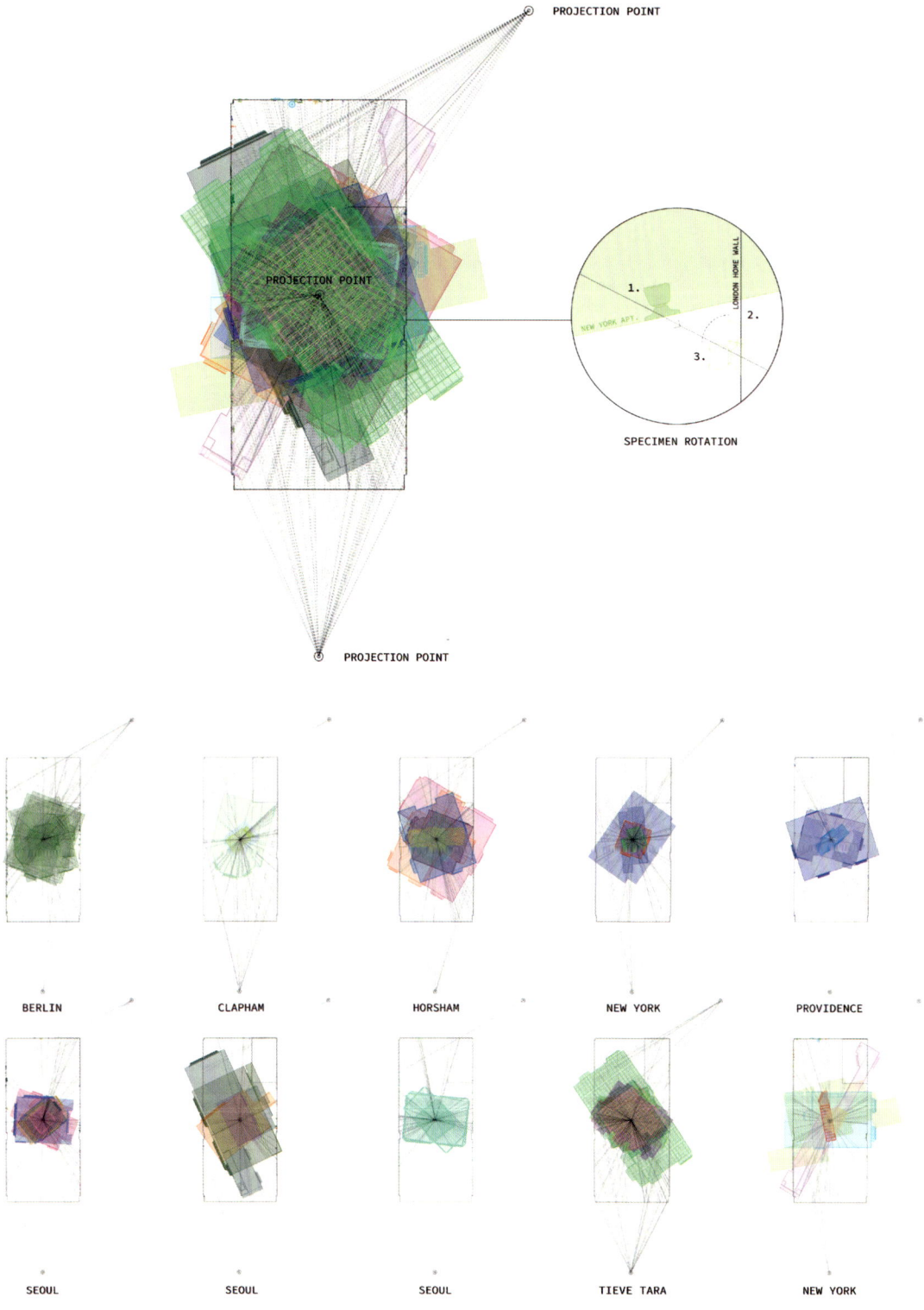

PROJECTION POINT

PROJECTION POINT

SPECIMEN ROTATION

1.
2.
3.

NEW YORK APT.
LONDON HOME WALL

BERLIN

CLAPHAM

HORSHAM

NEW YORK

PROVIDENCE

SEOUL

SEOUL

SEOUL

TIEVE TARA

NEW YORK

Each 'specimen' is modelled from past and present spaces occupied by the artist and his family. The spaces are overlaid onto one another and the objects from each of the walls are 'projected' back out onto the shell of Do Ho's current London apartment using a combination of manual- and computer-generated tools as if following an invisible projection line.

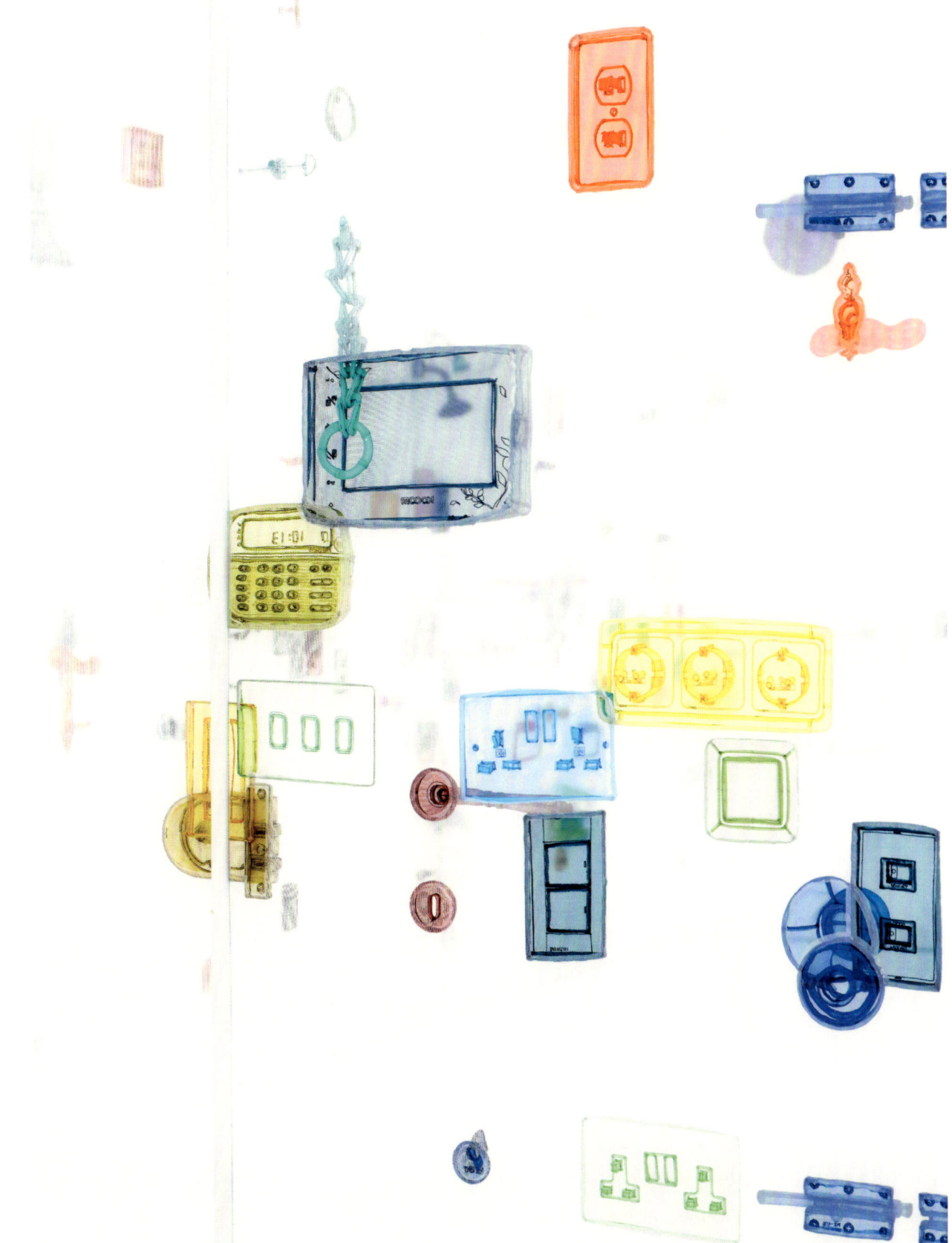

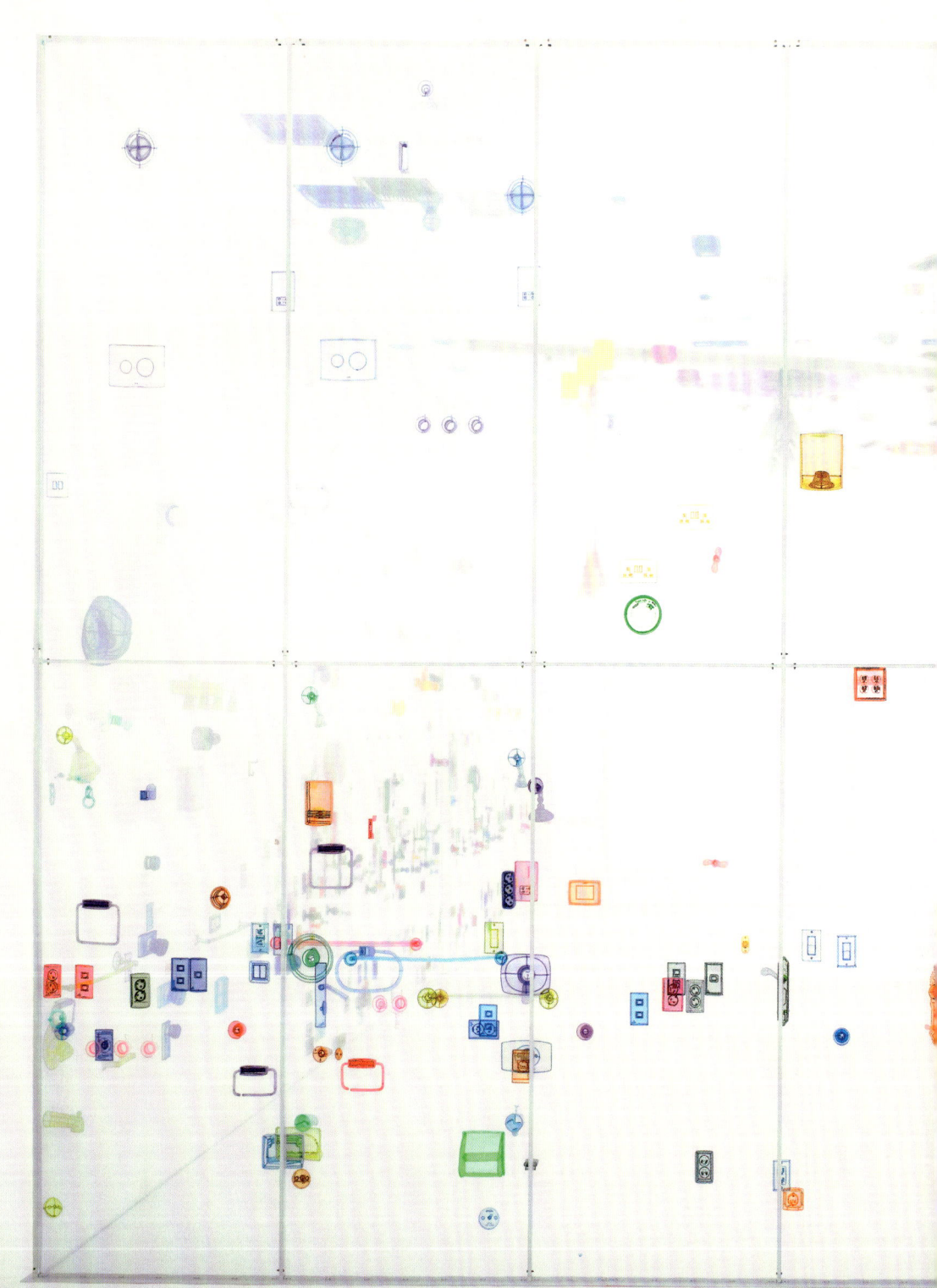

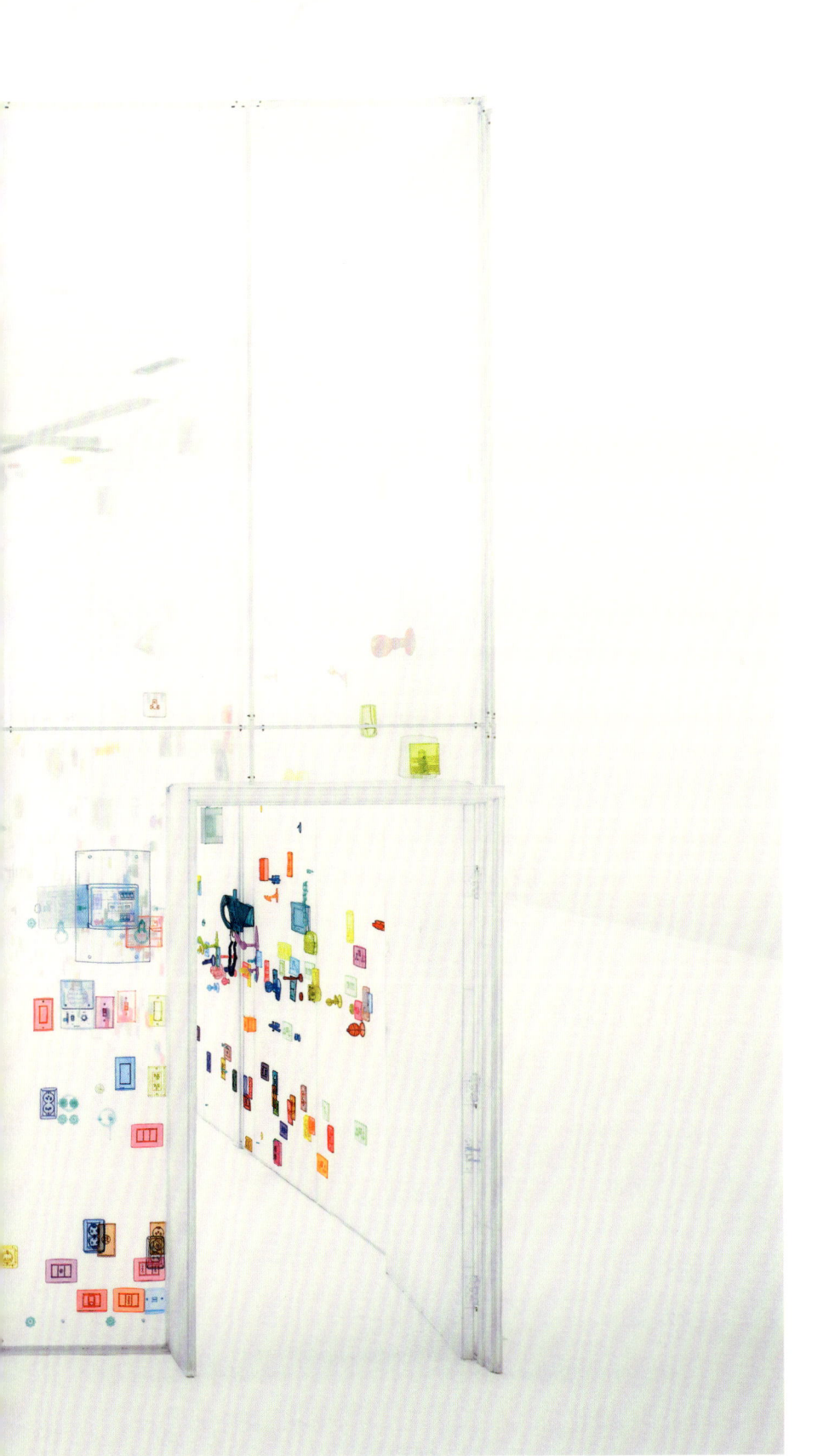

Bridge Project is an ongoing exploration in which Suh imagines his 'perfect home' at the central point of a bridge connecting London, Seoul and New York, while grappling with how this hypothetical gesture intersects with real-world social, political and ecological issues. Measuring the distances between these three important locations in his life, Suh found their midpoint to lie in the Arctic Ocean. The project began as early as 1999, with a work titled *A Perfect Home*, an ink and watercolour drawing of a house on a bridge. Since then, Suh has expanded the disciplinary boundaries of the project, working with specialists from a range of fields including architecture, engineering, industrial design, philosophy, anthropology and biology to reflect on both his personal experience of migration and more generally on the conditions of globalisation in contemporary life. The concept of a bridge which stretches across the globe, traversing countries and bodies of water, with a home at its centre in the Arctic Ocean, has unavoidable geopolitical and environmental implications. These raise for Suh essential questions regarding borders, land rights and the impact of human-made structures on the environment. Whose land would the bridge infringe upon? And what would the environmental impact be? These issues, coupled with the almost absurdist tone of *Bridge Project*, in which Suh imagines living isolated from friends and family in a virtually inaccessible location subject to extreme weather conditions, exposes the impossibility of the 'perfect home'. While the work has various ongoing physical outcomes in the form of videos, drawings and survival suits, at its core it exists in an imaginary space, acting as a provocation, a jumping-off point to think about how to locate home within our imperfect world. (KW)

Pages 165–75: *Bridge Project* 1999–ongoing
Pages 170–1: top left: The town of Utqiagvik at the northernmost point
in Arctic Alaska; top centre: Canada geese over shoreline

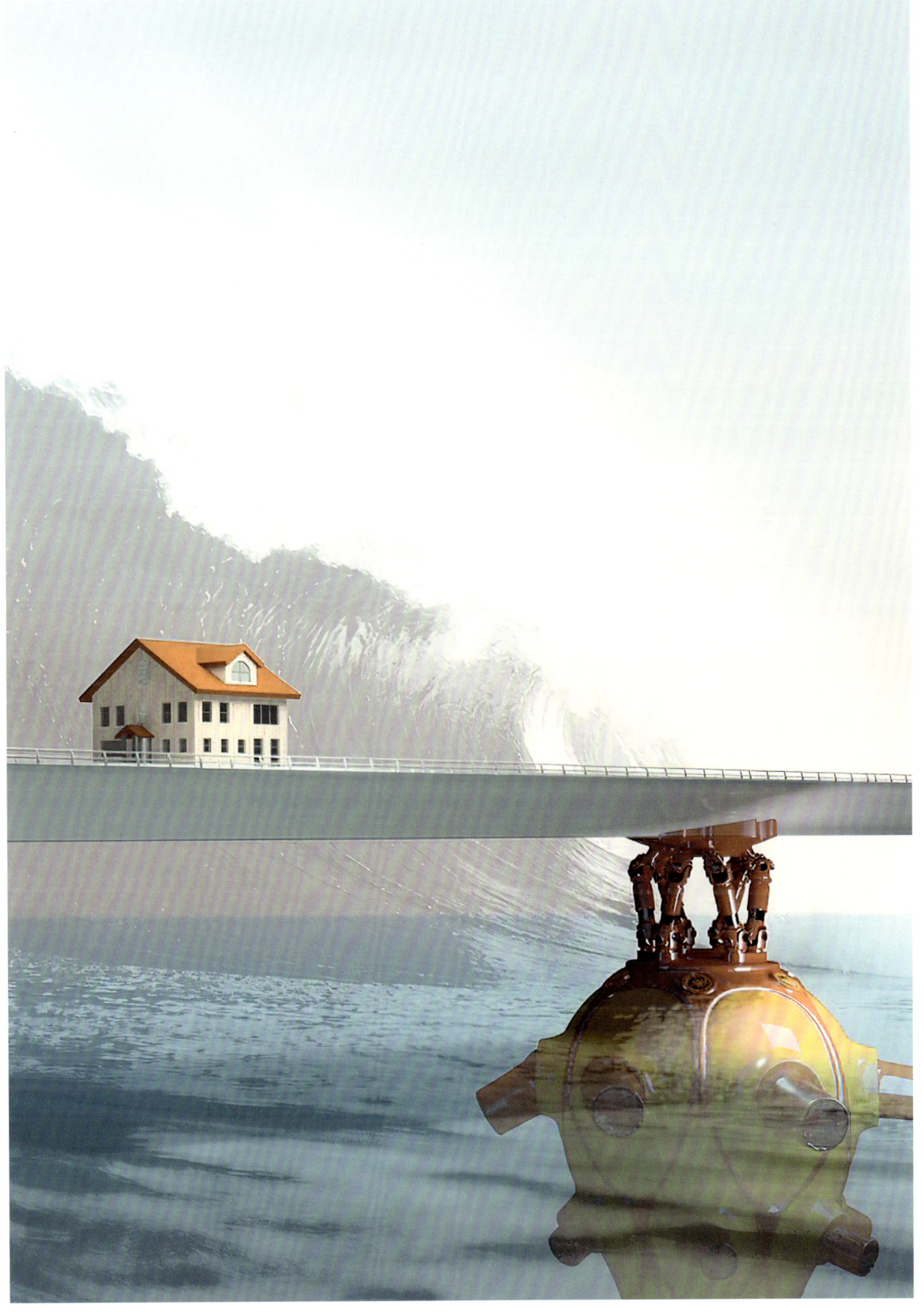

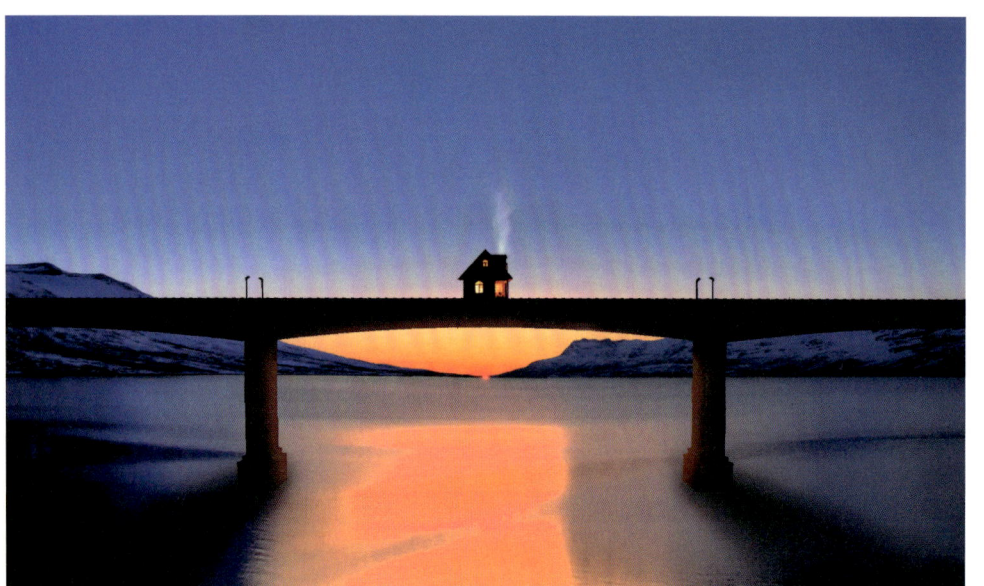

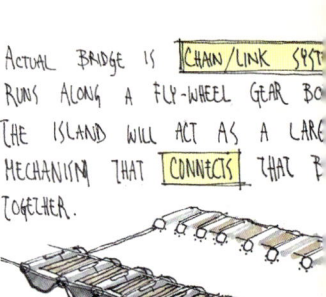

ACTUAL BRIDGE IS **CHAIN/LINK SYST**
RUNS ALONG A FLY-WHEEL GEAR BO
THE ISLAND WILL ACT AS A LARG
MECHANISM THAT **CONNECTS** THAT B
TOGETHER.

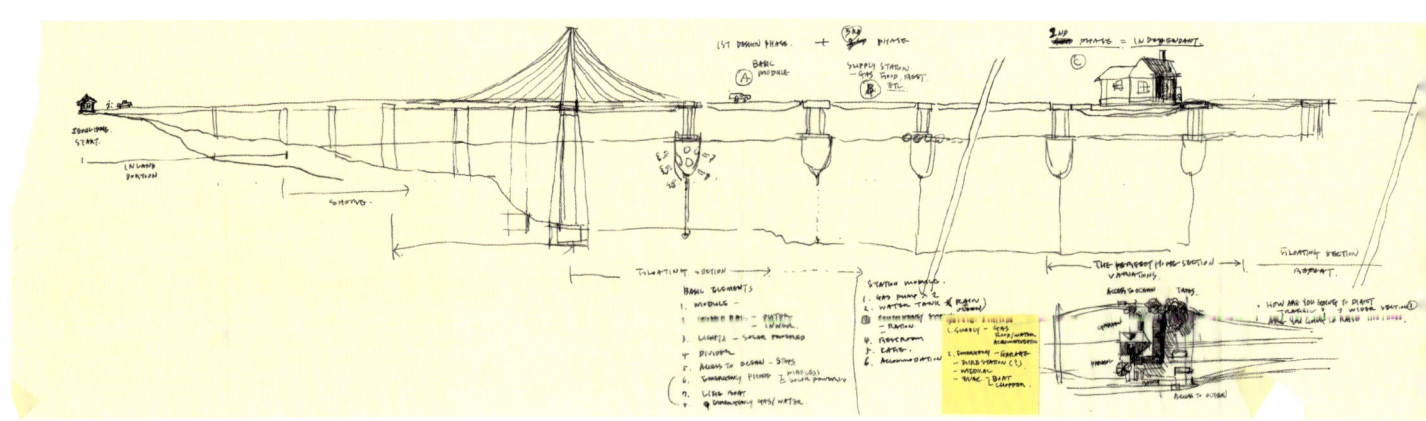

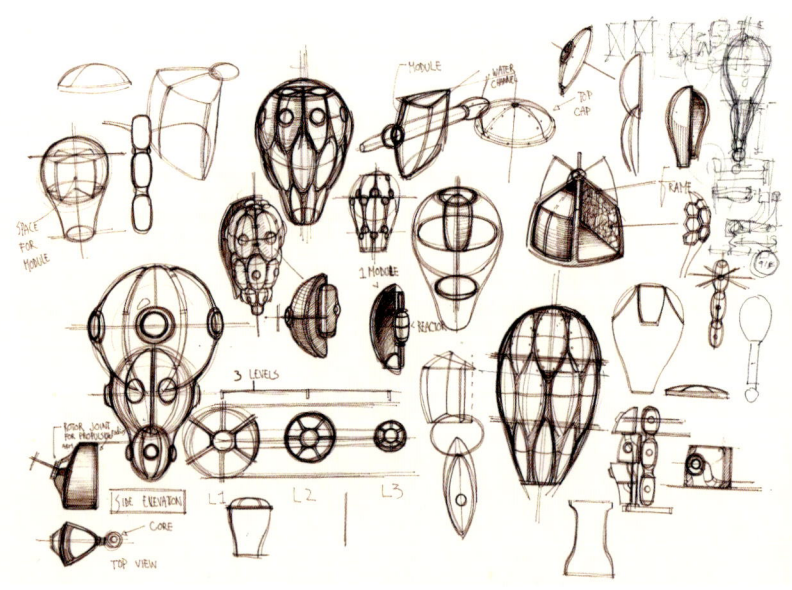

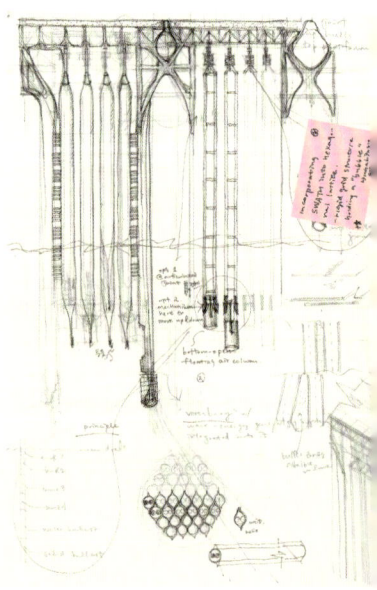

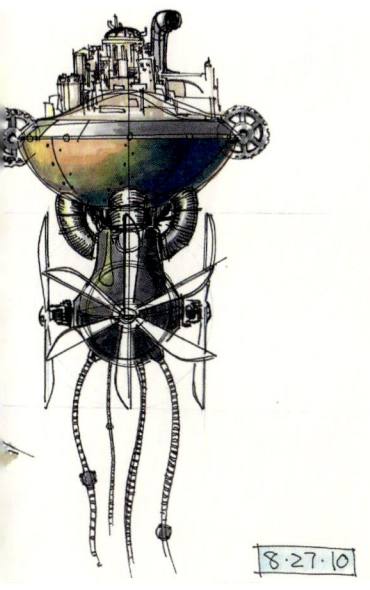

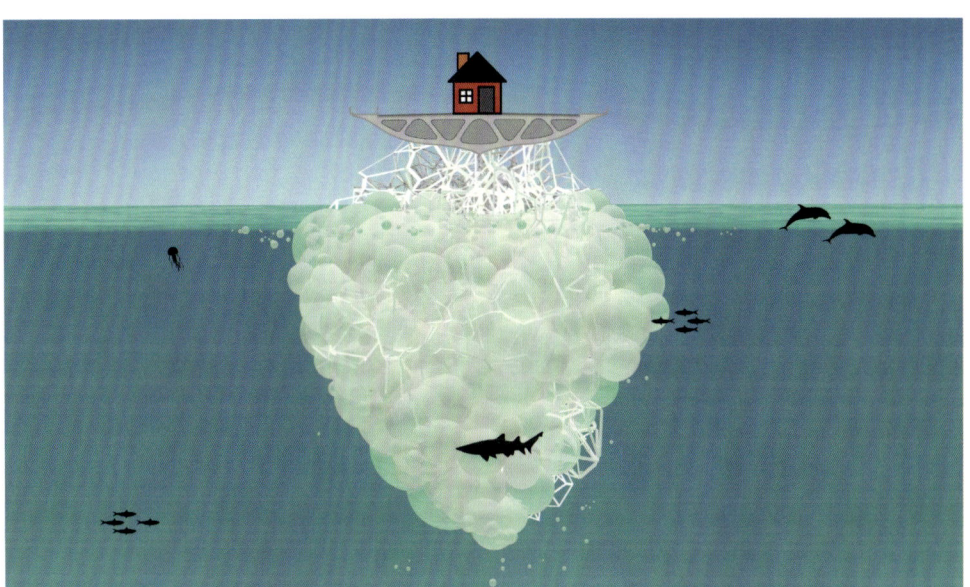

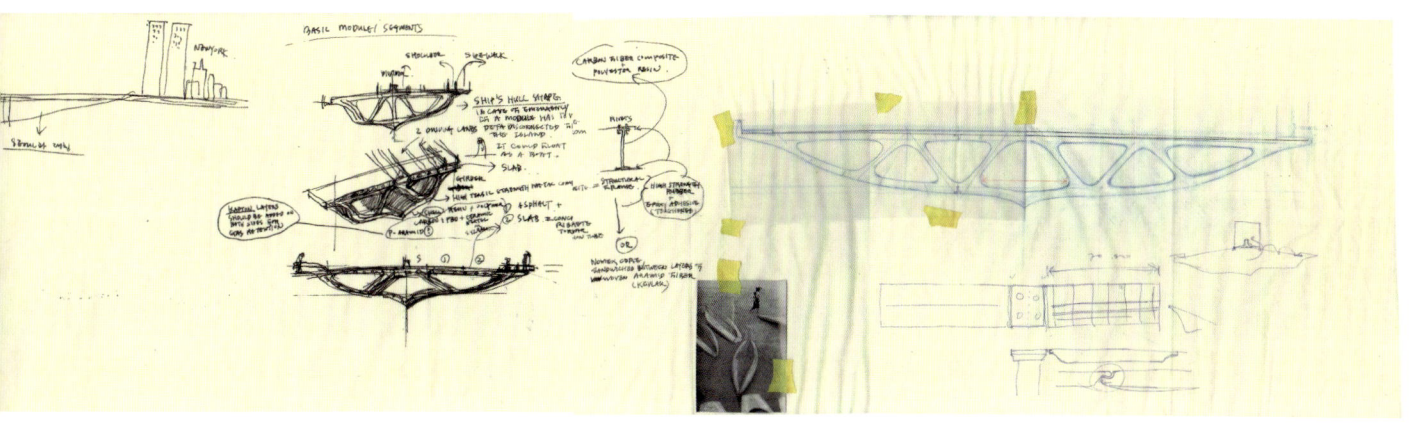

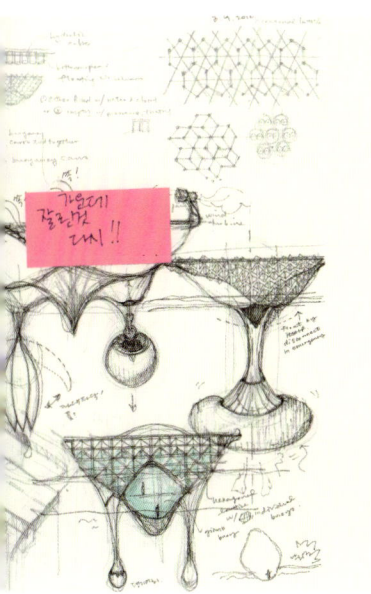

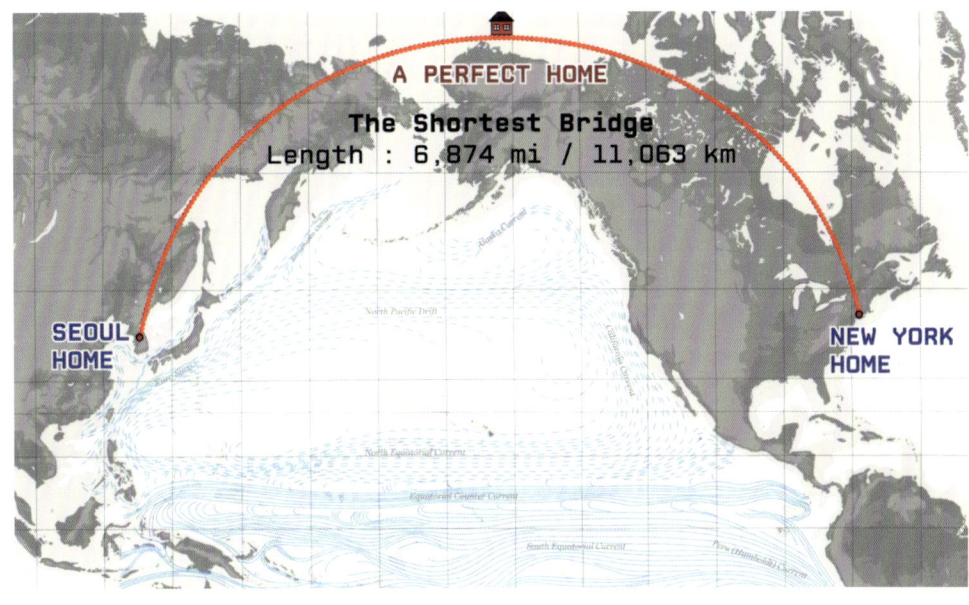

A PERFECT HOME

The Shortest Bridge
Length : 6,874 mi / 11,063 km

SEOUL
HOME

NEW YORK
HOME

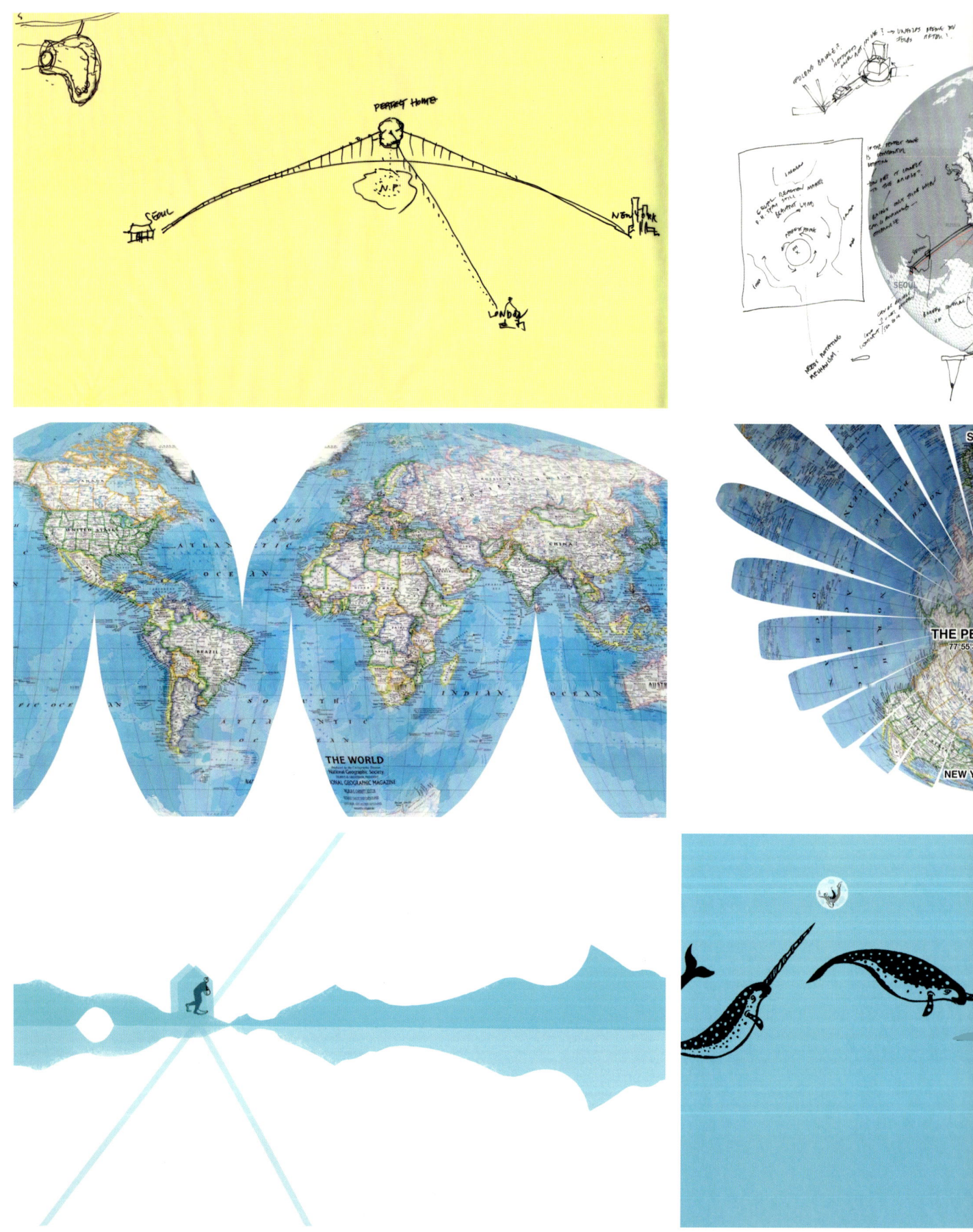

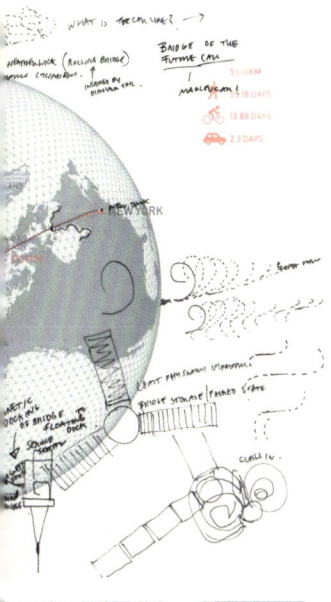

WHAT OR WHERE IS A 'PERFECT HOME'?

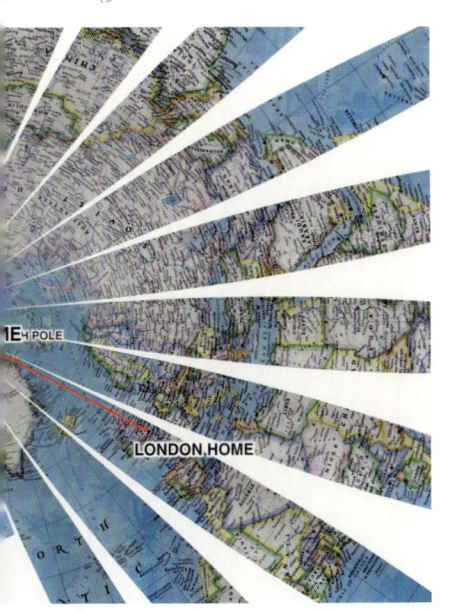

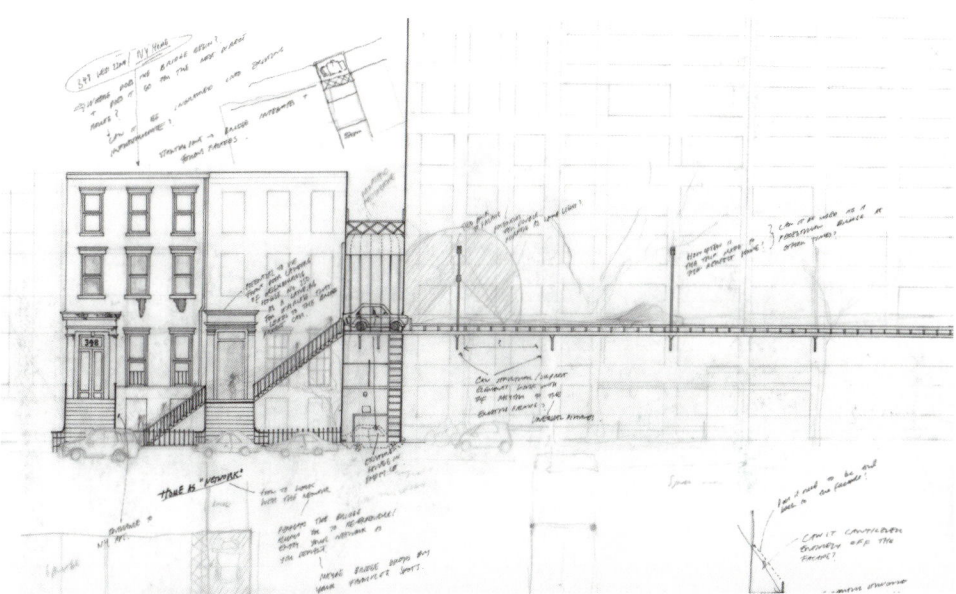

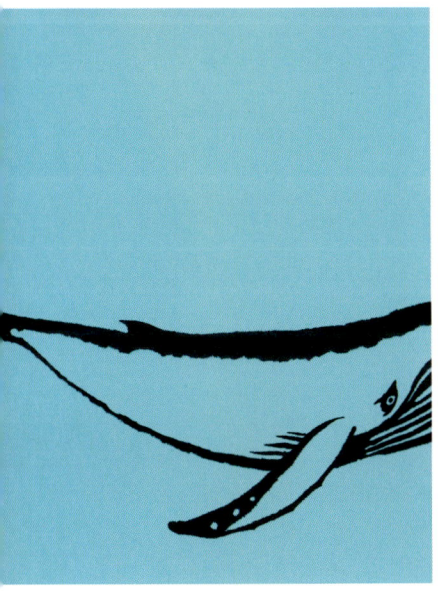

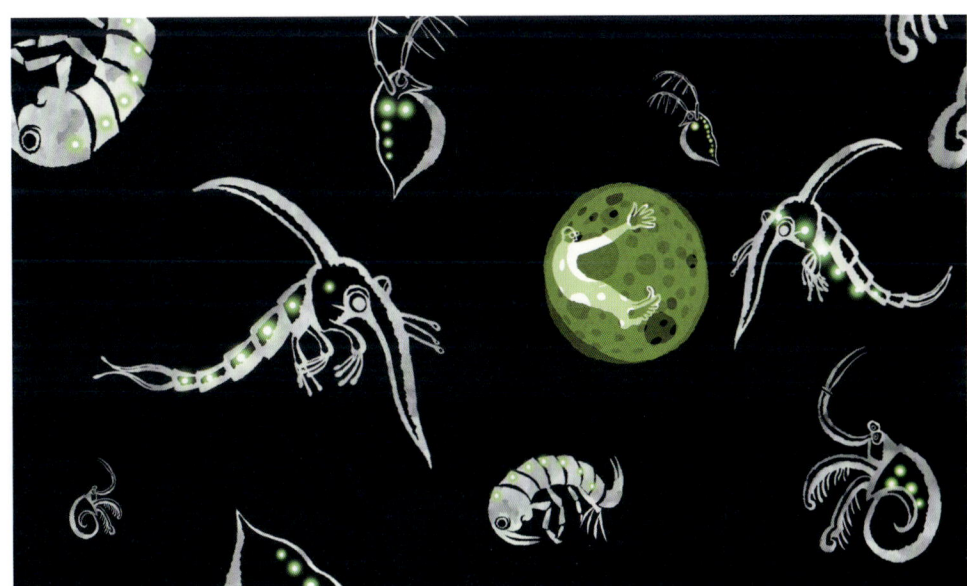

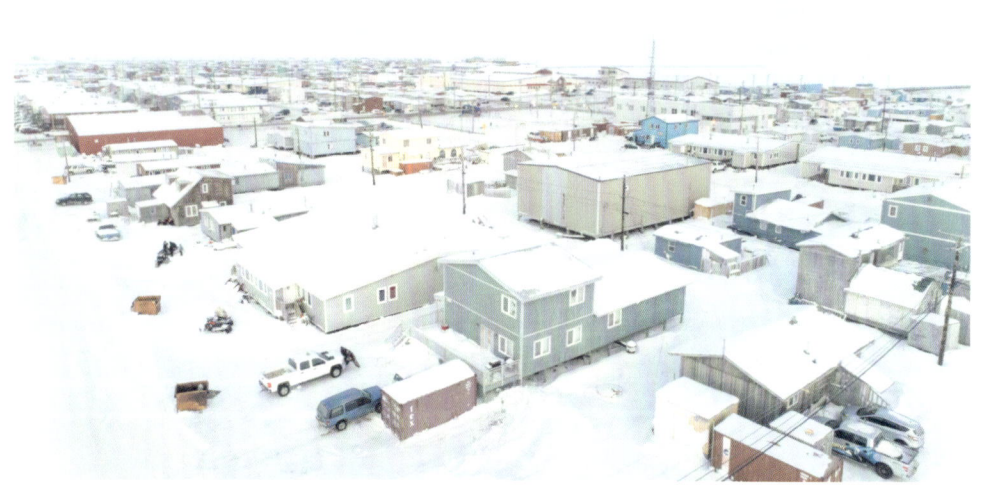
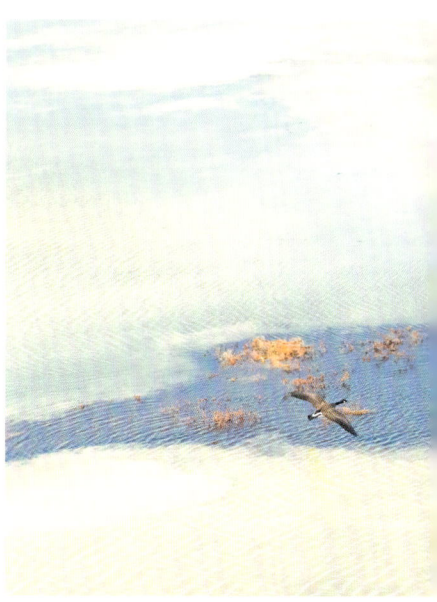
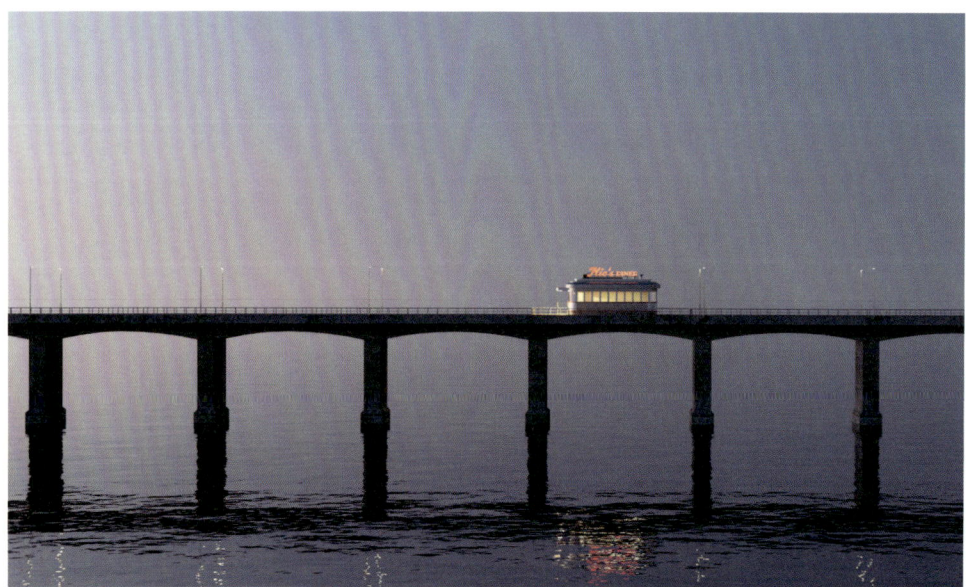
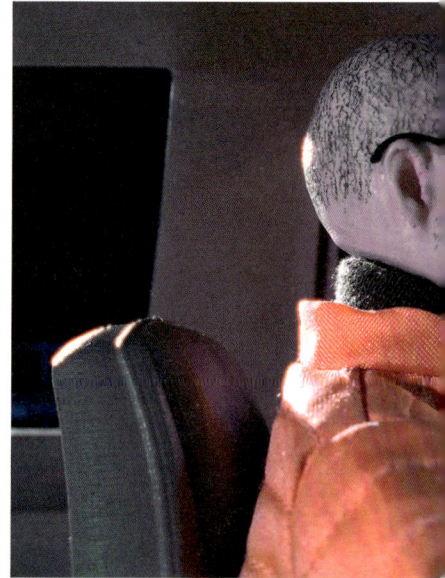
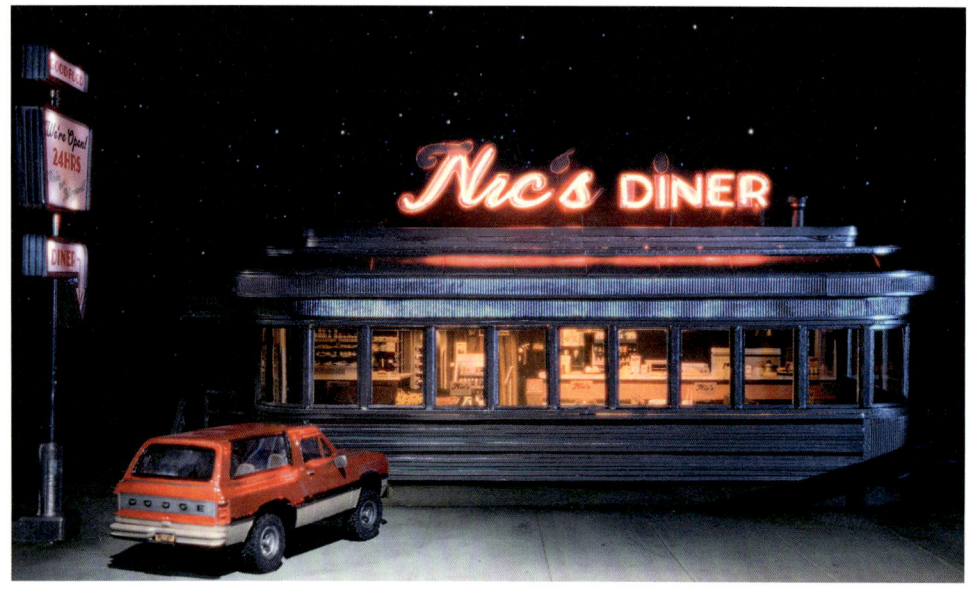
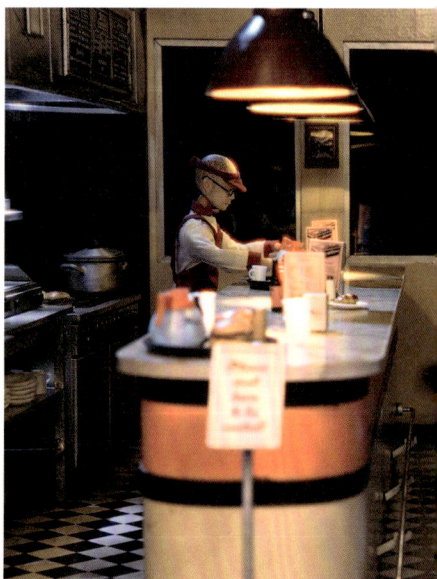

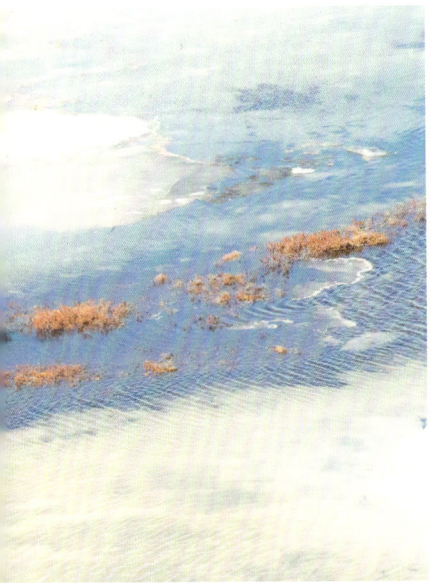
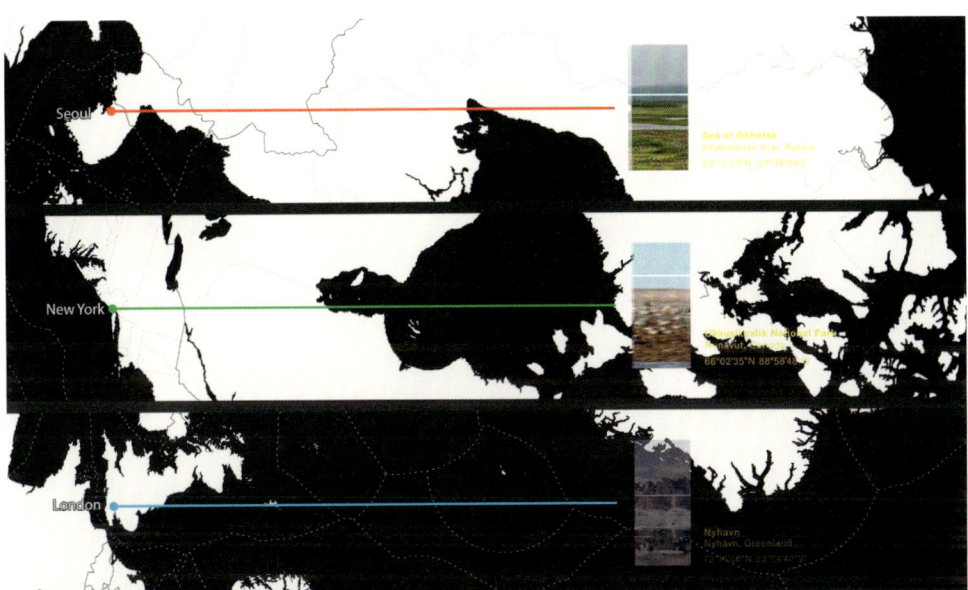
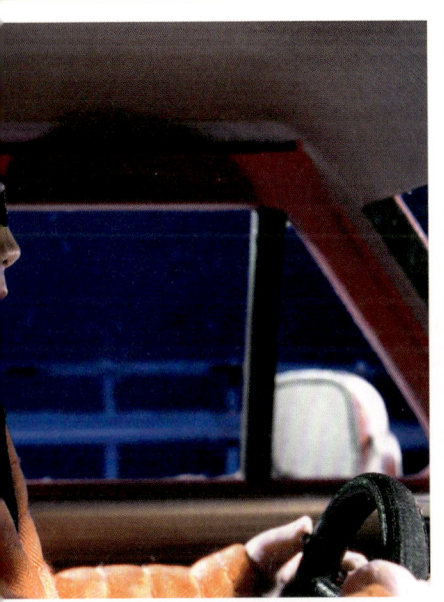
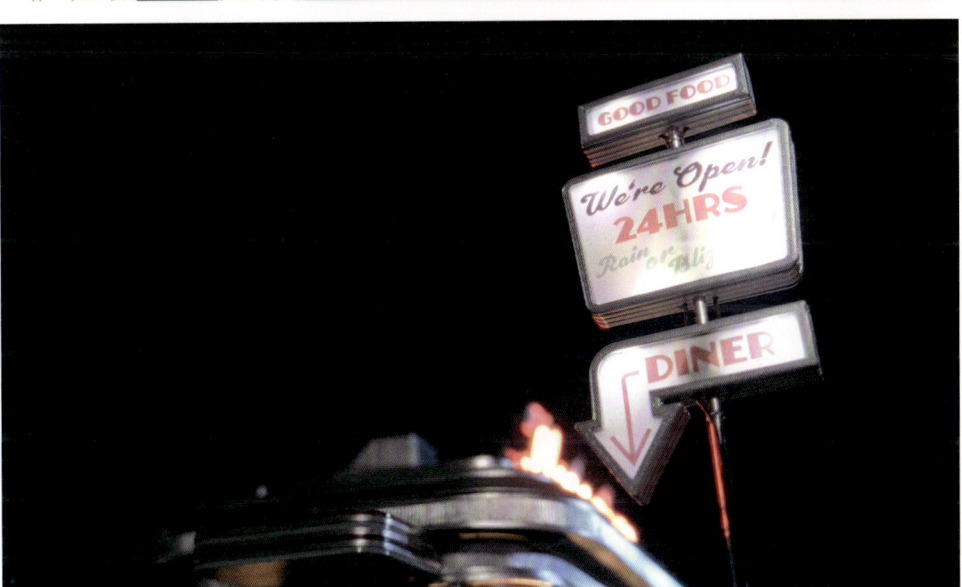
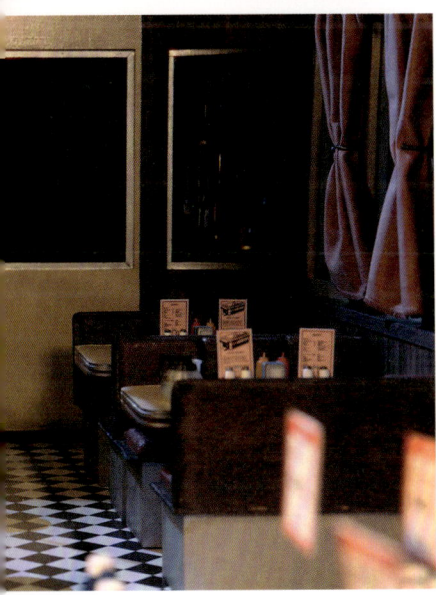
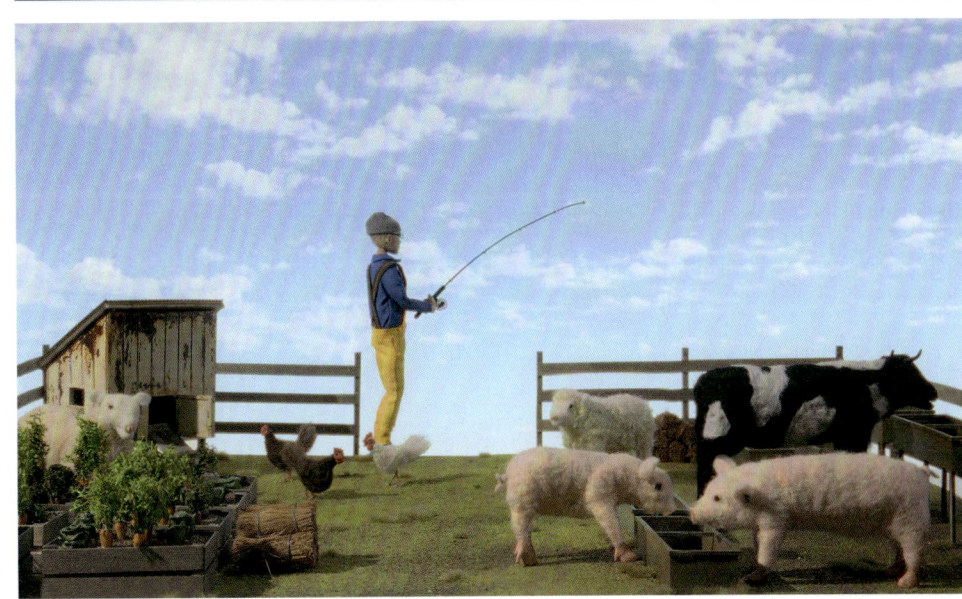

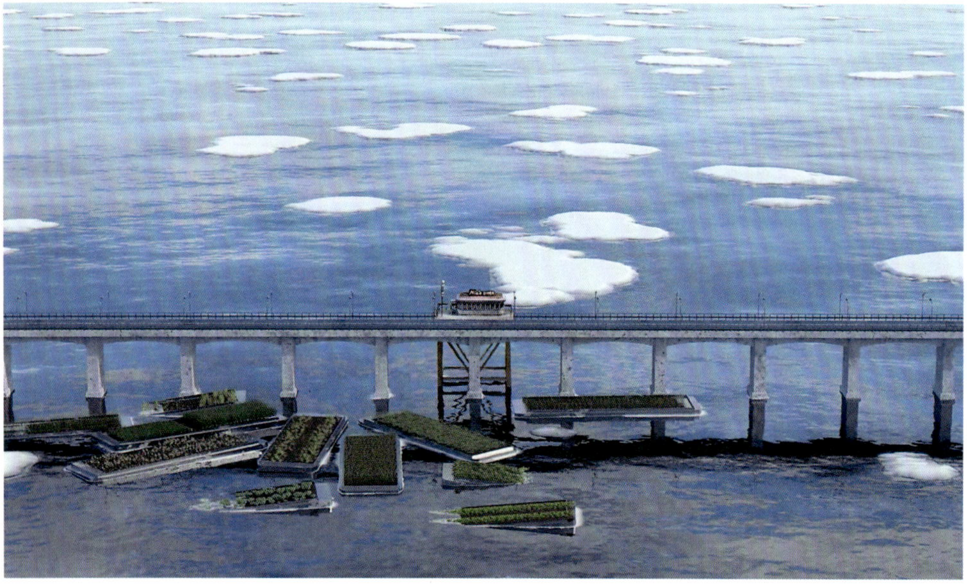

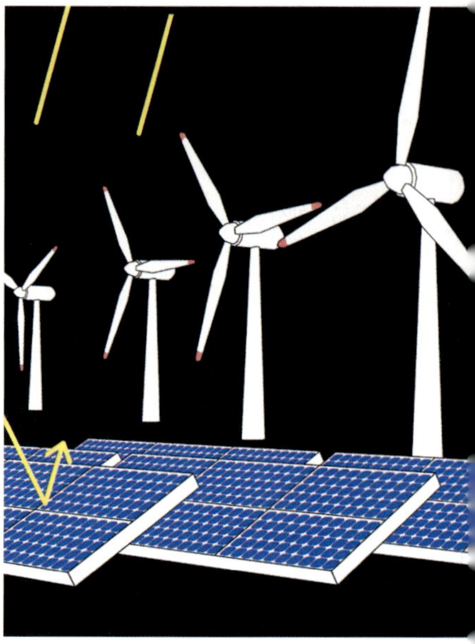

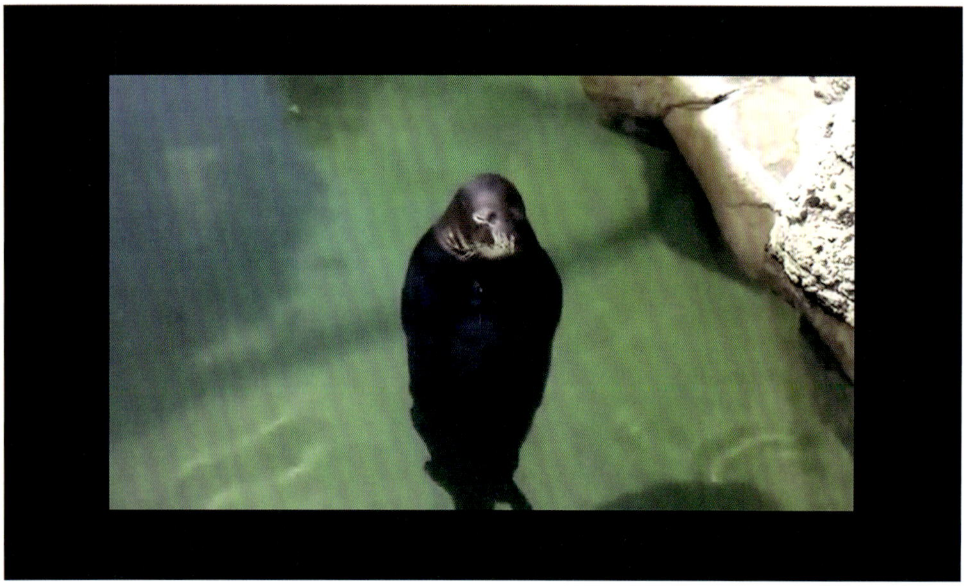

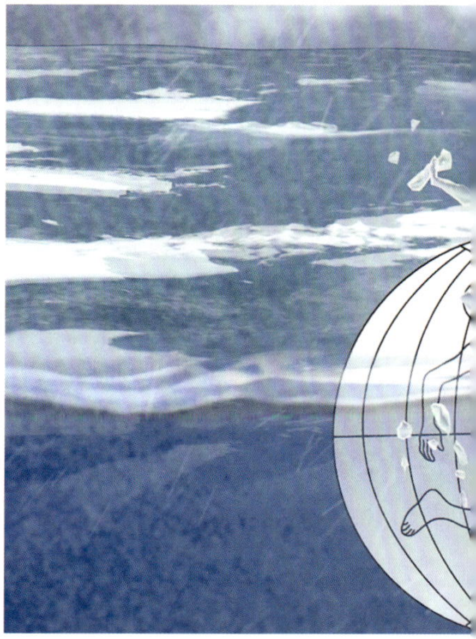

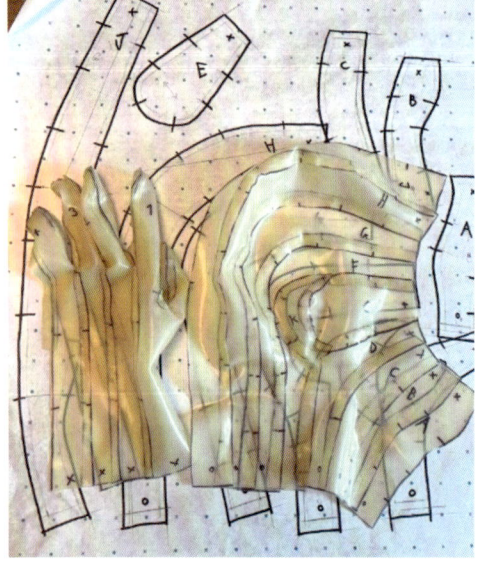

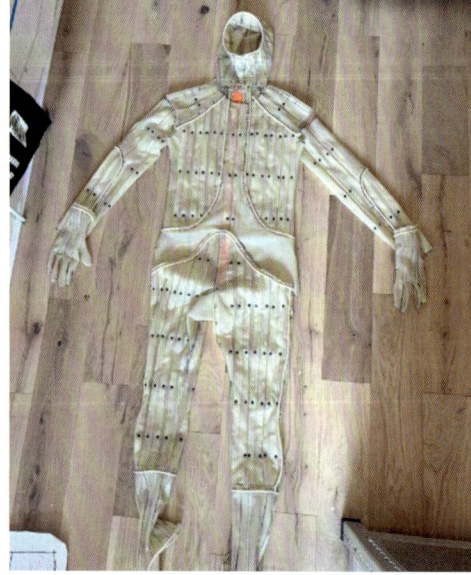

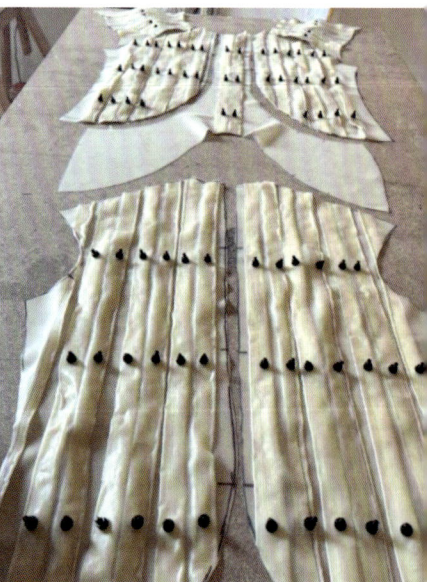

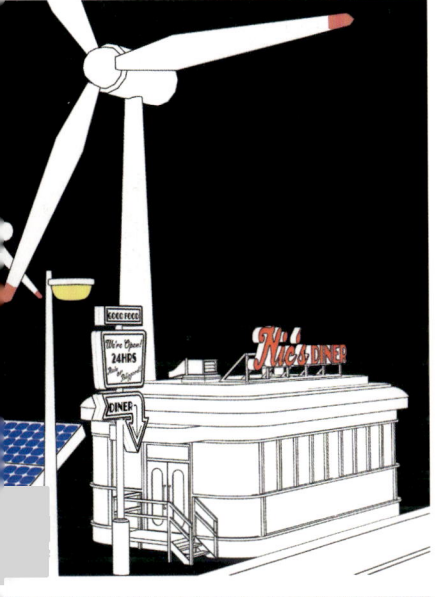

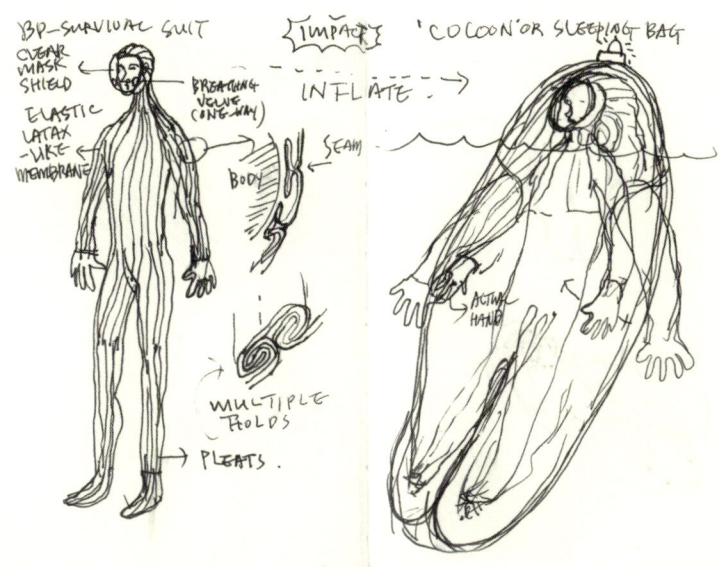

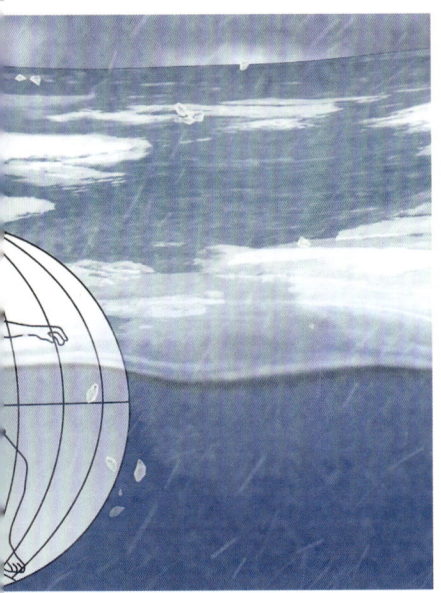

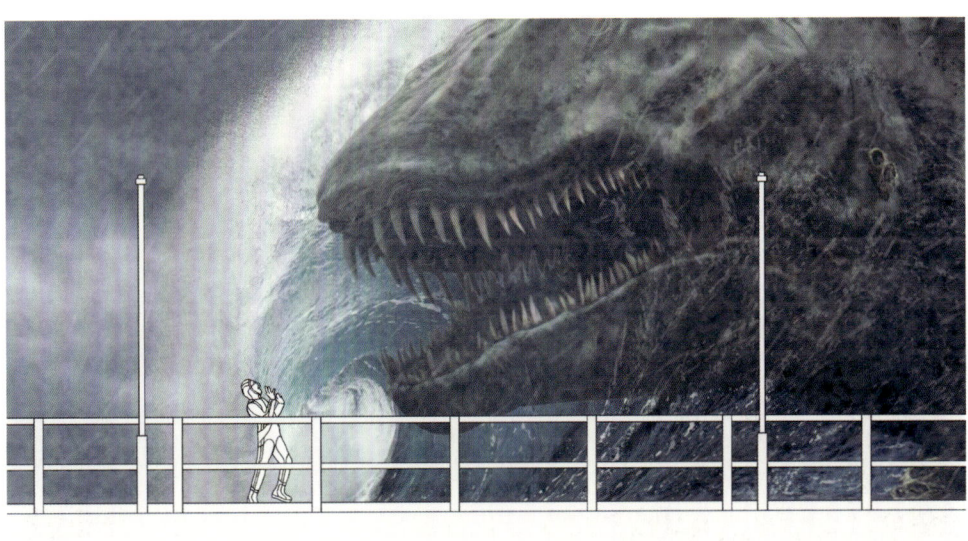

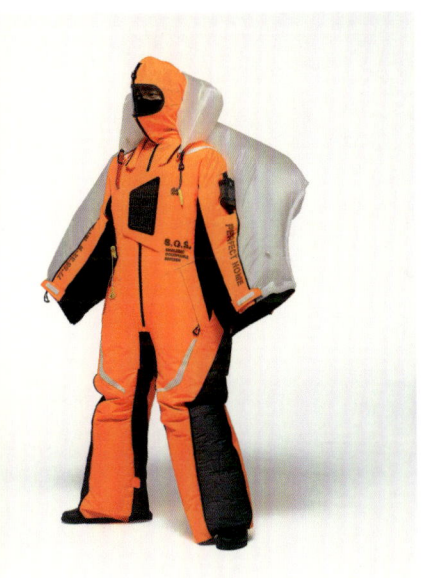

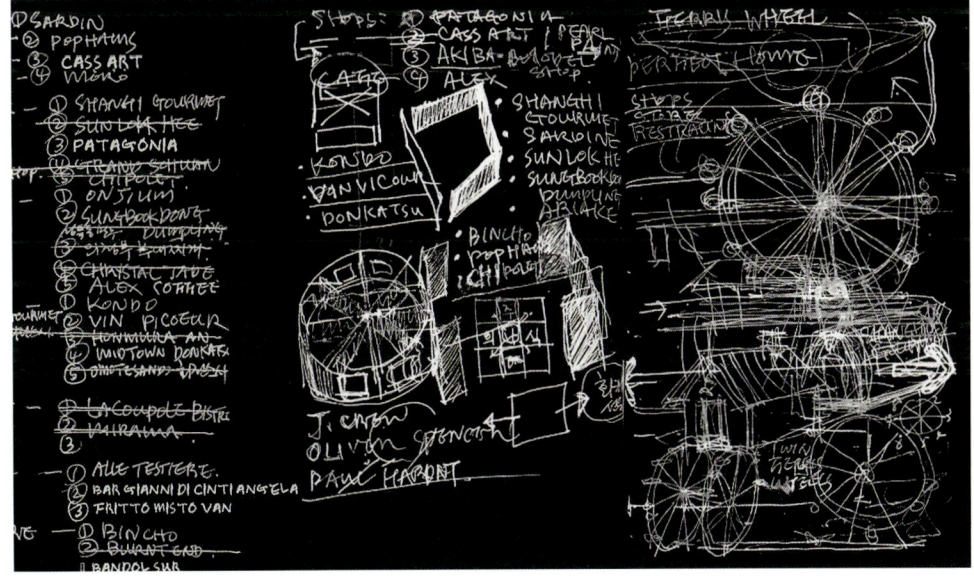

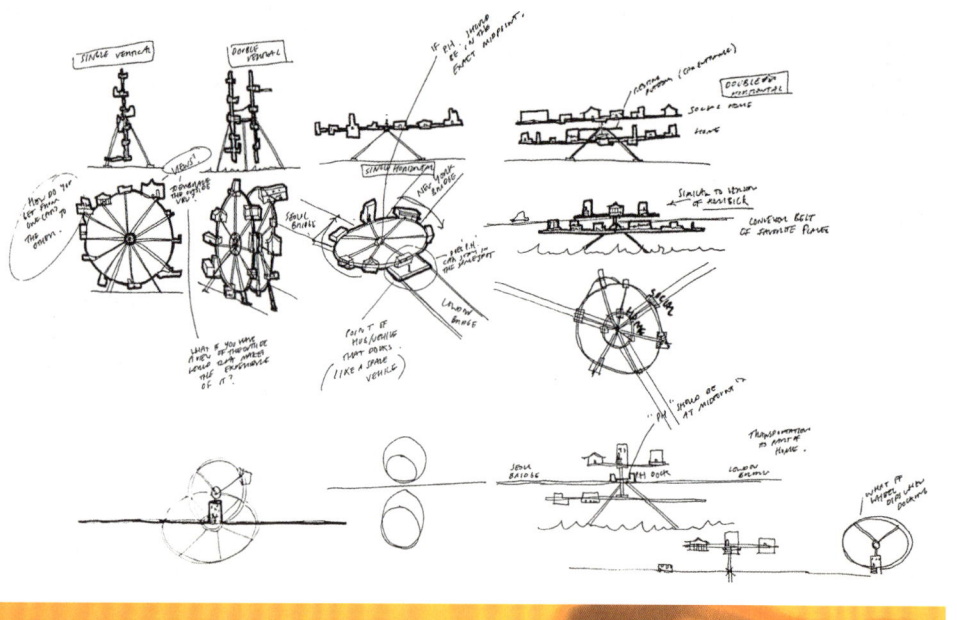
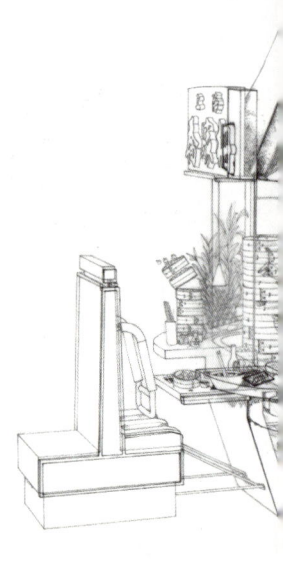
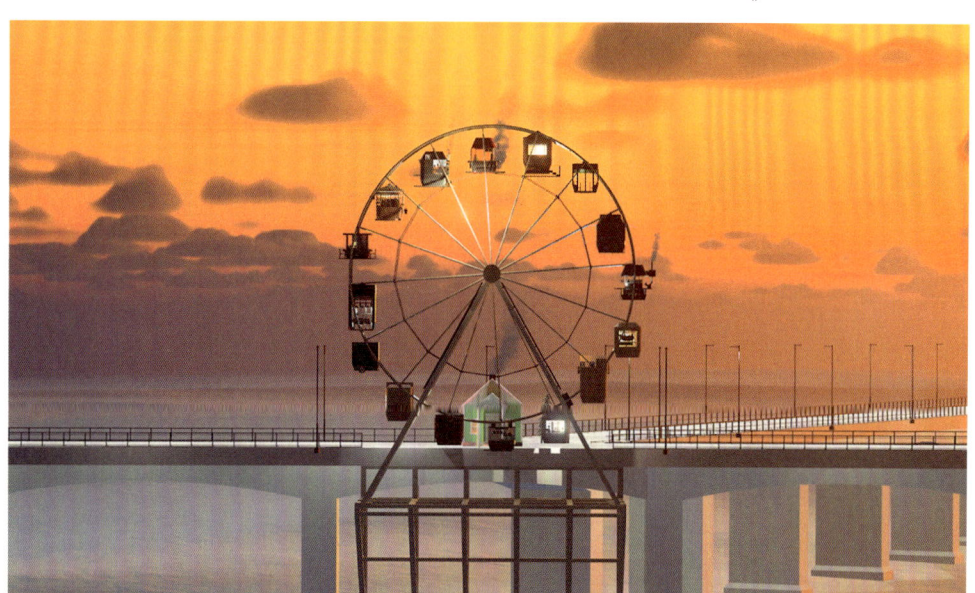
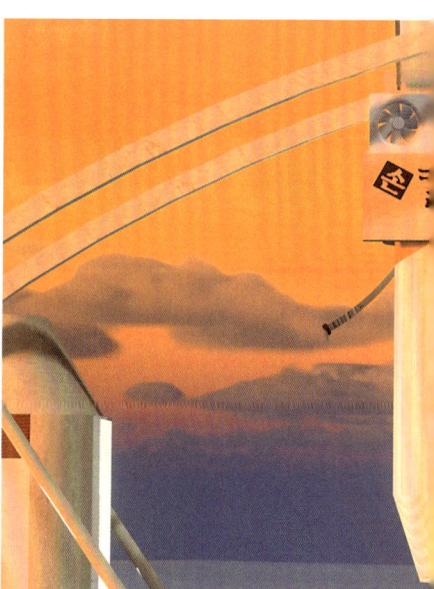
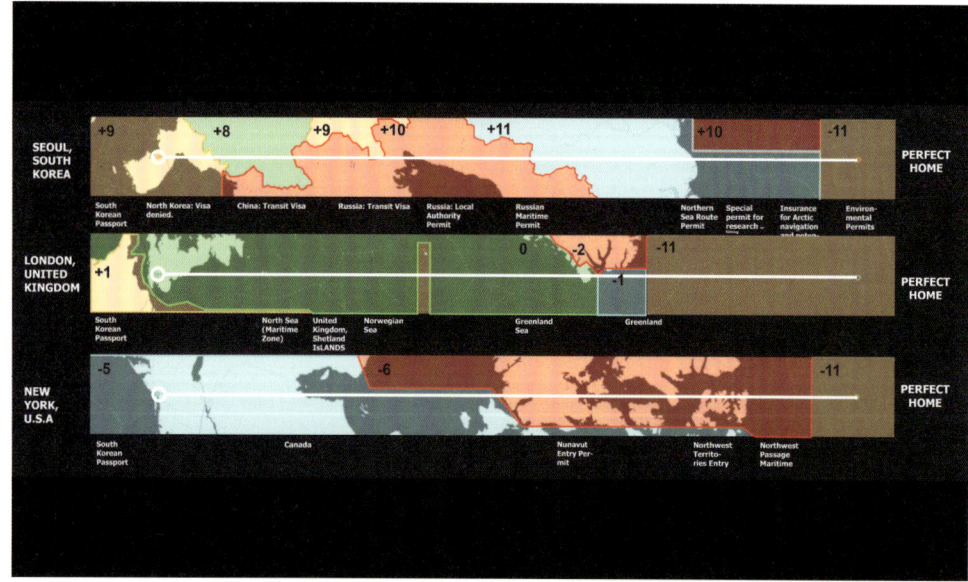

SEOUL, SOUTH KOREA	+9	+8	+9	+10	+11			+10		-11	**PERFECT HOME**
	South Korean Passport	North Korea: Visa denied.	China: Transit Visa	Russia: Transit Visa	Russia: Local Authority Permit	Russian Maritime Permit		Northern Sea Route Permit	Special permit for research ...	Insurance for Arctic navigation and return.	Environmental Permits
LONDON, UNITED KINGDOM	+1				0	-2	-11				**PERFECT HOME**
	South Korean Passport		North Sea (Maritime Zone)	United Kingdom, Shetland IsLANDS	Norwegian Sea	Greenland Sea	-1	Greenland			
NEW YORK, U.S.A	-5		-6				-11				**PERFECT HOME**
	South Korean Passport	Canada		Nunavut Entry Permit		Northwest Territories Entry	Northwest Passage Maritime				

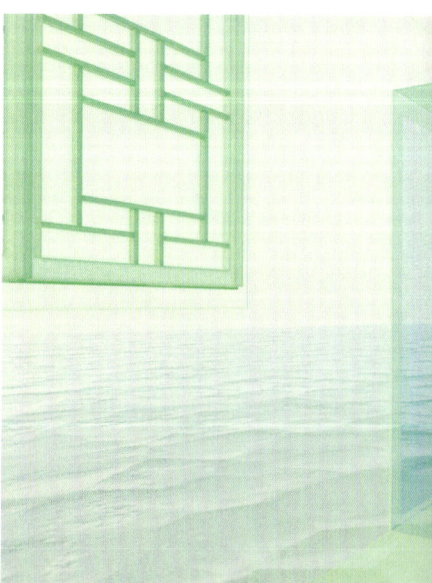

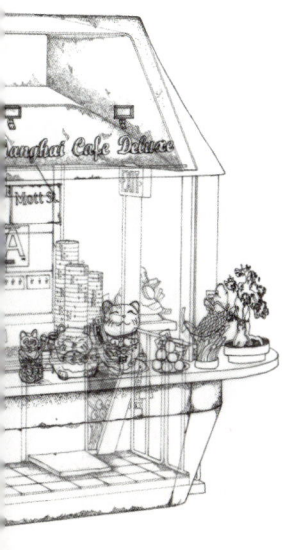

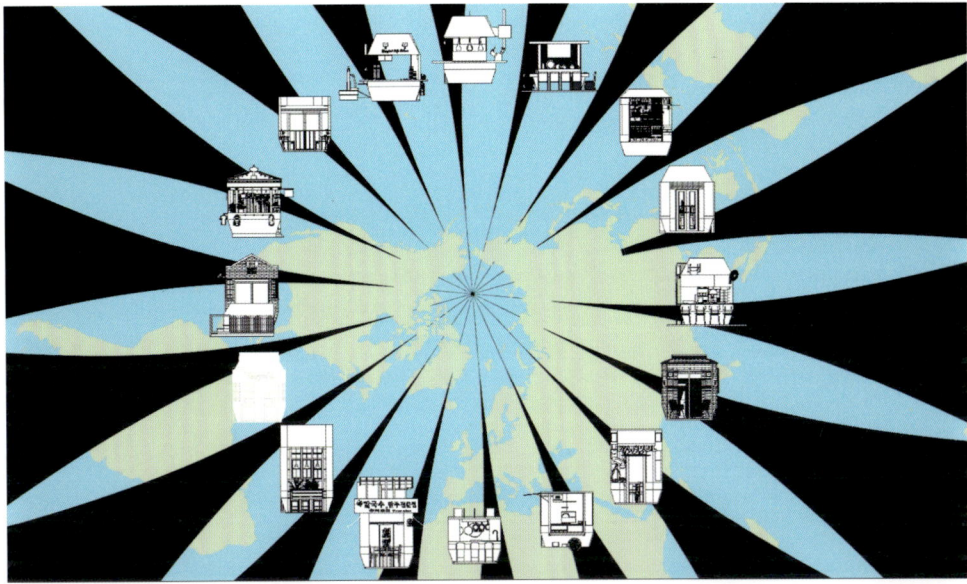

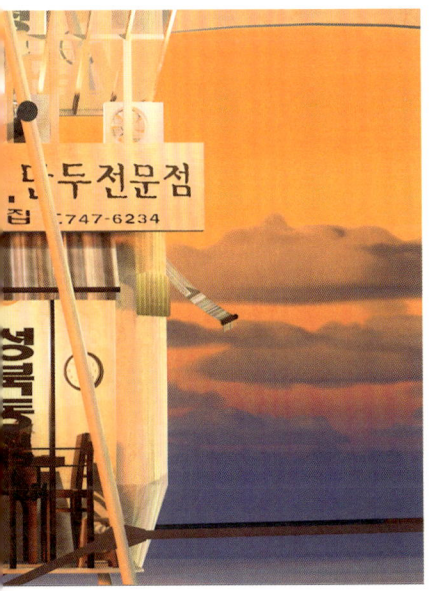

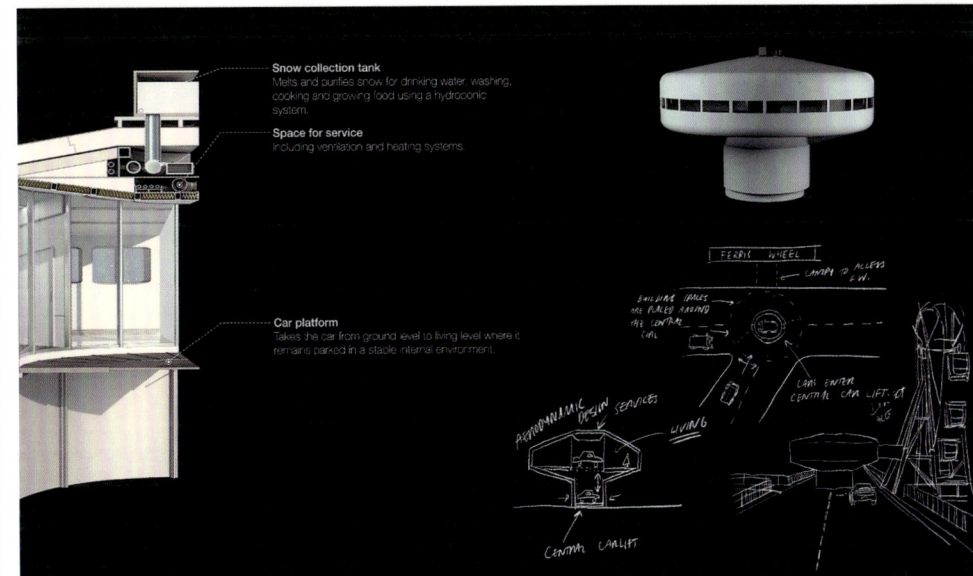

Snow collection tank
Melts and purifies snow for drinking water, washing, cooking and growing food using a hydroponic system.

Space for service
Including ventilation and heating systems.

Car platform
Takes the car from ground level to living level where it remains parked in a stable internal environment.

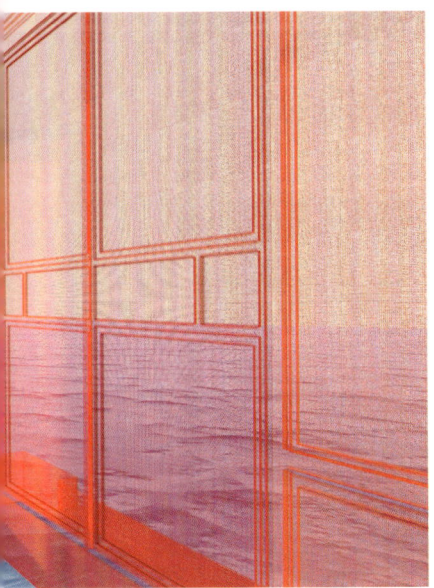

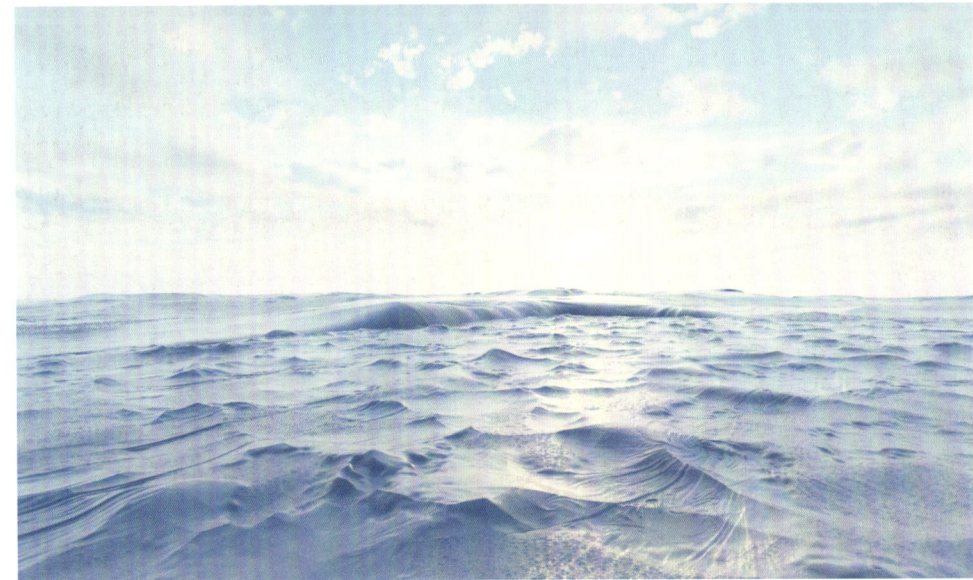

Born in Seoul, 1962
Lives and works in London

Education

1997 MFA Sculpture, Yale University
School of Art, New Haven
1994 BFA Painting, Rhode Island School
of Design, Providence
1987 MFA Oriental Painting, Seoul
National University
1985 BFA Oriental Painting, Seoul
National University

Selected Solo Exhibitions
*With accompanying catalogue /
publication

2025 *The Genesis Exhibition: Do Ho Suh*,
Tate Modern, London
2024 *Do Ho Suh: In Process*, Moody
Center for the Arts, Houston
Do Ho Suh: Speculations, Art Sonje
Center, Seoul
Do Ho Suh: Public Figures,
National Museum of Asian Art,
Washington D.C.
Do Ho Suh and Children: Artland,
Daegu Culture and Art Centre
Do Ho Suh: Tracing Time, National
Galleries of Scotland, Edinburgh
*Artland: An Installation by Do Ho
Suh and Children*, Brooklyn Museum
Atrium Project: Do Ho Suh, Museum
of Contemporary Art Chicago
Do Ho Suh: Portal, Museum of Fine
Arts Houston*
2022 *Do Ho Suh*, Museum of
Contemporary Art Australia, Sydney*
Do Ho Suh, Lehmann Maupin,
New York
Do Ho Suh and Children: Artland,
Buk-Seoul Museum of Art, Seoul*
2021 *Do Ho Suh: Proposal for
Sach'ŏnwang-sa*, Bloomberg
SPACE, London
2019 *Do Ho Suh: 348 West 22nd Street*,
Los Angeles County Museum of Art
Robin Hood Gardens, Victoria and
Albert Museum, London
Do Ho Suh, Museum Voorlinden,
Wassenaar*
2018 *Do Ho Suh: The Spaces in Between*,
Iris & B. Gerald Cantor Center for
Visual Arts, Stanford University

Do Ho Suh: Korridor, ARoS Aarhus
Kunstmuseum*
One: Do Ho Suh, Brooklyn Museum
Do Ho Suh: Specimens, Frist Center
for Visual Arts, Nashville
Do Ho Suh: Passage/s, Towada Art
Center
Do Ho Suh, Victoria Miro, Venice
Do Ho Suh: Almost Home,
Smithsonian American Art Museum,
Washington, D.C.
Do Ho Suh: Bridging Home, Art
Night and Sculpture in the City,
London
2017 *Do Ho Suh: Passage/s*, Bildmuseet,
Umeå
Do Ho Suh, Madison Museum of
Contemporary Art
Do Ho Suh: Passage/s, Victoria
Miro, London
Do Ho Suh: 95 Horatio Street,
Whitney Museum of Art Billboard
Project, New York
2016 *Entre Espacios*, NC-arte, Bogotá
Do Ho Suh, Museum of
Contemporary Art San Diego
Do Ho Suh: Passage, Contemporary
Arts Center, Cincinnati
2015 *Do Ho Suh: New Works*, Singapore
Tyler Print Institute
Do Ho Suh, Museum of
Contemporary Art, Cleveland
Do Ho Suh + Po Po, Mori Art
Museum, Tokyo
*Do Ho Suh: New York City
Apartment/Bristol*, Bristol Museum
& Art Gallery
2014 *Do Ho Suh*, The Contemporary
Austin
Do Ho Suh: Drawings, Lehmann
Maupin, New York
2013 *Do Ho Suh*, Lehmann Maupin,
Hong Kong
*Home Within Home Within Home
Within Home Within Home*, National
Museum of Contemporary Art, Seoul
In Between Hotel, Gwangju Folly II,
Gwangju
Do Ho Suh: Thread Drawings, Dieu
Donné, New York
2012 *Do Ho Suh: Perfect Home*, 21st
Century Museum of Contemporary
Art, Kanazawa*
Do Ho Suh: In Between, Hiroshima
City Museum of Contemporary Art*

Do Ho Suh: Fallen Star, Stuart Collection, University of California San Diego
Blueprint, Hiroshima City Museum of Contemporary Art, Hiroshima
Do Ho Suh: Home Within Home, Leeum, Samsung Museum of Art, Seoul*
Do Ho Suh: Cause & Effect, Western Washington University, Bellingham
Grass Roots Square, Regjeringskvartalet R6, Oslo

2011 *Do Ho Suh: Wielandstr. 18, 12159*, DAAD Galerie, Berlin
Do Ho Suh: Home within Home, Lehmann Maupin, New York
Do Ho Suh, Singapore Tyler Print Institute*
Do Ho Suh: Staircase-III, Tate Modern, London

2010 *Do Ho Suh: Cause & Effect*, The Hite Cultural Foundation, Seoul*
Do Ho Suh: A Perfect Home –The Bridge Project, Slade School of Fine Art, University College London; Storefront for Art & Architecture, New York*
Karma, Albright-Knox Art Gallery, Buffalo

2009 *Karma*, Kyungbang Times Square, Seoul

2007 *Do Ho Suh: Reflection*, Lehmann Maupin, New York
Do Ho Suh: Cause & Effect, Lehmann Maupin, New York
Do Ho Suh: Cause & Effect, Towada Art Center

2006 *The Speculation Project*, Sun Contemporary, Seoul

2005 *Staircase*, 21st Century Museum of Contemporary Art, Kanazawa
Do Ho Suh, The Fabric Workshop and Museum, Philadelphia
Do Ho Suh: Reflection, Maison Hermes, Tokyo

2004 *Do Ho Suh*, Galeria Soledad Lorenzo, Madrid*
The National Museum of Asian Art, Washington, D.C.
Lehmann Maupin, New York

2003 Brown University, Providence
Lehmann Maupin, New York
Do Ho Suh, Art Sonje Center, Seoul*
The Perfect Home, Kemper Museum of Contemporary Art, Kansas City

2002 *Some/One*, Nerman Museum of Contemporary Art, Overland Park
Unsung Founders Memorial, University of North Carolina, Chapel Hill
Do Ho Suh, Serpentine Gallery, London (Toured: Seattle Art Museum)*

2001 *Some/One*, Whitney Museum of American Art at Philip Morris, New York

2000 *Do Ho Suh*, Lehmann Maupin, New York

1999 *Seoul Home/L.A. Home*, Korean Cultural Center, Los Angeles
Do Ho Suh: Sight-Seeing, NTT InterCommunication Center, Tokyo

Selected Group Exhibitions

2025 *Future Fossils*, MassArt Museum, Boston

2024 *Spirit House*, Cantor Arts Center, Stanford University
In Memory, Utah Museum of Contemporary Art, Salt Lake City
Räume hautnah (Spaces Embodied), The Draiflessen Collection, Mettingen
Space Time Scenarios, Seoul Museum of Modern Art
Phenomena: Perspective for an Introduction to the MUSAC Collection, Museo de Arte Contemporáneo de Castilla y León

2023 *The Shape of Time: Korean Art after 1989*, Philadelphia Museum of Art (Toured: Minneapolis Institute of Art)
UNBUILD: A Site of Possibility, Drawing Room, London
Tomorrow is the Question, Storefront Futures Fund, New York
Time States – Contradiction and Accordance, Seoul National University Museum of Art
Narrative Threads: Fiber Art Today, Moody Center for the Arts, Houston
Please, Come In..., Art, Design & Architecture Museum, University of California Santa Barbara

2022 *Three Generations: Remembering Suh Se Ok*, Lehmann Maupin, Seoul
SHELTER: Flexible Fibers + Sustainable Solutions, Design Art Technology Massachusetts, CVPA Swain Gallery at University of Massachusetts, Dartmouth
The Distance From Here, Hayy Arts, Jeddah

2021 *The Contemporary Print: 20 Years at Highpoint Editions*, Minneapolis Institute of Art*
Colección Jumex: Ambient Temperature, Museo Jumex, Mexico City
Break the Mold: New Takes on Traditional Art Making, North Carolina Museum of Art, Raleigh
Global Asias: Contemporary Asian and Asian American Art from the Collections of Jordan D. Schnitzer and His Family Foundation, Palmer Museum of Art, University Park (Toured: Heckscher Museum of Art, Huntington)*
Likeness and Legacy in Korean Portraiture, Asian Art Museum, San Francisco*
Lightness of Being, K11 Foundation, Shanghai
Catastrophe and Recovery, National Museum of Modern and Contemporary Art, Gwacheon
Broken Landscapes: Have Our Cities Failed?, JUT Foundation, Taipei
Portable Sculpture, Henry Moore Institute, Leeds
Portals, NEON Foundation, Athens

2020 *MMCA Permanent Collection*

2020+, National Museum of Modern and Contemporary Art, Seoul
For a Dreamer of Houses, Dallas Museum of Art

2019 *Boundless Encounters: The 3rd Hangzhou Triennial of Fiber Art*, Zhejiang Art Museum, Hangzhou
When Home Won't Let You Stay: Migration Through Contemporary Art, Institute of Contemporary Art, Boston (Toured: Minneapolis Institute of Art, Iris & B. Gerald Cantor Center for Visual Arts, Stanford University)*
Waking Dream, Ruby City, San Antonio
CAB3: and other such stories, Chicago Architecture Biennial
Homo Faber: Craft in Contemporary Sculpture, Asia Culture Center, Gwangju
Crossing Lines, Constructing Home: Displacement and Belonging in Contemporary Art, Harvard Art Museums, Cambridge
Space Exploration, Gyeongnam Art Museum, Changwon
Lexicon: The Language of Gesture in 25 Years at Kemper Museum, The Kemper Museum, Kansas City

2018 *Altering Home*, 21st Century Museum of Contemporary Art & Culture City of East Asia, Kanazawa
Shelter in the Storm: A Look at the Exile in the MUSAC Collection, Museo de Arte Contemporáneo de Castilla y León
FREESPACE, Japan Pavilion, 16th International Architecture Exhibition, Venice
Speech Acts: Reflection, Imagination, Repetition, Manchester Art Gallery
Robin Hood Gardens: A Ruin in Reverse, La Biennale di Venezia with the Victoria and Albert Museum, 16th International Architecture Exhibition, Venice*
The House Imaginary, San José Museum of Art, San José
No Place Like Home, Museu Coleção Berardo, Lisbon

2017 7th Bi-City Biennale of Urbanism/Architecture, Shenzhen
OPENING SENTENCE, CCS Bard Hessel Museum, Annandale-On-Hudson
Out of Sight!: Art of the Senses, Albright-Knox Art Gallery, Buffalo
Atopia, Museum of Contemporary Art Lima, Lima
Victors for Art: Michigan's Alumni Collectors – Part II: Abstraction, University of Michigan Museum of Art, Ann Arbor
Lesson Zero, National Museum of Modern and Contemporary Art, Seoul
No Place Like Home, Jerusalem

2016 *On Site*, Petit Palais, FIAC, Paris
An Atlas of Mirrors, 5th Singapore Biennale, Singapore Art Museum*
Home Land Security, FOR-SITE Foundation, San Francisco
Don't Look Back: The 1990s at MOCA, The Geffen Contemporary at MOCA, Los Angeles
Transformation, CoBo House, Hong Kong
The Architecture of Life, Berkeley Art Museum and Pacific Film Archive

2015 *Going Public: The Cattelain Collection*, Museum Sheffield
Are you experienced?, Art Gallery of Hamilton, Ontario
Beyond the Buzz: New Forms, Realities, and Environments in Digital Fabrication, Minneapolis College of Art and Design
Apparitions: Frottages and Rubbings from 1860 to Now, Hammer Museum, Los Angeles (Toured: Menil Collection, Houston)*
Art Textiles, The Whitworth, Manchester*

2014 *Atopía: Migración, Legado y Ausenica de Lugar – Obras de la colección Thyssen-Bornemisza Art Contemporary, Vienna*, Museo de Arte de Zapopan, Guadalajara
M Home: Living in Space – RedStar Macalline Art Project, Ullens Center for Contemporary Art, Beijing
Margulies Collection at the WAREhOUSE, Miami
Entorno crítico, Centro de Arte Caja de Burgos
Beyond and Between, Leeum, Samsung Museum of Art, Seoul
Please Enter, Franklin Parrasch Gallery, New York
Shades of Time: An Exhibition from the Archive of Korean American Artists, Part Two 1989–2001, Queens Museum
Look at Me: Portraiture from Manet to the Present, Leila Heller Gallery, New York
Myth/History: YUZ Collection of Contemporary Art, YUZ Museum Shanghai, Shanghai
Striking Resemblance: The Changing Art of Portraiture, Zimmerli Art Museum, Rutgers University, New Brunswick
Perth International Arts Festival

2013 *Unknown Forces*, Tophanie-I Amire Gallery, Istanbul
Everyday Life, Asian Art Biennial, National Taiwan Museum of Fine Arts, Taichung
Power, Where Does the Beauty Lie?, Seoul Olympic Museum of Art
Homebodies, Museum of Contemporary Art Chicago
5th Auckland Triennial, Auckland Art Gallery
0 to 60: Contemporary Art, North Carolina Museum of Art, Raleigh

2012 *Dislocation*, Daegu Art Museum
Deoksugung Project, National Museum of Contemporary Art, Deoksugung, Seoul

Roundtable, The 9th Gwangju Biennale
San Antonio Collects Contemporary, San Antonio Museum of Art
Watch This Space: Works from the AGO's Contemporary Collection, Art Gallery of Ontario, Toronto

2011 *Luminous: The Art of Asia*, Seattle Art Museum
Haein Art Project, Haeinsa, Hapcheon
Against All Odds Project, Benaki Museum, Athens*
Korean Rhapsody, Leeum, Samsung Museum of Art, Seoul*
Dreamscapes, The Pulitzer Foundation for the Arts, St Louis*
Human Nature: Contemporary Art from the Collection, Los Angeles County Museum of Art
The Spirituality of Place, Gutstein Gallery, Savannah College of Art and Design

2010 *Mapping Identity*, Cantor Fitzgerald Gallery, Haverford College
The Hidden City: Selections from Martin Z. Margulies Foundation, Tampa Art Museum
Beyond/In Western New York 2010: Alternating Currents, Albright-Knox Art Gallery, Buffalo*
Touched, Liverpool Biennial*
Trust, Media City Seoul*
People Meet in the Architecture, Venice Architecture Biennale*
Setouchi International Art Festival, Shodoshima*

2009 *Innovations in the Third Dimension: Sculpture of Our Time*, Bruce Museum, Greenwich*
KAFA Awards Exhibition, Seoul National University Museum*
Papertrail v. 5: Intimate Gestures, Judi Rotenberg Gallery, Boston
The Kaleidoscopic Eye: Thyssen-Bornemisza Art Contemporary Collection, Mori Art Museum, Tokyo*
Your Bright Future, Los Angeles County Museum of Art (Toured: Museum of Fine Arts, Houston)*
Dress Codes: Clothing as Metaphor, Katonah Museum of Art*

2008 *METAMORPHOSES*, Espace Louis Vuitton, Paris*
Drawn in the Clouds, Kiasma Museum of Contemporary Art, Helsinki*
Transcendence: Modernity and Beyond in Korean Art, Singapore Art Museum
On the Margins, Mildred Lane Kemper Art Museum, St Louis*
Thyssen-Bornemisza Art Contemporary: Collection as Aleph, Kunsthaus Graz
Psycho Buildings, Hayward Gallery, London*
Second Lives, Museum of Arts & Design, New York

2007 *Tomorrow*, Kumho Museum and Artsonje Center, Seoul*
Red Hot: Asian Art Today from the Chaney Collection, Museum of Fine Arts Houston

Peppermint Candy: Contemporary Korean Art, Museo de Arte Contemporáneo, Santiago (Toured: National Museum of Fine Arts, Buenos Aires; National Museum of Contemporary Art, Gwacheon)*
System Error, Palazzo delle Papesse, Siena*
Façades, Krannert Art Museum, University of Illinois, Champaign
Downtown Expansion, Seattle Art Museum
Void in Korean Art, Leeum, Samsung Museum of Art, Seoul*

2006 *Collected Visions: Modern and Contemporary Works from the JPMorgan Chase Art Collection*, Pera Museum, Istanbul*
This Is Not For You, Thyssen-Bornemisza Art Contemporary, Vienna
New Works: 06.2, Artpace, San Antonio*
Facing East: Portraits from Asia, Freer + Sackler Galleries, Washington, D.C.
To the Human Future: Flight From The Dark Side, Contemporary Art Gallery, Art Tower Mito*
A Step in the Right Direction, Gammel Holtegaard Breda-Fonden, Holte

2005 *Monuments for the USA*, White Columns, New York*
St. Gauden's Memorial Award Exhibition, UBS Art Gallery, New York
ShowCase: Contemporary Art for the UK, Contemporary Art Society, Edinburgh
Identity and Nomadism, Palazzo delle Papesse-Centro Arte Contemporanea, Siena*
Sujeto, Museo de Arte Contemporáneo de Castilla y León*
The Elegance of Silence: Contemporary Art from East Asia, Mori Art Museum, Tokyo*
Contemporary Voice: The Contemporary American Art From Misumi Collection, Tottori Prefectural Museum*
Encounters with Modernism: Highlights from the Stedelijk Museum and the National Museum of Contemporary Art, Korea, National Museum of Contemporary Art, Seoul*
New Acquisitions 2004, National Museum of Contemporary Art, Gwacheon*

2004 *Contemplating War*, Johnson County Community College, Overland Park
Transcultures, National Museum of Contemporary Art, Athens*
Lustwarande 04: Disorientation of Beauty, Tilburg*
Siting: Installation Art 1969–2002, Museum of Contemporary Art, Los Angeles
Formed to Function, John Michael Kohler Arts Center, Sheboygan
Standing on a Bridge Part 1, Arario Gallery, Cheonan*
Stillness & Movement, Seoul Olympic Art Museum*
The Breath of a House, Yeongam Pottery Culture Center & Gurim Village*

The Snow Show, Rovaniemi Art Museum*
2003 *Home and Away*, Vancouver Art Gallery*
8th Istanbul Biennial: *Poetic Justice**
On the Wall: Wallpaper by Contemporary Artists, RISD Museum, Providence (Toured: The Fabric Workshop and Museum, Philadelphia)*
Living Inside the Grid, New Museum of Contemporary Art, New York*
Multiple/Multiples, Nassau County Museum of Art, New York
Undomesticated Interiors, Smith College Museum of Art, Northampton*
Hermès Korea Missulsang, Art Sonje Center, Seoul*
2002 *We Love Painting: Contemporary American Art from Misumi Collection*, Museum of Contemporary Art, Tokyo*
Constructed Fabric, Kobe Fashion Museum*
Mask or Mirror: A Play of Portraits, Worcester Art Museum
Multitude, Artists Space, New York
Asia Pacific Triennial of Contemporary Art, Queensland Art Gallery, Brisbane*
(The World May Be) Fantastic, 13th Biennale of Sydney*
Sculptura 02: International Art in Public Spaces, Falkenberg*
Collecting Contemporary Art: A Community Dialogue, Ackland Art Museum, Chapel Hill
International Contemporary Art, Museum of Modern Art, Mexico City
2001 *Lunapark: Contemporary Art from Korea*, Württembergischer Kunstverein Stuttgart*
Korean Pavilion, 49th Venice Biennale*
Plateau of Humankind, 49th Venice Biennale*
Uniform, Order and Disorder, Stazione Leopolda, Florence (Toured: MoMA PS1, New York)*
Made in Asia, Nasher Museum of Art at Duke University, Durham*
About Face, The Museum of Modern Art, New York
Subject Plural: Crowds in Contemporary Art, Houston Contemporary Art Museum*
BodySpace, The Baltimore Museum of Art
2000 *Greater New York*, MoMA PS1, New York*
Koreamericakorea, Art Sonje Center, Seoul; Art Sonje Museum, Kyungjoo*
Open Ends, The Museum of Modern Art, New York
My Home is Yours, Your Home is Mine, Rodin Gallery, Seoul (Toured: Tokyo Opera City Art Gallery)*
Currents in Korean Contemporary Art, Taipei Fine Arts Museum (Toured: Hong Kong Art Centre)*
1999 *Trippy World*, Baron/Boisante, New York
The Self, Absorbed, Bellevue Art Museum
Uniform, Center for Curatorial Studies, Bard College, Annandale-on-Hudson

1998 *Cross-Cultural Voices: Asian American Artists*, Staller Center for the Arts, State University of New York, Stony Brook
Editions '98, Brooke Alexander Editions, New York
Beyond the Monument, MetroTech Center Commons, Brooklyn
Electronically Yours, Tokyo Metropolitan Museum of Photography*
1997 *Do Ho Suh / Royce Weatherly*, Gavin Brown's Enterprise, New York
Promenade in Asia 1997, Shiseido Gallery, Tokyo*
Techno / Seduction, The Cooper Union, New York*
1996 *Arcos da Lapa Project*, Arcos da Lapa, Rio de Janeiro
Window Show, Gallery Hyundai, Seoul
Art at Home, Seomi Gallery, Seoul
1995 *6 Artists Now*, Gallery Hyundai, Seoul*
1994 *Invitational Exhibition*, Woods-Gerry Gallery, Rhode Island School of Design, Providence
1993 *Open Door*, Sol Koffler Gallery, Providence
1990 *Light from the East II*, Kiev City Museum*
Korean Contemporary Painting Exhibition, Hoam Gallery, Seoul*
Logos and Pathos, Kwanhoon Gallery, Seoul*
The Groping Youth 1990, National Museum of Contemporary Art, Gwacheon*
Seoul Print '90 Invitational Exhibition, Shinsegae Art Gallery, Seoul*
Exploration and Experiment, Seoul Gallery*
Seoul, March of 1990, 17 Artists, Kwanhoon Gallery, Seoul*
Image of Our Era: Korean Paintings in the 1990s, Gallery Hyundai, Seoul*
1989 20th São Paulo International Biennial*
1988 *Korean Contemporary Painting Exhibition: New Vision – Ink and Color Paintings*, Hoam Gallery, Seoul*
1987 *Leaders of 1980s Korean Painting*, The Third Art Museum, Seoul*
Vibrant New Generation, Gallery Yeh, Seoul*

Selected Public Collections

21st Century Museum of Contemporary Art, Kanazawa
Ackland Art Museum, University of North Carolina, Chapel Hill
Art, Design & Architecture Museum, University of California, Santa Barbara
Art Gallery of Ontario, Toronto
Art Sonje Center, Seoul
Baltimore Museum of Art
Brooklyn Museum
Buffalo AKG Art Museum (previously named Albright–Knox Art Gallery)
City Museum, St Louis
Daegu Museum of Art, Daegu

Garage Museum of Contemporary Art, Moscow
Guggenheim Abu Dhabi
Gwangju Biennale Foundation
Hammer Museum, Los Angeles
Jut Art Museum, Taipei
Leeum Museum of Art, Seoul
Los Angeles County Museum of Art
Mori Art Museum, Tokyo
Museo de Arte Contemporáneo de Castilla y León
Museo de Arte de Zapopan, Guadalajara
Museum of Contemporary Art, Chicago
Museum of Contemporary Art, Los Angeles
Museum of Contemporary Art, Tokyo
The Museum of Fine Arts, Houston
The Museum of Modern Art, New York
Museum Voorlinden, Wassenaar
Nasher Museum of Art, Duke University, Durham
National Museum of Contemporary Art, Athens
National Museum of Modern and Contemporary Art, Gwacheon
New Orleans Museum of Art
New York Public Library
Philadelphia Museum of Art
Rhode Island School of Design Museum, Providence
San Antonio Museum of Art, San Antonio
San Francisco Museum of Modern Art
Seattle Art Museum
Smithsonian American Art Museum, Washington, D.C.
Smithsonian National Museum of Asian Art, Washington, D.C.
Solomon R. Guggenheim Museum, New York
Stuart Collection, University of California, San Diego
Tate Modern, London
Thyssen-Bornemisza Art Contemporary, Vienna
Towada Art Center
University Museum of Contemporary Art, University of Massachusetts, Amherst
Vera List Center for Art and Politics, The New School, New York
Victoria and Albert Museum, London
Walker Art Center, Minneapolis
Whitney Museum of American Art, New York
Yale University Art Gallery, New Haven

Selected Publications

2025 Amie Corry and Louis Rogers (eds.), *Do Ho Suh: Anatomy*, London
2022 Amie Corry (ed.), *Do Ho Suh: Portal*, New York
2021 Martin Coomer, Allegra Pesenti and Sarah J.S. Suzuki (eds.), *Do Ho Suh: Works on Paper*, Singapore and New York
Liliane Wong and Markus Berger (eds.), *Interventions and Adaptive Reuse: A Decade of Responsible Practice*, Basel
2020 Mary Livingstone Beebe et al, *Landmarks: Sculpture Commissions for the Stuart Collection at University of California, San Diego*, 2nd edn, Oakland, CA
Roger Hallas (ed.), *Documenting the Visual Arts*, New York
2019 Jori Finkel (ed.), *It Speaks to Me: Art That Inspires Artists*, New York and Munich
Rebecca Morrill, Louisa Elderton and Catalina Imizcoz (eds.), *Vitamin T: Threads & Textiles in Contemporary Art*, London and New York
2018 Olivia Sand (ed.), *Contemporary Voices from the Asian and Islamic Art Worlds*, Milan
2017 Patrick Charpenel and Magnolia de la Garza (eds.), *Punto de Partida: Colección Isabel y Agustín Coppel*, Madrid
2016 Bridget Donlon, *Pure Pulp: Contemporary Artists Working in Paper at Dieu Donné*, New York and Munich
Danielle Krysa et al, *Art Installations: A Visual Guide*, Dublin
Margaret Lazzari and Dona Schlesier, *Exploring Art: A Global, Thematic Approach*, 5th edn, Boston, MA
2015 Melissa Bennett, (ed.), *Are You Experienced?*, London
David Midgley, Christian Emden, Henriette Steiner, Kristin Veel, et al, *Invisibility Studies: Surveillance, Transparency and the Hidden in Contemporary Culture*, Bern
Loren Olson (ed.), *Feelings: Soft Art,* New York.
Jonathan Openshaw (ed.), *Postdigital Artisans: Craftsmanship with a New Aesthetic in Fashion, Art, Design and Architecture*, Amsterdam
2014 Rochelle Steiner (ed.), *Do Ho Suh Drawings*, Munich
2013 Rina Arya (ed.), *Contemplations of the Spiritual in Art*, Bern
Kelly Grovier, *100 Works of Art That Will Define Our Age*, London
2011 Jin-Sook Lee (ed.), *Art Big Bang*, Seoul
Geun-Young Kwon (ed.), *I am an artist*, Seoul
Michael Petry, *The Art of Not Making: The New Artist/Artisan Relationship*, London
Jane Rendell, *Site-Writing: The Architecture of Art Criticism*, London
Fatos Üstek (ed.), *Unexpected Encounters: Situations of Contemporary Art and Architecture*, Istanbul
2010 Yuko Hasegawa (ed.), *A Guide to Contemporary Art for Young Women: The MOT Collection*, Tokyo.
Kyu-Hyun Lee (ed.), *Hello, Mr. Artist!*, Seoul
Jean Robertson and Craig McDaniel, *Themes of Contemporary Art: Visual Art after 1980*, 2nd edn, New York
2009 Jee-Sook Beck and Yoo-Mee Kang (eds.), *Endlessly battling between distinguishing oldness that no longer exists and newness that does not yet exist*, Paris

Furuichi Yasuko (ed.), *International Symposium 2008: Count 10 Before You Say Asia – Asian Art after Postmodernism*, Tokyo
Tae-hi Kang, Young-Jin Kwon and Young-Wook Lee (eds.), *Mapping of Korean Contemporary Art*, Seoul
Yujin Hwang, Jane Farver, Judy Kim and Sookeun Song (eds.), *Faces & Facts: Contemporary Korean Art in New York*, New York

2008 Taiyana Pimentel (ed.), *Implications of the Image*, Mexico City

2007 Robert Klanten and Lukas Ferireiss (eds.), *Spacecraft: Fleeting Architecture and Hideouts*, Berlin

2006 Brooke Hodge, Patricia Mears, Susan Sidlauskas et al, *Skin + Bones: Parallel Practices in Fashion and Architecture*, New York
Symptom of Adolescence, exh. cat., Leeum, Samsung Museum of Art, Seoul

2005 Youngna Kim (ed.), *Modern and Contemporary Art in Korea: Tradition, Modernity and Identity*, Seoul
Francesca Richer and Matthew Rosenzweig (eds.), *No.1: First Works by 362 Artists,* New York

2004 Sean Topham (ed.), *Move House*, Munich
Janet Bloor and John D. Sinclair (eds.), *RUBBER! Fun, Fashion, Fetish*, New York

2003 Elaine Kim, Sharon Mizota and Margo Machida, *Fresh Talk/Daring Gazes: Conversations on Asian American Art*, Berkeley, CA
Susan Sollins (ed.), *Art:21: Art in the Twenty-First Century 2*, New York

The list is organised by medium, then chronologically within each section, and alphabetically within years.

Measurements are given in centimetres, height before width and depth.

An asterisk (*) at the end of a medium line indicates that the work was produced at STPI – Creative Workshop & Gallery, Singapore, on handmade cotton paper.

All details were correct at the time of going to press.

Installations

Who Am We? (Multicoloured) 2000
Digital print on vinyl
Dimensions variable
Tate. Presented by the artist and Lehmann Maupin Gallery, New York 2009, accessioned 2012
Repurposing supported by Genesis

Rubbing/Loving: Company Housing of Gwangju Theater 2012
Graphite on paper, wooden structure; video, monitor, colour and sound (stereo)
522.8 × 1124 × 66.6
Courtesy the artist, Lehmann Maupin New York, Seoul and London and Victoria Miro
Repurposing supported by Genesis

Rubbing/Loving: Seoul Home 2013–22
Graphite on paper, aluminium, LED lighting; video, monitor, colour and sound (stereo)
527.6 × 827.3 × 803.6
Courtesy the artist, Lehmann Maupin New York, Seoul and London and Victoria Miro
Repurposing supported by Genesis

Rubbing/Loving: Unit 2, 348 West 22nd Street, New York, NY 10011, USA 2014–23
Coloured pencil on paper and stainless steel pins
244 × 664 × 17
Private Collection
Repurposing supported by Genesis

Nest/s 2024
Polyester fabric and stainless steel
410.1 x 375.4 x 2148.7
Courtesy the artist, Lehmann Maupin New York, Seoul and London
Creation supported by Genesis

Perfect Home: London, Horsham, New York, Berlin, Providence, Seoul 2024
Polyester fabric and stainless steel
455 × 575 × 1237
Courtesy the artist, Lehmann Maupin New York, Seoul and London
Creation supported by Genesis

Home Within Home (1/9 Scale) 2025
Resin
Four parts:
171.7 × 76.2 × 101
171.7 × 92.6 × 100.7
171.7 × 76.2 × 74.5
171.7 × 76.4 × 74.5
Installation dimensions variable
Courtesy the artist, Lehmann Maupin New York, Seoul and London and Victoria Miro
Creation supported by Genesis

Public Figures 2025
Jesmonite, nylon, aluminium and steel
284 × 209.4 × 275
Courtesy the artist, Lehmann Maupin New York, Seoul and London and Victoria Miro
Creation supported by Genesis

Bridge Project: Phase I & II 1999–ongoing
Video, projection, colour; sound (stereo); video, 4 flat screens, colour, no sound; works on paper; sound (stereo); polyester and polyamide; newspapers
Dimensions variable
Courtesy the artist, Lehmann Maupin New York, Seoul and London
Creation supported by Genesis

Videos

Robin Hood Gardens, Woolmore Street, London E14 0HG 2018
Video, colour and sound (stereo)
28 min, 33 sec
Courtesy the artist, Lehmann Maupin New York, Seoul and London and Victoria Miro
Commissioned by the Victoria and Albert Museum, London
Repurposing supported by Genesis

Dong In Apartments 2022
Video, colour, no sound
21 min
Courtesy the artist, Lehmann Maupin New York, Seoul and London and Victoria Miro
Repurposing supported by Genesis

Works on paper

A Perfect Home 1999
Ink and watercolour
on paper
25.1 × 35.4
Private Collection

*Seoul Home/L.A.
Home* 1999
Ink on paper
21 × 29.7
Private Collection

Fist 2002
Watercolour and
coloured pencil on
paper
10.5 × 14.5
Private Collection

Karma 2002
Ink on paper
32 × 24
Private Collection

*My Country / Our
Country* 2002
Ink on paper
28 × 21.5
Private Collection

Untitled 2002
Ink on paper
29.7 × 21
Private Collection

Dream Home 2003
Watercolour and
coloured pencil on
paper
15 × 9.8
Private Collection

Home Within Home
2003
Watercolour on paper
21 × 29.5
Private Collection

Father and Son
2004
Watercolour on paper
29.7 x 21
Private Collection

Reflection 2004
Coloured pencil on
paper
25.5 x 36
Private Collection

Figure Study 2006
Ink on paper
14.6 × 10.4
Private Collection

Self-Portrait 2006
Watercolour on paper
14.8 × 10
Private Collection

Sleepy Head 2008
Ink on polyester film
27.3 × 36.6
Private Collection

Untitled 2008
Ink on polyester film
24 × 7
Private Collection

Staircases 2009
Watercolour on paper
10.4 × 14.6
Private Collection

Flowers 2010
Lacquer on paper
26 × 18
Private Collection

Home Within Home
2010
Watercolour on paper
45.3 × 32
Private Collection

My Homes 2010
Thread embedded in
paper*
132 × 166
Private Collection

Fallen Star 2011
Watercolour and
coloured pencil on
paper
11.4 × 15.3
Private Collection

Staircase 2011
Watercolour on paper
15.3 × 10.5
Private Collection

Going Home 2013
Thread embedded in
paper
61 × 45.7
Private Collection

Karma Juggler 2013
Thread embedded in
paper
46 × 61
Private Collection

Myselves 2013
Thread embedded in
paper
35.6 × 27.9
Private Collection

My Home/s 2013
Thread embedded in
paper
36.8 × 29.2
Private Collection

Paratrooper 2013
Thread embedded in
paper*
46.9 × 35.8
Private Collection

Blueprint 2014
Thread embedded in
paper*
76.2 × 101.6
Private Collection

Facing Myself 2014
Thread embedded in
paper*
29.6 × 29.2
Private Collection

Home Clothing 2014
Watercolour on paper
14.8 × 10
Private Collection

Self-Portrait 2014
Watercolour and

graphite on paper
14.8 × 10
Private Collection

Spectators 2015
Ink on paper
29.7 × 21
Private Collection

Family Portrait 2016
Ink on paper
14.9 × 10
Private Collection

Myselves 2016
Lithograph on paper
56 × 38.5
Private Collection

Staircase 2016
Gelatine tissue and
thread embedded in
paper*
355 × 229
Private Collection

Fart in the Wind 2017
Ink on paper
14.6 × 10.6
Private Collection

Unfolded Room
2018
Graphite on paper
15.3 × 12
Private Collection

Haunting Home
2019
Thread embedded
in paper*
131.5 × 167
Private Collection

Separation Anxiety
2019
Ink on paper
14.7 × 21
Private Collection

Breathing Space
2020
Ink and watercolour
on paper

10 × 14.9
Private Collection

*Chapelle St-Louis de
la Salpêtrière* 2020
Watercolour and
graphite on paper
30.4 × 23
Private Collection

Clingy Home 2020
Ink on paper
21 × 14.8
Private Collection

Comfort Zone 2020
Ink and watercolour
on paper
10 × 14.9
Private Collection

Family Cuddle 2020
Ink on paper
14.8 × 10
Private Collection

Time Pockets 2021
Polyester, cotton and
assortment of objects
109 x 83 x 14.5
Private Collection

Time Pockets 2021
Polyester, cotton and
assortment of objects
109 × 83 × 14.5
Private Collection

Aami + Omi + Appa
2022
Ink on paper
29.7 × 21
Private Collection

Bangoopong 2022
Watercolour on paper
10 × 14.8
Private Collection

Circle 2022
Coloured pencil on
paper
14.8 × 10.5
Private Collection

Father and Daughter
2022
Thread embedded in
paper
35.8 × 28.4
Private Collection

Going Home 2022
Ink on paper
14.8 × 10.5
Private Collection

Illustrious Figure 2022
Ink on paper
42 × 29.6
Private Collection

Karma Juggler 2022
Coloured pencil on
paper
29.6 × 42
Private Collection

Myselves 2022
Graphite powder on
paper
14.8 × 10
Private Collection

Son and Father 2022
Ink on paper
29.7 × 41.9
Private Collection

Culture Shock 2023
Ink on paper
12.3 x 22
Private Collection

Self-Portrait 2023
Graphite and
watercolour on paper
14.8 x 10
Private Collection

*Self-Portrait (My
Journey)* 2023
Ink on paper
21 × 29.5
Private Collection

Spectators 2023
Charcoal on paper
244 × 152.4
Private Collection

Whisperer 2023
Graphite powder on
paper
10 × 14.8
Private Collection

Wise Man 2023
Thread embedded in
paper
244 × 212
Private Collection

Body/Building 2024
Ink on paper
14.8 x 10
Private Collection

Body/Building 2024
Ink on paper
14.9 x 10
Private Collection

Borderless Home
2024
Ink and coloured
pencil on paper
14.9 x 10.5
Private Collection

*Breath (348 West
22nd Street)* 2024
Ink on paper
14.7 x 10.5
Private Collection

Breathing Home
2024
Ink on paper
14.8 x 10
Private Collection

Breathing Home
2024
Watercolour and
coloured pencil on
paper
14.8 x 10
Private Collection

*Chapelle St-Louis
de la Salpêtrière*
2024
Watercolour and
coloured pencil on
paper

14.8 x 10.5
Private Collection

Convergence 2024
Ink on paper
14.7 x 10.3
Private Collection

Home Within Home
2024
Ink on paper
14.8 x 10.5
Private Collection

I am your conduit
2024
Coloured pencil on
paper
14.9 x 10.1
Private Collection

Journey 2024
Watercolour and
coloured pencil on
paper
14.7 x 10.5
Private Collection

Karma 2024
Watercolour and
coloured pencil on
paper
14.7 x 10.5
Private Collection

Leaving Home 2024
Watercolour and
coloured pencil on
paper
14.8 x 10
Private Collection

My Home/s 2024
Watercolour and
coloured pencil on
paper
21.3 x 30
Private Collection

Myselves 2024
Coloured pencil on
paper
14.8 x 10
Private Collection

Perfect Home 2024
Ink and coloured
pencil on paper
14.8 x 21
Private Collection

Possessed 2024
Ink on paper
14.8 x 10
Private Collection

Staircase/s 2024
Watercolour and
coloured pencil on
paper
14.8 x 10
Private Collection

I would like to extend my deepest gratitude to the many friends and collaborators who worked so hard to bring this exhibition to life.

My London studio: Kyle Bloxham Mundy, George Bolwell, Ringo Bunoan, Nicola Chan, Amie Corry, Amandine Couot-Garibal, Isobel Currie, Elisa Lapenna, SooMin Leong, Dominic Oliver, KC Poh, Louise Price, Zoe Sherwood, Graeme Smith and Andy Williams.

Genesis for making *Walk the House* possible.

Everyone at Tate. My particular thanks to Achim Borchardt-Hume, who is so deeply missed, and to Nabila Abdel Nabi and Dina Akhmadeeva for years of sensitive conversation and collaboration. I'm also grateful for the invaluable input of Tom Avery, Maria Balshaw, Nicola Bion, Neil Casey, Amy Dillman, Jarelle Francis, Karin Hindsbo, Sook-Kyung Lee, Rita Machado, Travis Miles, Phil Monk, Frances Morris, Alex Nichols, Kira Wainstein, Catherine Wood and Adam Wozniak.

Marwan Kaabour for this beautiful catalogue design, and to all the contributors, who have added so much to the conversation: Sean Anderson, Sarah Fine, Monica Juneja, Janice Kerbel, Rirkrit Tiravanija and Dylan Trigg.

Rachel Lehmann, David Maupin, Jen Mora, Adriana Elgarresta and everyone at Lehmann Maupin; and Victoria Miro, Glenn Scott Wright, Clare Coombes, Rachel Kent, Kathy Stephenson and everyone at Victoria Miro. Emi Eu and the team at STPI – Creative Workshop & Gallery, Singapore for decades of collaboration on my drawings. KOLON Sports for their support and collaboration on the *Bridge Project* Survival Suit. Daein, Darbyshire, Image Bakery, MDM Props, Jon Lowe and the many others who worked on the complex fabrication and installation of the work. I am hugely indebted to Hugh Brody, Claire Dacam, Craig Davies, Kalil Erazo and the engineering students at Rice University, James Kwang Ho Chung, Michael Mack, Rachel Naṇinaaq Edwardson, Doreen Nutaaq Simmonds and Piers Vitebsky for their expertise and generous insight.

Finally, a special thank-you to my family: Rebecca Boyle Suh, Aami Suh, Omi Suh, Min-Za Chung and Suh Se Ok, Wallace and Dorothy Boyle.

Artist's Acknowledgements

Opposite: *Flowers* 2013

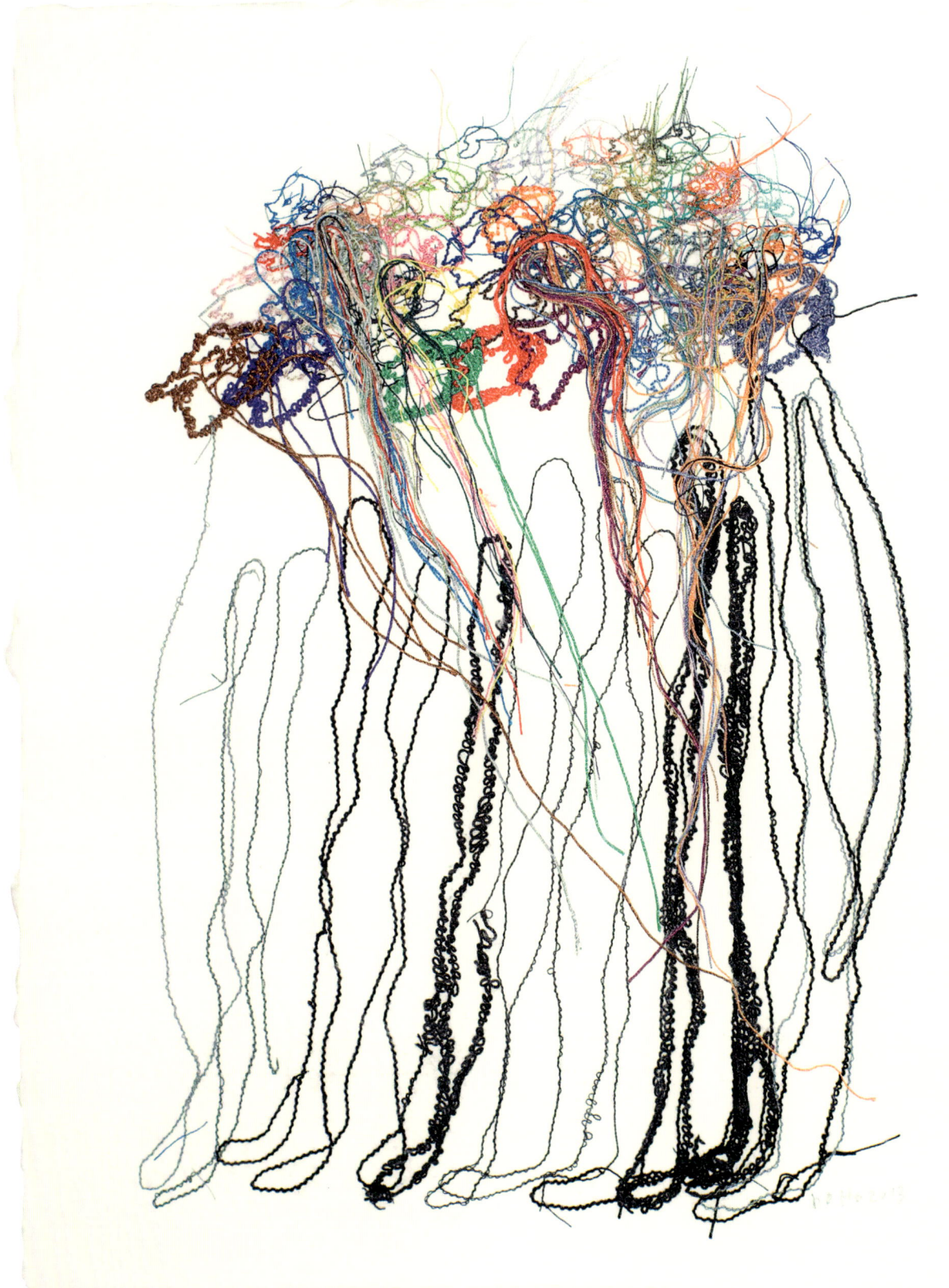

Copyright
© Do Ho Suh, courtesy Lehmann Maupin Gallery, New York, London and Seoul and Victoria Miro
pp.26–9, 84, 87: courtesy the artist and Museum of Contemporary Art Los Angeles
p.67: courtesy the artist and Tate
pp.56–7: courtesy the artist and Museum of Fine Arts, Houston
pp.68–70: courtesy the artist and Leeum Museum of Art, Seoul
pp.106 bottom, 111 bottom: courtesy the artist and KOLON Sports, Seoul
p.145: courtesy the artist and Victoria and Albert Museum, London

Photo Credits
Photo by Carlos Avendaño p.74
Photo by Thierry Bal p.19
Photo by Andrew Boyle p.140
Photo © Gautier Deblonde. All Rights Reserved, DACS 2025 pp.16, 141
Photo by Image Bakery pp.40–1, 81, 146–55
Photo by Sam Drake pp.118–19
Photo by Antoine van Kaam, Museum Voorlinden, Wassenaar, The Netherlands p.66
Photo by Hyunsoo Kim pp.2–3, 5, 6, 7, 8, 72, 77, 97, 100, 108
Photo by Soyeun Kim p.48
Photo by Anna Kucera p.86
Photo by Minjung Lee pp.49–52, 96 top, 99
Photo by Marcus Leith p.94
Photo by Paul Macapia p.34
Photo by Jessica Maurer pp.132–3
Photo by Sebastian Mrugalski pp.47, 53–5,
Photo by Christopher Payne pp.78, 101 bottom, 113–17, 102, 120, 142–3
Photo by Prudence Cuming Associates pp.4, 8–9 bottom centre, 38–9, 88 top, 91, 95, 109, 121, 135–9
Photo by Philipp Scholz Rittermann p.71
Photo by Shelby Ragsdale. Museum of Contemporary Art Chicago / Art Resource, NY p.33
Photo by Yuki Shima p.138
Photo by Jeon Taeg Su pp.21, 37 bottom, 42–5, 56–7, 68–70, 74–5, 77, 79, 80, 85, 96 bottom, 101 top, 122–31, 135–7, 157–9, 161–3
Photo by Kiliii Yuyan for National Geographic pp.170–1 top left and middle

Credits

Opposite: *Staircase/s* 2019

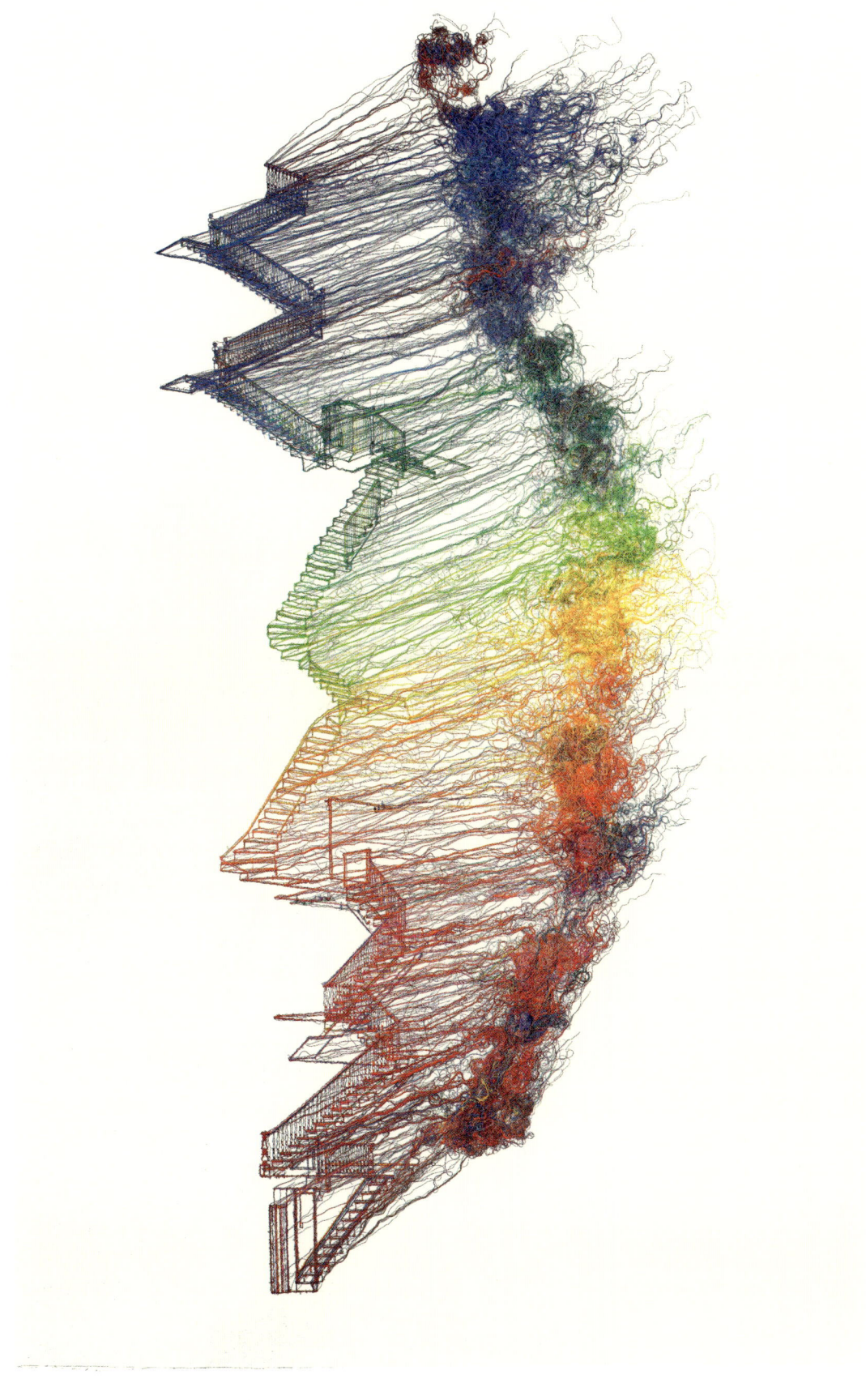

First published 2025 by order of the Tate Trustees by Tate Publishing,
a division of Tate Enterprises Ltd, Millbank, London SW1P 4RG

www.tate.org.uk/publishing

on the occasion of the exhibition

The Genesis Exhibition
Do Ho Suh: Walk the House

Tate Modern, London
1 May – 19 October 2025

In partnership with Genesis

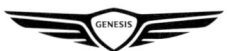

Supported by The Genesis Exhibition: Do Ho Suh Supporters Circle:
Lehmann Maupin, New York, Seoul and London
STPI – Creative Workshop & Gallery, Singapore
Victoria Miro
and Tate Members

The creation and repurposing of artworks in the exhibition has been
made possible with the generous support of Genesis

A catalogue record for this book is available from the British Library

ISBN 978-1-84976-967-9 (pbk)
ISBN 978-1-84976-938-9 (special edition)

Senior Editor: Nicola Bion
Production: Juliette Dupire
Picture Research: Roz Hill
Design: Marwan Kaabour

Printed by Graphicom SRL, Italy

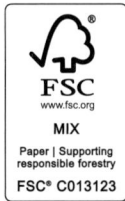